LEXICON AND ATLAS

OF THE MODERN WORLD

COINCIDING WITH

THE ANCIENT GREEK WORLD

*

JOSEPH R. LAURIN

authorHOUSE®

AuthorHouse™
1663 Liberty Drive
Bloomington, IN 47403
www.authorhouse.com
Phone: 1-800-839-8640

Published by AuthorHouse   01/03/2013

ISBN: 978-1-4772-9698-1 (sc)
ISBN: 978-1-4772-9697-4 (e)

Library of Congress Control Number: 2012923202

This book is printed on acid-free paper.

ACKNOWLEDGMENT

My gratitude goes first to the innumerable scholars
who transmitted, in the original or translation,
the texts used in the creation of this book.

My gratitude goes also to the few experts,
especially Alfred Lau,
who contributed to the technical and artistic
presentation of this book.

To my wife Joan and all the friends
who encouraged and supported me
in the pursuit of this time-consuming project,
my appreciation and sincere thanks.

Joseph R. Laurin

4

GENERAL CONTENTS

*   *   *

FOREWORD

For the Ancient Greeks, the earth was a flat oval sphere surrounded by a huge Ocean. The world, as they knew it, was longer from west to east than from north to south, as Aristotle attested in his *Meteorology* of about 350 BCE. In addition to Hellas (Greece), it encompassed the lands of Southern Europe, North Africa and Egypt, and West and Central Asia. In relation to the coinciding Modern World, it covered from the British Isles and Gibraltar in the west to western China and India in the east and from southern Germany, the Ukraine and Kazakhstan in the north to North Africa, Ethiopia and the Arabian Sea in the south.

From the Minoans of about 2,000 BCE to the Hellenistic Greeks of the 300's BCE, farmers, sailors, traders, explorers, athletes, warriors, politicians, poets, historians and philosophers told us in deeds and writings about the innumerable places they discovered, named and occupied or visited.

The usage of the resources and enjoyment of the beauty of the seas, rivers, mountains and plains and of the land where the cities stood contributed to molding the ancient Greeks' character and influenced the course of their lives. The knowledge they acquired about the world has remained to this day a significant factor in understanding not only who they were and what they did in relation to their friends and foes but also who we are and what we do in similar relations. The lineage from the Ancient Greek World to our Modern World remains unbreakable.

During the Classical Period of their history, in the fifth and fourth centuries BCE, the Ancient Greeks knew less than six percent of our Modern World, but in their small inhabited world they accomplished many of the greatest deeds of history. They did them in places where some names were kept intact to this day and where other names were either changed with the subsequent civilizations or remembered only as archaeological sites. In spite of the dearth and frequent vagueness of the information and of the shifting of borders as a result of military actions, political changes or natural forces, archaeologists and historians have made valuable contributions toward pinpointing the location of many places in the Ancient Greek World in relation to our Modern World.

The modern publications as lexicon or atlas of the Ancient Greek World are either monumental or relatively brief and specialized, usually without references to the Modern World. The purpose of this book is not to replace these excellent publications but to fill in a gap between them by providing alphabetical listings of places with a brief description and the support of maps and indexes, the main asset being convenience in clarity and brevity, yet with a comprehensive scope and general accuracy.

The foundations of this book are set in archaeology and ancient literature as well as in a few modern writings about the Ancient Greek World and our Modern World. The building erected upon these foundations has two entrances, one on each side, namely the Ancient Greek World and the Modern World. For example, the ancient Euesperides and the modern Benghazi are two entrances to the same location of a city in Libya, North Africa.

More often than not, the Greek transliteration is preferred here to the Latinized one commonly used by translators, for example **k** instead of c, **u** instead of y, **ai** instead of ae, as in Kithairon instead of Cithaeron. **Oi** also appears frequently in lieu of oe, for example Boiotia instead of Boeotia, **ei** instead of i, for example Peiraios instead of Piraeus. The ending of words in um or us usually appears as **on** or **os**, for example Drepanon instead of Drepanum and Epidauros instead of Epidaurus. In some cases, the Latinized version is preferred for practicality and ease in the use of the most common names, for example Aegean instead of Aigaion in reference to the Sea. Along the way, additional notes will guide the readers and facilitate their inquiries.

Also, the directional terms North, South, East, West, & Center, and their derivatives, are abbreviated by the capital letters: **N**, **S**, **E**, **W**, and **C**. The Ancient Greeks identified the directions by the prevailing wind for North (*Boreas*) and by the position of the sun in the morning, at noon and in the evening for East (*Eôs*), South (*Mesèmbria*) and West (*Espera*). The number in bold italic at the end of each description in the Lexicon refers to the page in the Atlas where the site is numbered with these directions and shown on a map. Continental Greece is divided into two large   regions: the Peloponnesos to the S and mainland Greece to the N of the Gulf of Corinth.

In spite of the careful and lengthy research leading to this publication, the result remains neither complete nor perfect by its own nature. Nevertheless, the nearly four thousand entries listed here should provide valuable assistance toward an easy and quick understanding of the physical Ancient Greek World and of part of our Modern World related to it. This Lexicon and Atlas remains a work in progress after its first edition. The future contributions by specialists will be appreciated for helping not only improve its quality but also extend its longevity. For this purpose, *LexiconandAtlas@yahoo.com* is the e-mail contact.

LEXICON

A

Abacaenum : inland town in the NE of the island of Sicily, in W Mediterranean Sea, W Europe. *236*

Abae : ancient town in NE Phokis, S of Huampolis, CS mainland Greece. *214*

Abanah : see Barada river. *256 & 258*

Abantes : 1. ancient city in Thesprotis, E Epeiros, exact location uncertain, in NW mainland Greece. *218*; -- 2. see Euboia. *212 & 228*

Abas : see Arachnaeos mountain. *202*

Abasa : early settlement, either close to Ephesos or Ephesos itself, in Lydia, CW Asia Minor, present-day CW Turkey. *254*

Abdera : 1. town of S Iberia (Spain), modern Adra, W of modern Almeria, along the Mediterranean Sea, in SW Europe. *232*; -- 2. city of the S coast of Thrace, near the mouth of the Nestos river, in NE Greece, opposite the island of Thasos in N Aegean Sea. *226*

Abia : city of SE Messenia, ancient Ire, on the NE side of the Gulf of Messenia, in SW Peloponnesos. *196*

Abii : tribe of N Sogdiana, located along the S shore of the Jaxartes river, in present-day W Kazakhstan, C Asia. *262*

Abisares : tribal area of ancient Bactria, located around the valley of Kashmir, covering NE Pakistan and NW India, in C Asia. *266*

Abivard : see Dara and perhaps Hekatompulos. *260*

Abu Dhabi : see Macetia. *246 & 264*

Abudos : 1. town on the S side of the Hellespontos, in Troas, NW Asia Minor, present-day NW Turkey. *250*; -- 2. city of C Egypt, on the W bank of the Nile river, N of Thebes, in NE Africa. *242*

Abula : city in SW Iberia (Spain), modern Ceuta, an enclave in NW Morocco, facing the Rock of Gibraltar across the strait of Gibraltar, in W Europe. *232 & 244*

Abu Simbel : modern town on an ancient site, in S Egypt, S of Aswan, on the W bank of the Nile river, in NE Africa. *244*

Acana : see Alalakh. *256*

Aces : ancient river flowing N through a ring of hills, into the S Caspian Sea, in C Asia. *260*

Acesines : river, modern Chenāb, flowing from the Himalayas, in the Punjab of NW India, W through Jammu and Kashmir, then SW through Pakistan, becoming tributary of the Zaradros (Sutlej) river, tributay of the Indus river, in C Asia. *266*; -- 2. river in the C of the island of Sicily, flowing S into the W Mediterranean Sea. *236*

Achaia : 1. region of N Peloponnesos, between the Gulfs of Patraikos and Korinthos to the N and the Panachaikon Mountains separating it from Arkadia to the SW, the regions of Elis to the SE and Korinthia to the E, and the Ionian Sea to the W. *188, 190, 192, 198, 200 & 214.* -- 2. see Phthiotis. *190, 192. 194, 200, 202 & 216*

Acharnae : town in C Attika, N of Athens, in SE mainland Greece. *210*

Acheloos : river, also called Peiros and Aspropotamos, flowing SW from the S Pindos mountain range of W Thessalia, across NW Aitolia, along the border with Akarnania, then through SE Akarnania, into the Ionian Sea at Oiniadai, in SW mainland Greece. *216 & 220*

Acheron : 1. river of Thesprotis, in E Epeiros, flowing W into the Ionian Sea. *218*; -- 2. major mythological river thought to be encircling the Underworld (Hades). *268*

Acherusia : 1. lake in S Thesprotis, E Epeiros, formed by the river Acheron, before reaching the Ionian Sea, in CW mainland Greece. *218*; -- 2. city on this lake. *218*

Achilles : 1. harbor on the SE side of the Gulf of Messenia, on the SW tip of Lakonia, in SE Peloponnesos. *198*; -- 2. kingdom of Achilles in Achaia Phthiotis, also called Hellas, where the Myrmidons had their land, In CE mainland Greece. *222*

Acradina : city on the SE island of Sicily, near Siracusa, in W Mediterranean Sea, W Europe. *236*

Acrae : inland town in the SE side of the island of Sicily, in the Heraei Mountains, W Mediterranean Sea. *236*

Acre : see Akko. *258*

Adana : 1. area of E Cilicia, along the river Puramos, W of the Gulf of Issos, in present-day SE Turkey. *256*; -- 2. major city in the Adana plain along this river, in SE Cilicia. *256*

Aden : gulf between Yemen to the N and Somalia to the S, connecting the Red Sea with the Arabian Sea, in W Asia. *188*

Adige : river meandering S and E from the Alps, through N Italy, and reaching the Adriatic Sea, N of the Po delta, in W Europe. *238*

Adra : see Abdera. *232*

Adramuttion : 1. gulf of the NE Aegean Sea, modern Edremit, opposite the island of Lesbos, in Mysia, in present-day NW Turkey, W Asia. *250*; -- 2. Aiolian town at the SE end of this gulf, S of Chruse. *250*

Adrano : see Hadranon. *236*

Adrasteia : Homeric city in Troas, near Apaisos, S of the Hellespontos, in present-day NW Turkey, W Asia. *250*

Adria : Etruscan seaport in NE Italy, in the deltas of the Po and Adige rivers, on the Adriatic Sea. *238*

Adrianople : see Uskudama. *226*

Adriatic : Sea as an arm of the NW Mediterranean Sea, N of the Ionian Sea, between Italy to the W and Illyria of the Balkan Peninsula to the E. *188, 190, 218, 240 & 258*

If a name is not found under Ae, look under Ai

Aea : city of Kolchis, at the NE end of the Euxine (Black) Sea, in present-day NE Turkey, W Asia. *248*

Aegean : sea, Greek Aigaion, as an arm of the CN Mediterranean Sea, between Greece to the W and Asia Minor, present-day Turkey, to the E, Macedonia and Thrace to the N and the Sea of Crete to the S. *188, 190, 220, 224, 226, 250 & 254*

Aegiae : city in SW Lakonia, W of Gutheion on the NW side of the Gulf of Lakonia, in CS Peloponnesos. *198*

Aegithallos : town in the W end of the island of Sicily, exact location uncertain, in W Mediterranean Sea, W Europe. *234*

Aegusa : small island W of the island of Sicily, in W Mediterranean Sea, W Europe. *234*

Aetionea : area along the W side of the Kantharos harbor, near Peiraios, in CW Attika, SE mainland Greece. *208*

Aetna : 1. mountain on the E side of the island of Sicily, in W Mediterranean Sea, W Europe. *236*; -- 2. inland town, also called Inessa, SE of Centuripa, in the CE of the island of Sicily. *236*

Afghanistan : country of CS Asia bordering on Iran to the W, Pakistan to the S and E, Turkmenistan, Uzbekistan & Tajikistan to the N, corresponding in its upper part to ancient Bactria. *188, 246, 260, 262 & 266*

Africa : Continent, the N referred to as Lybia in ancient times, present-day region S of the Mediterranean Sea between the Atlantic Ocean to the W and the Red Sea & the Indian Ocean to the E, with the Cape of Good Hope in the S. *187, 188, 242 & 244*

Aganippe : spring, also called Hippokrene (Horse's Spring), source of a stream flowing W from the foot of Mount Helikon in

Boiotia, through SE Phokis, into the Gulf of Korinthos, in CS mainland Greece. *212*

Agatha : 1. town along the Mediterranean Sea, W of Massalia, in SW France, W Europe. *232*; -- 2. see Agathurnum. *236*

Agathurnum : town, present-day Agatha, in the NE of the island of Sicily, on the coast of the CS Tyrrhenian Sea, in W Europe. *236*

Agbatana : major city in the high elevation of CW Media, also spelled Ecbatana, ancient Hangmatana and modern Hamadan, in present-day NW Iran, W Asia. *260*

Agea : town in CS Macedonia, E of Edessa, in NE mainland Greece, NW of the Gulf of Thermai, in NW Aegean Sea. *224*

Agia Irini : modern town on an ancient settlement, on the island of Kea, in the NE Cyclades, CW Aegean Sea. *230*

Agia Marina : modern town on an ancient site, on the NE coast of the island of Aigina, in the C Saronic Gulf, SE mainland Greece. *208*

Agia Triada : 1. site in the Laurion, near Agrileza, in SE Attika, SE mainland Greece. *208*; -- 2. modern city on an ancient site near Phaistos to the NW, E of the Gulf of Mesara, in CS island of Crete, C Mediterranean Sea. *204*

Agion Oros : 1. see Singitikos. *22*8 -- 2. see Akti. *228*

Agios Dhimitrios : modern name for an ancient seaport in the CE of the Peloponnesos, on the coast of the Ionian Sea, in ancient Triphulia, N Elis. *194*

Agios Ilias : town of NW Elis, on an ancient settlement, opposite the island of Zakynthos, in NW Peloponnesos. *194*

Agios Kosmas : modern name for an ancient town at the E end of the Gulf of Korinthos, on an ancient settlement, between Mainland Greece to the N and Peloponnesos to the S. *210*

Agios Nikolaos : 1. see Lato. *206*; -- 2. promontory at the city of Thorikos, on the coast of the Aegean Sea, separating the two harbors Frankolimani and Portomandri, in SE Attika, SE mainland Greece. *208*

Agora : 1. general site for people to assemble; -- 2. plateau S of the Akropolis of Athens, ancient name Kolonos Agoraios, civic center of the city, in C Attika, SE mainland Greece. *208*

Agraia : area in the N of Akarnania, near the SE end of the Gulf of Ambrakia, in SW mainland Greece. *216*

Agrapidochori : village in CW Elis, probable site of or contiguous to ancient Sandy Pulos, in NW Peloponnesos. *194*

Agrianes : 1. river of SE Thrace, tributary of the Maritsa river, in NE mainland Greece. *226*; -- 2. tribal area in the CN Macedonia, S of the Triballi, in present-day Kosovo, E Europe. *224*

Agrieliki : settlement, S of Marathon, in NE Attika, SE mainland Greece. *210*

Agrigento : see Akragas. *234*

Agrileza : 1. valley N of Cape Sounion in S Attika, in SE mainland Greece. *208*; -- 2. mining town in the N of this valley. *208*

Agrinion : city, also called Vrakhori, N of the Gulf of Patraikos and NW of Lake Trikhonis, in SW Aitolia, SW mainland Greece. *216*

Agurion : inland town in CE island of Sicily, modern San Filippo d'Argiro, near Enna, in W Mediterranean Sea, W Europe. *236*

Agylla : coastal town, on the NE side of the island of Corsica, in the Tyrrhenian Sea, W Europe. *232*

Ahhiyawa : area of SE Anatolia, bordering on the Hittite Territory, perhaps opposite the island of Cyprus, in W Asia, present-day SW Turkey. *256*

If a name is not found under Ai, look under Ae

Aiaia : mythical island or peninsula of goddess Kirke, perhaps along the W coast of Italy, exact location unknown, in W Europe. *269*

Aiane : town in CN Macedonia, NE mainland Greece. *224*

Aias : see Aoos river. *218*

Aigaeai : Aeolian town, N of Kume, in W Lydia, on the NW coast of Asia Minor, present-day NW Turkey. *250*

Aigai : 1. Homeric city on the S shore of the Gulf of Korinthos, W of Aigira, in NE Achaia, NE Peloponnesos. *200*; -- 2. Hesiodic mountain of E Boiotia, near the Gulf of Oropos, in SE mainland Greece. *212*; -- 3. town on the NW side of the island of Euboia, on the Gulf of Oropos. *228*; -- 4. town in Cilicia, on the CW coast of the Gulf of Issos, in present-day SE Turkey, W Asia. *256*; -- 5. see Vergina. *224*

Aigaion : see Aegean Sea. *190, 220, 224, & 226*

Aigaios : mythological river, in the land of the Phaeacians. *269*

Aigaleos :1. mount in NW Attika, E of the Bay of Salamis and W of Athens, in SE mainland Greece. *210*; -- 2. mountain range on the W side of Messenia, extending NS, in SW Peloponnesos. *196*

Aigeira : town, also called Huperesia, in CN Achaia, midway along the Gulf of Korinthos, in N Peloponnesos. *200*

Aigiale : seaport on the island of Amorgos, in the SE Cyclades, in CW Aegean Sea. *230*

Aigialos : 1. river of Paphlagonia, flowing N into the Euxine (Black) Sea, in present-day NW Turkey, W Asia. *252*; -- 2. area in CE Achaia, boundaries uncertain, in NE Peloponnesos. *200*

If a name is not found under Ai, look under Ae

Aigilips : Homeric site of uncertain location, on the island of Kephallenia, in CE Ionian Sea, off the coast of Akarnania, in CW mainland Greece. *216*

Aigina : 1. island in the C of the Saronic Gulf, near the W coast of Attika, S of Salamis, in SE mainland Greece. *208*; -- 2. city on the NW side of this island. *208*; -- 3. see Saronic Gulf. *208*

Aigion : 1. Homeric city near Argos, exact location uncertain, in CW Argolis, NE Peloponnesos. *202*; -- 2. port city, also known as Katharevousa, on the SW shore of the Gulf of Korinthos, also called Katharevousa, in CN Achaia, N Peloponnesos. *200*

Aigira : city on the S shore of the Gulf of Korinthos, E of Aigai, in NE Achaia, NE Peloponnesos. *200*

Aigiroëssa : Aiolian town, in NW Lydia, on the NW coast of Asia Minor, along the Aegean Sea. *250*

Aigition : ancient city, probably on the SE side of Aitolia, near the border with Ozolian Lokris, in CS mainland Greece. *216*

Aigospotami : port city of Hellespontine, on the S side of the Strait of Hellespontos, in present-day NW Turkey, W Asia. *250*

Aigosthena : town of NW Megaris, on the shore of the NE end of the Gulf of Korinthos, on the SW slopes of Mount Kithairon, in CS mainland Greece. *210*

Aiguptos : 1. see Egypt. *187 & 242*; -- 2. see Nile. *242*; -- 3. see Sinai. *242*

Aigussos : city, modern Tulcea, in NE Thrace, present-day E Romania, at the opening of the Danube delta, near the coast of the Euxine (Black) Sea, in SE Europe. *226 & 240*

Ai Khanoum : city in S Bactria, present-day NE Afghanistan, near Shortugai, on the border with Tajikistan, in C Asia. *262*

Aina : town, also called Kanli Kastelli, in the C of the island of Crete, C Mediterranean Sea. *206*

Ainis : small tribal region, bordered by Epeiros, Phthiotis, Malis and Aitolia, in C mainland Greece. *190, 214, 216 & 222*

Ainos : town of SE Thrace, on the Gulf of Melas, NE coast of the Aegean Sea, in NW Turkey, SE Europe. *226*

Aiolia : group of small islands, N of the E end of the island of Sicily, W of SW Italy, in the S Tyrrhenian Sea, W Europe. *238*

Aiolis : region of NW Asia Minor, including the islands of Lesbos and Tenedos, between Troas and Ionia, along the Aegean Sea, in W Anatolia, present-day W Turkey. *190 & 250*

Aipeia : Homeric town near Pherai, in SE Thessalia, NE mainland Greece. *220*

If a name is not found under Ai, look under Ae

Aipu : 1. Homeric city of S Elis, also called Tupanaei, exact
location unknown, in CW Peloponnesos. *194*; -- 2. seaport city
on the Ionian Sea, N of Pulos, in CW Messenia, SW
Peloponnesos. *196*

Aisageia : Homeric hill, probably in Lydia, CW Asia Minor,
present-day CW Turkey. *254*

Aisepos : river flowing W from the Ida mountain range, in C
Troas, near Skepsis, past Zeleia, into the Aegean Sea, in NW Asia
Minor, present-day NW Turkey. *250*

Aisume : Homeric city in Thrace, exact location unknown, in NE
mainland Greece. *226*

Aithaia : site probably located in CE Messenia, SW Peloponnesos.
196

Aithices : tribal area of CN Macedonia, N of the Pindos
mountains, in CN mainland Greece. *224*

Aithiopia : region of NE Africa, where the Nile river has its source,
presently bordered by Eritrea in the N, Kenya in the S, Somalia in
the E and Sudan in the W, probably including Sudan in antiquity.
187 & 244

Aitolia : region surrounded by Akarnania and the Acheloos river
to the W, Epeiros to the N, Ainis, Lokris, Phokris to the E and the
Gulf of Korinthos to the S, in SW mainland Greece. *190, 214,
216 & 218*

Aitos : town on the W side of Akarnania, S of Oiniadai, on the
coast of the Ionian Sea, in SW mainland Greece. *216*

Aixone : town S of Peiraios, near the coast of the Saronic Gulf, in
SW Attika, SE mainland Greece. *208*

Akakeson : town in SW Arkadia, between Megalopolis to the E and
Phigalia to the W, in CS Peloponnesos. *192*

Akanthos : coastal town of the E Chalkidike, in the N of the
peninsula Akti, in NW Aegean Sea. *224 & 228*

Akarnania : region on the SW coast of mainland Greece, squeezed
between the Gulf of Ambrakia of the Ionian Sea to the W, and
the river Acheloos and Mount Thuamos to the E, Epeiros to the
N and the mouth of the Gulf of Korinthos to the S. *190, 216 &
218*

Akhmim : 1. city on the E bank of the Nile river, also called
Chemmis, in C Egypt, NE Africa. *242*; -- 2. island on a lake,
probably near this city, in Egypt, NE Africa. *242*

Akidos : see Iardanos river. *194*

Akko : seaport at the E end of the Mediterranean Sea, in Ancient
Palestine, modern Acre, in present-day NW Israel, W Asia. *258*

Akovitika : seaport city in SW Messenia, at the N end of the Bay of Navarino, in SW Peloponnesos. *196*

Akra :1. cape at the S tip of the peninsula Malea, in SE Lakonia, SE Peloponnesos. *198*; -- 2. cape at the W end of the peninsula Mimas, in Lydia, CW Asia Minor, present-day CW Turkey. *250*

Akragas : 1. coastal town, modern Agrigento, in the CS side of the island of Sicily, where the Hypsas and Akragas rivers meet before running into the W Mediterranean Sea. *234*; -- 2. river of CS of Sicily, in W Europe. *234*

Akraia : Hill SE of Mukenae, opposite the sanctuary of Hera (Heraion), in NW Argolis, NE Peloponnesos. *202*

Akraiphia : territory in NE Boiotia, near the Gulf of Oropos, in SE mainland Greece. *212*

Akraiphnion : town on the E side of Lake Kopais, in C Boiotia, SE mainland Greece. *212*

Akriae : town of CW Lakonia, on the NE coast of the Gulf of Lakonia, in SE Peloponnesos. *198*

Akritas : mountain at the S tip of S Messenia, in SW Peloponnesos, extending as a cape between the Gulf of Messenia to the E and the Ionian Sea to the W, opposite the island of Theganussa to the S. *196*

Akrokeraunia : promontory above the NE Ionian Sea, in NW Epeiros, NW mainland Greece, near the border with Illyria. *218*

Akrokorinthos : mount in Korinthia, NW Argolis, overlooking the SE end of the Gulf of Korinthos, above the S terraces of the city of Korinthos, in NE Peloponnesos. *202*

Akropolis : 1. mount in the center of Athens, in Attika, SE mainland Greece. *208*; -- 2. similar mounts in other Greek cities.

Akroterion : town on the island of Zakinthos, in the CE Ionian Sea. *194*

Akrothoi : city near the SE coast of the peninsula Akti, in the E Chalkidike, NW Aegean Sea, NE mainland Greece. *228*

Akrotiri : 1. town in the S of the island of Thera, in the S Cyclades, SW Aegean Sea, *230*; -- 2. peninsula between the Gulf of Khania and the Bay of Souda, in the NW island of Crete, C Mediterranean Sea. *204*; -- 3. town on the NW side of this peninsula. *204*; -- 4. peninsula in CS of the island of Cyprus, E Mediterranean Sea. *256*; -- 4. town on this peninsula. *256*

Akte : shore area at the S end of the peninsula of Peiraia, in CW Attika, SE mainland Greece. *208*

Akti : 1. peninsula opposite the Peiraia peninsula in CW Attika, SW of Athens, in SE mainland Greece. *208*; -- 2. the E peninsula of the Chalkidike, modern Agion Oros, in NW Aegean Sea, NE mainland Greece. *228*

Aktion : promontory of the S peninsula forming the Gulf of Ambrakia, in N Akarnania, S mainland Greece. *216*

Alaca : town in CN of Cappadocia, ancient Hittite territory, NE of Hattusa, in present-day CN Turkey, W Asia. *248*

Alagonia : town in CW Lakonia, in the hills of Mount Kalathios, in SW Peloponnesos. *198*

Alalakh : ancient Syrian city, modern Tell Acana, near the NE end of the Mediterranean Sea, in the Orontes river valley, present-day E Turkey. *256*

Alalia : coastal town, also known as Aléria, on the E side of the island of Corsica, in the Tyrrhenian Sea, W Europe. *232*

Alalkomenae : city of Boiotia, on the Herkune river, NW of Koroneia, in SE mainland Greece. *212*

Alashiya : see Cyprus. 2*56*

Alassa : see Lassaia. *206*

Albania : region of the ancient Albani tribe, modern country on the coast of the S Adriatic and N Ionian seas, surrounded by Greece, Macedonia, Kosovo and Montenegro, in the W Balkans, SE Europe. *188, 218 & 240*

Albion : large island W of mainland Europe in the Atlantic Ocean, modern Britain and England. *240*

Al- Biqã : valley, also known as Bekaa, between the Lebanon and Anti-Lebanon mountain ranges, connecting Lebanon with Syria, in W Asia. *256 & 258*

Alea : town in NE Arkadia, near the border with Argolis, in CE Peloponnesos. *192*

Aleion : plain, in SW Cilicia, near the NE coast of the Mediterranean Sea, in SE Asia Minor, present-day SE Turkey. *256*

Alepotrupa : cave at Diros in the Mani Peninsula, in Lakonia, SE Peloponnesos. *198*

Aleppo : city in present-day N Syria, ancient Halab, on the trading route between the Western World and Asia. *258*

Aléria : see Alalia. *232*

Alesia : city near the Alps, in E Gaul, present-day NE France, W Europe. *232*

Alesion : 1. Homeric town, somewhere on a rocky mount in W Elis, on the coast of the Ionian Sea, in NW Peloponnesos. *194*; -- 2. mountain in Arkadia, E of the Ophis river, in CE Peloponnesos. *192*

Alexander's Harbor : harbor city, modern Karachi, in ancient Sangada, on the N Arabian Sea, in present-day SE Pakistan, C Asia. *264*

Alexandretta : 1. gulf in the NE Mediterranean Sea, also called Iskenderun, N Phoenicia, present-day SE Turkey, near N Lebanon

W Asia. *256*; -- 2. city, also called Iskenderun and Alexandria-at-Issos, on the E side of this gulf. *256*

Alexandria : (in alphabetical order) 1. town in W Arachosia of ancient Parthia, present-day Kandahãr, rebuilt many times, in SE Afghanistan, C Asia. *262*; -- 2. town in Areia, see modern Herat. *260*; -- 3. city in S Carmenia, modern Gulashkird, in present-day SE Iran, W Asia. *264*; -- 4. city known as Alexandria-in-Caucasus (Hindu Kush), ancient Nicaea, in S Bactria. present-day NE Afghanistan, C Asia. *262*; -- 5. Alexandria-Charax, modern Basra, near the estuary of the Euphrates and Tigris rivers into the Persian Gulf, in S Mesopotamia, present-day S Iraq, W Asia. *258*; -- 6. Mediterranean seaport city at the W edge of the Nile Delta in Egypt, NE Africa. *242*; -- 7. town, ancient Eschate, modern Khodjend and Leninabad, in the area of Escharta, N Sogdiana, present-day Kazakhstan, C Asia. *262*; -- 8. city known as Alexandria-in-India, in NW India, C Asia. *266*; -- 9. city known as Alexandria-at-Issos, see Alexandretta. *256*; -- 10. city known as Alexandria-Kapisu, ancient Cartana and modern Bagrãm, N of Kabul, in present-day NE Afghanistan. *262*; -- 11. town in Margiane, near Margiana, in the Merv Oasis, W Bactria, present-day Turkmenistan, C Asia. *260*; -- 12. town known as Alexandria-Nicaea, near the Hydaspes river, in Bactria, N India, C Asia. *266*; -- 13. town known as Alexandria-in-Opiene, E of the Hydaspes river, in Bactria, present-day N India, C Asia. *266*; -- 14. town known as Alexandria-in-Oreitidae, modern Las Bela, in Sangada, present-day SE Pakistan, C Asia. *264*; -- 15. town in Prophthasia, Drangiana, present-day C Afghanistan, C Asia. *260*; -- 16. town known as Alexandria-at-Rambacia, N of Cocala, in present-day S Pakistan, C Asia. *264*; -- 17. town known as Alexandria-at-Rohri, also called Sogda, in Arachosia, W of the Thar Desert of India, in SE Pakistan, C Asia. *266*; -- 18. city known as Alexandria-in-Susiana, in Elam, SW Persia, present-day SW Iran, W Asia. *258*; -- 19. town in N Thrace, along the Vedea river, in present-day S Romania, E Europe. *226*; -- 20. city known as Alexandria-in-Troas, also called Sigeion, at the entrance to the Hellespontos, in NW Asia Minor, present-day NW Turkey. *250*

Alexandropolis : capital city of the Maidi, renamed by Alexander the Great, in the Kumli valley, along the Strumon river in W Thrace, present-day Bulgaria, E Europe. *226*

Algeria : country of NW Africa on the Mediterranean coast, between present-day Morocco and W Sahara to the W, Tunisia and Libya to the E, and Mauritania, Mali & Niger to the S. *188, 232 & 244*

Algerian : sea N of Algeria, NW Africa, at the W end of the Mediterranean Sea, surrounded by Spain, France, and the islands of Corsica and Sardinia. *244*

Aliakmon : river, also called Vistritsa, flowing from NE Pindos Mountains, SE through S Macedonia, into the N of the Gulf of Thermaikos, arm of the NE Aegean Sea. *224*

Aliki : town on the SE coast of the island of Thasos, in N Aegean Sea. *228*

Alimos : village S of Phaleron, in CW Attika, SE mainland Greece. *208*

Alinda : inland city of Caria, SE of Miletos, in SW Asia Minor, present-day SW Turkey. *254*

Alipheira : town in CW Arkadia, NW of Theisoa, in C Peloponnesos. *192*

Alishar : town of Anatolia, in CN of the Hittite territory, SE of Hattusa, in present-day NE Turkey, W Asia. *248*

Alkimedon : plain between the E slopes of Mount Mainalos and the city of Mantinea, in □ Arkadia, CE Peloponnesos. *192*

Allana : town on the W side of the island of Crete, exact location uncertain, in C Mediterranean Sea. *204*

Allia : river in the Latium, tributary of the Tiber, N of Rome, in CW Italy, W Europe. *238*

Al-Marj : see Barce. *244*

Almeria : 1. gulf of the W Mediterranean Sea, in SE Iberia, present-day SE Spain, W Europe. *232*; -- 2. city on the N side of this gulf. *232*

Al Mina : seaport of Phoenicia, at the mouth of the Orontes river, on the NE Mediterranean Sea, in modern NW Syria, W Asia. *256*

Almirou : gulf where the city of Rithumna is located, south of the Bay of Souda, in NW island of Crete, CS Mediterranean Sea. *204*

Almopia : tribal area in the CW Macedonia, NE mainland Greece. *224*

Almunécar : see Sexi. *232*

Almuros : site of an ancient cemetery at modern Almuros, on the W side of the Gulf of Pagassai, in Phthiotis, NE mainland Greece. *222*

Al- Mygdoniae : town, N of Arbela, in N Mesopotamia, on the E side the Tigris river, in present-day N Iraq, W Asia. *258*

Alonnisos : island of the Thessalian Sporades, in CW Aegean Sea. *228*

Alope : 1. spring near Eleusis, in the NW of Attika, SE mainland Greece. *210*; -- 2. city of E Opuntian Lokris, in CE mainland Greece, on the Gulf of Oropos, separating it from N island of Euboia. *214*

Alopeoe : suburb S of Athens, in CW Attika, SE mainland Greece. *208*

Alos : 1. Hesiodic city in Aitolia, exact location unknown, in CS mainland Greece. *216*; -- 2. see Halos. *222*

Alpheios : river flowing NW from the Parrhasios mountain range in SW Arkadia, past Olumpia through Elis where it meets several tributaries, before discharging into the Ionian Sea, in NW Peloponnesos. *192 & 194*

Alps : mountains of CS Europe, covering SE France, N Italy, S Switzerland, W Germany, Croatia and Austria. *188, 232 & 240*

Altinum : harbor city of the N Adriatic Sea, modern Venice, in NE Italy, C Europe. *238*

Alube : Homeric city of Phrygia, S of the Euxine (Black) Sea, in NW Asia Minor, present-day NW Turkey. *252*

Aluntium : coastal city in the NE of the island of Sicily, S of the Gulf of Messina, on the Sicilian Sea, W Europe. *236*

Al-Utaybah : Lake into which the river Barada discharges, E of Damascus, in S Syria, W Asia. *258*

Aluzia : town in SW Akarnania, S of Aitos, in SW mainland Greece. *216*

Amanos : mountain range between E Cilicia, in SE Turkey, and NW Syria, in W Asia. *256 & 258*

Amardus : river, modern Sefid Rud, flowing N from the Parachoathras mountains into the Caspian Sea, in W Asia. *260*

Amarna : city of C Egypt, also known as Tell el-Amarna, on the E bank of the Nile river, in NE Africa. *242*

Amastris : see Sesamos. *252*

Amathus : town in SW of the island of Cyprus, near Limassol, in the NE Mediterranean Sea. *256*

Amaxitos : city of Troas, N of Larissa, near the Aegean Sea, in present-day NW Turkey, W Asia. *250*

Ambrakia : 1. gulf of the Ionian Sea, also called Arta, in NW Akarnania, NE of the island of Leukas, in NW mainland Greece. *216*; -- 3. area N of this gulf. *216*; -- 4. city in this area. *216*

Ambrosos : city SE of Delphi, in CS Phokis, CS mainland Greece. *214*

Ameselum : inland town in the CE of the island of Sicily, W Mediterranean Sea. *236*

Amilos : town N of Mount Trachu, in NE Arkadia, C Peloponnesos. *192*

Amisos : town, modern Samsun, E of Sinope, at the CS of the Euxine (Black) Sea, between the deltas of the rivers Kizil and Yesil, in Phrygia, present-day NW Turkey, W Asia. *252*

Ammonium : city of NW Egypt, ancient Zeus Ammon and modern Siwa, in the oasis of Siwa, on the border with Kyrenaika, in NE Africa. *242*

Amnisos : seaport city in the NE of the island of Crete, C Mediterranean Sea. *206*

Amorgos : island on the SE side of the Cyclades, in SW Aegean Sea. *230*

Ampelos : seaport city below a promontory, in the S of the peninsula Sithonia of the Chalkidike, in the N Aegean Sea, NE mainland Greece. *228*

Amphanae : village near the seaport city of Pagassai, in SE Thessalia, NE mainland Greece. *220*

Amphaxitis : area of C Macedonia, between the Axios and Strumon rivers, including the Charadros river, N of the Gulf of Thermai, in NE mainland Greece. *224*

Amphia : city of CE Messenia, near the border with Lakonia, in SW Peloponnesos. *196*

Amphiareion : 1. small territory of the Oropians on the NE border between Attika and Boiotia, near the coast of the Gulf of Petalion, in SE mainland Greece. *210*; -- 2. island in C Aegean Sea, W of the island of Chios. *230*

Amphigeneia : Homeric city in CW Messenia, near Pulos, on the coast of the Ionian Sea, in SW Peloponnesos. *196*

Amphikaea : ancient city in N Phokis, also known as Amphiklea, SW of Tithronion, in CS mainland Greece. *214*

Amphiklea : see Amphikaea, *214*

Amphilochia : area of NW Aitolia, E of the Gulf of Ambrakia, in SW mainland Greece. *216*

Amphipolis : city, once called Ennea Hodoi, on a plateau above the river Strumon in SW Thrace, E of the Chalkidike peninsulas, NE of the Gulf of Orfanou, in NE mainland Greece. *226*

Amphirho : Hesiodic mythical river, meaning Surrounding, probably in Greece. *269*

Amphissa : town in NE Ozolian Lokris, NW of Delphi and W of Mount Parnassos in Phokis, in CS mainland Greece. *214*

Amphitrope : town in CW Attika, on the Saronic Gulf, in SE mainland Greece. *208*

Amphitos : river in NW Messenia, flowing S and joining the Pamisos river as a tributary, in SW Peloponnesos. *196*

Amu Darya : see Oxus river. *260 & 262*

Amudon : town of NE Macedonia, in NE mainland Greece, present-day W Bulgaria, in SE Europe. *224*

Amuklai : town of NW Lakonia, S of Sparta, on the bank of the river Eurotas, in SE Peloponnesos. *198*

Amuros : Hesiodic town on the plain of Dotion, E of Larissa, in CN Thessalia, NE mainland Greece. *220*

Anaguros : town in SW Attika, on the SE side of the Humettos mountain range, in SE mainland Greece. *208*

Anaktorion : town S of the Gulf of Ambrakia, N of Medeon, in N Akarnania, SW mainland Greece. *216*

Anamis : river flowing from Carmenia, in present-day SE Iran, into the Gulf of Oman, W Asia. *264*

Anaphe : island in CS of the Cyclades, E of Thera, in CS Aegean Sea. *230*

Anaphlustos : town, modern Anavusos, in Paralia, SW Attika, SE mainland Greece. *208*

Anapos : 1. river probably in E Akarnania, flowing SW into the Ionian Sea, in SW mainland Greece. *216*; -- 2. river fowing E into the harbor of Siracusa, on the SE side of the island of Sicily, in W Mediterranean Sea. *236*

Anatolia : region covering mostly the Asiatic portion of present-day Turkey, ancient Asia Minor, from the Aegean Sea in the W, the Mediterranean Sea in the S, including the Hittite territories, to N Iran in the E, in W Asia. *190, 246, 248, 250 & 252*

Anavusos : see Anaphlustos. *208*

Anchesmos : mount, N of ancient Athens, modern Lukavettos, in the center of present-day Athens, in C Attika, SE mainland Greece. *208*

Anchisia : mountain in CE Arkadia, S of Orchomenos, in C Peloponnesos. *192*

Ancyra : town of SE Bithynia, S of the Euxine (Black) Sea, NE of Gordion, in present-day CN Turkey, W Asia. *252*

Andalusia : modern region of S Spain, in W Europe. *232*

Andania :town of NE Messenia, on the W bank of the river Charadros, in SW Peloponnesos. *196*

Andritsaina : town near Bassai, in SW Arkadia, C Peloponnesos. *192*

Andros : 1. most N of the islands of the Cyclades, S of the island of Euboia, in the Aegean Sea. *230*; -- 2. city on the E coast of this island. *230*

Anemoreia : city in S Phokis, CN of the Gulf of Korinthos (Krisa), in CS mainland Greece. *214*

Anemosa : town in CS Arkadia, E of Mount Phalanthos, in C Peloponnesos. *192*

Anigraia : area covering Dine and the W of Dine, along the W coast of the Gulf of Argolis, in SW Argolis, NE Peloponnesos. *202*

Anigros : river known for its bad smell, flowing W from mount Lapithos in CW Arkadia, through SE Elis, into the Ionian Sea, S of Sarnia, in CW Peloponnesos. *194*

Ano : palace site W of Zakros at the E end of the island of Crete, in C Mediterranean Sea. *206*

Anopolis : site above Aradaena, in SW of the island of Crete, C Mediterranean Sea. *204*

Anshan : 1. area in SW Media (Persia), present-day SW Iran, W Asia. *260*; -- 2. city, NW of Susa, in this area. *260*

Antakya : see Antioch. *256*

Antalya : 1. gulf of the Mediterranean Sea, in Pamphylia, CS of Turkey, W Asia. *256*; -- 2. seaport city, also known as Attalia and Perga, modern Murtina. at the NW corner of the same gulf. *256*

Antandros : Aiolian town at the E end of the gulf of Edremit, S of Mount Ida, opposite the island of Lesbos, in E Mysia, NW Asia Minor, present-day NW Turkey. *250*

Antariatae : lake in NW Illyria, present-day Croatia, along the NE side of the Adriatic Sea, in W Europe. *218*

Anthedon : town on the CE coast of Boiotia, near the Strait of Euripos, N of Aulis, in CE mainland Greece. *212*

Antheia : Hesiodic city in SE Thessalia, near the border with Achaia Phthiotis, NE mainland Greece. *220*

Anthela : city on the border between Opuntian Lokris and Malis, near Thermopulai, on the coast along the Gulf of Malis, in CE mainland Greece. *214*

Anthemoëssa : mythological islands of the Sirens, probably along the W Coast of Italy, in W Europe. *269*

Anthemos : inland city of SE Macedonia, N of Chalkidike, in NE mainland Greece. *224*

Anthene : see Athene. *202*

Anthylla : city near the Canobia (Rosetta) branch of the W Delta of the Nile river, in NW Egypt, NE Africa. *242*

Antigoneia : 1. town of W Macedonia, modern Negotino, W of the Axios river, in N mainland Greece. *224*; -- 2. inland city of Chaonia, in NW Epeiros, NW mainland Greece. *218*

Antigori : town on the SE of the island of Sardinia, on the W side of the Tyrrhenian Sea, in W Europe. *232*

Antikura : 1. bay in the N side of the Gulf of Korinthos, in CS Phokis, CS mainland Greece. *214*; -- 2. port city at the top W side of this bay. *214*; -- 3. city of E Malis, near the coast of the Gulf of Malis and the mouth of the Spercheios river, in NE mainland Greece. *214*; -- 4. city in SW Ozolian Lokris, near the border with Aitolia, on the N side of the entrance to the Gulf of Korinthos, in SW mainland Greece. *214*

Antikuthera : island between the NW of the island of Crete and the island of Kuthera, S of Lakonia in the SE Peloponnesos, C Mediterranean Sea. *204*

Anti-Lebanon : mountain range from the N plain of Syria in the N to Mount Hermon in the S, separating NW Syria from Lebanon and following a track parallel to the E of the Lebanon mountain range, in W Asia. *256*

Antimacheia : mythological land of the Meropians, blind people. *269*

Antioch : 1. city of ancient Syria, now Antakya of SE Turkey, near the mouth of the Orontes river, in W Asia. *256*; -- 2. see Pythopolis. *254*

Antiocheia : city of Pisidia, near the NE end of lake Hoyran, in present-day C Turkey, W Asia. *256*

Antissa : coastal town on the W side of the island of Lesbos, in NE Aegean Sea, E of Aiolia in Asia Minor. *228*

Antron : Homeric town in NE Achaia Phthiotis, NE mainland Greece. *222*

Anysis : town in the C Nile Delta, N Egypt, NE Africa. *242*

Aoos : river, also called Aias, flowing N from the Pindos mountains of Epeiros, modern Macedonia, past Konitsa, then W on the border with Illyria and into the Adriatic Sea, in SE Europe. *218*

Aornos : 1. town in the area of Khulm (Tashkurghan), in ancient Bactria, ancient Pir Sarai and modern Savnob, in N Afghanistan, C Asia. *262*; -- 2. steep ridge, in ancient Bactria, W of the Indus and N of the Buner rivers, S of Kashmir, modern Pir Sarai, in N Pakistan, C Asia. *266*

Apaisos : town on the S side of the Hellespontos, where it reaches the Sea of Propontis, in NW Asia Minor, Present-day NW Turkey. *250*

Apameia : city in NW Syria, on the E bank of the Orontes river, in W Asia. *256*

Apameia Murleia : see Kelainae, in Lydia, Asia Minor. *254*

Apeire : mythical town in the land of Phaecians, perhaps Crete. *269*

Apennines : mountain range crossing C Italy from N to S, in W Europe. *238*

Aperopia : island S of the peninsula of Argolis, opposite Cape Buporthmos, in SE Argolis, NE Peloponnesos. *202*

Apesas : mountain in NW Argolis, SW of Korinthos, in NE Peloponnesos. *202*

Aphaia : town near the NE coast of the island of Aigina, in the S Saronic Gulf, SE mainland Greece. *208*

Aphetae : 1. site on the coast of the Magnesia peninsula, in SE Thessalia, NE mainland Greece. *220*; -- 2. site in Kolchis, on the E coast of the Euxine (Black) Sea, in present-day Georgia, E Europe. *248*

Aphidna : village in NE Attika, on the river Charadra, in SE mainland Greece. *210*

Aphousa : small island, modern Avsa, in the SW of the Sea of Propontis, W of the island Pasalimani, in present-day NW Turkey, W Asia. *250*

Aphrodisia : 1. city of Messenia, somewhere on the coast of the Ionian Sea, in SW Peloponnesos. *196*; -- 2. city of Lakonia, probably near Koturta, both precise locations unknown, in SE Peloponnesos. *198*; -- 3. city of CW Arkadia, near the river Arsen, in C Peloponnesos. *192*

Aphroditopolis : town in N Egypt, on the E bank of the Nile river, S of Memphis, in NE Africa. *242*

Aphtis : city in the CE Delta of the Nile river, N Egypt, NE Africa. *242*

Aphutis : coastal city of the W Chalkidike, in S Macedonia, on the CE side of the Peninsula Kassandra (Pallene), in NE mainland Greece. *228*

Apis : ancient town on the NW side of Egypt, near the border with Kyrenaica, in NE Africa. *242*

Apollinopolis : town of S Egypt, modern Edfu, on the W bank of the Nile river, N of Aswan, in NE Africa. *242*

Apollo : site of a sanctuary of Apollo, E of Lake Kopais and N of lake Hulika, in C Boiotia, SE mainland Greece. *212*

Apollonia : 1. town in NW Epeiros, N mainland Greece, on the SE Ionic Gulf, where the Adriatic Sea meets the Ionian Sea. *218*; -- 2. seaport of Kyrenaica, near Kyrene, in E Libya, NE Africa. *244*; -- 3. town of SE Macedonia, in Mugdonia, NE of Salonika, in NE mainland Greece. *224*; -- 4. town of CE Thrace, on the CW coast of the Euxine (Black) Sea, in present-day Bulgaria, SE Europe. *226*; -- 5. town in the NE of the island of Sicily, on the coast of the Tyrrhenian Sea, exact location uncertain, in W Europe. *236*; -- 6. see Eleutherna. *206*

Apostana : city S of Gogana, on the E shore of the Persian Gulf, in W Carmania, S Persia, present-day SW Iran. *264*

Apsilaea : area of Scythia, in present-day S Russia, W Asia. *248*

Apsus : river of W Macedonia, flowing W into Epeiros, S of the Genusus river, and into the Adriatic Sea, in NW mainland Greece. *224*

Aptera : town in the NW end of the island of Crete, on the Bay of Souda, C Mediterranean Sea. *204*

Apulia : region of SE Italy along the Adriatic Sea, also known as Puglia, in W Europe. *246*

Aqaba : 1. gulf of the NE Red Sea, extending between the Sinai Peninsula and NW Saudi Arabia, in SW Asia. *258*; -- 2. port on this gulf at the SW corner of Jordan. *258*

Arabaya : region in the NE of Egypt, between the N end of the Red Sea and the Gulf of Aqaba, in NE africa. *242*

Arabia : Desert peninsula in SW Asia between the Red Sea to the W and the Persian Gulf to the E, the Arabian Sea to the S and Jordan & Iraq to the N. *187 & 258*

Arabian : 1. sea in the NW Indian Ocean, between India on the E side and the coast from the strait of Oman in the N to Yemen in the S, in S Asia. *188, 246 & 264*; -- 2. in ancient times, included both the present-day Arabian Sea and Red Sea. *187*

Arabis : river of Oreitis, also called Purali, in S Pakistan, flowing E through E Baluchistan, past Alexandria-in-Oreitidae, before emptying in the Indian Ocean, S of Karachi, in C Asia. *264*

Arachnaeos : mountain range, also called Abas, in C Argolis, NW of Epidauros, in NE Peloponnesos. *202*

Arachosia : region between Bactria to the N, Gedrosia & the Arabian Sea to the S, Drangiana to the W and the Indus river and India to the E, covering mostly modern Afghanistan and N Pakistan, in C Asia. *246, 262 & 266*

Aradaena : 1. river with gorges, flowing SE from the White mountains of Crete into the Libyan Sea. *204*; -- 2. ancient city along a gorge of this river, exact location uncertain, in C Mediterranean Sea. *204*

Arados : island city of C Phoenicia, on the E Mediterranean Sea, off the coast of present-day Lebanon, in W Asia. *256*

Arae : Ionian city on the coast of the CE Aegean Sea, S of Teos, in CW Asia Minor, present-day SW Turkey. *254*

Arainon : city of C Lakonia, on the NW coast of the Gulf of Lakonia, S of Las, in CS Peloponnesos. *198*

Arakunthos : 1. mount in SW Aitolia, SW mainland Greece. *216*; -- 2. plain at the foot of this mount, once a site of the ciy of Pleuron. *216*

Aral : sea E of the Caspian sea, the N in modern SW Kazakhstan and the S in modern Uzbekistan, in C Asia. *187, 188, 246 & 260*

Arantia : town in the hills of NW Argolis, SW of Nemea, in NE Peloponnesos. *202*

Araphen : coastal town of CE Attika, on the Gulf of Petalion, in SE mainland Greece. *210*

Ararat : mountain in Armenia, S of the Araxes river, in W Asia. *248*

Araros : 1. one of five rivers flowing from the Carpathian mountains, between the Pyretus and Tiarantus rivers, into the Danube river, in Scythia, present-day Romania, E Europe. *240*, -- 2. city on this river. *240*

Aras : see Araxes/Caspian. *248*

Araxes : 1. river of C Asia, modern Aras river, rising from the mountains of E Turkey, flowing E through Armenia, between Azerbaijan in the N and Turkey & Iran in the S, joining the Kuros river in Cadusia, before discharging into the Caspian Sea, in C Asia. *248*, -- 2. river, also called Pulvar, flowing S From Elam (Susiana) into the Persian Gulf, in Persis, present-day S Iran, W Asia. *264*

Araxos : cape in the NW corner of Achaia, S of the Gulf of Patraikos, in NW Peloponnesos. *200*

Arbela : town, modern Irbil, in N Mesopotamia, S of Kirkuk, on the E side the Tigris river, in present-day N Iraq, W Asia. *258*

Archandropolis : city in the NW Delta of the Nile river, near Anthylla, in N Egypt, NE Africa. *242*

Archanes : town near the C of the island of Crete, S of Herakleion, in C Mediterranean Sea. *206*

Arcia : area of Bactria, covering modern N Afghanistan, in C Asia. *262*

Arda : river flowing from the Rhodope mountains of Thrace, present-day Bulgaria, through Greece, joining the Maritsa river, W of Uskudama (Edirne) in European Turkey. *226*

Ardakan : inland city in N Persis, S Persia, present-day S Iran, W Asia. *264*

Ardeskos : Hesiodic river, probably in Aitolia, SW mainland Greece. *216*

Ardiaei : tribal land located in Illyria, S of Autoriatae, in NW Balkan Peninsula, present-day Croatia, along the NE Adriatic Sea. *218*

Areia : area in E Parthia, in present-day NW Afghanistan, C Asia. *246 & 260*

Areiopagos : hill, just W of the Akropolis of Athens, in Attika. *208*

Arene : seaport city in NW Messenia, on the Ionian Sea, in CW Peloponnesos. *196*

Ares : small island at the SE end of the Euxine (Black) Sea, in W Asia. *248*

Arethurea : town in E Achaia, exact location uncertain, in N Peloponnesos. *200*

Arethusa : 1. spring in CE Elis, somewhere along the Alpheios river, in NW Peloponnesos. *194*, -- 2. spring on the island of Ortugia, near Siracusa, in SE Sicily, W Mediterranean Sea, W Europe. *236*, -- 3. inland city of ancient Syria, beyond the E end of the Mediterranean Sea, in W Asia. *256*; -- 4. town of Bisaltia, N of Bromiskos, N of the Chalkidike peninsulas, in E Macedonia, NE mainland Greece. *224*

Arezzo : see Arretium. *238*

Argilos : city in SE Macedonia, on the N coast of Gulf of Orfanou, in N Aegean Sea, E of the Chalkidike and SW of Amphipolis of SW Thrace, in NE mainland Greece. *224*

Arginos : cape most W in Lydia, on the peninsula Mimas, opposite the island of Chios, in CW Asia Minor, present-day Turkey. *250*

Arginusai : Aiolian islands in W Mysia, opposite the island of Lesbos, in NW Asia Minor, present-day NW Turkey. *250*

Argissa : town in CE Thessalia, CN mainland Greece. *220*

Argolid : see Argolis. *202*

Argolis : 1. gulf surrounded by S Argolis, also called Gulf of Argos, N of the Mirtóön Sea, in NE Peloponnesos. *202*; -- 2. region around the Gulf of Argolis, including the area along the W side of the Gulf, N of Lakonia, and the Peninsula between the Gulf of Argolis to the W and the Saronic Gulf to the E. *190, 192, 198, 200 & 202*; -- 3. peninsula in the S of this region, E of the gulf, in the CN Mediterranean Sea. *202*

Argos : 1. city of CW Argolis, at the foot of Mount Larissa, N of the Gulf of Argolis, NW of Tiruns, in NE Peloponnesos. *202*; -- 2. see Gulf of Argolis. *202*; -- 3. town of NW Aitolia, referred to as Amphilochian Argos, E of the Gulf of Ambrakia, in SW mainland Greece. *216*

Argupheia : seaport city on the Ionian Sea, S of Arene, in Messenia, CW Peloponnesos. *196*

Argura : city in CN Achaia, near the SW shore of the Gulf of Korinthos, NE of Patrai, in CN Peloponnesos. *200*

Ariaspi : see Sistan. *260 & 264*

Aricia : town of the Latium, S of Rome, in C Italy, W Europe. *238*

Aridanos : tributary river, joining the river Peneios in the plain of Thessalia, in N mainland Greece. *220*

Arigaeum : city in NW India, S of the valley of Kashmir, C Asia. *266*

Arima : mythological site of the Underworld. *268*

Arimaspia : legendary world of the Gryphons, perhaps the Caucasus region, between the Euxine (Black) Sea and the Caspian Sea, in W Asia. *269*

Arisbe : 1. city on the S side of the Hellespontos in Troas, NW Asia Minor, present-day NW Turkey. *250*; -- 2. ancient site on the island of Lesbos, in NE Aegean Sea. *228*

Aristerai : small island, S of the island Pitiussa, off the SW coast of the peninsula of Argolis, in the N Mirtóön Sea. *202*

Aristonautae : port on the SE side of the Gulf of Korinthos, in NE Achaia, near the border with Argolis, in NE Peloponnesos. *200*

Arkades : town in the C island of Crete, C Mediterranean Sea. *204*

Arkadia : region in C Peloponnesos, S of Achaia and E of Elis, W of Argolis and N of Messenia and Lakonia. *190, 192, 194, 196, 198, 200 & 202*

Arkesine : town on the island of Amorgos, in the Cyclades, CW Aegean Sea. *230*

Arkines : village in Lakonia, exact location uncertain, in the SE Peloponnesos. *198*

Arkolochori : 1. village, SE of Herakleion, in C island of Crete, CS Mediterranean Sea. *206*; -- 2. cave near this village. *206*

Arkoudiotissa : town in the N of the peninsula Akrotiri, NW Island of Crete, C Mediterranean Sea. *204*

Arktonnessos : ancient island in the SW of the Sea of Propontis, later made a peninsula called Cyzicus, modern Kapidagi, in Phrygia, present-day NW Turkey, W Asia. *250*

Arkturos : see Phasis river. *248*

Armenia : region between the Euxine (Black) Sea and the Caspian Sea, S of the Caucasus mountains and N of Media (Iran), in W Asia. *188, 246 & 248*

Armenoi : inland town, near the mouth of the Puknos river, at the Bay of Souda, in NW island of Crete, C Mediterranean Sea. *204*

Arne : 1. see Chaironeia. *212* -- 2. town in the Chalkidike, unknown location, in NE mainland Greece. *228*

Arnisa : town in NW Macedonia, S of lake Begoritis, in NE mainland Greece. *224*

Arnus : river of Toscana, flowing from the Apennines mountains, first S then W, past Faesulae, into the Ligurian Sea near Pisae, in C Italy, W Europe. *238*

Aroanios : 1. mountain range running EW in N Arkadia, source of the river Stux, in CN Peloponnesos. *192*; -- 2. river in NW Arkadia, tributary of the river Erumanthos, in CN Peloponnesos. *192*; -- 3. city in NW Arkadia, near the border with Achaia to the N and Elis to the E, in NE Peloponnesos. *192*

Arrapkha : city, modern Kirkuk, E of the Tigris river, in NE Mesopotamia, present-day Iraq, W Asia. *258*

Arretium : 1. Etruscan region in CN Italy, modern Arezzo, in W Europe. *238*; -- 2. main town in this region. *238*

Arsen : river of NW Arkadia, tributary of river Ladon in Elis, C Peloponnesos. *192*

Arsinoë : town in the CN of the island of Crete, adjacent to or identical with Rithumna, in C Mediterranean Sea *204*

Arsissa : see Van Lake. *248*

Arta : 1. modern city in S Epeiros, above the Gulf of Ambrakia in NW Aitolia, SW mainland Greece. *218*; -- 2. see Ambrakia. *216*

Artakia : mythical spring on the island of the Laestrygonians, perhaps Corsica, in the Tyrrhenian Sea, W Europe. *269*

Artacoana : city of Areia, near Herat, in present-day W Afghanistan, C Asia. *260*

Artanes : river in Thrace, course unknown, in NE mainland Greece. *226*

Artemision : 1. cape on the NE coast of the island of Euboia, E of mainland Greece. *228*; -- 2. town on the same cape. *228*; -- 3. mount on the CW side of Argolis, on the border with CE Arkadia, in CE Peloponnesos. *202*

Arvi : village on the S coast in CE of the island of Crete, in C Mediterranean Sea. *206*

Arzawa : territory covering SW Anatolia, neighboring the Hittite territories to the E, in present-day SW Turkey, W Asia. *252*

Ascalon : city, present-day Ashqelon in Philistia, S of Ashdod, at the SE end of the Mediterranean Sea, in S ancient Palestine, present-day SW Israel, W Asia. *258*

Asculum : town in Picene, SE Italy, W Europe. *238*

Asea : town in SE Arkadia, E of Megalopolis, in C Peloponnesos. *192*

Ashdod : see Azotus. *258*

Ashqelon : see Ascalon. *258*

Asia : 1. largest of the present-day continents, between the Arctic Ocean to the N, the Indian Ocean to the S, the Pacific Ocean, except in the Ancient Greek World, India only to the E, and roughly the Ural Mountains, W Turkey & the Red Sea to the W. *187, 188, 246, 258, 260, 262, 264, 266*; -- 2. mount near the NW coast of the Gulf of Lakonia, W of Arainon and Las, in CS Peloponnesos. *198*

Asia Minor : region of present-day Asiatic Turkey, between the Sea of Marmara and the Euxine (Black) Sea to the N, the Aegean Sea on the W side, the Mediterranean Sea to the S, and covering the W portion of ancient Anatolia which extends to the Euphrates river in Kurdistan, W Asia. *190, 230, 246 & 252*

Asine : 1. town of SW Argolis, ancient site of Talioti, S of Nauplia, on the Gulf of Argolis, in NE Peloponnesos. *202*; -- 2. harbor town of SE Messenia, on the SW coast of the Gulf of Messenia, also known as Koroni, in SW Peloponnesos. *196*

Askania : Homeric city in Troas, S of the Hellespontos, in present-day NW Turkey, W Asia. *250*

Askanos : river flowing W through Hellespontine, E of the Rhundakos river, in NW Asia Minor, present-day Turkey, into the Aegean Sea. *250*

Askitario : town of the E coast of Attika, along the Gulf of Petalion, in SE mainland Greece. *210*

Askra : hamlet S of Keressos and E of the Valley of Muses, in S Boiotia, SE mainland Greece. *212*

Askulepios : city in the C of the peninsula of Argolis, site of a sanctuary, in NE Peloponnesos. *202*

Asopios : port city of SE Lakonia, on the E side of the Gulf of Lakonia, on the Peninsula of Mani, in SE Peloponnesos. *198*

Asopos : 1. city of CE Lakonia, on the NE coast of the Gulf of Lakonia, in SE Peloponnesos. *198*; -- 2. river flowing NE from NW Argolis, past Phlios and Sikuon, in NW Argolis, NE Peloponnesos, into the Gulf of Korinthos. *202*; -- 3. river flowing E from the highlands near Leuktra in W Boiotia, through S Boiotia, past Tanagra, in SE mainland Greece, into the Gulf of Petalion. *212*; -- 4. river flowing NE from the mountains of Aitolia, through Malis, NE into the Gulf of Malis, in NE mainland Greece. *214*; -- 5. river flowing N from Mount Ida in S Phrygia, near Skepsis, through Troas and into the Hellespontos, near Zeleia, in present-day NW Turkey. *198*

Aspadana : city of Media, modern Isfahan, on the W side of the Desert of kavir, in S Media, present-day C Iran, W Asia. *260*

Aspasii : tribal land in NW India, S of Kashmir, in C Asia. *266*

Aspendos : city near the mouth of the Eurymedon river, on the coast of the NE Mediterranean Sea, W of Side, in Pamphylia, SW Asia Minor, present-day SW Turkey. *256*

Aspis : hill SW of Argos, next to Mount Larisa, in CW Argolis, in NE Peloponnesos. *202*

Aspledon : town in NW Boiotia, N of Orchomenos, in CE mainland Greece. *212*

Asprochaliko : site on the shore of the river Louros, in CE Epeiros, NW mainland Greece. *218*

Aspropotamos : meaning White River, a surname given to many major rivers of Ancient Greece, especially the Acheloos river in NW Mainland Greece. *216 & 220*

Assa : town at the NW of the peninsula Akti, in the E Chalkidike, N of the Aegean Sea, NE mainland Greece. *228*

Assaceni : tribal land located in NW India, S of the valley of Kashmir, C Asia. *266*

Assesus : city of Lydia, near Sardis, in CW Asia Minor, present-day CW Turkey. *252*

Assinaros : river in the SE of the island of Sicily, S of the Cacyparis river, flowing SE into the Mediterranean Sea, in W Europe. *236*

Assorus : inland town in the CE of the island of Sicily, in W Mediterranean Sea, W Europe. *236*

Assos : Aeolian port city on the N shore of the Gulf of Edremit, in Troas, opposite the offshore island of Lesbos, in present-day NW Turkey, W Asia. *250*

Assur : city of Assyria, W of the Tigris river, in N Mesopotamia, present-day N Iraq, W Asia. *258*

Assyria : region of N Mesopotamia, present-day N Iraq, W Asia. *258*

Astakos : town in CW Akarnania, near the Ionian Sea, in SW mainland Greece. *216*

Asterion : 1. river of NW Argolis, flowing from Mount Tretos, past E of Mukenae, joining the river Inachos as a tributary, in NE Peloponnesos. *202*; -- 2. Homeric city of CE Thessalia, S of lake Boibeis, in CN mainland Greece. *220*

Asteris : 1. small island of the Ionian Sea, N of the island of Leukas, off the coast of Akarnania. *216*; -- 2. harbor city on this island. *216*

Astibos : city of W Macedonia, in the Almopia area, in N mainland Greece. *224*

Astraios : Hesiodic river, later called Kaikos, flowing from the Tamnus Mountains of Lydia, through Mysia, into the E Aegean Sea, in CW Asia Minor, present-day CW Turkey. *250*

Astros : town in SW Argolis, S of Lerna, near the Gulf of Argolis, in NE Peloponnesos. *202*

Astupalaia : 1. mythological site in the land of the Meropians, blind people. *269*; -- 2. the most NW island of the Rhodian Dodekanesoi, in the SE Aegean Sea. *230*; -- 3. cape at the S tip of the island of Rhodes, in SE Aegean Sea. *230*

Aswan : modern city of S Egypt, ancient Syene, N of the first cataract of the Nile river, opposite the island of Elephantine, NE Africa. *242*

Asyût : see Lykopolis. *242*

Ataburion : 1. mountain in the CW of the island of Rhodes, in SE Aegean Sea. *230*; -- 2. mountain of ancient Palestine, between Jerusalem in present-day Israel and Damascus in present-day Syria, in W Asia. *258*

Atalanta : island in the Gulf of Oropos, between Opuntian E Lokris in CE mainland Greece and the N of the island of Euboia. *214*

Atalante : city of SE Macedonia, along the Axios river, S of Gortunia, in NE mainland Greece. *224*

Atarbechis : town on the island of Prosopitis, in the Nile Delta, exact location unknown, in N Egypt, NE Africa. *242*

Atarneus : Aiolian town in W Mysia, opposite the S of the island of Lesbos, in present-day NW Turkey, W Asia. *250*

Atbara : river flowing N from Aithiopia, across E Sudan and joining the Nile river as a tributary, in NE Africa. *244*

Atella : town in SW Italy, on the coast of the Tyrrhenian Sea, in W Europe. *238*

Athena : site of a sanctuary of Athena in Opuntian Lokris, E of Elatheia, CS mainland Greece. *214*

Athenai : see Athens. *208*

Athenaion : 1. city in CN Achaia, on the SW shore of the Gulf of Korinthos, in CN Peloponnesos. *200*; -- 2. city in the NW of Lakonia, near the border with Messenia to the W and Arkadia to the N, in C Peloponnesos. *198*

Athene : coastal city, probably the same as Anthene, on CW Gulf of Argolis, SE of Thurea, in SW Argolis, NE Peloponnesos. *202*

Athens : major city of C Attika, Greek Athenai, a short distance from the Bay of Phaleron in the Saronic Gulf to the SW, mount Anchesmos to the N and the N of the Hymettos mountains to the E, in SE mainland Greece. *208*

Athos : mount in the S of the E peninsula Akti of the Chalkidike, in SE Macedonia, along the NW Aegean Sea, in NE mainland Greece. *228*

Athribis : town in the C Nile Delta, N Egypt, NE Africa. *242*

Atintania : tribal area on the Ionian Sea, W of Molossia in NW Epeiros, NW mainland Greece. *218*

Atlantic : ocean separating Europe and Africa to the E from N and S America to the W. *188, 232 & 244*

Atlantis : mythological region, probably located near Gibraltar, at the W end of the Mediterranean Sea. *269*

Atlas : 1. mountain range running NE from NE Morocco, through Algeria, to SW Tunisia, in NW Africa. *187, 188 & 244*; -- 2. river, also called Auras, flowing from NE Haemos mountains, through Scythia, modern Romania, into the Euxine (Black) Sea, in SE Europe. *226*

Atok : area in N Hyrcania, E of SE Caspian Sea, in N Persia (Media), present-day N Iran, W Asia. *260*

Atropatene : see Media Atropatene. *258*

Attalia : see Antalya. *256*

Attika : region shaped as a peninsula jutting S from Boiotia, into the Mediterranean Sea, on the E side of S mainland Greece. *190, 208, 210, 212 & 228*

Attok : area of the NW Punjab, along the E bank of the Indus river, in NW Pakistan, C Asia. *266*

Augeiae : 1. city in CN Lakonia, exact location unknown, in SE Peloponnesos. *198*; -- 2. Homeric city of Opuntian Lokris, E of Thermopulai, on the Gulf of Oropos, in CE mainland Greece. *214*

Augila : town W of the Sahara desert, in present-day W Mauritania, NW Africa. *244*

Aulis : seaport city of CE Boiotia, in SE mainland Greece, on the strait of Euripos, connecting the Gulfs of Petalion to the S and Oropos to the N, opposite Chalkis on the island of Euboia. *212*

Aulon : 1. town in SE Macedonia, N of the Chalkidike Peninsula, probably near Lake Bolbe, in NE mainland Greece. *224*; -- 2. town on the border between NW Messenia and SW Elis, near the coast of the Ionian Sea, in SW Peloponnesos. *194*

Auras : see Atlas river. *226*

Ausonia: see Italy. *187 & 238*

Austria : country of CS Europe surrounded by Switzerland, Germany, Czechoslovakia, Hungary, Slovenia and Italy. *188 & 240*

Autariatae : tribe located in NW Illyria, N of Ardiaei, in NW Balkan Peninsula, present-day Croatia, along the NE Adriatic Sea, in E Europe. *218*

Autokane : Homeric hill, probably in Troas, NW Asia Minor, present-day NW Turkey. *250*

Avaris : city, later renamed Ramsës, on the E side of the Nile Delta, in N Egypt, NE Africa. *242*

Avenos : see Euenos. *216 & 220*

Avsa : see Aphousa. *250*

Axios : 1. river of Macedonia, modern Vardar, flowing SE from the Sar mountains through the N Balkan region and N Greece into the Gulf of Thermaikos (Salonika), in NW Aegean Sea. *224*; -- 2. see Orontes. *256*

Axos : village, ancient Oaxos, on the N slope of Mount Ida, SE of Rithumna, in NW Crete, C Mediterranean Sea. *204*

Azania : area of NW Arkadia, in C Peloponnesos. *192*

Azerbaijan : modern country, SE of the Caucasus mountains, bordering on Russia to the N, the Caspian Sea to the E, Iran to the S and Georgia & Armenia to the W, in W Asia. *188, 246 & 248*

Aziris : coastal town of Kyrenaica in NE Africa, along the Mediterranean Sea. *244*

Azotus : city in ancient Philistia, S Palestine, modern Ashdod in present-day Israel, on the SE Mediterranean Sea, in W Asia. *258*

Azov : 1. see Maeotis. *248*; -- 2. see Tanais city. *248*

Az- Saqādiq : modern town on ancient site in the CE Nile Delta, along the Damietta branch, in NE Egypt, NE Africa. *242*

B

Baalbek : city of NE Phoenicia, later called Heliopolis, present-day Lebanon, at the pass into NW Syria, W Asia. *252*

Babylon : major city of Babylonia, ancient Shankhar, on the Euphrates river, in S Mesopotamia, modern S Iraq, W Asia. *258*

Babylonia : see Sumer. *258*

Bactra : principal city of Bactria, also called Vahlika, probably modern Balkh, in present-day S Uzbekistan, C Asia. *262*

Bactria : region, also called Zariaspa, covering Uzbekistan, Tahkistan & N Afghanistan and, at its largest, extending into Turkmenistan to the W and the Hindu Kush of N Pakistan to the E, in C Asia. *246, 260. 262 & 266*

Badakhshan : area in the far NE Afghanistan, C Asia. *266*

Badis : town in E Harmozia, N of the Strait of Oman, in present-day SE Iran, W Asia. *264*

Bagia : city of Gedrosia, on the coast of the Arabian Sea, in present-day SW Pakistan, C Asia. *264*

Bagisara : city, in ancient S Gedrosia, W of Ormara, on the N coast of the Arabian Sea, in present-day S Pakistan, C Asia. *264*

Bagistane : city of W Media, SW of Agbatana, in present-day W Iran, W Asia. *260*

Bagrām 1. area NE of Kabul in Bactria, NE Afghanistan, C Asia. *262*; -- 2. see Alexandria-Kapisu. *262*

Bahariya : oasis of NW Egypt, in NE Africa. *242*

Bahce : pass in NE Cilicia, between SE Turkey, and NW Syria, W Asia. *256*

Bahrain : small country on a peninsula of the W Persian Gulf, surrounded by Saudi Arabia and Qatar, in SW Asia. *188*

Baleares : islands of the W Mediterranean Sea, off the E coast of Iberia (Spain), in W Europe. *232*

Balkans : region, called Haemos by the Ancient Greeks, shaped as a peninsula into the Mediteranean Sea, bordered in the N and E by the Drava river, Danube river and Aegean Sea, in the S by the Mediterranean Sea and in the W by the Adriatic and Ionian seas, including Croatia, Bosnia, Herzegovina, Kosovo, Serbia, Montenegro, Macedonia, Albania & Greece on the W side, and Bulgaria and NW Turkey on the NE side. *240*

Balkh : 1. area in ancient Bactria, covering present-day NW Afghanistan, bordering to the N on Turkmenistan and Uzbekistan, C Asia. *262*; -- 2. river flowing along the S border of this area. *262*; -- 3. city, see Bactra. *262*

Balkhash : lake in modern CE Kazakhstan, opposite the Aral Sea, in C Asia. *262*

Baluchistan : region of ancient Gedrosia, also called Makrãn, on the Arabian Sea, in present-day SW Pakistan and S Afghanistan, W of the Makrãn mountain range and the region of Brahui, in C Asia. *246 & 264*

Balura : river flowing NE from Mount Ithome, tributary of river Elektra, in CN Messenia, SW Peloponnesos. *196*

Bam : town of Persia, S of the Desert of Lut, in present-day CE Iran, C Asia. *264*

Bambyce : city in N Caria, later called Hierapolis, identified with modern Denizli, in SW Turkey, W Asia. *254*

Baphuras : navigable river, connecting the city of Dion with the Aegean Sea, in SE Macedonia, NE mainland Greece. *228*

Barada : 1. lake in the Anti-Lebanon mountains, also called Chrusorrhoas, in NW Syria, W Asia, *256 & 258*; -- 2. river of Syria, Greek Chrusorrhoas and Biblical Abanah, flowing SE from lake Barada, fanning out at Damascus, drying up in E desert toward lake Al-Utaybah, in W Asia. *256 & 258*

Barce : 1. city of Kyrenaica, modern Al-Marj in NE Libya, N of Euesperides, near the Mediterranean coast, in NE Africa. *244*; -- 2. city of C India, on the Son river, in C Asia. *266*

Basilicata : see Lucania. *238*

Basra : see Alexandria-Charax. *258*

Bassai : town in SW Arkadia, near the border with Messenia, in SW Peloponnesos. *192*

Bastarnae : tribal land of E Thrace, located between the E Carpathian mountains and the Euxine (Black) Sea, from the Upper valley of the Dnestr river to the Danube Delta, mostly in present-day Romania, SE Europe. *226*

Batieia : mound in the middle of the plain below Troy, also called Murine's grave, in Troas, present-day NW Turkey, W Asia. *250*

Battus : town of Lycia, near the mountains N of Xanthos, in SW Asia Minor, present-day SW Turkey. *254*

Bathymasi : city on the NE shore of the Sea of Propontis, in present-day European Turkey. *252*

Bazira : city of Sogdiana, S of the valley of Kashmir, in NW India, C Asia. *266*

Beãs : see Hyphasis river. *266*

Bebryces : tribal land in Bithynia, along the SE coast of the Sea of Propontis, in NW Asia Minor, present-day Turkey. *252*

Begoritis : lake in SW Macedonia, NE mainland Greece. *224*

Behistun : village on a rock, also called Bisitun and Bhagasthena, in the foothills of the Zagros mountains, SW of Agbatana, in NW Media, present-day NW Iran, W Asia. *260*

Beirut: see Beroth. *258*
Bekaa : see Al-Biqã. *256 & 258*
Belarus : country of E Europe, surrounded by Poland, Lithuania, Russia and Ukraine. *188*
Belemina : area of S Arkadia overlapping upon NW Lakonia, in CS Peloponnesos. *192 & 198*
Belen : town in SE Cilicia, near the border with Syria, N of the NE Mediterranean Sea, in present-day SE Turkey, W Asia. *256*
Belgium : country of W Europe, surrounded by France, Germany and Holland, on the North Sea. *188*
Belgrade : city of Serbia, at the confluence of the Danube and Sava rivers, in the Balkans, SE Europe. *240*
Beneventum : town of CS Italy, E of Neapolis (Naples), in W Europe. *238*
Bengal : bay E of the Indian peninsula, part of the Indian Ocean, in C Asia. *188 & 246*
Benghazi : see Euesperides. *244*
Berbati : town of CW Argolis, N of Tiruns, exact location uncertain, in NE Peloponnesos. *202*
Berezean : small island in the N Euxine (Black) Sea, S of Scythia, present-day S Ukraine, SE Europe. *248*
Bergama : see Pergamon. *250*
Beroia : 1. town in SE Macedonia, NE mainland Greece. *224*; -- 2. town in CN Thrace, present-day Romania, SE Europe. *226*
Beroth : city, modern Beirut, in N Lebanon, on the coast of the NE Mediterranean Sea. *258*
Bessa : Homeric town in Opuntian Lokris, on the Gulf of Oropos, in CE mainland Greece. *214*
Bessi : tribal land of C Thrace, located W of the Maritsa river, in NE mainland Greece. *226*
Bhagasthena : see Behistun. *260*
Bias : river in SE Messenia, flowing from Mount Mathia, NE into the Gulf of Messenia, in SW Peloponnesos. *196*
Bilbeis : town in the SE Nile Delta, in N Egypt, NE Africa. *242*
Biblis : mythological spring into which the goddess Biblis was changed after her death. *269*
Birket Kârûn : large lake in N Egypt, below sea level, near the W bank of the Nile river, N of lake Moeris, in NE Africa. *242*
Bisaltia : tribal area near the border between SE Macedonia and SW Thrace, near lake Kerkinitis, in NE mainland Greece. *224*
Bisanthe : town of S Thrace, later called Rhaidestos, on the NW coast of the Sea of Propontis, in present-day European Turkey.
Bisitun : see Behistun. *226*
Bist : town of Arachosia, W of Kandahãr, in C Afghanistan, C Asia. *262*

Bithynia : region extending from the S shore of the Sea of Propontis, along the Bosporos, to the S shore of the W Euxine (Black) Sea, in NW Asia Minor, present-day NW Turkey. *250 & 252*

Bithynion : town in Bithynia, modern Bolu, in present-day NW Turkey, W Asia. *252*

Bitter : lake, N of the Gulf of Suez, in NE Egypt, NE Africa. *242*

Black : 1, see Euxine Sea. *188, 190, 214, 226, 240, 246, 248 & 252*; --2. forest in SW Germany, source of the Danube river, in W Europe. *232*

Boagrios : Homeric river of Opuntian Lokris, flowing NE into the Gulf of Oropos, in CE mainland Greece. *214*

Bodrum : 1. peninsula of SW Caria, on the Gulf of Kerameikos off the Aegean Sea, in SW Asia Minor, present-day SW Turkey. *254*; -- 2. modern city, on this Peninsula, near Hallikarnassos. *254*

Boeai : town in SE Lakonia, on the SE side of the Gulf of Lakonia, in SE Peloponnesos. *198*

Bogaianzköy : village of ancient Hittite territories, near Hattusa, exact location uncertain, in CN Turkey, W Asia. *248*

Boghazköy : see Hattusa. *248*

Bohemia : ancient region in present-day W Czech Republic, SE Europe. *240*

Boibe : Homeric town, on lake Boibeis, N of Pagassai, in SE Thessalia, NE mainland Greece. *220*

Boibeis : ancient lake, along the plain of Dotion, in CE Thessalia, NE mainland Greece. *220*

Boion : one of a group of four cities, with kitinion, Erineos and Pindos, in the valley of the Pindos river, in Doris, CS mainland Greece. *214*

Boiotia : region, formerly called Kadmeia especially in the CS, located N of Attika, Megaris and the NE end of the Gulf of Korinthos, E & S of Phokis, S of Opuntian Lokris and opposite the island of Euboia to the E, in SE mainland Greece. *190, 210, 212, 214 & 228*

Bolãn : 1. pass in ancient Bactria, from modern Quetta, in present-day CW Pakistan, going S through mountains, valleys and plains, in C Brahui, Baluchistan, into Sind, SE Pakistan, C Asia. *262*; -- 2. river flowing S from the Kalāt highlands, through the Kachi plain and Baluchistan, S Pakistan, into the Arabian Sea, C Asia. *264*

Bolbe : lake of E Macedonia, in Mugdonia, N of the Chalkidike and W of the Gulf Orfanou, in NE mainland Greece. *224*

Bolina : city in CN Achaia, near the SW shore of the Gulf of Korinthos, E of Argura, in CN Peloponnesos. *200*

Bolinaeos : river of CN Achaia, flowing N into the Gulf of Korinthos, near Bolina, in CN Peloponnesos. *200*

Bolissos : town on the island of Chios, probably on the NW side, in CE Aegean Sea. *230*

Bolu : see Bithynion. *252*

Bonifacio : strait separating Corsica to the N from Sardinia to the S, in the Tyrrhenian Sea, W Europe. *232*

Boreos : mountain in SE Arkadia, S of Pallantion, in SE Peloponnesos. *192*

Borysthenes : 1. river, modern Dnieper, flowing from the Valdai Hills, NW of Moscow, in W Russia, past Kiev in Ukraine and discharging into the Euxine (Black) Sea, near Odessa, in SE Europe. *248*; -- 2. see Olbia. *248*

Bosnia : country of the W Balkans, contiguous to Herzegovina, with Croatia to the N and W, Albania to the S and Serbia to the E, in SE Europe. *188, 218, 224 & 240*

Bosporos : 1. strait connecting the Sea of Propontis (Marmara) and the Euxine (Black) Sea, in present-day NW Turkey, separating Europe and Asia. *252*; -- 2. Cimmerian, see Kerch. *248*

Bottia : town in the plain along the Orontes river, near Antioch, in ancient Syria, present-day Turkey. *256*

Bottiaia : 1. see Bottike. *224*; -- 2. city in this area. *224*

Bottike : 1. land of the Bottians, N of the Peninsula Chalkidike, in SE Macedonia, NE mainland Greece. *224*; -- 2. city in this area. *224*

Boudeion : Homeric city on the peninsula of Magnesia, in SE Thessalia, NE mainland Greece. *220*

Boudinoi : tribal area of Scythia, N of the Euxine (Black) Sea, in W Asia. *248*

Bouga : Town in CS Achaia, S of Kallithea, in CN Peloponnesos. *200*

Bounomos : see Pella. *224*

Bouprasion : 1. Homeric area in NW Elis, along the coast of the Ionian Sea, NW Peloponnesos. *194*; -- 2. city in this area, S of cape Araxos, in the N of this area in W Achaia. *194*

Brahui : region of hills in ancient W Gedrosia, S of Quetta, in present-day SW Pakistan, E of Baluchistan, N of the Arabian Sea, C Asia. *264*; -- 2. mountain range in this region, running N-S in S Pakistan. *264*

Branchidai : see Diduma. *254*

Branichevo : town of C Thrace, in NE mainland Greece, present-day NE Bulgaria, SE Europe. *226*

Brasiai : city on the coast of the Mirtóön Sea, in NE Lakonia, near the border with S Argolis, in CE Peloponnesos. *198*

Brauron : ancient town near the Gulf of Petalion, in CE Attika, SE mainland Greece. *208*

Brea : town NE of the Chalkidike peninsulas, near the border between Macedonia and Thrace, N of the Aegean Sea, in NE mainland Greece. *224*

Brentesion : seaport, modern Brindisi, in SE Italy, on the S Adriatic Sea, in W Europe. *239*

Brenthe : town in SW Arkadia, between Trapezos to the SE and Gortus to the NW, in CS Peloponnesos. *192*

Bricinniae : town in the CE of the island of Sicily, in W Mediterranean Sea, W Europe. *236*

Brilessos : see Pentelikon. *210*

Brindisi : see Brentesion. *238*

Britain : see Albion, present-day England, Scotland and Wales. *188 & 232*

Bromion : city in SE Macedonia, S of Bottiaia, N of the Chalkidike, in NE mainland Greece. *224*

Bromiskos : seaport city in SE Macedonia, N of the Chalkidike, where Lake Bolbe connects with the Aegean Sea, in NE mainland Greece. *224*

Brooks : see Rheiti. *210*

Bruseia : Homeric city, S of Sparta, in NW Lakonia, SE Peloponnesos. *198*

Bubassos : peninsula in SW Caria, most to the SW Asia Minor, present-day SW Turkey, N of the island of Sumi, in SE Aegean Sea. *254*

Bubastis : city, modern Tall Bastah, S of modern Az-Zaqãdiq, on the Damietta branch of the CE Delta of the Nile river, in N Egypt, NE Africa. *242*

Bublos : ancient seaport in N Phoenicia, at the E end of the Mediterranean Sea, in present-day N Lebanon, W Asia. *258*

Bucharest : city of C Romania, near the Danube river, in SE Europe. *240*

Budoron : site of a fort, in SE Megaris, probably NW of the island of Salamis, in S mainland Greece. *210*

Bug : see Hypanis river. *248*

Buhen : city of S Egypt on the bank of the Nile river, in NE Africa. *244*

Buhtan : river of N Assyria, flowing W as a tributary of the Tigris river, in present-day N Iraq, W Asia. *258*

Bukephala : 1. cape in the SW of the peninsula of Argolis, CE Argolis, NE Peloponnesos. *202*; -- 2. city in N India, near the Hydaspes river, in C Asia. *266*

Bukhara : 1. region in W Sogdiana, present-day C Uzbekistan, C Asia. *262*; -- 2. city in the C of the oasis in this region. *262*

Bulazoia : town in CW Macedonia, on the Axios river, exact location uncertain, in N mainland Greece. *224*

Bulgaria : country of SE Europe, covering the E part of ancient Thrace, W of the Euxine (Black) Sea, E of Serbia and Macedonia, S of Romania and N of NE Greece & NW Turkey. *188, 224, 226 & 240*

Bulis : port city in SE Phokis, on the SE side of the Bay of Antikura, in CS mainland Greece. *214*

Buner : 1. region of ancient Bactria, in present-day N Pakistan, S of Kashmir, in C Asia. *266*; -- 2. river flowing E through this region, into the Indus river as its tributary. *266*

Buphagion : town in SW Arkadia, between Gortus to the SE and Melainiai to the NW, in CS Peloponnesos. *192*

Buporthmos : cape in CS of the peninsula of Argolis, in SE Argolis, NE Peloponnesos. *202*

Bura : 1. inland city of CN Achaia, W of the river Buraikos, in CN Peloponnesos. *200*; -- 2. city in the area of Kaludonia, in SW Aitolia, SW mainland Greece. *216*

Buraikos : river flowing N from CN Arkadia, through E Achaia, into the Gulf of Korinthos, near Bura, in CN Peloponnesos. *192 & 200*

Bursa : see Prusa. *252*

Busantion : city at the entrance of the Bosporos from the Sea of Propontis, renamed later Constantinople and Istanbul, in present-day NW Turkey, on the border between E Europe and W Asia. *252*

Busiris : city in the center of the Delta of the Nile River, in N Egypt, NE Africa. *242*

Buto : city in the center of the Delta of the Nile River, in N Egypt, NE Africa. *242*

C

If a name is not found under C, look under K

Cacyparis : river in the SE of the island of Sicily, N of the Assinaros river, flowing SE into the Mediterranean Sea, in W Europe. *236*

Cacyrum : inland town in the CS of the island of Sicily, probably a short distance NW of Siracusa. in W Mediterranean Sea, W Europe. *236*

If a name is not found under C, look under K

Cadites : see Gaza city. *258*

Cadiz : 1. large gulf in SW Iberia, mostly in present-day SW Spain, W Europe. *232*; -- 2. see Gedeira. *232*

Cadrusi : city in ancient Bactria, near Alexandria-Kapisu, exact location unknown, in the Kabul valley, present-day NE Afghanistan, C Asia. *262*

Cadusia : tribal area, SW of the Caspian Sea, in Media, present-day NW Iran, W Asia. *246 & 260*

Cadytis : see Gaza. *258*

Caere : town of S Etruria in C Italy, W Europe. *238*

Caicinos : river of the SW tip of Italy, in W Europe, E of the Halex river, flowing S into the Mediterranean Sea. *238*

Cairo : Modern city in N Egypt, at the juncture between the Nile river and the Delta, in NE Africa. *242*

Cakitsuya : river of W Cilicia, flowing SE from the Taurus Mountains and joining the Saros river as tributary, in present-day SE Turkey, W Asia. *256*

Calabria : region at the S tip of Italy, in W Europe. *238*

Callatebos : inland town of Lydia, near Manisa, NE of Smyrna (Izmir), along the Hermos river, in CW Asia Minor, present-day CW Turkey. *250*

Callatis : town on the CW coast of the Euxine (Black) Sea, in Thrace, present-day Romania, E Europe. *240*

Calpe : 1. city on the SW coast of the Euxine (Black) Sea, about halfway between Bisantion and Herakleia to the E, in Bithynia, NW Asia Minor, present-day Turkey. *252*; -- 2. see Gibraltar. *232*

Calycadnus : river of CS Anatolia, present-day CS turkey, W Asia, flowing S from the Taurus mountain range, across Cilicia, as W border of Tracheia, into the NE Mediterranean Sea. *256*

Camarina : coastal town on the SE side of the island of Sicily, SE of Gela, in W Mediterranean Sea, W Europe. *236*

Camicus : inland area around Akragas, in the CS of the island of Sicily, in W Mediterranean Sea, W Europe. *234*

Campania : region of SW Italy, along the Tyrrhenian Sea, in W Europe. *238*

Canaan : region covering present-day Lebanon, S Syria and Israel, often identified as ancient Palestine, W Asia. *258*

Canate : city of Gedrosia, on the coast of the Arabian Sea, between Dagaseira and Talmena, on the border between present-day Iran and Pakistan, in C Asia. *264*

Candath : gulf of the E Aegean Sea, between the Mimas Peninsula and the coast of Lydia, also called Gulf of Izmir, in CW Asia Minor, present-day CW Turkey. *250*

If a name is not found under C, look under K

Canobia : 1. see Rosetta river. *242*; -- 1. see Rosetta city. *242*

Canopus : city in the NW of the Nile Delta, on the Mediterranean coast, E of Alexandria, in NW Egypt, NE Africa. *242*

Cappadocia : CS region of Anatolia, N of the Taurus Mountains of Cilicia and S of Paphlagonia, E of Phrygia and W of Armenia, present-day C Turkey, W Asia. *248, 252 & 256*

Caralis : coastal town, at the S end of the island of Sardinia in the Tyrrhenian Sea, N of Nora, in W Europe. *232*

Carchemish : city in SE Hittite territories, on the Euphrates river, in present-day NW Syria, W Asia. *258*

Caria : region along the SE Aegean Sea, between Lydia in the N and Lycia in the S & E, and the Mediterranean Sea in the S, in SW Asia Minor, present-day SW Turkey. *190 & 254*

Carmana : town in C Carmania, present-day SE Iran, W Asia. *264*

Carmania : region of Persia, covering modern S Iran, E of Persis, and SW Pakistan, N & W of Gedrosia, along the Persian Gulf and the Gulf of Oman, in C Asia. *246 & 264*

Carmona : inland city of Iberia, present-day Spain, in W Europe. *232*

Carpathian : mountain range in CE Europe, crossing Czecho-slovakia, Hungary and Romania. *240*

Cartana : see Alexandria-Kapisu. *262*

Carthage : city on the CN coast of Africa, identified with modern Tunis, in Tunisia. *244*

Casius : 1. mount in N Phoenicia, W of Aleppo, in present-day NW Syria, W Asia. *256*; -- 2. mount in S Palestine, N of the Sinai desert, near Gaza, at the SE end of the Mediterranean Sea, in W Asia. *258*

Caspian : 1. inland sea, also called Tanais or Hyrcanian Sea, E of the Caucasus Mountains, surrounded by modern Azerbaijan to the W, Kazakhstan to the NE, Turkmenistan to the E and Iran to the S, its N side in SE Europe and S side in C Asia. *187, 188, 246, 248. 258 & 260*; -- 2. gate like a narrow pass, called Sialek and Sardar, in SW Hyrcania, NW of the desert of Kavir, in Media, present-day NE Iran, W Asia. *260*

Cassiterides : islands of the Atlantic Ocean, modern Isles of Scilly, S of England, in W Europe. *232*

Catana : coastal town on the CE side of the island of Sicily, modern Catania, in W Mediterranean Sea, W Europe. *236*

Catania : see Catana. *236*

Cataracts : five rapids in the Nile river: 1. S of Aswãn, in S Egypt, NE Africa. *242*; -- 2. on the border between S Egypt and N Nubia (Sudan). *244*; -- 3. in NE Nubia. *244*; -- 4. in NE Nubia, S of the

preceding one. *244*; -- 5. in NE Nubia, S of the preceding one.
244

If a name is not found under C, look under K

Caucasus : 1. mountain range in present-day SW Russia, SE
Europe, between the Euxine (Black) Sea and the Caspian Sea, N
of Georgia and Azerbaijan, the latter in NW Asia. *187, 188, 248
& 262*; -- 2. see Parapamisus (Hindu Kush}. *262 & 266*
Celones : city on the border between N Mesopotamia and Media,
present-day Iraq and Iran, in W Asia. *258*
Celtic : vast region in the N of Europe. *187*
Centuripa : inland town in the CE of the island of Sicily, N of
Inessa, in W Mediterranean Sea. *244*
Cephaloedium : coastal town in the CN of the island of Sicily, on
the coast of the S Tyrrhenian Sea. *234*
Cercasorus : town on a small island at the opening of the Nile
Delta, in N Egypt, NE Africa. *242*
Ceuta : see Abula. *232 & 244*
Ceyhan : city along the Puramos river, E of Adana, in SW Cilicia,
present-day CS Turkey. *256*
Ceyhan Nehri : see Puramos river. *256*
Chad : country of N Africa, S of Libya, between Niger and Sudan.
188 & 244
Chaironeia : town in NW Boiotia, ancient Arne, W of Orchomenos,
in SE mainland Greece. *212*
Chalandriani : town on the island of Suros, in CN Cyclades, CW
Aegean Sea. *230*
Chaldaea : area of S Babylonia, N of the Persian Gulf, in present-
day S Iraq, W Asia. *258*
Chalkedon : city of Bithynia, also called Nikomedia, on the E side
of the Bosporos, at the Sea of Propontis, opposite Busantion, in
W Asia. *252*
Chalkidike : large peninsula, present-day Salonika or
Thessaloniki, with three finger-like peninsulas stretching S into
the N Aegean Sea, in ancient times in SE Macedonia, NE
mainland Greece,. *190, 224 & 228*
Chalkis : 1. city in SW Aitolia, on the N coast of the Gulf of
Patraikos, near the estuary of the Euenos river, in CW mainland
Greece. *216*; -- 2. town in CW of the island of Euboia, in CW
Aegean Sea, along the Strait of Euripos dividing the island into N
and S and separating it from mainland Greece. *228*
Chalybes : Tribal land along the shore of the SE Euxine (Black)
Sea, beween the Halys river and the city of Trapezos, in present-
day CN Turkey, W Asia. *252*

Chantsa : town in the N of Boiotia, NE of lake Kopais, in C mainland Greece. *212*

Chaon : mountain in CW Argolis, SW of Mount Larisa and Argos, in NE Peloponnesos. *202*

Chaonia : small tribal area, in W Epeiros, on the NW coast of the Ionian Sea, opposite the N end of the island of Kerkura, in E Aegean Sea. *218*

Charadra : 1. river, usually a dry bed, flowing E from mount Parnes in CN Attika, into the Gulf of Petalion, in SE mainland Greece. *210*; -- 2. town along this river, in NE Attika. *210*; -- 3. town in NW Phokis, NW of Lilaia, in CS mainland Greece. *214*

Charadros : 1. river of CN Achaia, flowing N into the Gulf of Korinthos, near Argura, in CN Peloponnesos. *200*; -- 2. river flowing from Mount Artemision, E through Argolis, past Argos, into the Gulf of Argolis, in CW Argolis, NE Peloponnesos. *202*; -- 3. river of N Messenia, flowing W and joining river Elektra, N of Mount Ithome, in SW Peloponnesos. *196*; -- 4. river of C Macedonia, flowing from Mount Dusoron in the N, into the Gulf of Thermai in the S, near Rhekaios, in NE mainland Greece. *224*

Charakopid : town in SW Messenia, on the W side of the Gulf of Messenia, in SW Peloponnesos. *196*

Charax : see Alexandria-Charax. *258*

Chardan : island on the W edge of the Tyrrhenian Sea, modern Sardinia, S of Corsica, in W Europe. *232*

Charente : river in SW France, flowing NW into the Atlantic Ocean, in W Europe. *232*

Charman : city on the border between CW Pakistan and SE Afghanistan, NW of Quetta, in C Asia. *262*

Charsadda : town of Bactria, NW of Taxila, on the W side of the Indus river, in present-day N India, C Asia. *266*

Charybdis : in mythology, this whirlpool refers with Scylla to the Strait of Messina, between SW Italy and NE island of Sicily, in W Europe. *236 & 268*

Cheimarros : river in SW Argolis, flowing E into the NW Gulf of Argolis, N of Lerna, in NE Peloponnesos. *202*

Chelidoria : mountain in SE Achaia, E of Pellene, in NE Peloponnesos. *200*

Chemmis : city of C Egypt, later called Panopolis and modern Akhmim, on the E bank of the Nile river, S of Asyüt, in NE Africa. *242*

Chenāb : see Acesines river. *266*

Cherna : river in Thrace, present-day Bulgaria, flowing SE from the SE Rhodope mountains, tributary of the Arda river, in SE Europe. *226*

Cheronia : city of E Phokis, W of Phanotis, in CS mainland Greece. *214*

Chersonesos : 1. town of SW Korinthia, on the coast of the Saronic Gulf, in CN Argolis, NE Peloponnesos. *202*; -- 2. region extending from the Peninsula of Gallipoli, N of the Hellespontos and the Sea of Propontis, in S Thrace, present-day NW Turkey, to the Crimea, especially the SW as Taurica, where an ancient town was located, N of the Euxine (Black) Sea, in present-day S Ukraine, SE Europe. *226 & 248*

Chesmeh- i- Ali : see Stiboates river. *260*

Chimerion : harbor city on the Ionian Sea, in S Thesprotis, SW Epeiros, CW mainland Greece. *218*

China : large country of Far E Asia. *188, 246 & 266*

Chionistra : see Olympos, on the island of Cyprus. *256*

Chios : 1. island of the CE Aegean Sea, off the coast of Ionia, opposite the peninsula of Mimas, in Asia Minor, present-day CW Turkey. *190, 230 & 250*; -- 2. harbor city on the E side of this island. *230*; -- 3. harbor city on the SE coast of the Sea of Propontis, in Bithynia, NW Asia Minor, present-day NW Turkey. *252*

Choanes : tribal land in the NW of Epeiros, on the SE coast of the Adriatic Sea, in present-day Albania, E Europe. *218*

Choarene : 1. area on the E side of the Desert of Kavir, in NE Media, present-day NE Iran, W Asia. *260*; -- 2. city in this area. *260*

Choaspes : 1. river in present-day Iran, also called Eulaeus, modern Karkheh, flowing S from the Zagros mountains, through Elam, past Susa, joining the Pasitigris river as its tributary into the Persian Gulf, near the border with Iraq, in W Asia. *258*; -- 2. river in present-day Afghanistan, also called Swat, from the Parapamisus (Hindu Kush) mountain range to the Indus valley where it becomes a tributary of the Kabul river, in C Asia. *262*; -- 3. valley, modern Swat, in the Malakand region, ancient Bactria, W of the Indus river, in present-day NW Pakistan, C Asia. *262*

Choerades : islets along the NE coast of the Gulf of Taranto, in SE Italy, W Europe. *238*

Choerea : city of Eretria, in C of the island of Euboia, E of the N end of the Gulf of Petalion, in CW Aegean Sea. *228*

Choerios : river flowing from Mount Taleton in Lakonia, N and then E into the Gulf of Messenia, between Abia to the N and Gerenia to the S, on the border between Lakonia and Messenia, in CS Peloponnesos. *196 & 198*

Cholarges : town along the W bank of the river Kephisos, W of Mount Anchesmos, in N Attika, SE mainland Greece. *210*

Chorasmia : region, modern Khwãrezm, in C Asia, E of the Caspian Sea and S of the Aral Sea, mostly in present-day Uzbekistan and Turkmenistan. *260*

Chorienes : steep rock in N Sogdiana, modern S Kazakhstan, in C Asia. *262*

Christos : site near Hersonissos, in CN of the island of Crete, C Mediterranean Sea. *206*

Chruse : Homeric town, S of Mount Ida, in Mysia, present-day NW Turkey, W Asia. *250*

Chrusorrhoas : 1. see Barada lake. *256*; -- 2. see Barada river. *256 & 258*

Chrusovitsa : site in Akarnania, exact location unknown, in SW of mainland Greece. *216*

If a name is not found under C, look under K

Cilicia : region of CS Anatolia, along the N coast of the E Mediterranean Sea and surrounded by the Taurus mountains, in present-day CS Turkey, W Asia. *256*

Cimmeria : ancient region of a displaced people, mostly in SE of the Euxine (Black) Sea, in W Asia. *248*

Cinyps : 1. river in Tripolitania, Libya, flowing N into the Mediterranean Sea, in CN Africa. *244*; -- 2. town at the mouth of this river. *244*

Cirenic : sea S of the island of Crete, in the larger Mediterranean Sea, N of Libya, in NE Africa. *204*

Cissia : ancient city of Elam, near Susa, in SW Media (Persia), present-day Iran, W Asia. *260*

Citium : town on the S coast of the island of Cyprus, near present-day Larnaka, in W Asia. *256*

Clashing Rocks : see Plagktas. *236*

Cleft Way : site in C Phokis, between Delphi and Daulis, in CS mainland Greece. *214*

Clusium : Etruscan town in Arezzo, C Italy, W Europe. *238*

Cocala : coastal city of E Gedrosia, in present-day S Pakistan, on the Arabian Sea, C Asia. *264*

Coele Syria : in ancient times extended to all Syria, in W Asia, later restricted to the Al-Biqã (Bekaa) valley, between present-day C Lebanon and N Syria. *256 & 258*

Comana : city of N Cappadocia, on the border with Pontos, S of the E Euxine (Black) Sea, in C Anatolia, present-day C Turkey, W Asia. *252*

Comisene : area on the E side of the Desert of Kavir, in NE Media, present-day NE Iran, W Asia. *260*

If a name is not found under C, look under K

Comlekci : settlement in Caria, on a hill near Kaunos, on the S
coast of Asia Minor, near the SE Aegean Sea, in present-day SW
Turkey. *254*

Commagene : region of N ancient Syria, also called Kummuh, at
the E end of the Mediteranean Sea, S of Cappadocia, with Cilicia
to the W and the bend of the Euphrates river to the E, in present-
day SE Turkey, W Asia. *256*

Constanta : see Tomis. *226 & 240*

Constantinople : see Busantion. *252*

Continental Greece : the Peloponnesos and Mainland Greece
without the surrounding Greek islands. *187- 202 & 208- 226*

Cophas : city, E of Gwatar Bay of the Arabian Sea, on the S coast
of ancient Gedrosia, present-day S Pakistan, in C Asia. *264*

Cophen : river of C Asia, modern Kabul river, flowing from the
Sanglãkh mountain range, NW of the city of Kabul, through E
Afghanistan, into W Pakistan, past Peshawar, and joining the
Indus river, near Islamabad, in NE Pakistan. *262*

Coptos : town in S Egypt, on the E bank of the river Nile, N of the
road to the Red Sea, in NE Africa. *242*

Corcyra : see Kerkura. *218*

Corfu : see Kerkura. *218*

Corinth : see Korinthos. *202*

Corsica : island of the Mediterranean Sea, S of France and W of
Italy, N of Sardinia, in the N Tyrrhenian Sea, W Europe. *188 &
232*

Cossaea : region in CW Media, present-day CW Iran, C Asia. *260*

Cotinusa : see Gadira. *232*

Crete : 1. large island, in the CS Mediterranean Sea, Homeric
Krete, also called Kandia, S of the Cyclades and N of Libya in
Africa. *188, 190, 204, 206 & 244* ; -- 2. sea N of the island of
Crete, S boundary of the Aegean Sea, in the larger Mediterra-
nean Sea. *204 & 206*

Crimea : peninsula called Taurica, in E Chersonesos, extending S
into the N Euxine (Black) Sea, W of the Sea of Azov, S of Scythia,
in S Ukraine, SE Europe. *246 & 248*

Crimissus : river in the C of the island of Sicily, flowing W of the
river Halicus, into the Mediterranean Sea, in W Europe. *234*

Crithote : city of the Chersonesos, at the NE end of the Strait of
Hellespontos, in present-day NW Turkey, SE Europe. *226*

Crna : see Erigon river. *224*

Croatia : country along the NE coast of the Adriatic Sea, E of N
Italy, S of Austria and W of Hungary, in the NW Balkan Peninsula,
CS Europe. *188, 218, 238 & 240*

If a name is not found under C, look under K

Crocodilônpolis : 1. city In N Egypt, near the W bank of the Nile river, between Aphroditopolis and Herakleopolis, in NE Africa. *242*; -- 2. City in C Egypt, S of Thebes, on the W bank of the Nile river, in NE Africa. *242*

Cromna : 1. river of Paphlagonia, flowing N into the Euxine (Black) Sea, in Asia Minor, present-day CN Turkey. *252*; -- 2. city along this river. *252*

Croton : port city of Calabria, near the W entrance to the Gulf of Taranto, on the E coast of S Italy, in W Europe. *238*

Ctesiphon : city in C Mesopotamia, on the E shore of the Tigris river, in present-day C Iraq, W Asia. *258*

Cudi- Dag : mountain range spreading on the border between SE Turkey and NE Syria, S of Mount Ararat, in the Urartu region, W Asia. *248*

Cumae : city on the W side of S Italy, NW of Neapolis, in the region of Campania, along the E Tyrrhenian Sea, in W Europe. *238*

Curium : town on the S coast of the island of Cyprus, in NE Mediterranean Sea, W Asia. *256*

Cusae : town in C Egypt, on the W bank in a bend of the Nile river, between Hermopolis and Lykopolis Magna, in NE Africa. *242*

Cyclades : circular group of islands in CW Aegean Sea, S of Attika and E of the Peloponnesos. *190 & 230*

Cyclops : mythological island, perhaps in the Sicilian Sea, off the city of Catania, in NE Sicily, W Europe. *269*

Cydnos : river flowing S from the Taurus Mountains, in W Cilicia, SW Asia, past Tarsus, into the NE Mediterranean Sea. *256*

Cyprus : island with the ancient name of Alashiya, Homeric Kupros, near the NE end of the Mediterranean Sea, S of Turkey, N of Egypt and W of Lebanon. *188, 244, 246 & 256*

Cyrenic : see Libyan Sea. *204 & 244*

Cyreschata : see Cyropolis. *262*

Cyropolis : town of E Sogdiana, also known as Cyreschata, in present-day S Kazakhstan, C Asia. *262*

Cyrrhestis : region between Cilicia to the N, Phoenicia to the S and Syria to the S & E, in W Asia, near the NE coast of the Mediterranean Sea. *258*

Cyzicus : 1. see Arktonnessos peninsula. *250*; -- 2. major town at the entrance to this peninsula. *250*

Czech Republic : country of W Europe, N portion of previous Czechoslovakia, S of Poland and Germany. *240*

D

Dabarosa : town of S Egypt, on the banks of the Nile river, near the Second Cataract, in NE Africa. *244*

Dagaseira : town in E Harmozia, N of the Strait of Oman, in present-day SE Iran, near the border with Pakistan, in W Asia. *264*

Dahae : region E of the Caspian Sea and N of Hyrcania & Margiana, separated in the E from Sogdiana by the Oxus river, in present-day Turkmenistan & Kazakhstan, C Asia. *246 & 260*

Dahan- i- Gulahan : city in the area of Zranka, S of a small desert, in present-day Pakistan, C Asia. *262*

Dakhla : oasis of CW Egypt, in NE Africa. *242*

Dalmatia : region on the W side of the Balkans, along the NE coast of the Adriatic Sea, in present-day Croatia, E Europe. *218, 238 & 240*

Damanhür : city on the W side of the Nile Delta, later called Hermopolis Parva, in N Egypt, NE Africa. *242*

Damascus : city of SW Syria, at the base of the Qasiyun mountains, S of the Barada river, in W Asia. *258*

Damghan : city of S Hyrcania, E of Tehrãn, on the N edge of the Desert of Kavir, in present-day N Iran, C Asia. *260*

Damietta : 1. E branch of the Nile Delta, in NE Egypt, NE Africa. *242*; -- 2. city, S of the mouth of this branch, W of Port Said. *242*

Danube : river, also called Ister, flowing SE from the Black Forest of SW Germany, gathering water from many tributaries through Austria, Slovakia, Hungary, Croatia, Serbia, then along its border with Romania, further turning NE across Romania, touching on Moldova and Ukraine, finally discharging as a delta at Tulcea, into the Euxine (Black) Sea, in SE Europe. *187, 226 & 240*

Daphnae : ancient city of Egypt, also called Defenneh, in the NE Delta of the Nile river, NE Africa. *242*

Daphni : 1. small suburb NW of Athens, in C Attika, SE mainland Greece. *208*; -- 2. port giving access to Mount Athos in the E peninsula Akti of the Chalkidike, in NE mainland Greece. *228*; -- 3. area of many villages such as Naupaktos in SW Ozolian Lokris and Nemea in NW Argolis. *202 & 228*

Dara : 1. village in C Messenia, SW Peloponnesos. *196*; -- 2. town, modern Abivard and perhaps Hekatompulos, E of Tehrãn, in S Hyrcania, present-day N Iran, W Asia. *260*

Dardanelles : see Hellespontos. *250*

Dardania : 1. tribal land of ancient N Illyria, located in present-day Bosnia and Macedonia, in the Balkans, E Europe. *218 & 224*

Dardanos : river flowing W along the border between SW Arkadia and NE Messenia, S of the river Neda, into the Ionian Sea, in CW Peloponnesos. *196*; -- 2. ancient city of Troas, along the S coast of Hellespontos, in present-day NW Turkey, W Asia. *250*

Darya : see Amu Darya (Oxus) river. *260*

Daseae : town W of Megalopolis, in SW Arkadia, CE Peloponnesos. *192*

Daskon : site of the fort of Siracusa, W of the Bay, in CE of the Mediterranean island of Sicily, W Europe. *236*

Daskulion : city of Bithynia, near the CS coast of the Sea of Propontis, in Asia Minor, present-day NW Turkey. *250*

Dassaretis : area between N Epeiros and Macedonia, in N mainland Greece. *218*

Dasteira : town in W Armenia, S of the SE Euxine (Black) Sea, in W Asia. *248*

Daulis : city of CE Phokis, W of Phanotis, in CS mainland Greece. *214*

Daunia : area of SE Italy, in N Apulia, along the Adriatic Sea, in W Europe. *238*

Dead Sea : inland body of water, salty and below sea level, between Israel and Jordan, in W Asia. *258*

Decapolis : region of N Jordan, on the E side of the Jordan river, in ancient Palestine, W Asia. *258*

Defenneh : see Daphnae. *242*

Deipnias : village near Larissa, in CN Thessalia, NE mainland Greece. *220*

Deiras : ravine between two mounts, Larisa and Aspis, S of Argos in CW Argolis, NE Peloponnesos. *202*

Dekeleia : town of NE Attika, N of Leipsudrion, in SE mainland Greece. *210*

Deli : river of E Cilicia, flowing W from Mount Amanos, into the NE Gulf of Issos, in present-day SE Turkey, W Asia. *256*

Delion : town, later called Siphae, in SE Boiotia, near the NW coast of the Gulf of Petalion, in SE mainland Greece. *212*

Delos : island on the E side of the Cyclades, S of Mikonos (Nisos), in CW Aegean Sea. *230*

Delphi : major city in CW Phokis, ancient Putho, S of mount Parnassos, near the N side of the Gulf of Korinthos, in CS mainland Greece. *214*

Delphinion : harbor city, on the NE side of the island of Chios, N of the city of Chios, in CE Aegean Sea. *230*

Demetrias : town with two harbors on the coast of the Gulf of Pagassai, in SE Thessalia, NE mainland Greece. *220*

Demir Kapija : town in E Macedonia, NE mainland Greece, in W Agrianes, in present-day Macedonia. *224*

Demonesi : group of nine tiny islands, in the Sea of Propontis (Marmara), SE of Busantion, in Asia Minor, present-day NW Turkey. *252*

Dendera : town on the W bank of the Nile river, N of Thebes, in C Egypt, NE Africa. *242*

Dendra : site in CW Argolis, next to Midea, in NE Peloponnesos. *202*

Denizli : seé Bambyce. *254*

Derveni : site in Mugdonia, SE Macedonia, NE mainland Greece. *224*

Desert : vast region of arid land, especially in Africa, Arabia and C Asia. *187*

Despoina : site of a temple at Lukosura, in SW Arkadia, C Peloponnesos. *192*

Dhikaios : mountain in the center of the island of Kos, in the Dodekanesoi, SE Aegean Sea. *230*

Dhiktaion : mythological cave, probably in the Dhikte mountain, in CE of the island of Crete, CS Mediterranean Sea. *269*

Dia : 1. small island N of the C of the island of Crete, in CS Mediterranean Sea. *206*; -- 2. seaport town on this island. *206*

Diagon : river flowing N from the mountains of Triphulia, in SE Elis, along the border with Arkadia, and merging with river Erumanthos, in NW Peloponnesos. *194*

Dicaearchia : town on the coast facing the E Tyrrhenian Sea, in SW Italy, W Europe. *238*

Diduma : Ionian town in Caria, also called Branchidai by the name of the inhabitant tribe, S of Miletos, on the coast of the Aegean Sea, in CW Asia Minor, present-day CW Turkey. *254*

Didume : Aiolian island N of NE island of Sicily and W of SW Italy, in SE Tyrrhenian Sea, W Europe. *238*

Didumi : city in the hills SW of the E peninsula of Argolis, in SE Argolis, NE Peloponnesos. *202*

Didumoi : twin hills of SE Thessalia, in the plain of Dotion, near Amuros, in NE mainland Greece. *220*

Dii : tribal land of SE Thrace, N of Abdera, on the N Aegean Sea, in NE mainland Greece. *226*

Dikaia : 1. town of S Macedonia, on the W side of the Gulf of Thermai, in NE mainland Greece. *224*; -- 2. town in CS Thrace, on the coast of the N Aegean Sea, in NE mainland Greece. *226*

Dikili Tash : town near the CN coast of the Aegean Sea and the border with Macedonia, E of the Chalkidike peninsula, in SW Thrace, NE Mainland Greece. *226*

Dikte : mountain range in the region of Lasithi, CE of the island of Crete, CS Mediterranean Sea. *204*

Dimini : site N of the Gulf of Pagassai, closer to the Aegean sea in ancient time, perhaps the same as Iolkos and Pagassai, S of Sesklo, in SE Thessalia, NE mainland Greece. *220*

Dina : town in CS Lydia, present-day CW Turkey, W Asia. *254*

Dinar : see Kelainae. *254*

Dinaric : mountain range along the E Adriatic Sea, extending the Alps to the S, in CS Europe. *240*

Dindymus : mountains in C Lydia, in CW Asia Minor, present-day CW Turkey. *254*

Dine : city of Anigraia, in SW Argolis, on the W coast of the Gulf of Argolis, in NE Peloponnesos. *202*

Diolkos : place of haulage in Megaris, between the SE end of the Gulf of Korinthos and the NW Saronic Gulf, in NE Peloponnesos. *210*

Dion : 1. town in the NW peninsula Akti, on the SE side of the Gulf Singitikos, in E Chalkidike, NW Aegean Sea. *228*; -- 2. town in the SW peninsula Akti, on the SE side of the Gulf Singitikos, in E Chalkidike, NW Aegean Sea. *228*; -- 3. Homeric city on a hill of the island of Euboia, exact location uncertain, in the CW Aegean Sea. *228*; -- 4. town on the border between NE Thessalia and CS Macedonia, on the CW side of the Gulf of Thermai, in NE mainland Greece. *220 & 224*

Dioskurias : town at the NE end of the Euxine (Black) Sea, in present-day Russia, SE Europe. *248*

Dipaia : town in CS Arkadia, W of Mount Mainalos, near the source of the Helisson river, in C Peloponnesos. *192*

Dirmil : city of Doris, near the coast of SE Aegean Sea, in SW Asia Minor, present-day SW Turkey. *254*

Diros : town on the Mani Peninsula, archaeological site of caves, in SE Lakonia, SW Peloponnesos. *198*

Divari : village and cemetery in Messenia, SW Peloponnesos. *196*

Djibouti : small country surrounded by Ethiopia, Eritrea and Somalia, on the W side of the Red Sea, in N Africa. *188 & 246*

Diyala : see Gyndes river. *258*

Diz : see Oroatis. *258*

Dnestr : river flowing from the Carpathian Mountains of NW Romania, through Moldova and into the Euxine (Black) Sea, near Odessa in S Ukraine, SE Europe. *240*

Dnieper : see Borysthenes. *248*

Doberos : city of CE Macedonia, W of Mount Kerkine in W Thrace, in NE mainland Greece. *224*

Dobruja : region along the W Euxine (Black) Sea, in present-day Romania and Bulgaria, E Europe. *240*

Dodekanesoi : a group of twelve islands, also called Sporades, around the major island of Rhodes, in SE Aegean Sea. *230*

Dodona : city of Thesprotis, in the CN of Epeiros, in the NW of mainland Greece. *218*

Dolopia : 1. Ancient city of N Thessalia, near Homeric Ithome, in NE mainland Greece, *220*; -- 2. land of the Dolopians, along the Ionian Sea, N of the Thuamos mountain range, in SW Epeiros, NW mainland Greece. *218*

Don : see Tanais river. *248*

Donussa : town in NE Achaia, near the S coast of the Gulf of Korinthos. E of the river Krios, in NE Peloponnesos. *200*

Dor : city on the coast of E Mediterranean Sea, in ancient Palestine, present–day Israel, W Asia. *258*

Dorion : town W of Polichne, in CN Messenia, SW Peloponnesos. *196*

Doris : 1. region of C mainland Greece, surrounded by Aitolia, Ainis, Malis, Phokis and the two Lokris. *190 & 214*; -- 2. region most to the S of Asia Minor, along the SE Aegean Sea, in present-day SW Turkey. *190 & 254*

Doriskos : inland town of S Thrace, near the NE Aegean Sea, N of the Chersonesos, in NW Turkey, SE Europe. *226*

Dortyol : inland town in Cilicia, SE of Issos, near the NE end of the Gulf of Issos, in present-day SE Turkey, W Asia. *256*

Doruk : town of Cilicia, near the NW coast of the Gulf of Issos, in present-day SE Turkey, W Asia. *256*

Dotion : 1. Hesiodic plain, near NW lake Boibeis, in SE Thessalia, NE mainland Greece. *220*; -- 2. city on this plain. *220*

Douro : river, also called Duero, flowing W from CN Spain, through N Portugal, into the Atlantic Ocean, in W Europe. *232*

Drabeskos : city of Edonia, N of Amphipolis, in SW Thrace, NE mainland Greece, on the NE side of the Gulf of Orfanou, In N Aegean Sea. *226*

Dragmos : town on the NE coast of the island of Crete, between Zakros and Vai, SE of Setaia, in C Mediterranean Sea. *206*

Drago : see Hypsas river. *234*

Drangiana : region between Carmenia and Arachosia, in present-day C Afghanistan, C Asia. *246 & 262*

Drapano : cape on the S side of the bay of Souda, in NW island of Crete, C Mediterranean Sea. *204*

Drapsaca : see Konduz city. *262*

Drava : river flowing E from the mountains of S Austria and joining the Danube river as a tributary on the W border of Hungary, in E Europe. *240*

Drepanon : 1. cape in NW Achaia, at the W entrance to the Gulf of Korinthos, in NW Peloponnesos. *200*; -- 2. seaport town, modern Trapani, in the CW of the island of Sicily, opposite the island of Stagnone, in W Mediterranean Sea, W Europe. *234*

Dreros : inland village in the NE end of the island of Crete, on the W side of the Gulf of Megambellou, in C Mediterranean Sea. *206*

Drilon : river of ancient Illyria, present-day Albania, in the W Balkan Peninsula, flowing W from Mount Skardos, into the Adriatic Sea, in E Europe. *218*

Drin : river of the Balkans, flowing W from the area of Kosovo, across Albania, into the Adriatic Sea, in SE Europe. *240*

Driopia : land of the Driopians, in W Aitolia, SW mainland Greece. *216*

Drumaia : city in CN Phokis, NW of Tithronion, in CS mainland Greece. *214*

Drumoussa : small Ionian island in the Gulf of Candath of the Aegean Sea, in W Lydia, CW Asia Minor, present-day CW Turkey. *230*

Druopis : town of W Phokis, near the border with Doris, in CS mainland Greece. *214*

Druoskephalae : pass through Mount Kithairon, between Boiotia and Attika, in SE mainland Greece. *212*

Dubai : see Macetia. *188, 246 & 264*

Duero : see Douro. *232*

Dulichion : Homeric island of the Ionian Sea, perhaps the same as Leukas, off the coast of Akarnania in SW mainland Greece. *216*

Dumaion : Homeric site, S of Teikhos, in NW Elis, NW Peloponnesos. *194*

Dume : city of NW Achaia, near the S shore of the Gulf of Patraikos, E of Cape Araxos, in NW Peloponnesos. *200*

Dunamene : ancient river, flowing S from the Geraneia mountain range, through Megaris and, between Pherusa and Nisaia, into the Saronic Gulf, in SE mainland Greece. *210*

Dunax : mountain of NE Macedonia, S of Mount Skombros in the land of the Agrianes, in N mainland Greece. *224*

Dura Europos : town in C Mesopotamia, on the W bank of the Euphrates river, in present-day N Iraq, W Asia. *258*

Durrachion : see Epidamnos. *218*

Dusoron : mount in CE Macedonia, NE mainland Greece, N of the Chalkidike Peninsula, in N Aegean Sea. *224*

Duspontion : city of CW Elis, SE of Letrini, in NW Peloponnesos. *194*

Duvanlij : town in CN Thrace, in present-day Romania, SE Europe. *226*

E

Ecbatana : see Agbatana. *260*

Echelidai : town W of the Kephissos river and Athens, in C Attika, SE mainland Greece. *208*

Echetia : inland city on the SE side of the island of Sicily, exact location uncertain, in W Mediterranean Sea, W Europe. *236*

Echinades : ancient group of small islands, later called Strophades, in CE Ionian Sea, off the coast of Akarnania, in SW mainland Greece. *216*

Echinae : islet of the CE Ionian Sea, E of Ithaca, off W Akarnania, in SW mainland Greece. *216*

Echinos : town of CN Phthiotis, in the Othris mountain range, E of the Spercheios river, in NE mainland Greece. *222*

Edessa : 1. town in CW Macedonia, on the W side of the Aliakmon river, in NE mainland Greece. *224*; -- 2. city in Kurdistan, ancient Harran, modern Urfa, in present-day SE Turkey, near the border with NW Iraq, in W Asia. *258*

Edfu : see Apollinopolis. *242*

Edirne : see Uskudama. *226*

Edonia : tribal area of SW Thrace, N of Mount Pangaion, in NE mainland Greece. *226*

Edremit : 1. see Adramuttion **gulf**. *250*; -- 2. see Adramuttion city. *250*

Eetionea : site of a breakwater on the W side of the harbor at Peiraios, in CW Attika, SE mainland Greece. *208*

Egesta : city in the NW of the island of Sicily, W Mediterranean Sea, W Europe. *234*

Egypt : country in NE Africa, Greek Aiguptos, along the Nile river, from Nubia (Sudan) in the S to the Mediterranean Sea in the N and fron Lybia in the W and the Gulf of Aqaba and the Red Sea in the E. *187, 188, 242, 244 & 246*

Egyptian : 1. river of Egypt, Greek Aiguptos, along the N Sinai, in NE Africa, S of Gaza in Palestine. *242*; -- 2. see Red Sea. *242*

Eilei : city in CS of the peninsula of Argolis, SE Argolis, NE Peloponnesos. *202*

Eileithuia : cave near the seaport of Amnisos in CN Crete, C Mediterranean Sea. *206*

Eilesion : Homeric town of SE Boiotia, also called Ilesion, near Thebes, in SE mainland Greece. *212*

Eion : seaport city in SE Macedonia, on the N coast of Gulf of Orfanou in N Aegean Sea, W of Amphipolis in SW Thrace, NE mainland Greece. *224*

Eïonae : Homeric city, probably between Epidauros and Troizen, on the E side of the peninsula of Argolis, in CE Argolis, NE Peloponnesos. *202*

Eira : river in N Messenia, S of the river Neda, in SW Peloponnesos. *196*

Eiresiai : Homeric city, near Aigai, on the NW side of the island of Euboia, on the Gulf of Oropos. In CW Aegean Sea. *228*

Elafonissi : small island, SW of the island of Crete, in CS Mediterra-nean Ses. *204*

Elaia : Aiolian town in NW Lydia, at the NE end of the Gulf of Candath, facing the S end of the island of Lesbos in the NE Aegean Sea. *250*

Elaios : town at the tip of the peninsula of Chersonesos, at the NW entrance to the Strait of Hellespontos, in present-day NW Turkey, *226* -- 2. mountain in SW Arkadia, on the border with Messenia, in C Peloponnesos. *192*

Elam : region E of the Tigris river and N of the Persian Gulf, also called Susiana, in Persia, present-day SW Iran, SW Asia. *258 & 260*

El- Amarna : see Amarna. *242*

Elaphonisos : island of the S Mirtóön Sea, between the S tip of the peninsula Malea, in SE Lakonia, SE Peloponnesos, and the island of Kuthera. *198*

Elaphos : river in SE Arkadia, tributary of the Helisson river, in CE Peloponnesos. *192*

El- Arish : town of NE Egypt, NE Africa, on the coast of the Mediterranean Sea. *242*

Elassa : small island off the NE end of the island of Crete, in C Mediterranean Sea. *206*

Elasson : modern town in CE Thessalia, S of ancient Oloösson, in area of Perrhaibia, CN Mainland Greece. *220*

Elatae : see Elatheia. *214*

Elatea : city in NE Phokis, between Erochos and Vranesi, in CS mainland Greece. *214*

Elatheia : ancient town in NW Opuntian Lokris, also called Elatae, near the Sanctuary of Athena, in CE mainland Greece. *214*

Elba : island of the N Tyrrhenian Sea between the island of Corsica and the coast of C Italy, in W Europe. *238*

Elbo : ancient island in the Nile Delta of N Egypt, exact location unknown, in NE Africa. *242*

Elburz : see Parachoathras. *260*

Elea : 1. city of Lucania, in SW Italy, SE of Paestum, W Europe. *238*; -- 2. city of Calabria, on the E side of the S tip of Italy, near the Strait of Messina, in W Europe. *238*

Elearchos : village near Axos, on the N slope of Mount Ida, SE of
Rithumna, in NW Crete, C Mediterranean Sea. *204*

Elafonissi : island off the SW coast of the island of Crete, in the
Cyrenic Sea. *204*

Elefsina : see Eleusis bay. *210*

Elektra : river Flowing from the Nomia mountain range in NE
Messenia, joining with several tributaries on the NE of Mount
Ithome, then brought by the river Pamisos to the CN of the Gulf
of Messenia, in SW Peloponnesos. *196*

Eleon : Homeric city of Boiotia, exact location unknown, in SE
mainland Greece. *212*

Elephantine : island in the Nile river, opposite the modern city of
Aswan, in S Egypt, NE Africa. *242*

Eleusis : 1. see bay of Salamis. *210*; -- 2. city of NW Attika,
modern Elefsina, N of this Bay and NW of Athens, opposite the
island of Salamis, in SE mainland Greece. *210*

Eleutherae : fortified town of NW Attika, at the Kaza pass to
Boiotia, in SE mainland Greece. *210*

Eleutherna : inland town, also known as Apollonia, SE of
Rithumna and SW of Knossos, on the NE slope of Mount Ida, in
the CN of the island of Crete, C Mediterranean Sea. *206*

Elimia : tribal area of N Thessalia, in NE mainland Greece. *220*

Eliomenos : town at an unknown location on the Island of Leukas,
in E Ionian Sea, off the coast of Akarnania, in SW mainland
Greece. *216*

Elis : 1. region in the NW of the Peloponnesos, along the Ionian
Sea, bordering Achaia to the N, Arkadia to the E and Messenia to
the S. *190, 192, 194, 196 & 200*; -- 2. inland city in the NW of
this region. *194*

El-Kab : town on the E bank of the Nile River, S of Thebes,
in C Egypt, NE Africa. *242*

Elone : Homeric city, later called Leimone, near Larissa, in CN
Thessalia, NE mainland Greece. *220*

Elthuna : town in the C of the island of Crete, in the area of
Rithumna, exact location uncertain, C Mediterranean Sea. *204*

Elumi : region in the NW end of the island of Sicily, in W Mediterranean Sea, W Europe. *234*

Eluros : inland city in the SW of the island of Crete, near the
Libyan Sea, in C Mediterranean Sea. *204*

Elysian Fields : in mythology, the fortunate abode of the dead.
268

Emãmshar : see Sharud. *260*

Emathia : see Oisume. *226*

Embatum : town at an unknown location in E Ionia, probably near Eruthrae, in CW Asia Minor, opposite the island of Chios, in E Aegean Sea. *254*

Emborio : town in the S of the island of Chios, in C Aegean Sea. *230*

Emirates : modern countries of W Asia, surrounded by the Persian Gulf in the N, the Gulf of Oman and the Arabian Sea in the E & S, and Saudi Arabia and Yemen in the W. *188, 246 & 264*

Emporion : town along the W Mediterranean Sea, in Iberia, present-day NE Spain, W Europe. *232*

Enchelea : tribal land in NW Illyria, present-day Croatia, in NW mainland Greece. *218*

Enete : area of Paphlagonia, tribal land of the Aneti, around Amisos, along the Aigialos river, in the CS of the Euxine (Black) Sea, present-day NW Turkey, W Asia. *252*

England : see Albion. *232*

English : channel of the Atlantic Ocean, between England and France, in W Europe. *188*

Engyum : inland town in the CN of the island of Sicily, in W Europe, W Mediterranean Sea. *236*

Enienae : Homeric town, at the foot of Mount Olumpos, near Lektos, in CN Thessalia, NE mainland Greece. *220*

Enipeos : river of Phthiotis, flowing N into W Thessalia, joining the Aridanos river and together the Peneios river, in N mainland Greece. *220 & 222*

Enispe : Homeric city of Arkadia, precise location unknown, in C Peloponnesos. *192*

Enna : inland town, high on a mount, in the CE of the island of Sicily, W Mediterranean Sea. *236*

Ennea Hodoi : see Amphipolis. *226*

Enneakrounos : fountains, supplied by the stream Kallirhoe, in Athens, CW Attika, SE mainland Greece. *208*

Enope : Homeric city of SW Messenia, E of Pulos, in SW Peloponnesos. *196*

Entella : inland town in CW of the island of Sicily, in W Europe, W Mediterranean Sea. *234*

Enualios : site somewhere on the peninsula of Minoa, in SE Megaris, W of Salamis, in SE mainland Greece. *210*

Eordaia : tribal area of CW Macedonia, S of Almopia, in NE mainland Greece. *224*

Eordaikos : river of S Illyria, flowing W past Pelion, in present-day Albania, into the Adriatic Sea, in C Europe. *218*

Epano Englianos : town on the island of Sphakteria, also known as Palace of Nestor, S of Pulos, in SW Messenia, SW Peloponnesos. *196*

Epardus : see Margush river. *262*

Epeiros : region of NW Greece and S Albania, along the W coast where the S Adriatic and the N Ionian seas meet, present-day Albania, with the Pindos Mountains of Thessalia to the E, Illyria, modern Albania, in the N and the Gulf of Ambrakia in the S, separating it from Aitolia and Akarnania, and Phthiotis in the SE. *190, 214, 216, 218, 220, 222 & 224*

Ephesos : Ionian city, W of Lydia, in the CW of Asia Minor, S of the Kaustros river, on the E coast of the Aegean Sea. *254*

Ephura : 1. Homeric city of Thesprotis, S of Dodona, in C Epeiros, NW mainland Greece. *218*; -- 2. see Korinthos. *202*

Epidamnos : town along the SE Adriatic Sea, also called Durrachion, in Antiquity on an isthmus of Illyria, present-day Albania, CS Europe. *218*

Epidauros : 1. city on the CE side of Argolis, near the W coast of the Saronic Gulf, opposite the island of Aigina, in NE Peloponnesos. *202*; -- 2. harbor town on the SE side of Lakonia, modern Momenvasia, on the Mirtóön Sea, one with the site of Limera, in SE Peloponnesos. *198*

Epidelion : seaport city of SE Lakonia, on the coast of the Mirtóön Sea, in SE Peloponnesos. *198*

Epipolae : site in the SE of the island of Sicily, W Europe, W Mediterranean Sea. *236*

Epion : Minyan town in Elis, exact location unknown, in CW Peloponnesos. *194*

Erannoboas : small river flowing N, E of the Son river and joining the Ganges river near Patna, in present-day India, C Asia. *266*

Erasinos : river of CW Argolis, flowing from the ancient lake Stumphalis, S of Argos, into the N end of the Gulf of Argolis, in NE Peloponnesos. *202*

Erchia : town NE of Paeania, in C Attika, SE mainland Greece. *208*

Erebos : mythological river in Hades. *268*

Erebuni : palatial site in Armenia, ancient N Urartu and modern S Russia, W Asia. *248*

Erech : see Uruk. *258*

Eresos : coastal town on the W side of the island of Lesbos, in CE Aegean Sea, opposite Aiolia in CW Asia Minor. *228*

Eretria : area in C of the island of Euboia, E of the N end of the Gulf of Petalion, in CW Aegean Sea. *228*; -- 2. city, S of Chalkis, in this area. *228*

Erganos : inland village W of mount Dikte, in CE of the island of Crete, C Mediterranean Sea. *206*

Ergines : river flowing from CE Thrace, tributary of the river Maritsa, into the Aegean Sea, in NE mainland Greece. *226*

Ericussa : small Aiolian island N of NE island of Sicily and W of SW Italy, in SE Tyrrhenian Sea, W Europe. *238*

Eridanos : 1. river flowing from Mount Anchesmos, S through Kerameikos and Agora, W of Athens, into the Ilisos river as its tributary, in CW Attika, SE mainland Greece. *208*; -- 2. river in N Italy, modern Po, flowing SE from the Alps, then E into a delta of the NW Adriatic Sea, in W Europe. *238*

Erigon : river of W Macedonia, modern Crna river, tributary of the Axios river, in N mainland Greece. *224*

Erineos : 1. city in CN Achaia, NW of Rhupes, on the S shore of the Gulf of Korinthos, in CN Peloponnesos. *200*; -- 2. one of a group of four cities, with Boion, Kitinion, and Pindos, in the valley of the Pindos river, in Doris, CS mainland Greece. *214*; -- 3. small river in the SE of the island of Sicily, exact location unknown, possibly S of the Cacyparis river, in W Mediterranean Sea, W Europe. *236*

Eritrea : small country on the SW coast of the Red Sea, N of Ethiopia and E of Sudan, in NE Africa. *188 & 246*

Erochos : town in CN Phokis, SE of Tithronium, in CS mainland Greece. *214*

Eronos : town on the N side of the Lasithi Plateau, in the NE of the island of Crete, C Mediterranean Sea. *206*

Ertaea : town in the area of Herakleion, exact location uncertain, in C of the island of Crete, C Mediterranean Sea. *206*

Erumanthos : 1. mountain range of NE Elis and CS Achaia, along the border with Arkadia, in CN Peloponnesos. *194 & 200*;-- 2. river flowing from NW Arkadia, along the border between Elis to the W and Arkadia to the E, tributary of river Alpheios, in CN Peloponnesos. *194*;-- 3. mythological mount, probably in C Lydia, CW Asia Minor, present-day CW Turkey. *269*

Erutheia : mythological island, referred to as the Red Isle, somewhere in the W side of the river Okeanos, W of Europe. *268*

Eruthini : Homeric site of a fortress in Paphlagonia, S of the Euxine (Black) Sea, in Asia Minor, present-day NW Turkey. *252*

Eruthrae : 1. Ionian seaport on the Mimas peninsula of CW Asia Minor, present-day CW Turkey, opposite the island of Chios in the Aegean Sea. *254*; -- 2. Ancient city in CS Boiotia, S of the Asopos river and near the border with Attika, in SE mainland Greece. *212*

Erymandrus : river, modern Helmand river, mostly in Bactria, flowing through SW Afghanistan, into the Sistãn swamps, on the S Pakistani-Iranian border, in C Asia. *262 & 264*

Eryx : 1. mount in the NW of the island of Sicily, W Mediterranean Sea, W Europe. *234*; -- 2. town at the foot of this mountain, near Segesta. *234*

Escharta : area of N Sogdiana, along the Jaxartes river, in present-day SE Uzbekistan, C Asia. *262*

Eschate : city, also known as Khodjend, modern Leninabad. in Escharta, C Asia. *262*

Esfahan : see Aspadana. *260*

Esna : town on the W bank of the Nile River, S of Thebes, in C Egypt, NE Africa. *242*

Eteonos : Homeric city in Boiotia, exact location unknown, SE mainland Greece. *212*

Ethiopia : see Aithiopia. *188 & 246*

Etiani : site at the SE end of the island of Crete, in C Mediterranean Sea. *206*

Etone : Town NE of Larissa, on the Peneios river, in CN Thessalia, NE mainland Greece. *220*

Etruria : region on the CW coast of Italy, also called Tyrrhenia, on the Tyrrhenian Sea, inhabited by Etruscans, N of Latium, in W Europe. *238*

Eua : 1. village SW of Thurea, modern Hellenikon, in SW Argolis, near the border with Arkadia to the W and Lakonia to the S, in CE Peloponnesos. *202*; -- 2. mount in C Messenia, S of Messene, in SW Peloponnesos. *196*

Euboia : 1. island, also called Abantes, parallel to the coast of Attika and Boiotia, in the W Aegean Sea. *190, 212, 222 & 228*; -- 2. gulf separating this island from mainland Greece, made of the Gulfs of Petalion in the S and Oropos in the N, connected by the Strait of Euripos. *228*; -- 3. hill SE of Mukenae, near the sanctuary of Hera (Heraion), in NW Argolis, NE Peloponnesos. *202*; -- 4. inland city on the SE side of the island of Sicily, in W Mediterranean Sea. *236*

Euenos : 1. Hesiodic river in N Phrygia, S of the Hellespontos, exact course uncertain, in Asia Minor, present-day NW Turkey. *252*; -- 2. river, also called Avenos and Nessos, flowing SW from the Pindos Mountains of Thessalia on the E side of the Acheloos river, through Aitolia, into the Gulf of Patraikos, in SW mainland Greece. *216 & 220*

Euesperides : seaport of Kyrenaica, present-day Benghazi in Libya, NE Africa, along the Mediterranean Sea. *244*

Eulaeus : see Choaspes river. *258*

Eumelos : village near Larissa, in CN Thessalia, NE mainland Greece. *220*

Eupalion : city in W Ozolian Lokris, N of the Gulf of Korinthos, NE of Naupaktos in SE Aitolia, in CS mainland Greece. *214*

Eupatoria : city of CW Crimea, also called Kerkinitis, in CN Euxine (Black) Sea, SE Europe. *248*

Euphrates : river, also called Puratta, flowing from the E Taurus
mountains of present-day E Turkey, SE through Mesopotamia, W
of the Tigris river, through modern N Syria and the length of
Iraq, to end in the S marshes and the Persian Gulf, in W Asia.
The Euphrates and Tigris rivers may have remained separate to
the S end until the fourth century BCE. *187, 248 & 258*

Euripos : strait off CW island of Euboia, near the Lelantine plain,
between the gulfs of Petalion to the S and Oropos to the N, in
CW Aegean Sea. *212 & 228*

Europe : continent between the Mediterranean Sea, the Euxine
(Black) Sea & the Caucasus Mountains to the S and the Arctic
Ocean to the N, Asia to the E, as far as the Ural Mountains in the
NE and the Aegean Sea in the SE, and the Atlantic Ocean to the
W. *187, 188, 232, 238, 240 & 248*

Europos : city of S Macedonia, on the W bank of the Axios river, S
of Atalante, in NE mainland Greece. *224*

Eurotas : 1. river flowing from N Lakonia, past E of Sparta, into
the CN Gulf of Lakonia, in SE Peloponnesos. *198*; -- 2. valley
where Sparta is located, in SE Peloponnesos. *198*

Eurution : city of SW Thessalia, later called Oichalia, W of the
Othris mountain range, in CN mainland Greece. *220*

Euryelus : site in the SE of the island of Sicily, W Mediterranean
Sea, W Europe. *236*

Eurymedon : 1. river of Pamphylia flowing from the C mountains
of Pisidia into the NE Mediterranean Sea, in present-day CS
Turkey, W Asia. *256* -- 2. city, near Aspendos, at the mouth of
this river. *256*

Eutresis : town in SW Boiotia, NW of Eleutherae in NW Attika, SE
mainland Greece. *212*

Euxine : inland sea of SE Europe, also called Black Sea or Pontos,
surrounded by Asia Minor and the Hittite Territories, modern
Turkey, to the S, the Caucasus Mountains, present-day Georgia
and Russia, to the E, the Crimea and present-day Ukraine to the
N, and E Thrace, modern Moldovia, Romania and Bulgaria, to the
W, connected with the Mediterranean Sea by the Bosporos, the
Sea of Marmara, the Hellespontos and the Aegean Sea. *187,
190, 226, 240, 246, 248 & 252*

Exampaeus : salty spring in Scythia, between the rivers
Borysthenes and Romanian Hypanis, overflowing into this river,
in Scythia, present-day NW Turkey. *248*

F

Faesulae : Etruscan town in C Italy, W Europe. *238*
Fair Havens : see Lasaia. *206*
Faiyûm : 1. large depression of the NW desert of Egypt, SW of
   Cairo, in NE Africa. *242*; -- 2. modern city in this area *242*
Falassarua : town in the SW of the peninsula of Grambousa, NW
   of the island of Crete, C Mediterranean Sea. *204*
Falerii : city of the Latium in C Italy, W Europe, a short distance E
   of Rome, near Praeneste. *238*
Farafra : oasis in CW Egypt, between the oases Dakhla to the S
   and Barîya to the N, in NE Africa. *242*
Farah : 1. see Prophthasia area. *260*; -- 2. city in this area, W Asia.
   260 -- 3. river flowing SW from the mountains of C Afghanistan,
   past the city of Farah, into the Sistãn swamps, near the SW
   border with Iran, C Asia. *260, 262 & 264*
Felsina : Etruscan town in Toscana, CN Italy, W Europe. *238*
Ferghana : 1. mountain range in ancient N Sogdiana, at the
   juncture of Tajikistan, Uzbekistan and Kazakhstan, in CN Asia.
   262; -- 2. city in the fertile valley along this mountain range.
   262; -- 3. gate like a pass connecting Kazakhstan and Tajikistan
   via Uzbekistan, in CN Asia. *262*
Fethiye : see Telmessos. *254*
Fevzipasa : city of NE Cilicia, near the border with Syria, in
   present-day SE Turkey, SW Asia. *258*
Firdawsi : town of Persis, present-day Iran, in CS Asia. *264*
Foinikia : village a short distance E of Knossos, in CN of the island
   of Crete, C Mediterranean Sea. *206*
Fraktin : city in the C of the Hittite territories, in Anatolia, C of
   present-day Turkey, W Asia. *252*
France : modern country of W Europe bordering the English
   Channel & Belgium to the N, Germany, Switzerland & Italy to the
   E, the Mediterranean Sea and Spain to the S and the N Atlantic
   Ocean to the W. *188 & 232*
Franchthi : cave in the SW of Argolis, on the N shore of the Gulf of
   Argolis, S of Tiruns, in CW Argolis, NE Peloponnesos. *202*
Frankolimani : harbor city on the N side of the promontory of
   modern Agios Nikolaos, at Thorikos, opposite the harbor
   Portomandri, in SE Attika, SE mainland Greece. *208*
Frattesina : Etruscan village N of Felsina, in NE Italy, W Europe.
   238
Frogs : mythological lake crossed by Dionysus and Xanthias in the
   Underworld. *268*

G

Gabès : 1. gulf of SW Mediterranean Sea, also spelled Qabes and called Syrtis Minor, in E Tunisia, CN Africa. *244*; -- 2. town on this gulf. *244*

Gadara : 1. city in ancient Palestine, called Gadara Decapolis, on the E side of the Jordan river, in present-day N Jordan, W Asia. *258*; -- 2. city of ancient Palestine, called Gedara Perea, S of Gedara Decapolis, in present-day C Jordan, W Asia. *258*

Gadira : island in the Atlantic Ocean, modern Cotinusa, off the coast of SW Spain, opposite Gedeira (Cadiz), in W Europe. *232*

Gaidhouronisi : small island off the SE coast of the island of Crete, in CS Mediterranean Sea. *206*

Galatia : region of CN Anatolia, S of Paphlagonia, in present-day CN Turkey, W Asia. *252*

Galepsos : town on the SE side of the Gulf of Orfanou, E of the Chalkidike Peninsula, in SW Thrace, NE mainland Greece. *226*

Galeria : inland town in the CE of the island of Sicily, in W Mediterranean Sea, W Europe. *236*

Gallipoli : 1. narrow peninsula at the NE end of the Hellespontos, in S Thrace, W part of the Chersonesos, in present-day NW Turkey, SE Europe. *226*; -- 2. port city on this peninsula, modern Gelibolu, on the European side of the Hellespontos, opposite Lampsakos. *226*

Gandak : river flowing from the Himalaya Mountains through Nepal and SW through India until it joins the Ganges river near Patna, in C Asia. *266*

Gandhãra : area of E Bactria, E of the Indus river, NW of the Himalayas, in NW Pakistan and N India, C Asia. *246 & 266*

Ganges : major river flowing from the Himalaya Mountains, E of the Hyphasis river, N to S through India and Bangladesh into the Bay of Bengal, in C Asia. *266*

Garama : inland city of SW Libya, in NE Africa. *244*

Garamantes : inland area of W Libya, in NE Africa. *244*

Garates : river flowing from SE Arkadia, past E of Tegea, then E and S toward the river Tanaos as its tributary, in SW Argolis, CE Peloponnesos. *192 & 202*

Gardez : city of Bactria, S of Kabul, in present-day Afghanistan, C Asia. *262*

Gargara : Aiolian town in the N of the gulf of Adramuttion, near Lamponion, in W Mysia, NW Asia Minor, present-day NW Turkey. *250*

Gargaron : peak of Mt Ida, in C Troas, NW Asia Minor, present-day NW Turkey. *250*

Gargettos : inland town of Attika, SW of Marathon, in SE mainland Greece. *210*

Garumna : river in SW France, modern Gironde, flowing NW from the Pyraenaei mountains, into the Atlantic Ocean, in W Europe. *232*

Gathea : town in CS Arkadia, near the border with Lakonia, in SE Peloponnesos. *192*

Gatheatas : river of CS Arkadia, flowing N into river Karnion as a tributary, in SE Peloponnesos. *192*

Gaudos : Greek island of the Libyan Sea, S of the W side of the island of Crete, in C Mediterranean Sea. *204*

Gaugamela : town in ancient Assyria, near Arbela, in NE Iraq, W Asia. *258*

Gaul : region of W Europe, consisting mainly of present-day France, Belgium, Holland and SW Germany. *232*

Gaza : 1. SW portion of Philistia, S area of ancient Palestine, in modern West Bank territory, NE of Egypt and W of Israel, in W Asia. *258*; 2. major town, ancient Cadites, in this region. *258*

Gazaca : city in the C plain of Media, present-day N Iran, W Asia. *260*

Gazara : city of ancient Israel, biblical Gezer, NW of Jerusalem, in W Asia. *258*

Gazi : village W of Herakleion, on the CN coast of the island of Crete, in C Mediterranean Sea. *206*

Gedeira : seaport of SW Iberia, modern Cadiz, on the Atlantic Ocean, in SW Spain, SW Europe. *232*

Gediz : see Hermos river. *250, 252 & 254*

Gedrosia : ancient desert region, in modern Baluchistan of S Pakistan, N of the Arabian Sea and W of the Indus river, in C Asia. *246 & 264*

Gela : coastal city on the SE side of the island of Sicily, W of Camarina, in W Mediterranean Sea, W Europe. *236*

Gelas : river in the C of the island of Sicily, past Gela, flowing S into the Mediterranean Sea, W Europe. *236*

Gelibolu : see Gallipoli city. *226*

Gelonos : ancient city of Sauromatai, in N Scythia, present-day Ukraine, SE Europe. *248*

Gelydonia : cape at the W entrance to the gulf of Antalya, on the CS Turkish coast of the Mediterranean Sea, in W Asia. *256*

Gennesaret : lake in N Jordan river, N Palestine, p Israel, W Asia. *258*

Genoa : city on the coast of the Ligurian sea, in E Italy, W Europe. *232*

Genusus : river of W Macdonia, flowing W from the E side of Lake Luchnites, near the Epeiros border, and into the Adriatic Sea, in NW mainland Greece. *224*

Georgia : see Iberia. *246 & 248*

Geraistos : cape at the S tip of the island of Euboia, in CW of the Aegean Sea. *228*

Geraneia : mountain range on the border between NE Argolis and Megaris, E of the Isthmus of Korinthos, in NE Peloponnesos. *202 & 210*

Gerasa : city of ancient Palestine, in present-day Jordan, near the E bank of the Jordan river, in W Asia. *258*

Gerenia : city in the NW corner of Lakonia, near the border with Messenia, between the coast of the Gulf of Messenia to the W and Mount Kalathios to the E, in CS Peloponnesos. *198*

Gerenon : Hesiodic city of CW Messenia, in Nestor's kingdom, SW Peloponnesos. *196*

Geresia : ancient area of Nestor's kingdom, near Pulos, in CW Messenia, SW Peloponnesos. *196*

Germany : modern country in NW Europe, bordering on Denmark and the North & Baltic Seas to the N, Poland & Czechoslovakia to the E, Austria & Switzerland to the S and France, Belgium & Holland to the W. *188 & 232*

Geronthrae : city in CN Lakonia, SE of Selinos, in SE Peloponnesos. *198*

Gerrha : town on the SW side of the Persian Gulf, in present-day E Saudi Arabia, W Asia. *264*

Gerrhos : river of the Saromatai region of Scythia, branch of the delta of the Danube river discharging into the Euxine (Black) Sea, in present-day Romania, SE Europe. *242*

Getae : area of NE Thrace, present-day Romania, N of the Haemos Mountain, in SE Europe. *226*

Gezer : see Gazara. *258*

Ghazni : city of Bactria, SW of Kabul, in present-day Afghanistan, C Asia. *262*

Gianisadhes : small islands in the Sea of Crete, opposite the NE of the island of Crete. *206*

Gibraltar : 1. rocky peninsula, ancient Calpe, at the SW end of Spain extending into the Mediterranean Sea, in W Europe. *232 & 244*; 2. strait between Spain to the N and Morocco to the S, connecting the Mediterranean Sea and the Atlantic Ocean. *232 & 244*

Gigonos : city of S Macedonia, in NW Chalkidike, NE mainland Greece, on the E coast of the Gulf of Thermai, in NW Aegean Sea. *224*

Giophurakia : village in CN of the island of Crete, exact location uncertain, C Mediterranean Sea. *206*

Girga : town on the W bank of the Nile river in C Egypt, N of Thebes, in NE Africa. *242*

Gironde : see Garumna river. *232*

Gîza : funerary site in N Egypt, near the W bank of the Nile river, SW of Cairo, in NE Africa. *242*

Gla : 1. in Antiquity an island in Lake Kopais, N Boiotia, SE mainland Greece. *212*; -- 2. town made of the island, later attached to N Boiotia, E of Orchomenos, in SE mainland Greece. *212*

Glaphurai : ancient city S of lake Boibeis, in SE Thessalia, NE mainland Greece. *220*

Glauke : town near Mukale, exact location unknown, in SW Caria, Asia Minor, present-day SW Turkey. *254*

Glaukos : river of W Achaia, flowing W into the Gulf of Patraikos, in NW Peloponnesos. *200*

Glausae : tribal land located in Kashmir, ancient Bactria, present-day NE Pakistan, C Asia. *266*

Glechon : Hesiodic city of N Boiotia, near Orchomenos, along the Kephisos river, in SE mainland Greece. *212*

Glisas : Homeric city NE of Teumesos, in CE Boiotia, in SE mainland Greece. *212*

Gluppia : city in CE Lakonia, SE of Marios, in SE Peloponnesos. *198*

Gogana : city N of NW Apostana, on the E shore of the Persian Gulf, in W Carmania, S Persia, present-day SW Iran, W Asia. *264*

Gogarene :area of Armenia, N of Mount Ararat, in W Asia. *248*

Golovita : lake in SE Bulgaria where the Hamangia culture flourished in ancient time, in SE Europe. *240*

Gonies : village in CN of the island of Crete, C Mediterranean Sea. *204*

Gonoëssa : Homeric city near Argos, exact location uncertain, in CW Argolis, NE Peloponnesos. *202*

Gordaia : town in CW Macedonia, NE mainland Greece. *224*

Gordion : town of N Galatia. in CN Asia Minor, present-day CN Turkey. *252*

Gordyene : area of Assyria, along the E side of the Tigris river, in present-day N Iraq, W Asia. *258*

Gorgãn : city near the SE corner of the Caspian Sea, in Hyrcania, present-day NE Iran, C Asia. *260*

Gorgippa : town of the Crimea, along the Euxine (Black) Sea, S of Hermonassa and the Sea of Maeotis, in SE Europe. *248*

Gortunia : city of C Macedonia, on the W bank of the Axios river, SE of Idomene, in NE mainland Greece. *224*

Gortunios : river of SW Arkadia, also called Lusios, flowing S past Gortus, into the Alpheios river as its tributary, in C Peloponnesos. *192*

Gortus : 1. city in SW Arkadia, NE of Rhaeteae, in C Peloponnesos. *192*; -- 2. ancient city on the W side of the plain of Mesara, NE of Phaistos, in CS of the island of Crete, C Mediterranean Sea. *204*

Gournia : town on the E side of the island of Crete, at the S end of the Gulf of Megambellou, in C Mediterranean Sea. *206*

Gourtsouli : see Ptolis. *192*

Gozo : see Ogugia. *244*

Graia : Homeric city, probably a short distance from Tanagra, in SE Boiotia, CE mainland Greece. *212*

Grambousa : 1. peninsula at the far end of the NW island of Crete, between the CS Mediterranean Sea and the Gulf of Kissamos. *204*; -- 2. island N of this peninsula. *204*

Grammos : mountain of W Macedonia, in N mainland Greece. *224*

Granikos : 1. river flowing from N Mysia, W through Hellespontine and Troas, in NW Asia Minor, into the Aegean Sea. *250*; -- 2. town near the estuary of this river. *250*

Granis : river of Persis, in S Persia, ancient Sitaces, modern Mand river, flowing W into the Persian Gulf, in present-day S Iran, W Asia. *264*

Gravisca : Etruscan seaport, on N Tyrrhenian Sea, W of the town of Tarquinii, in Etruria, CW Italy, W Europe. *238*

Great Prespa : see Prespa. *224*

Greece : S portion of the Balkan peninsula, including also many islands of the Aegean and Ionian seas and, as Magna Graecia, Asia Minor in the W region of Turkey, along the Aegean Sea, and the S region of Italy & Sicily together with the neighboring islands of the Mediterranean Sea. *187, 188, 190- 202, 208- 226 & 240*

Gritsa : town of SE Phthiotis, in E mainland Greece. *222*

Grotta : site in the N of the island of Naxos, in the Cyclades, CW Aegean Sea. *230*

Gruneia : Ionian town, in SW Mysia, on the NW coast of Asia Minor, present-day CW Turkey, along the Aegean Sea. *250*

Guadalquivir : river in the SW of Spain, W Europe, flowing W into the Atlantic Ocean. *232*

Guadiana : river of S Iberia, flowing W from CS Spain, then S along the border with Portugal, into the Atlantic Ocean, on the N side of the Gulf of Cadiz, in W Europe. *232*

Guge : Homeric lake in the C of Lydia, CW Asia Minor, present-day CW Turkey. *250*

Gulashkird : see Alexandria-in-Carmenia. *264*

Gumal : 1. river flowing from the mountains of S Waziristan, in NE
   Afghanistan, between the Khyber and Bolān passes, into
   Pakistan where it joins the Kundar river, a tributary to the Indus
   river, in C Asia. *262 & 266*; -- 2. pass in ancient Bactria, from
   this river valley in present-day CE Afghanistan, through the S of
   the Sulaimān mountains, to NE Pakistan. *262*

Guphtokastro : 1. pass between Attika and Boiotia, on the W side,
   between Boiotian Plataia and NW of Eleutherae, in NW Attika, SE
   mainland Greece. *210*; -- 2. hill of S Aitolia, near the W entrance
   to the Gulf of Korinthos where Pleuron was once located, in SW
   mainland Greece. *216*

Gupsades : site in the CS of the island of Crete, exact location
   uncertain, in C Mediterranean Sea. *206*

Gurae : rocky headland, like cliffs, in E Macedonia, NE mainland
   Greece, somewhere along the N Aegean Sea. *224*

Guraei : tribal land located in NW India, S of Kashmir, in C Asia.
   266

Gurob : harem settlement of the Faiyum region, SW of Cairo, in
   NW Egypt, NE Africa. *242*

Gurtone : town of C Thessalia, in NE mainland Greece. *220*

Gutheion : seaport of CW Lakonia, on the NW side of the Gulf of
   Lakonia, in SE Peloponnesos. *198*

Gwadar : city, E of Cophas, on the S coast of ancient Gedrosia,
   present-day S Pakistan, in C Asia. *264*

Gwatar : bay in the N Arabian Sea, off the coast of ancient
   Gedrosia, present-day S Pakistan, in C Asia. *264*

Gyndes : river of N Mesopotamia, also called Diyala, tributary of
   the Tigris river, in persent-day N Iraq, W Asia. *258*

H

Habu : see Medinet. *242*

Hades : mythological resting place of the dead beneath the earth,
   also referred to as the Underworld. *268*

Hadranon : inland town in the CE of the island of Sicily, also
   known as Adrano, along the river Simeto, on the W side of
   Mount Aetna, in W Mediterranean Sea, W Europe. *236*

Haemos : 1. mountain range of E Thrace, between Odrusia to the
   S and Getae to the N, in present–day N Bulgaria, SE Europe. *226*;
   -- 2. see Balkans. *240*

Haimoniae : town SE of Megalopolis, in C Arkadia, C Peloponnesos. *192*

Halab : see Aleppo. *258*

Halaesa : town in the NE of the island of Sicily, near the coast of the Tyrrhenian Sea, in W Europe. *236*

Halai : 1. city in the NE corner of Boiotia, on the Gulf of Oropos, near the border with Opuntian Lokris, in SE mainland Greece. *212*; -- 2. site of a cemetery near Thebes, in CS Boiotia, SE mainland Greece. *212*

Halex : river of the SW tip of Italy, W of the Caicinos river, flowing S into the Mediterranean Sea, in W Europe. *238*

Halfa : city of S Egypt, on the border with Nubia (Sudan), in NE Africa. *244*

Halicus : river in the C of the island of Sicily, flowing S into the Mediterranean Sea, W of Akragas, in W Europe. *234*

Haliartos : Homeric city, S of Lake Kopais, E of Koroneia, in C Boiotia, SE mainland Greece. *212*

Halieis : seaport city in SE Argolis, on the E side of the entrance of the Gulf of Argolis, SW on the peninsula of Argolis, opposite the island of Pitiussa, in SE Argolis, NE Peloponnesos. *202*

Halikarnassos : ancient harbor city of SW Caria, near modern Bodrum, on the Bodrum Peninsula of SW Asia Minor, present-day SW Turkey, on the Gulf of Kerameikos, off the Aegean Sea. *254*

Halizonia : area of Cappadocia, S of the Euxine (Black) Sea, in present-day CN Turkey, W Asia. *252*

Halos : Homeric town of Achaia Phthiotis, on the W side of the Gulf of Pagassai, in NE mainland Greece. *222*

Halys : major river, also called Kizil, flowing from the high mountains of NC Anatolia, first in a SW direction, then N through the Pontos region, separating it from Paphlagonia to the W, and emptying into the Euxine (Black) Sea, in present-day NW Turkey, W Asia. *248 & 252*

Hama : Phoenician city, modern Hmãh, in the Lebanon mountains, N of Homs, in present-day NW Syria. W Asia. *256*

Hamadan : see Agbatana. *260*

Hamãh : see Hama. *256*

Hamangia : ancient area covering E Bulgaria and Romania, between the Danube River and the Euxine (Black) Sea, mostly around Lake Golovita, in SE Europe. *240*

Hammamet : gulf in E Tunisia, S of Tunis, in S Mediterranean Sea, CN Africa. *244*

Hangmatana : see Agbatana. *260*

Harirûd : 1. river flowing from the W slopes of the SW Hindu Kush mountain range, in C Afghanistan, W through the area of Herat, then N along the Iranian border and into the Kara-Kum desert of

Turkmenistan, where it is called Tedzhen river, in C Asia. *260 &
262*; -- 2. fertile valley with oasis, along this river, where the city
of Herat is located. *260*

Harma : Homeric city, NE of Thebes, in CE Boiotia, SE mainland
Greece. *212*

Harmozia : 1. region N of the Strait of Oman, between the Persian
Gulf and the Arabian Sea, in present-day SE Iran, W Asia. *264*; --
2. town in this region. *264*

Harnai : pass in SW Pakistan, from Quetta to the E, past Ziãrat-e-
shah-Maqsûd and Loralei, in C Asia. *262*

Harpina : city of CE Elis, at the juncture of the rivers Harpinates
and Alpheios, in CW Peloponnesos. *194*

Harpinates : river of CE Elis, merging with the Alpheios river near
Harpina, in CW Peloponnesos. *194*

Harpus : see Tigres. *269*

Harran : see Edessa. *258*

Hasanbeyli : town, S of the Bahce Pass, in NE Cilicia, present-day
SE Turkey, W Asia. *256*

Hasarlik **:** city of Doris, exact location uncertain, on the S coast of
Asia Minor, near the SE Aegean Sea. *254*

Hatti : see Hittite. *248*

Hattusa : city, modern Boghazköy, in CN of the Hittite territories,
surrounded on three sides by the Halys river, in Hatti, W Asia.
248

Hebros : see Maritsa river. *226*

Hekatompulos : see Shahrud or Dara (Abivard). *260*

Helene : island near the coast of SE Attika, in CW Aegean Sea. *208*

Helike : 1. lake like a delta of river Selinos, near the Gulf of
Korinthos, in NE Peloponnesos. *200*; -- 2. town on this lake, N of
Kerunia. *200*

Helikon : mountain range from Lake Kopais in C Boiotia to the
Gulf of Korinthos in the S, especially the mount NW of Thisbe, in
SW Boiotia, SE mainland Greece. *212*

Heliopolis : 1. city, also called Ôn, E of the opening of the Nile
Delta, N of Cairo, in N Egypt, NE Africa. *242*; -- 2. see Baalbek.
256

Helisson : 1. river of SE Arkadia, flowing NS from the Phalantos
mountain range, then W through the city of Megalopolis, and
further W joining the Alpheios river as its tributary, in C Peloponnesos, *192*; -- 2. town of C Arkadia, somewhere along this
river. *192*; -- 3. river flowing from the NE border of Arkadia,
through NW Argolis, N of Sikuon, into the Gulf of Korinthos, in
NE Peloponnesos. *202*

Hellas : 1. ancient name for Greece, *187 & 190*; -- 2. see Achilles.
222

Hellenikon : see Eua. *202*

Hellespontos : strait, modern Dardanelles, between Troas in NW Asia Minor and the Peninsula of Gallipoli in SE Europe, joining the Aegean Sea and the Sea of Marmara, in present-day NW Turkey. *190, 226 & 250*

Hellespontine : narrow region S of the Hellespontos, between the Aegean Sea and the Sea of Propontis (Marmara), in present-day NW Turkey, W Asia. *250*

Hellopia : see Molossis. *218*

Helmand : see Erymandrus. *262 & 264*

Heloros : town on the SE island of Sicily, S of Siracusa, on the coast of the Mediterranean Sea, in W Europe. *236*

Helos : 1. city in C Lakonia, near the NE shore of the Gulf of Lakonia, in SE Peloponnesos. *198*; -- 2. ancient city in W Messenia, in Nestor's kingdom, near Pulos, in SW Peloponnesos. *196*

Hephaisti : see Hiera. *238*

Heptaporos : see Kebrene river. *250*

Heraei : mountains in the SE of the island of Sicily, in the W Mediterranean Sea, W Europe. *236*

Heraia : city of CW Arkadia, N of the Alpheios river, in C Peloponnesos. *192*

Heraion : 1. city N of ancient Argos, in NW Argolis, NE Peloponnesos. *202*; -- 2. cape adjacent to Epidauros, in CE Argolis, into the Saronic Gulf. *202*; -- 3. city on the S side of the island of Samos, in E Aegean Sea, off the coast of Caria, near the C of Asia Minor, CW Turkey. *230*

Herakleia : 1. city of CS Elis, NW of Olumpia, in NW Peloponnesos. *194*; -- 2. town in SE Illyria, near the border with Epeiros, in NW mainland Greece. *218*; -- 3. city in the area of Trachis, in E Malis, near Thermopulai, in CE mainland Greece. *214*; -- 4. town at the NW end of the gulf of Taranto, SW of Metapontion, in S Italy, W Europe. *238*; -- 5. town of Bithynia, in SW of the Euxine (Black) Sea, in present-day Turkey, W Asia. *252*

Herakleia Minoa : coastal town near the SW of the island of Sicily, in W Mediterranean Sea, W Europe. *234*

Herakleion : 1. town in CW Attika, S of the Bay of Eleusis and W of the Kephisos river, in SE mainland Greece. *210*; -- 2. bay in the CN coast of the island of Crete, in CS Mediterranean Sea. *206*; -- 3. city on the S shore of this gulf, NW of Knossos. *206*

Herakleopolis : city, modern Ihnasya el-Medina, in C Egypt, near the W bank of river Nile, N of Oxyrhynchos, in NE Africa. *242*

Herat : 1. area in the region of Areia, in present-day W Afghanistan, near the border with Iran and Turkmenistan, in C Asia. *260*; -- 2. city, ancient Alexandria-in-Areia, on the Harirûd river,

S of the Parapamisus mountain range, in the NW of this area.
260

Herbessus : inland town in the Heraei Mountains of SE island of Sicily, in W Mediterranean Sea, W Europe. *236*

Herbita : inland city near Engyum, in the CN of the island of Sicily, W Mediterranean Sea, W Europe. *236*

Herkune : river of CW Boiotia, flowing E into Lake Kopais, in SE mainland Greece. *212*

Hermione : coastal town at the CS end of the peninsula of Argolis, on the W side of the Saronic Gulf, in SE Argolis, NE Peloponnesos. *202*

Hermon : mount, also called Sirion and Senir, W of Damascus, on the border between Lebanon and Syria, source of the Jordan river, near the E end of the Mediterranean Sea, in W Asia. *258*

Hermonassa : town of the Crimea, along the N Euxine (Black) Sea, S of the Sea of Maeotis, in Scythia, SE Europe. *248*

Hermonthis : village on the W bank of the Nile river, between Thebes and Crocodilônpolis, in S Egypt, NE Africa. *242*

Hermopolis Magna : see Khmun. *242*

Hermopolis Parva : see Damanhür. *242*

Hermos : ancient river, modern Gediz, near the Hyllus river, flowing from Mount Sardene and contributing to Lake Guge in C Lydia, then across N Ionia, into the Aegean Sea, in CW Asia Minor, present-day CW Turkey. *250, 252 & 254*

Hermoupolis : port city of the island of Suros, in the C of the Cyclades, CW Aegean Sea. *230*

Herronisos : city, modern Kissamos, S of the Gulf of Kissamos, in NW island of Crete, CS Mediterranean Sea. *204*

Hersonissos : coastal city in the NE of Crete, on a peninsula E of Herakleion, in SC Mediterranean Sea. *206*

Herzegovina : country of the W Balkans, one with Bosnia, with Croatia to the N and W, Albania to the S and Serbia to the E, in SE Europe. *188, 218, 224 & 240*

Hesidros : see Zaradros river. *266*

Hestiaeotis : area of Macedonia, E of the N of the Pindos mountains, in CN mainland Greece. *224*

Hiera : small Aiolian island, also called Hephaisti, N of NE end of the island of Sicily, W of SW Italy, in S Tyrrhenian Sea, W Europe. *234 & 238*

Hierakônpolis : town in S Egypt, on the W bank of the Nile river, N of Edfu and opposite El-Kãb, in NE Africa. *242*

Hierapolis : see Bambyce. *254*

Hieraputna : coastal town, also called Kirva, in the SE of the island of Crete, in C Mediterranean Sea. *206*

Hieratis : city of W Carmania, on the N side of the Persian Gulf, in SW Persia, present-day Iran, W Asia. *264*

Himalayas : high mountain range along the borders of Nepal, India and Pakistan to the W and China to the E, in CS Asia. *266*

Himera : coastal town on the NW side of the island of Sicily, near Panormos, at the mouth of the river Himeras, on the coast of the S Tyrrhenian Sea, in W Europe. *234*

Himeraion : town of SE Macedonia, on the coast of the N Aegean Sea, near the border with Thrace, exact location unknown, in NE mainland Greece. *224*

Himeras : river of the N island of Sicily, flowing into the Tyrrhenian Sea, in W Europe. *234*

Hindu Kush : see Parapamisus. *246, 260, 262 & 266*

Hingol : see Mulla river. *262 & 264*

Hippana : inland town in the C of the island of Sicily, in W Mediterranean Sea, W Europe. *234*

Hippo : city along the Mediterranean Sea, in present-day N Algeria, N Africa. *244*

Hippokrene : see Aganippe. *212*

Hippola : inland city in SW Lakonia, E of Cape Thurides, in SE Peloponnesos. *198*

Hipponion : town on the W side of the S tip of Italy, along the Tyrrherian Sea, in W Europe. *238*

Hire : Homeric city of SW Messenia, near Pulos, in SW Peloponnesos. *196*

Hispalis : city of Andalusia, modern Sevilla, in the S of Iberia, present-day Spain, SW Europe. *232*

Hissos : river flowing SE of Athens, outside the ancient wall, in Attika, SE mainland Greece. *208*

Histiaia : town, also called Oreos, in the N of the island of Euboia, W of the Cape Artemision, in CE mainland Greece. *228*

Histriani : tribal land of N Thrace, near the Danube Delta, W of the NW coast of the Euxine (Black) Sea, in present-day Romania, SE Europe. *226*

Hittite : territories, also known as Hatti, covering from present-day C Turkey to NW Syria in the E, so called after the name of its inhabitant Hittites, in E Anatolia, W Asia. *248*

Holland : country of W Europe, also known as The Netherlands, on the North Sea, N of Belgium and W of Gernany. *188*

Homs : city of NW Syria, between Damascus in the S and Aleppo in the N, in W Asia. *258*

Honikas : village W of ancient Argos, exact location uncertain, in CW Argolis, NE Peloponnesos. *202*

Hormuz : 1. strait connecting the Persian Gulf with the Gulf of Oman in the SE, between modern Iran and the Arabian

Peninsula, in W Asia. *264*; -- 2. island in this Strait. *264*; -- 3. settlement on this island. *264*

Horse's Spring : Greek Hippokrene, see Aganippe. *212*

Houpian : city in ancient Bactria, near Alexandria-Kapisu, in the Kabul valley, present-day NE Afghanistan, C Asia. *262*

Hoyran : lake in Pisidia, present-day C Turkey, W Asia. *256*

Hua : 1. see Huampolis area. *214*; -- 2. see Huampolis city. *214*

Huampolis : 1. area in NE Phokis, also called Hua, E of the river Kephissos, in CS mainland Greece. *214*; -- 2. city in this area, also called Hua, N of Abae. *214*

Hudra : island of the W Sporades, off SE Argolis, near the island Sphaeria, off the S Troizen territory, in the SW Saronic Gulf. *202*

Hudrea : island at the W entrance to the Saronic Gulf, S of the peninsula of Argolis, in NE Peloponnesos. *202*

Hudria : town on the E coast of the Gulf of Petalion, in SE Boiotia, near Delion, in CE of mainland Greece. *212*

Huelva : city in the CN of the gulf of Cadiz, on the Atlantic Ocean, in SW Iberia (Spain), W Europe. *232*

Huesca : see Osca. *232*

Hule : town of NE Achaia, near the S shore of the Gulf of Korinthos, on the border with Argolis, in NE Peloponnesos. *200*

Hulika : lake N of Thebes, in C Boiotia, SE mainland Greece. *212*

Hullaikos : harbor of the city of Kerkura, on the NE coast of the Island of Kerkira, in the NE Ionian Sea. *218*

Hullikos : river in the SE of the Peninsula of Argolis, flowing N from the hills around Troizen, into the Saronic Gulf, in SE Argolis, NE Peloponnesos. *202*

Humettos : mountain range of C Attika, running NS from E of Athens in the NE and Anaguros in the SE, in SE mainland Greece. *208*

Hungary : country of NE Europe, surrounded by Croatia, Austria, Slovakia and Romania. *188 & 240*

Hupata :1. city of NW Phokis, N of Mount Oita, near the border with Malis, in CS mainland Greece. *214*; -- 2. city in SW Thessalia, on the Spercheios river, in N mainland Greece. *220*

Hupatos : mountain in CE Boiotia, SW of Mount Messapios, in SE mainland Greece. *212*

Hupereia : 1. fountain near Argos, exact location uncertain, in CW Argolis, NE Peloponnesos. *202*; -- 2. spring in Phthiotis, some- where S of Pherai, in SE Thessalia, on the W side of the gulf of Pagassai, in NE mainland Greece. *222*; -- 3. mythological land of the Phaecians. *269*

Huperesia : see Aigeira. *200*

Huperteleaton : inland city in SE Lakonia, between Epidauros Limera to the E and Asopos to the W, in SE Peloponnesos. *198*

Hupoplakia : see Thebe. *250*
Hupsos : mountain in CS Arkadia, E of the Gortunios river, in CE Peloponnesos. *192*
Huria : city of SE Boiotia, on the NW shore of the Gulf of Petalion, S of Aulis, in SE mainland Greece. *212*; -- 2. ancient city in S Thessalia, exact location unknown, in NE mainland Greece. *220*
Hurmine : Homeric city in NW Elis, on the cost of the Ionian Sea, opposite the island of Zakinthos, in NW Peloponnesos. *194*
Hurria : tribal land in NE Mesopotamia, mostly in the N of present-day Iraq, between the Tigris river and the Zagros mountains, in W Asia. *258*
Husiai : 1. inland town in SW Argolis, between the NW coast of the Gulf of Argolis and Arkadia, in NE Peloponnesos. *202*; -- 2. city in CS Boiotia, NW of Eruthrae and NE of Mount Kithairon, in SE mainland Greece. *212*
Hüyük : see 1. Alaca. *248*; -- 2. Alishar. *248*
Hybla Geleatis : coastal town, probably near Catana, in the CE of the island of Sicily, W Mediterranean Sea, W Europe. *236*
Hyblaea : see Megara Hyblaea. *236*
Hyccara : coastal town on the NW side of the island of Sicily, on the coast of the S Tyrrhenian Sea, in W Europe. *234*
Hydaspes : river, modern Jhelum, flowing S from Wular lake, on the Indian side of the region of Kashmir, through the Punjab, in NE Pakistan, where it joins the Hyphasis (Beãs) river in NW India, C Asia. *266*
Hyde : town of E Lydia, in CW of Asia Minor, present-day CW Turkey. *250*
Hydraotes : river, modern Rãvi, in present-day NW India and NE Pakistan, flowing from lake Wular in the Indian Himalayas, SE into Pakistan and the Punjab where it joins the Acesines (Chenãb) river, in C Asia. *266*
Hylias : ancient river, exact location unknown, probably near the Sybaris river in SE Italy, W Europe. *238*
Hyllus : ancient river flowing from Mount Sardene, N of the Hermos river and contributing to Lake Guge, in C Lydia, CW Asia Minor, present-day CW Turkey. *250 & 252*
Hypacyris : see Hypanis in Romania. *238 & 240*
Hypanis : 1. branch of the delta of the Danube river, also called Hypacyris, discharging into the Euxine (Black) Sea, in Scythia, present-day Romania, SE Europe. *240*; -- 2. ancient river, also known as Bug, modern Kuban, in S Russia, flowing N from the Caucasus mountains, then W into the Euxine (Black) Sea, at the entrance to the Sea of Maeotis, in SE Europe. *248*
Hyparna : coastal town in SW Lycia, in present-day SW Turkey, on the NE Mediterranean Sea, in W Asia. *254*

Hyphasis : river, modern Beâs river, flowing from the Himalaya Mountains of NW India, first S then W through the Punjab, where it joins the Zaradros (Sutlej) river and enters the Indus river as a tributary, in C Asia. *266*

Hypsas : river, also called Drago, flowing in the CS side of the island of Sicily, W Europe, where it joins the Akragas river before running into the W Mediterranean Sea. *234*

Hyrcania : 1. region SE of the Caspian Sea, W part of the Parthian empire, modern Gorgãn, in present-day NE Iran, C Asia. *246 & 260*; -- 2. see Caspian Sea. *248 & 260*

Hyssus : 1. river flowing N in CN Anatolia, into the SE Euxine (Black) Sea, in present-day CN Turkey, W Asia. *248*; -- 2. seaport city at the mouth of this river. *248*

I

Ialusos : town at the N end of the island of Rhodes, in SE Aegean Sea, W Asia. *230*

Ianessos : gulf NE of the peninsula Akti of the Chalkidike, in NW Aegean Sea. *228*

Iaphos : small island of the E Ionian Sea, E of the island of Leukas, off the coast of N Akarnania, in SW mainland Greece. *216*

Iapygia : ancient area at the SE tip of Italy, in the W Ionian Sea, W Europe. *238*

Iapygium : cape at the S end of Iapygia, in W Europe. *238*

Iardanos : 1. Homeric (Iliad) river, later called Akidos, flowing NW, then S into the Anigros river as its tributary, in SE Elis, CW Peloponnesos. *194*; -- 2. Homeric (Odyssey) river, modern Platanias river, flowing from the W White Mountains of Crete, into the Gulf of Khanion, near Platanias city, in the NW of the island, CS Mediterranean Sea. *204*

Iasos : 1. gulf along the SE Aegean Sea, on the coast of Doris, in SW Asia Minor. *254*; -- 2. Ionian town on the CE coast of this Gulf, S of Miletos. *254*

Iberia : 1. peninsula of SW Europe, comprising present-day Spain and Portugal. *187 & 232*; -- 2. ancient region in the SW of the Caucasus mountains, present-day Georgia, along the SE Euxine (Black) Sea, N of Turkey and Armenia, in E Europe. *248*

Ichthos : cape of CW Elis, into the Ionian Sea, near Phaia, in NW Peloponnesos. *194*

Ida : 1. S peak mountain in the Idhi mountain range, also called Psiloritis, C of the island of Crete, C Mediterranean Sea. *204*; -- 2. cave on the N side of this mountain. *204*; -- 3. mountain range shared by Mysia, Phrygia and C Troas, in NW Asia Minor, present-day NW Turkey. *250*; -- 4. in mythology, applied to any wooded mountain. *269*

Idakos : town of the Chersonesos, exact location unknown, in SE Europe. *226*

Idhi : mountain range, running NS in the C of the island of Crete, in C Mediterranean Sea. *204*

Idomene : 1. city of SW Epeiros, probably somewhere N of the area of Amphilochia in NW Aitolia, CW mainland Greece. *218*; -- 2. city of C Macedonia, on the W bank of the Axios river, NW of Gortunia, in NE mainland Greece. *224*

Iduma : city NE of the Gulf Kerameikos, E of Keramos, in Caria, SW Asia Minor, present-day SW Turkey. *264*

Ienysos : seaport city of S Palestine, E of modern Rafah, in present-day SE Gaza Territory, at the SE end of the Mediterranean Sea, in W Asia. *258*

Ieraputna : coastal town, also called Kirva, in the NE of the island of Crete, CS Mediterranan Sea. *206*

Ierne : island W of Albion (Britain) in the NE Atlantic Ocean, modern Ireland, W Europe. *232*

Ietae : site of a fort, probably near Siracusa, on the SE of the Island of Sicily, in W Mediterranean Sea, W Europe. *236*

Igoumenitsa : modern city on the coast of the Ionian Sea, opposite the island of Kerkura (Corfu), in NW Epeiros, NW mainland Greece. *218*

Ihnasya el- Medina : see Herakleopolis. *242*

Ikãr : see Oskios. *226*

Ikaria : 1. island of CE Aegean sea, W of the island of Samos, W of Caria in Asia Minor. *230*; -- 2. gulf as an arm of the CE Aegean Sea, between the island of Samos and the coast of Ionia, at the mouth of the Maeander river, in Caria, Asia Minor, present-day Turkey. *254*

Ikarion : inland town of NE Attika, SW of Marathon, in SE mainland Greece. *210*

Ikos : island of the Thessalian Sporades, E of the island of Skiathos, in CW Aegean Sea. *228*

Ila : harbor city of Carmania, on the E Persian Gulf, in SW Persia, present-day Iran, C Asia. *264*

Ilesion : see Eilesion. *212*

Ilias : see Agios Ilias. *194*

Ilios : see Troy. *250*

Ilisos : river flowing from the stream Kallirhoe, on the E side of Athens, passing S of Athens and joining the Kephisos river as its tributary to the W, in CW Attika, SE mainland Greece. *208*

Illyria : region of the NW Balkan peninsula, N of Epeiros and W of Macedonia, present-day Croatia and Bosnia, in C Europe, along the NE coast of the Adriatic Sea, at one time including Albania, with many tribes and variable frontiers. *190, 218, 224 & 240*

Imbros : island of the Thracian Sporades, in the NE Aegean Sea, near the entrance to the Hellespontos. *228*

Inachos : 1. river flowing N from the N of the mountain Artemision, in SW Argolis, then SE into the N end of the Gulf of Argolis, in NE Peloponnesos. *202*; -- 2. town along this river, exact location uncertain, in SW Argolis. *202*

Inatos : ancient seaport on the CS shore of the island of Crete, servicing the inland city of Priansos, on the Libyan Sea. *204*

India : ancient region, present-day large country, in CS Asia, extending like a peninsula into the Indian Ocean between the Arabian Sea to the W, Pakistan to the NW & N, the Bay of Bengal, Bangladesh, Nepal and China to the E and the Kunlun mountains to the NE. *187, 188, 246, 262, 264 & 266*

Indus : major river flowing from the Himalaya Mountains in SW Tibet, NW to Jammu & Kashmir and SW through the length of Pakistan, with many tributaries and fertile plains, especially in the Punjab, and ending with a delta SE of Karachi, into the Arabian Sea, in C Asia. *187, 262, 264 & 266*

Inessa : see Aetna. *236*

Ingul : ancient river, tributary of the Bug river, in Scythia, present-day Ukraine, E Europe. *248*

Inopos : stream on the island of Delos, in the Cyclades, CW Aegean Sea. *230*

Inycum : inland town in the CS of the island of Sicily, in W Mediterranean Sea, W Europe. *234*

Ioannina : 1. lake in E Epeiros, NE of Dodona, in NW mainland Greece. *218*; -- 2. modern city around this lake. *218*

Iolkos : ancient town of SE Thessalia, probably identified with either Pagassai (Volos) or Dimini, in NE mainland Greece, at the N end of the Gulf of Pagassai of CW Aegean Sea. *220*

Ionia : Region of W Asia Minor covering the land along the coast of Asia Minor, present-day CW Turkey, S of Aiolis and N of Caria, including the islands of Samos and Chios. *190 & 254*

Ionian : 1. sea, an arm of the CN Mediterranean Sea, between Greece to the E side and Italy & Sicily to the W side, S of the Adriatic Sea. *188, 190, 194, 200, 216, 218 & 238*;- 2. islands of the Ionian Sea, from Kerkura (Corfu) in the N to Paxos in the S. *218*

Ionic : gulf where the Adriatic Sea meets the Ionian Sea, between SE Italy, in SW Europe, and NW Epeiros, in NW mainland Greece. *218*

Ios : island in CS Cyclades, N of Thera, in the E Aegean Sea. *230*

Ipsos : town of Phrygia, in CE of Anatolia, present-day Turkey, W Asia. *252*

Iran : modern country of SW Asia, stretching from the Caspian Sea in the N to the Persian Gulf & the Gulf of Oman in the S, E of Turkey, Iraq and the Persian Gulf, W of Turkmenistan, Afghanistan and Pakistan, identified in Ancient Times with Media, Persis and W Parthia. *188, 246, 258, 260 & 264*

Iraq : modern country of SW Asia, same general region as Mesopotamia, bordering on modern Turkey in the N, Syria and Jordan in the W, Kuwait and Saudi Arabia in the S, and Iran in the E. *188, 246 & 258*

Irbil : see Arbela. *258*

Ire : see Abia. *196*

Ireland : see Ierne and Tin islands. *188 & 232*

Iria : 1. town in CE Argolis, on the W side of the Troizen territory, at cape Struthos, on the E coast of the Gulf of Argolis, in NE Peloponnesos. *202*; -- 2. site on the island of Naxos, in the Cyclades, CW Aegean Sea. *230*

Iris : see Yesil river. *252*

Is : 1. river of C Mesopotamia, tributary of the Euphrates river, in present-day C Iraq, W Asia. *258*; -- 2. town on this river. *258*

Isauria : area of CS Cilicia, between the NE Mediterranean Sea and the W range of Taurus mountains, in SE Anatolia, present-day SE Turkey, W Asia. *256*

Ischia : island of the E Tyrrhenian Sea, near the entrance to the Gulf of Naples, in W Europe. *238*

Isfahan : see Aspadana. *260*

Isin : ancient city of Babylonia, near Larsa, in present-day S Iraq, W Asia. *258*

Iskenderun : 1. see Issos Gulf. *256*; -- 2. see Alexandretta. *256*

Islamabad : major city of present-day NE Pakistan, C Asia. *266*

Ismaros : 1. mountain in CS of Thrace, N of the Aegean Sea, in present-day S Bulgaria and NW Turkey, SE Europe. *226*; -- 2. town of the Kikonos tribe, at the foot of this mountain. *226*

Ismenos : river flowing N from the hills W of Thebes, into Lake Hulika, in CE mainland Greece. *212*

Israel : 1. ancient land of the Israelites, covering the major portion of Canaan and Palestine. *188, 246 & 258*; -- 2. modern country, presently sharing with the West Bank and Gaza territories this ancient land of Israel, between the E

Mediterranean Sea on the W side, and Syria and Jordan on the E side, S of Lebanon and N of Egypt. *246*

Issedones : town of NW Asia, present-day NW Turkey, exact location unknown. *252*

Issos : 1. gulf, also called Iskenderun, in Cilicia, in present-day SE Turkey, W Asia, near the NE corner of the Mediterranean Sea. *256*; -- 2. plain adjacent to the gulf *256*; -- 3. city in the plain E of the Gulf. *256*

Istanbul : see Busantion. *252*

Ister : see Danube. *226 & 240*

Isthmia : city in W Megaris, in NE Peloponnesos, at the SE end of the Gulf of Korinthos where the place of haulage (*diolkos*) was located from there to the Saronic Gulf, present-day village of Kura Vrusi. *210*

Isthmos : land bridge connecting the Gulf of Korinthos with the Saronic Gulf, in Megaris, and serving as border between the Peloponnesos and mainland Greece. *210*

Istone : mount in the N of the island of Kerkura (Corfu), in E Ionian Sea, opposite Epeiros, in NW mainland Greece. *218*

Istra : see Istria peninsula. *238*

Istria :1. peninsula of Croatia, also known as Istra, extending into the NE Adriatic Sea, between the Gulf of Venice to the W and the Gulf of Kvarner to the E, in C Europe. *238*; -- 2. town of NE Thrace, also called Istros, at the W end of the Euxine (Black) Sea, N of Tomis, in present-day E Romania, E Europe. *226*

Istron : town S of Agios Nikolaos, on the SW side of the Gulf of Megambellou, in the NE of the island of Crete, C Mediterranean Sea. *206*

Istros : see Istria in Romania. *226*

Isvoria : village in C Macedonia, near Lefkadia, exact location uncertain, in NE mainland Greece. *224*

Italy : large peninsula of SW Europe, present-day country between the Tyrrhenian Sea to the W and the Adriatic & Ionian seas to the E, extending from the Alps in the N to the Mediterranean Sea and Sicily in the S. *187, 188, 236. 238 & 240*

Itanos : site at the NE end of the island of Crete, in C Mediterranean Sea. *206*

Iteia : town NW of Praisos, exact location uncertain, in the NE of the island of Crete, C Mediterranean Sea. *206*

Ithaka : island of the Ionian sea, E of the N end of the island of Kephallenia, off the coast of W Akarnania, in CW mainland Greece. *216*

Ithome : 1. Homeric city of CW Thessalia, in N mainland Greece. *220*; -- 2. mountain in N Messenia, N of Messene, in SW Peloponnesos. *196*

Iton : Homeric city in S Thessalia, near Phthiotis, exact location uncertain, NE mainland Greece. *220*

Izmir : 1. see Smyrna. *254*; -- 2. see Candath. *250*

Iznik : 1. area of Bithynia, on the SE shore of the Sea of Propontis (Marmara), in present-day NW Turkey, W Asia. *252*; -- 2. inland lake, S of SE Sea of Propontis. *252*; -- 3. see Nicaea. *252*

J

Jaffa : see Joppa. *258*

Jalalabad : see Jalalkot. *262*

Jalalkot : city, modern Jalalabad in E Afghanistan, at the entrance to the Laghman and Kunar valleys, in C Asia. *262*

Jammu : mountainous region of ancient Sogdiana, NW of Kashmir, N of the Siwalik mountain range, in present-day NE Pakistan and NW India, C Asia. *266*

Jaxartes : river, modern Syrdarya, in Sogdiana, flowing NW from the E Ferghana valley, through present-day Tajikistan, Uzbekistan and Kazakhstan into the NE Aral Sea, in CN Asia. *187, 260 & 262*

Jerabius : see Thapsacus. *258*

Jericho : city of ancient Palestine, now in the West Bank Territory, N of the Dead Sea and W of the Jordan valley, near the E end of the Mediterranean Sea. *258*

Jerusalem : major city, near the C of ancient Palestine, present-day Israel, W of the Jordan river, at the E end of the Mediterranean Sea, in W Asia. *258*

Jhelum : 1. see Hydaspes river. *266*; -- 2. area of the Punjab, in Bactria, present-day NE Pakistan, W of this river, in C Asia. *266*; -- 3. city in this area, also W of the river. *266*

Jonah : pass between SE Cilicia and NW Syria, through the Amanos mountain range, in W Asia. *256*

Joppa : city of Palestine, modern Jaffa and Tel-Aviv in Israel, on the E Mediterranean coast, in W Asia. *258*

Jordan : 1. river flowing S from Mount Hermon at the S end of the Anti-Lebanon mountains, across ancient Palestine, into the Dead Sea, parallel to the E end of the Mediterranean Sea. *258*; -- 2. country on the E side of the Jordan river, bordering on Syria in the N, Iraq in the E, Saudi Arabia in SE and Egypt, the West Bank & Israel in the W. *188, 246 & 258*

Juktas : site on a mount, in the C of the island of Crete, CS
Mediterranean Sea. *206*
Jumma : river flowing SW from the Himalaya mountains through
NW India into the Ganges river as a tributary, in C Asia. *266*

K

If a name is not found under K, look under C

Kabeiri : site of a sanctuary, W of Thebes, in CS Boiotia, SE
mainland Greece. *212*
Kabesos : town, also known as Kavissos, on the border between
Macedonia and Thrace, in NE mainland Greece. *224*
Kabul : 1. valley of Bactria, in present-day E Afghanistan, C Asia.
262; -- 2. city on the W side of this valley. *262*; -- 3. see Cophen
river. *262*
Kabura : town of the Hindu Kush, N of the Kabul river, in present-
day NE Afghanistan, C Asia. *262*
Kabyle : town of C Thrace, now in ruins, N of the W end of the
Euxine (Black) Sea, N of Yambol, in present-day CE Bulgaria, E
Europe. *226*
Kabylia : 1. region, E of Algiers, along the coast of the SW
Mediterranean Sea, in Algeria, NW Africa. *244*; -- 2. mountain
range, Grande, Petite and de Collo, covering this region. *244*
Kachi : plain of ancient Gedrosia, in present-day Baluchistan, SW
of Sibi area and Bolãn river, in CS Pakistan, C Asia. *264*
Kadesh : ancient city of NW Syria, on the Orontes river, in W Asia.
256
Kadmea : site of the citadel of Thebes, in Boiotia, SE mainland
Greece. *212*
Kadmeia : see Boiotia. *212*
Kaffa : see Theodosia. *248*
Kaiadas : site of the prison for the city of Sparta, in CW Lakonia,
CS Peloponnesos. *198*
Kaikos : see Astraios. *250*
Kainepolis : seaport city on the E side of the SW tip of Lakonia, on
the Gulf of Messenia, in SE Peloponnesos. *198*
Kakovatos : town of SW Elis, near Purgos, near the coast of the
Ionian Sea, in W Peloponnesos. *194*
Kalamai : city of CE Messenia, in the N of the Gulf of Messenia, in
SW Peloponnesos. *196*

If a name is not found under K, look under C

Kalamas : see Thuamis. *218*

Kalamata : see Makaria. *196*

Kalambaka : town of C Thessalia, W of Larisa, in NE mainland Greece. *220*

Kalandriani : island in NE Cyclades, S of Andros, in C Aegean Sea. *230*

Kalapodi : town in the area of Huampolis in Phokis, in CS mainland Greece. *214*

Kalãt : 1. area in ancient W Gedrosia, present-day Baluchistan, SW Pakistan, between the Bolãn and Mulla rivers, C Asia. *260*; -- 2. city on the W side of this area. *264*

kalathios : mountain in CW Lakonia, S of the river Choerios and of the border with Messenia, in SE Peloponnesos. *198*

Kalauria : city on the SW coast of the island of Sphaeria, in SW Saronic Gulf, NE Peloponnesos. *202*

Kaleakte : town in the NE of the island of Sicily, on the coast of the Tyrrhenian Sea, in W Europe. *236*

Kalindoea : city of E Macedonia, on the S side of Lake Bolbe in Mugdonia, N of the Chalkidike, in NE mainland Greece. *224*

Kalliaros : Homeric city in Opuntian Lokris, near Thermopulai, CE mainland Greece. *214*

Kallichoros : Homeric spring, N of the Bay of Eleusis, in NW Attika, SE mainland Greece. *210*

Kallidromon : mount in NE Malis, on the border with Opuntiian Lokris, along the NW Gulf of Oropos, allowing only a narrow pass at Thermopulai between mainland Greece and the Gulf. *214*

Kallikolone : Homeric hill near the river Simois, in Troas, present-day NW Turkey, W Asia. *250*

Kallipolis : town on the NE side of the island of Sicily, exact location uncertain, in W Mediterranean Sea, in W Europe. *236*

Kallirhoe : stream supplying the fountain Enneakrounos, in Athens, CW Attika, SE mainland Greece. *208*

Kallithea : 1. town in CE Achaia, on the S side of the Gulf of Korinthos, exact location uncertain, in CN Peloponnesos. *200*; -- 2. modern name of a town on an ancient site SW of Athens, in C Attika, SE mainland Greece. *208*

Kaludnae : island of the Aegean Sea, off the coast of Caria in SW Asia Minor. *230*

Kaludon : Homeric city of SW Aitolia, E side of modern Mesolongion, N of the Gulf Patraikos, at the W entrance of the Gulf of Korinthos, in SW mainland Greece. *216*

If a name is not found under K, look under C

Kaludonia : area of SW Aitolia, around the city of Kaludon, in SW mainland Greece. *216*

Kalumnos : island N of the island of Kos, in the N of the Rhodian Dodekanesoi, in SE Aegean Sea. *230 & 254*

Kamakaea : city of E Macedonia, near Kalindoea, on the S shore of Lake Bolbe in Mugdonia, N of the Chalkidike, in NE mainland Greece. *224*

Kamalia : modern city in CN Pakistan, SW of Lahore, in C Asia. *266*

Kaman : village in Elis, exact location unknown, in W Peloponnesos. *194*

Kamares : cave in CS of the island of Crete, exact location uncertain, in C Mediterranean Sea. *204*

Kambos : site of C Messenia, at the top of the Gulf of Messenia, in SW Peloponnesos. *196*

Kambunion : mountain on the border between Thessalia to the SE and Macedonia to the NW, in CN mainland Greece. *220*

Kameiros : city on the N side of the island of Rhodes, in SE Aegean Sea, W Asia. *230*

Kamenskoe : town along the S Borysthenes river, in present-day Ukraine, SE Europe. *248*

Kamilari : site in the CS of the island of Crete, C Mediterranean Sea. *204*

Kanastraeon : cape in the S of the W peninsula Kassandra (Pallene) of the Chalkidike, in the NW Aegean Sea, NE mainland Greece. *228*

Kandahãr : area, also spelled Qandahãr, in SE Afghanistan, C Asia. *262*; -- 2. city, see Alexandria-in-Arachosia. *262*

Kandia : 1. see island of Crete. *204 & 206*; -- 2. see Sea of Crete. *204 & 206*

Kanli Kastelli : see Aina. *206*

Kantharos : 1. largest harbor, on the W side of the peninsula of Peiraia, in CW Attika, SE mainland Greece. *208*; -- 2. city on this harbor. *208*

Kaoshan ; pass high in the Parapamisus (Hindu Kush) mountains, N Pakistan, C Asia. *266*

Kapakli : site in SE Thessalia, near the border with Phthiotis, in NE mainlad Greece. *220*

Kaparisso : see Tainaron. *198*

Kaphirio : settlement in S Messenia, near the SW coast of the Gulf of Messenia, in SW Peloponnesos. *196*

Kaphuae : town N of Mount Knakalos, in NE Arkadia, CE Peloponnesos. *192*

If a name is not found under K, look under C

Kapidagi : see Arktonnessos. *250*
Kapija: see Demir. *224*
Kapisu : 1. area of Bactria, in present-day NE Afghanistan, C Asia,
	262; -- 2. see Alexandria-Kapisu. *262*
Kara- Bogaz : saline gulf on the CE side of the Caspian Sea, in
	present-day Turkmenistan, C Asia. *248 & 260*
Karachi : see Alexander's Harbor. *264*
Karakali : mountain range in SW Armenia, near the SE Euxine
	(Black) Sea, in W Asia. *248*
Kara Kum : desert in SW Turkmenistan, into which the river
	Tadzen ends its course, S of the Aral Sea, in C Asia. *260*
Karamoti : town of SW Thrace, E of Neapolis (Kavala) on the CN
	coast of the Aegean Sea, E of the Chalkidike peninsula. *226*
Karanova : ancient site in NW Bulgaria, SE Europe. *240*
Karaoglan : city E of the Sea of Propontis, in the NW of the Hittite
	territories, CN Anatolia, present-day CN Turkey. *252*
Karasu : 1. city of Bithynia, on the CS coast of the Euxine (Black)
	Sea, at the mouth of the Sangarios river, in CN Asia Minor,
	present-day CN Turkey. *252*; -- 2. river of NW Syria, flowing S
	from the Amanos mountains, past Sochi, into the E Mediterra-
	nean Sea, in W Asia. *252*
Kardamule : 1. Homeric city of SW Messenia, E of Pulos, in SW
	Peloponnesos. *196*; -- 2. inland city of CW Lakonia, near the E
	side of the Gulf of Messenia, in SE Peloponnesos. *198*; -- 3. city
	in the N of the island of Chios, in CE Aegean Sea. *230*
Kardia : city of the NE Chersonesos, on the N shore of the Sea of
	Propontis, in NE mainland Greece, present-day NW Turkey, SE
	Europe. *226*
Karditsa : city of C Thessalia, S of Trikala, in NE mainland Greece.
	220
Karesos : river flowing from Mount Ida, through Troas and
	Phrygia, into the Hellespontos, in NW Asia Minor, present-day
	NW Turkey. *250*
Karkheh : see Choaspes. *258*
Karnak : same site as Egyptian Thebes. *242*
Karnion : river of CS Arkadia, flowing NW and joining the Alpheios
	river as a tributary, in CW Arkadia, C Peloponnesos. *192*
Karpathos : see Krapathos. *230*
Karphi : village in the Dikte mountains, CE of the island of Crete,
	CS Mediterranean Sea. *206*
Karteria : town of N Ionia, probably S of Phokaia, in CW Asia
	Minor, present-day CW Turkey. *250*

If a name is not found under K, look under C

Karuai : city of CN Lakonia, near the border with Arkadia, in CE Peloponnesos. *198*

Karuanda : area on the Bodrum Peninsula, in Caria, SW Asia Minor, present-day SW Turkey. *254*

Karustos : city at the S end of the island of Euboia, between the Gulf of Petalion and the CW Aegean Sea. *228*

Kashan : modern city of Iran, between Rhagae (Tehrãn) to the N and Ispahan to the S, in W Asia. *260*

Kashmir : fertile valley of ancient Sogdiana, one with Jammu, surrounded by high mountains, in present-day NE Pakistan and NW India, N of the Siwalik mountain range of India, in C Asia. *188 & 266*

Kaska : region in NE of the Hittite territories, S of the Euxine (Black) Sea, in NE Anatolia, present-day C Turkey, W Asia. *248*

Kasmenai : town in the SE of the island of Sicily, in the Heraei Mountains, W Mediterranean Sea, W Europe. *236*

Kasos : island of the Dodekanesoi, in SE Aegean Sea, near Krapathos, in SE Aegean Sea. *230*

Kassandra : 1. one of the three peninsulas of the Chalkidike, the one on the W side, also called Pallene, in NW Aegean Sea, NE mainland Greece. *228*; -- 2. gulf between the peninsulas Kassandra in the W and Sithonia in the C of the Chalkidike, in NW Aegean Sea. *228*

Kassandreia : see Potidaia. *228*

Kassope : town in SW Epeiros, near the Ionian Sea, N of the Gulf of Ambrakia, on the CW side of mainland Greece. *218*

Kastalia : spring in the NE of Delphi, in S Phokis, in CS of mainland Greece. *214*

Kastellorizon : see Megiste. *230*

Kasthanaia : town of CE Thessalia, in NE mainland Greece, along the NW Aegean Sea. *220*

Kastoria : 1. Lake in W Macedonia, NW mainland Greece. *224*; -- 2. area around this lake, *224*; -- 3. town, see Keletron. *224*

Kastraki : town of SE Thessalia, N of the Gulf of Pagassai, in N mainland Greece. *220*

Kastri : 1. city on the SE side of the island of Kuthera, S of the Gulf of Lakonia in SE Peloponnesos. *198*; -- 2. town in SW Boiotia, N of Eutresis, in SE mainland Greece. *212*

Kastritsa : village S of lake Ioannina in E Epeiros, NW mainland Greece. *218*

Kastro : city in SE Argolis, on the coast of the Gulf of Argolis, exact location unknown, in NE Peloponnesos. *202*

If a name is not found under K, look under C

Katakolou : site on the SE coast of the island of Euboia, in W Aegean Sea. *228*

Katara : pass between Thessalia and Epeiros, in NW mainland Greece. *220*

Katerini : town of Pieria, in S Macedonia, near the CW coast of the Gulf of Salonika, in NE mainland Greece. *224*

Kathaei : tribal land along the Himalaya mountain range, N of Sangala, between the Hydraotes and Zaradros rivers, in Bactria, N India, C Asia. *266*

Katharevousa : see Aigion, in Achaia. *200*

Kato Suli : town N of Marathon, in NE Attika, SE mainland Greece. *210*

Katri : town in the NW of the island of Crete, exact location uncertain, C Mediterranean Sea. *204*

Katsambas : seaport city E of Herakleion, in CN of the island of Crete, in C Mediterranean Sea. *206*

Kaulonia : town on E side of the S tip of Italy, along the Ionian Sea, in W Europe. *238*

Kaunos : seaport city of Caria, E of peninsula Bubassos, in SW Asia Minor, present-day SW Turkey. *254*

Kaustros : river, sometimes called Little Maeander, flowing from the Tmolos mountains, N of the Maeander (Menderez) river, through Lydia and Ionia, into he Aegean Sea, near Ephesos, in CW Asia Minor, present-day CW Turkey. *254*

Kavala : 1. bay of the CN Aegean Sea, in SW Thrace, NE mainland Greece. *226*; -- 2. see Neapolis. *226*

Kave : town in the hills N of Delphi, S of Mount Parnassos, in C Phokis, CS mainland Greece. *214*

Kavir : large desert in present-day NE Iran, from Hyrcania in the N to Persis in the S and from Afghanistan in the E to the Zagros mountains in the W, in C Asia. *260*

Kavissos : see Kabesos. *224*

Kavousi : town in the SE of the Gulf of Megambellou, in NE of the island of Crete, C Mediterranean Sea. *206*

Kavrochori : site in CN of the island of Crete, in C Mediterranean Sea. *206*

Kayio : see Psamathos for Porto Kayio. *198*

Kaza : pass near Eleutherae in NW Attika, through the Kithairon mountain, to Plataia and Thebes in Boiotia, SE mainland Greece. *210*

Kazakhstan : country bordering on Russia to the N, China to the E, Kyrkystan and Uzbekistan to the S and the Caspian Sea & Turkmenistan to the W, in CN Asia. *188, 246, 248, 260 & 262*

If a name is not found under K, look under C

Kazmaci : city in CE Cilicia, on the Ceyhan river, in present-day SE Turkey, W Asia. *256*

Kea : island in NW Cyclades, S of Kephala, in C Aegean Sea. *230*

Kebrene : 1. river in the Troas, probably the Homeric Heptaporos, tributary of the River Simois, in present-day NW Turkey, W Asia. *250*; -- 2. town along this river. *250*

Kedros : village in C Thessalia, on the S edge of the Thessalian plain, near Karditsa, in NE mainland Greece. *220*

Keiros : Phrygian town S of the Euxine (Black) Sea, in present-day NW Turkey, W Asia. *252*

Kekruphalia : small island in the Saronic Gulf, W of Aigina, in NE Peloponnesos. *202*

Keladon : river tributary of the Alpheios river, flowing from the SW border of Arkadia with Messenia, in CW Peloponnesos. *192*

Kelainae : 1. town of Phrygia, S of the Sea of Propontis (Marmara), exact location uncertain, in NW Asia Minor, present-day Turkey. *250*; -- 2. town of Lydia, in C Asia Minor, near the source of the Maeander river, called Apameia Murleia in Hellenistic Time and now covered by the modern town of Dinar, in CW Turkey, W Asia. *254*

Kelames : village, W of Athens and SW of Kolonos Hippios, in CW Attika, SE mainland Greece. *208*

Keleae : town in NW Argolis, at a S fork of the Asopos river, in NE Peloponnesos. *202*

Kelenderis : 1. port city on the SE side of the peninsula of Argolis, opposite the island of Sphaeria, on SW Saronic Gulf, in SE Argolis, NE Peloponnesos. *202*; -- 2. town of Cilicia on the NE coast of the Mediterranean Sea, in present-day SE Turkey, W Asia. *256*

Keletron : town, modern Kastoria, on the shore of Lake Kastoria, in W Macedonia, NW mainland Greece. *224*

Kelif : city in ancient NE Margiane, on the Oxus river, in present-day N Afghanistan, near the border with Turkmenistan, in C Asia. *262*

Kellatis : town of E Thrace at the W end of the Euxine (Black) Sea, in present-day Bulgaria, in SE Europe. *226*

Kenaion : cape at the N end of the island of Euboia, in CW Aegean Sea. *228*

Kenchreai : 1. port town of CN Argolis, serving the city of Korinthos, on the S side of the Isthmus of Korinthos, on the NW coast of the Saronic Gulf, in NE Peloponnesos. *202*; -- 2. inland city, W of Lerna, in SW Argolis. *202*

If a name is not found under K, look under C

Keos : island in the N of the Cyclades, S of Sounion in S Attika, CW Aegean Sea. *230*

Kephala : 1. island in NW Cyclades, W of Andros. *230*; -- 2. village in the SE end of the island of Crete, in C Mediterranean Sea. *206*

Kephale : town in CS Attika, SE mainland Greece. *208*

Kephali : ancient site in CS of the island of Crete, C Mediterranean Sea. *204*

Kephallenia : island of the NE Ionian Sea, also called Same, facing the Gulf of Patraikos, off the S coast of Akarnania, in SW mainland Greece. *190 & 216*

Kephalos : town at the W end of the island of Kos, in SE Aegean Sea. *230*

Kephisia : village in C Attika, in the S foothills of Mount Pentelikon, in SE mainland Greece. *210*

Kephisos : 1. river flowing first NE from the N side of Mount Parnassos in N Phokis, near Lilaia, then SE receiving the Parapotamii river as its tributary, where the city is located, and emptying into the Gulf of Argolis, in NE Peloponnesos. *214*; -- 2. same river flowing from Mount Parnassos in N Phokis, bifurcating E through Boiotia, past S of Orchomenos, into Lake Kopais, in SE mainland Greece. *212*; -- 3. river flowing S from both mounts Parnes and Pentelikon in N Attika, between Acharnae and Kephisia, past W of mount Anchesmos and crossing the W section of the city of Athens, in Attika, into the Bay of Phaleron, E of Peiraia, in SE mainland Greece. *208 & 210*; -- 4. river flowing SE from Mount Kithairon in NW Attika, past Oinoë and Eleusis, into the Bay of Eleusis, N Saronic Gulf, SE mainland Greece. *210*

Keraia : ancient village, modern Rokka, just W of Kissamos on the NE side of a large rock, on the Gulf of Kissamos, in NW island of Crete, CS Mediterranean Sea. *204*

Kerameikos : 1. area of the cemetery NW of the ancient Agora in Athens, in SE mainland Greece. *208*; -- 2. Gulf of the SE Aegean Sea, between the Bodrum and Bubassos peninsulas, in SW Caria of Asia Minor, present-day SW Turkey. *254*

Keramos : city N of the Gulf of Kerameikos, in SW Caria, between Halikarnassos and Iduma, in SW Asia Minor, present-day SW Turkey. *254*

Kerasous : town at the SE end of the Euxine (Black) Sea, in present-day NW Turkey, W Asia. *248*

Keraunia : mountain range across Albania, from its S border with Greece to Cape Linguetta along the Adriatic Sea, in SE Europe. *240*

If a name is not found under K, look under C

Kerch : 1. strait, also known as Cimmerian Bosporos, connecting the Sea of Maeotis (Azov) to the CN Euxine (Black) Sea, in SE Europe. *248*; -- 2. see Pantikapaion. *240 & 248*

Kerdulion : hill near Amphipolis, in the estuary of the Strumon river into the N Aegean Sea, precise location unknown, in SE Macedonia, NE mainland Greece. *224*

Keressos : town in CS Boiotia, N of Askra, in SE mainland Greece. *212*

Kerinthos : town on NE coast of the island of Euboia, in CW Aegean Sea. *228*

Kerkennah : 1. see Kerkine mountain. *226*; -- 2. see Kerkine island. *244*

Kerkine : 1. mount in CW Thrace, also called Kerkennah, E of the river Strumon, separating Paeonia from Sintia, in NE mainland Greece. *226*; -- 2. island of the SW Mediterranean Sea, modern Kerkennah, off the coast of Tunisia, N of the Gulf of Gabès, in CN Africa. *244*

Kerkinitis : 1. lake formed by the S river Strumon, ancient lake Prasias, N of Murkinos, on the Thracian side of the border with Macedonia, in NE mainland Greece. *224*; -- 2. see Eupatoria. *248*

Kerkis : town of S Egypt, on the W bank of the Nile river, S of the island of Elephantine, in NE Africa. *244*

Kerkura : 1. Island of the NE Ionian Sea, off the coast of Epeiros in NW Greece, also known as Corcyra and present-day Corfu. *190 & 218*;-- 2. city on the NE side of this island. *218*

Kerman : city of C Media, SE of modern Tehrãn, CS Iran, W Asia. *260*

Keros : island in SE Cyclades, SE of Naxos, in CW Aegean Sea. *230*

Kerunia : inland town S of Helike, in CN Achaia, near the coast of the Gulf of Korinthos, in CN Peloponnesos. *200*

Kerunites : river of E Achaia, flowing N into the Gulf of Korinthos, near Kerunia, in CN Peloponnesos. *200*

Kestrine : tribal area, N of the river Thuamis, in SW Epeiros, opposite the N end of the island of Kerkura (Corfu), in NE Ionian Sea. *218*

Khabur : river of N Assyria, S of the Bhutan river, flowing W and becoming tributary of the Tigris river, in present-day N Iraq, W Asia. *258*

Khalki : island of the Dodekanesoi, NW of the island of Rhodes, in SE Aegean Sea. *230*

Khanates : tribal land located mostly in present-day Uzbekistan, E of the Caspian Sea, C Asia. *260*

Khani : see Nirou. *206*

If a name is not found under K, look under C

Khania :town on the SE coast of the gulf of Khanion, NW end of the Island of Crete, in CS Mediterranean Sea. *204*

Khanion : gulf between the peninsulas of Rodopou to the W and Akrotiri to the E, in NW island of Crete, CS Mediterranean Sea. *204*

Khãrga : oasis of CW Egypt, between Thebes and the Dakhla oasis, in NE Africa. *242*

Khash : 1. river flowing SW from the mountains of C Afghanistan, SE of the Farah river, into the Sistan swamps, near the SW Pakistani border with Iran, C Asia, *260 & 262*; -- 2. city along this river. *260*

Khasia : mountain on the border between Thessalia in the S and Macedonia in the N, in CN mainland Greece. *220*

Khawak : pass in Bactria, between the Panjshir valley of N Pakistan, through the Hindu Kush mountain, and Kabul in NE Afghanistan, C Asia. *262*

Khirokitia : see Khoirokoitia. *256*

Khmün : town, also called Hermopolis Magna, about halfway between Cairo and Luxor, on the W bank of the Nile river, in C Egypt, NE Africa. *242*

Khodjend : see Eschate. *262*

Khoirokoitia : city in the CS of the island of Cyprus, E Mediterranean Sea, W Asia. *256*

Khorãsãn : major area of ancient Parthia, SE of the Caspian Sea, in present-day NE Iran, extended for a period of time into portions of Turkmenistan and Afghanistan, in C Asia. *246 & 260*

Khrusoskalitissa : town on the SW coast of the island of Crete, exact location uncertain, in C Mediterranean Sea. *204*

Khulm : area, also called Tashkurghan, in ancient Bactria, between Balkh and Konduz, in present-day N Afghanistan, C Asia. *262*

Khwãrezm : see Chorasmia. *260*

Khyber : 1. mountain range, S of the Cophen (Kabul) river, in NE Afghanistan and NW Pakistan, C Asia. *262*; -- 2. important pass through these mountains, connecting Kabul in Afghanistan and Peshãwar in Pakistan. *262*; -- 3. area, see vale of Peshãwar. *262*

Kiata : village in NE Achaia, near the border with Argolis, W of Sikuon, S of the Gulf of Korinthos, in NE Peloponnesos. *200*

Kikonos : tribe, perhaps mythological, with land in S Thrace, N of Troas, in NW Turkey, W Asia. *226 & 269*

Kiliaris : see Puknos. *204*

Killa : Aiolian town, in Troas, near Troy, in present-day NW Turkey, W Asia. *250*

If a name is not found under K, look under C

Kimmeria : mythical region described by Homer as gloomy. *269*
Kimmerikon : town of the Crimea along the N Euxine (Black) Sea,
  S of the Sea of Maeotis, in W Asia. *248*
Kirke : see Aiaia. *269*
Kirkuk : see Arrapkha. *258*
Kirphis : mountain in CS Phokis, SE of Delphi, in CS mainland
  Greece. *214*
Kirrha : 1. city at the top of the gulf of Korinthos, on the border
  between Ozolian Lokris and Phokis, in CS mainland Greece. *214*;
  -- 2. Hesiodic town of NW Achaia, in the plain along the Krathis
  river, near Aigeira and the S shore of the Gulf of Korinthos, in
  NE Peloponnesos. *200*
Kirva : see Ieraputna. *206*
Kis Kulesi : town in Cilicia, on the CE coast of the Gulf of Issos,
  near the Pass of Jonah, in present-day SE Turkey, W Asia. *256*
Kissamos : 1. gulf at the NW end of the island of Crete, in CS
  Mediterranean Sea. *204*; -- 2. see Herrosinos, on this gulf. *204*
Kissavos : see Ossa. *220*
Kissos : tumulus for burial in Messenia, SW Peloponnesos. *196*
Kithairon : mount S of Thebes and Plataia, in CS Boiotia, on the
  border with Megaris and Attika, near the NE end of the Gulf of
  Korinthos, in SE mainland Greece. *210 & 212*
Kitinion : one of a group of four cities, with Boion, Erineos and
  Pindos, in the valley of the Pindos river, in Doris, CS mainland
  Greece. *214*
Kition : seaport in CS of the island of Cyprus, in E Mediterranean
  Sea, W Asia. *256*
Kizil : see Halys river. *248 & 252*
Kizil Kum : city of Chorasmia, in present-day Uzbekistan, CN Asia.
  260
Kladeos : river flowing S from the mountains of CE Elis, in NW
  Peloponnesos and, as a tributary, joining the Alpheios river near
  Olumpia in C Elis, before reaching the Ionian Sea to the W. *194*
Klaros : ancient site, S of Kolophon, in Caria, near the SE of the
  coast of Asia Minor, in present-day SW Turkey. *254*
Klazomenae : Ionian town of CW Asia Minor, at the entrance to
  the Bay of Smyrna, opposite the island of Chios, in CE Aegean
  Sea. *254*
Kleitor : town surrounded by mountains, S of Kunaitha, in CN
  Arkadia, in N Peloponnesos. *192*
Klenies : quarry in NE Arkadia, somewhere N of Tripolis, in N
  Peloponnesos. *192*

If a name is not found under K, look under C

Kleonae : 1. town E of ancient Nemea, S of Korinthos. in NW Argolis, NE Peloponnesos. *202*; -- 2. city on the SW side of the Peninsula Akti, in the E Chalkidike, NE mainland Greece. *228*

Klimax : city NE of Melangea, in CE Arkadia, on the border with NW Argolis, in CN Peloponnesos. *192 & 202*

Klithi : town on Mount Vodomatis, N of the modern city of Ioaninna, in CN Epeiros, NW mainland Greece. *218*

Klitoria : town in W Arkadia, exact location unknown, in NW Peloponnesos. *192*

Knakalos : mountain in NE Arkadia, NW of Orchomenos, in CE Peloponnesos. *192*

Knemis : mountain range parallel to the coast of Opuntian Lokris, along the Gulf of Oropos, in CE mainland Greece. *214*

Knidos : city of Caria, on the Peninsula Bubassos, in SW Asia Minor, present-day Turkey, opposite the island of Kos in the Aegean Sea. *254*

Knossos : major city near the CN of the island of Crete, in C Mediterranean Sea. *206*

Kokcha : area on the S border of the city of Ai Khanoum, in S Bactria, present-day NE Afghanistan, in C Asia. *262*

Kokkinopulos : site in CS Epeiros, N of the Gulf of Ambrakia in Akarnania, CW mainland Greece. *218*

Kokutos : branch of the mythological river Stux, tributary of the river Acheron in Hades, also called Konkutos. *268*

Kolchis : region S and E of the Caucasus mountains, between the Euxine (Black) Sea and the Caspian Sea, in present-day Georgia and Azerbaijan, SE Europe. *248*

Kolias : cape, probably on the SE side of the Bay of Phaleron, in CW Attika, SE mainland Greece. *208*

Kolokithia : island near the coast of NE island of Crete, on the W side of the Gulf of Megambellou, in C Mediterranean Sea. *206*

Kolonides : inland city of SE Messenia, near the SW coast of the Gulf of Messenia, NW of Asine, in SW Peloponnesos. *196*

Kolonna : site at the N end of the harbor, SW of the island of Aigina, in the S of the Saronic Gulf, SE mainland Greece. *208*

Kolonos : 1. qualified Agoraios, see Agora. *208*; -- 2. qualified Hippios, grove identified by Sophokles for the place of Oedipus' death, a short distance NE of Athens. *208*

Kolophon : Ionian city, N of Ephesos, in Lydia, near the C of the W coast of Asia Minor, in present-day CW Turkey. *254*

Kolossai : town in CS Lydia, in CW Asia Minor, present-day Turkey. *254*

If a name is not found under K, look under C

Koluergia : cape at the SW tip of the peninsula of Argolis, in SE
   Argolis, NE Peloponnesos. *202*
Kolumbari : town in the SE of the peninsula Rodopou, in NW
   island of Crete, CS Mediterranean Sea. *204*
Komaros : seaport town of the Ionian Sea, present-day Mutika, W
   of modern Nikopolis in SW Epeiros, SW mainland Greece. *218*
Komlekci : site of an ancient fortress on a hill near Kaunos, in
   Caria, SW Asia Minor, present-day SW Turkey. *254*
Kommos : seaport city on the CS coast of the island of Crete, on
   the Gulf of Mesara, in C Mediterranean Sea. *204*
Konduz : also spelled Qonduz, 1. area of Bactria, S of the Hindu
   Kush, in present-day NE Afghanistan, C Asia. *262*; -- 2. river
   flowing through this area. *262*; -- 3. town on this river, ancient
   Drapsaca, N of Kabul. *262*
Konitsa : town on the NW slope of the Pindos mountain range , in
   the valley where the Aoos and Voidomatis rivers meet in
   Epeiros, near the border with Illyria, in NW mainland Greece.
   218
Konkutos : see Kokutos. *268*
Kontadesdos : river of SE Thrace, joining the Agrianes river as a
   tributary of the Maritsa river, in NE mainland Greece. *226*
Konya : city of Lycaonia, in CS Anatolia, present-day CS Turkey.
   256
Kopae : Homeric city of C Boiotia, N of the E end of Lake Kopais,
   in SE mainland Greece. *212*
Kopais : lake, now dry land, E of Orchomenos, in N Boiotia, SE
   mainland Greece. *212*
Kopanos : town NE of Lefkadia, in CE Macedonia, NE mainland
   Greece. *224*
Kophinas : village in the CS of the island of Crete, exact location
   uncertain, in C Mediterranean Sea. *206*
Kophosa : harbor of Torone, in the SW of the peninsula Sithonia
   of the C Chalkidike, in the N Aegean Sea. *228*
Koprinka : town of C Thrace, in present-day Bulgaria, SE Europe.
   226
Korakou : town of NW Argolis, on the Isthmus of Korinthos, exact
   location uncertain, in NE Peloponnesos. *202*
Korax : rock near the spring of Arethusa, in NE Elis, NW
   Peloponnesos. *194*
Korçë : see Koritsa. *218*
Korinthia : area around the city of Korinthos, in NW Argolis, NE
   Peloponnesos. *190, 202 & 210*

If a name is not found under K, look under C

Korinthos : 1. gulf separating the Peloponnesos from mainland Greece except for the isthmus, ancient name Krisaean Gulf, in CS mainland Greece. *190, 200, 202, 210, 212 & 214*; -- 2. bay, also called Krisa, between Ozolian Lokris and Phokis, at the NE end of the Gulf, in SW Boiotia. *202 & 214*; -- 3. isthmus in N Argolis, between the SE end of the Gulf of Korinthos and the Saronic Gulf, like a bridge connecting the Peloponnesos with mainland Greece. *202*; -- 4. city at the SE end of the Gulf, Homeric Ephura, modern Corinth, N of Argos and S of the port of Lechaion, in NW Argolis, NE Peloponnesos. *202*

Koritsa : plain in Illyria, present-day Korçë in SE Albania, in Molossis, on the border with Epeiros, NW mainland Greece. *218*

Korone : city of SE Messenia, on the NW coast of the Gulf of Messenia, E of Mount Mathia, in SW Peloponnesos. *196*

Koroneia : city in C Boiotia, on the river Phalaros, SW of Lake Kopais, in SE mainland Greece. *212*

Koroni : 1. see Asine. *196*; -- 2. see Messenia. *196*

Koronta : site probably near Stratos, in C Akarnania, near the border with Aitolia, in SW mainland Greece. *216*

Koropissos : town in Cilicia, N of modern Mut, at the foot of the Taurus mountain, in present-day CS Turkey, W Asia. *256*

Korsea : town in NE Boiotia, NE of Kurtone, in SE mainland Greece. *212*

Korthion : port city, on the coast of the island of Andros, S of the city of Andros, in the N of the Cyclades, CW Aegean Sea. *226*

Korudallos : 1. region of CW Attika, E of the Bay of Eleusis. *210*; -- 2. major city in this region. *210*; -- 3. ancient city of SE Lycia, on the SW side of the Gulf of Antalya, along the Mediterranean Sea, in SW Asia Minor, present-day Turkey. *254*

Korukos : mount, S of Eruthrae, in Ionia, CW of the coast of Asia Minor, present-day CW Turkey. *254*

Korupedion : town of Lydia, NW of Sardis, on the coast of the Aegean Sea, in present-day CW Turkey. *250*

Koruphasion : 1. promontory at the N end of the Bay of Navarino, in SW Messenia, SW Peloponnesos. *196*; -- 2. Hesiodic town E of Pulos, on this Bay. *196*

Koruphon : mount SE of the Kunortion mountain, in the C of the peninsula of Argolis, in CE Argolis, NE Peloponnesos. *202*

Kos : 1. island of the Dodekanesoi, in SE Aegean Sea, N of the island of Rhodes, *190, 230 & 254*; -- 2. city on the NE coast of this island. *230*

If a name is not found under K, look under C

Kosovo : 1. country in the CN Balkan Peninsula, surrounded by
Albania to the W, Serbia to the N and E, and Macedonia to the S,
in E Europe. *224 & 240*; -- 2. major city of this region. *240*

Kotiliusa : mountain in SW Arkadia, N of Phigalia, in C Peloponnesos. *192*

Koturta : city of Lakonia, probably near Aphrodisia, both precise
locations unknown, in SE Peloponnesos. *198*

Koukounara : village with tholos tombs on the E side of
Messenia, in SW Peloponnesos. *196*

Koumasa : ancient site in CS of the island of Crete, in C
Mediterranean Sea. *206*

Kouphia Rachi : site in SE Epeiros, exact location uncertain, in C
mainland Greece. *218*

Kouphonisi : 1. small island near the SE end of the island of
Crete. *206*; -- 2. seaport on the same island. *206*

Kourion : town on the SW of the island of Cyprus, in the NE
Mediterranean Sea, W Asia. *256*

Kourtes : town in CS of the island of Crete, NW of Phaistos, in C
Mediterranean Sea. *204*

Kozan : town in CN Cilicia, S of the Taurus mountains, in present-
day SE Turkey, W Asia. *256*

Kranae : 1. city on the CE side of the island of Kephallenia, in CE
Ionian Sea, W of Akarnania, in CW mainland Greece. *216*; -- 2.
islet off the port of Gutheion, in the NW of the Gulf of Lakonia,
CW Lakonia, SE Peloponnesos. *198*

Kranidhion : town of SW Argolis, W of Tiruns, exact location
uncertain, along the Gulf of Argolis, in NE Peloponnesos. *202*

Kranon : town of C Thessalia , NW of Pharsalos, in NE mainland
Greece. *220*

Krapathos : island of the Rhodian Dodekanesoi, modern
Karpathos, near Kasos, between the islands of Crete and
Rhodes, in SE Aegean Sea. *230*

Krathis : 1. mountain in NE Arkadia, near the border with Achaia,
in NE Peloponnesos. *192*;-- 2. river flowing N from Mount
Krathis in Arkadia, through E Achaia, into the Gulf of Korinthos,
near Aigai, in NE Peloponnesos. *200*; -- 3. river flowing from the
mountains of Calabria, by Sybaris, into the Gulf of Taranto, in S
Italy, W Europe. *238*

Kreine : springs on the coast of S Akarnania, opposite the island
of Ithaka, in SW mainland Greece. *216*

Krenae : town of Amphilochia, in NW Aitolia, SW mainland Greece.
216

If a name is not found under K, look under C

Krenides : inland city, renamed Philippi, near the bay of Kavala, E of the Chalkidike and N of the island of Thasos, in SW Thrace, NE mainland Greece, on the center N coast of the Aegean Sea. *226*

Krestonia :tribal land in SE Macedonia, E of the Axios river and N of Mugdonia, N of the Gulf of Thermai, in NE mainland Greece. *224*

Krete : see Crete. *204 & 206*

Kretea : town in SW Arkadia, S of Mount Lukaion, in C Peloponnesos. *192*

Kreusis : town in CS Boiotia, on the coast of the E end of the Gulf of Korinthos, in SE mainland Greece. *212*

Krios : river in E Achaia, flowing N into the Gulf of Korinthos, W of Donussa, in NE Peloponnesos. *200*

Krisa : 1 gulf, see Korinthos. *202, 212 & 214*; -- 2. bay, see Korinthos. *202 & 214*; -- 3. city in CS Phokis, in the valley of the foothills of Mount Parnassos, N of Kirrha and SW of Delphi, in CS mainland Greece. *214*

Kritsana : ancient site in C Macedonia, exact location unknown, in NE mainland Greece. *224*

Krokeae : 1. city of NW Lakonia, N of the Gulf of Lakonia, in SE Peloponnesos. *198*; -- 2. quarry near Sparta, in Lakonia, SE Peloponnesos. *198*

Krokule : ancient city of Aitolia, exact location unknown, in C mainland Greece. *216*

Krokuleia : Homeric city on the island of Leukas, exact location uncertain, in CE Ionian Sea. *216*

Kromi : town in CS Arkadia, between the rivers Karnion to the E and Gatheatas to the W, in CS Peloponnesos. *192*

Kromion : town of NE Argolis, on the S side of the Isthmus of Korinthos, on the N coast of the Saronic Gulf, in NE Peloponnesos. *202*

Kropia : town of CE Attika, probably W of Sphettos, in SE mainland Greece. *208*

Krounoi : ancient city of SW Elis, in SW Triphulia, on the coast of the Ionian Sea, near the border with Messenia, in CW Peloponnesos. *194*

Krusis : tribal area in SE Macedonia, NE mainland Greece, along the E coast of the Gulf of Thermai, in NW Aegean Sea. *224*

Kuaneia : 1. legendary shifting rocks, also called Symplegades, in a narrow stretch of the Hellespontos, in N Troas, NW Asia Minor. *250 & 269*; -- 2. small islands, near Melos, in SW Cyclades, SW Aegean Sea. *230*

If a name is not found under K, look under C

Kuban : see Russian Hypanis river. *248*

Kudonia : seaport city on the S coast of the Gulf of Khanion, in NW island of Crete, C Mediterranean Sea. *204*

Kudrara : ancient city of N Lydia, on the border with Phrygia, in NW Asia Minor, present-day NW Turkey. *250*

Kuh- e- Daman : valley in Bactria, N of Kabul, in present-day NE Afghanistan, C Asia. *262*

Kullene : 1. port city of NW Elis, in the area of Bouprasion, on the coast of the Ionian Sea, in NW Peloponnesos. *194*; -- 2. mountain range in NE Arkadia, bordering on Achaia to the N and Argolis to the E, in CN Peloponnesos. *192*

Kum : ancient city of Media, modern Qom, SW of Rhagae (Tehrãn), in present-day NW Iran, W Asia. *260*

Kumbaca : modern city of SE Lycia, on the SW side of the Gulf of Antalya, E of Korudallos, along the Mediterranean Sea, in SW Asia Minor, present-day Turkey. *256*

Kume : Aiolian city of Lydia, also called Panopeios and Phrikonis, between Elaia to the N and Phokaia to the S, on the CW coast of Asia Minor, present-day Turkey. *250*

Kumli : valley, on the border between Macedonia and Thrace, along the Strumon river, in N mainland Greece. *224 & 226*

Kummuh : see Commagene. *256*

Kunaitha : town N of Kleitor and Lousoi, in CN Arkadia, near the border with Achaia, in NW Peloponnesos. *192*

Kunar : valley in Bactria, in present-day NE Afghanistan, on the border with Pakistan, in C Asia. *266*

Kunaxa : town N of Babylon, on the W bank of the Euphrates river, in Babylonia, S Mesopotamia, present-day S Iraq, W Asia. *258*

Kundar : river of C Pakistan, tributary of the Indus river, in C Asia. *262*

Kunlun : mountain range in NW China, N of the Plateau of Tibet, in C Asia. *266*

Kunortion : mountain on the C of the peninsula of Argolis, below the city of Epidauros, NW of Mount Koruphon, in CE Argolis, NE Peloponnesos. *202*

Kunos : Homeric city on the coast of SE Opuntian Lokris, near Thermopulai, on the Gulf of Oropos, in CE mainland Greece. *214*

Kunosarges : area outside the walls of Athens, on the S bank of the river Ilisos, in C Attika, SE mainland Greece. *208*

Kunoskephalai : range of hills in SE Thessalia, W of Volos, in NE mainland Greece. *220*

If a name is not found under K, look under C

Kunossema : 1. cape in the SW Chersonesos, in E Ancient Thrace, on the N side of the Hellespontos, pushing it to its narrowest exit into the Sea of Marmara, in NW Asia Minor, present-day NW Turkey. *226*; -- 2. city on this cape. *226*

Kunosura : 1. peninsula on the N side of the Bay of Marathon, along the Gulf of Petalion, in NE Attika, SE mainland Greece. *210*; -- 2. town on this peninsula. *210*

Kunouria : plain W of the city of Astros, in SW Argolis, NE Peloponnesos. *202*

Kunthos : mountain on the island of Delos, in the Cyclades, CW Aegean Sea. *230*

Kunuria : see Thurea. *202*

Kuparisseis : 1. Homeric territory, part of the Nestor's kingdom, N of Pulos, in CW Messenia, SW Peloponnesos. *196*; -- 2. river crossing this area, flowing NW from Mount Ithome to the Ionian Sea. *196*; -- 3. Homeric city of NW Messenia, near the coast of E Ionian Sea. *196*

Kuparission : cape along the E Ionian Sea, on the coast of NW Messenia, in SW Peloponnesos. *196*

Kuparissos : Homeric city of Phokis, SE of Delphi, in CS mainland Greece. *214*

Kuphanta : city in CE Lakonia, near the coast of the Mirtóön Sea, in SE Peloponnesos. *198*

Kuphos : port city on the W Aegean Sea, in E Thessalia, NE mainland Greece. *220*

Kuprianon : quarry near Sparta in NW Lakonia, SE Peloponnesos. *198*

Kupros : see Cyprus. *256*

Kupsela : site of a fort in Parrhasia, CW of Arkadia, CN Peloponnesos. *192*

Kura Vrusi : see Isthmia. *210*

Kurdistan : region of ancient E Anatolia, presently mostly inhabited by the Kurds in E Turkey and N Iraq and Iran, in W Asia. *258*

Kuros : river flowing E from the S Caucasus mountains, between the Euxine (Black) Sea and the Caspian Sea, in W Asia. *248*

Kurrhos : town in C Macedonia, W of Atalante, in CN of mainland Greece. *224*

Kurtkulak : town in C Cilicia, W of Issos, in present-day SE Turkey, W Asia. *256*

Kurtone : town in NE Boiotia, NE of Orchomenos, in SE mainland Greece. *212*

If a name is not found under K, look under C

Kush : 1. region along the Nile river, S of Egypt, also known as Nubia, present-day Sudan. *244*; -- 2. see Hindu Kush. *266*

Kuthera : island of the S Mirtóön Sea, off the SE coast of Lakonia, at the entrance to the Gulf of Lakonia, near the peninsula Malea, in SE Peloponnesos. *190 & 198*; -- 2. city in the center of this island. *198*

Kuthnos : island on the NW side of the Cyclades, in the Aegean Sea, S of Attika. *230*

Kuthoros : 1. mount near the CS coast of the Euxine (Black) Sea, near Sesamos, in Asia Minor, present-day NW Turkey. *252*; --2. Homeric city on this mount. *252*

Kuwait : small country in E Arabia, on the N Persian Gulf, between present-day Saudi Arabia and Iraq, in W Asia. *246 & 258*

Kvarner : gulf in the NE Adriatic Sea, E of the peninsula of Istria, in Croatia, C Europe. *238*

Kyra : see Kyreskhata. *262*

Kyrenaica : region covering the NE portion of Libya, W of Egypt, on the Mediterranean Sea, in NE Africa. *242 & 244*

Kyrene : seaport city of Kyrenaica, modern Shahbat, E of the gulf of Sidra, in NE Libya, NE Africa. *244*

Kyrenia : city on the CN coast of the island of Cyprus, in NE Mediterranan Sea, W Asia. *256*

Kyreskhata : fort city of Sogdiana, also called Kyra, near Alexandria-in-Escharta, along the Jaxartes river, in present-day SE Uzbekistan, C Asia. *262*

Kyrgyzstan : modern country of ancient Sogdiana, bordering on Kazakhstan to the N, China to the E and S, Uzbekistan and Tajikistan to the W, in CN Asia. *188, 246, 262 & 266*

L

Laas : Homeric city of Lakedaimon, near Sparta, in CW Lakonia, exact location unknown, in CS Peloponnesos. *198*

Labda : see Leptis Magna. *244*

Labdalum : inland city near the SE end of the island of Sicily, in W Mediterranean Sea, W Europe *236*

Labeati : tribal land located in ancient NW Illyria, near the coast of the NE Adriatic Sea, present-day Croatia, E Europe. *218*

Lade : 1. Ionian city in Caria, near Miletos, on the coast of the E Aegean Sea, in Asia Minor, present-day CW Turkey. *254*; -- 2. little island of the E Aegean Sea, off the coast of the Ionian city of Miletos, in SW Asia Minor, present-day SW Turkey. *230*

Ladochori : site of a cemetery, on the coast of the Ionian Sea, S of Igoumenitsa, in NW Epeiros, NW mainland Greece. *218*

Ladon : river of NE Elis, tributary of river Peneios, in NW Peloponnesos. *194*

Ladonas : river flowing from Mount Oruxis in NE Arkadia, SW to CW Arkadia where it joins with the river Alpheios, in CE Peloponnesos. *192*

Laechon : seaport in CN Achaia, on the S side of the Gulf of Korinthos, exact location uncertain, in CN Peloponnesos. *200*

Lagash : 1. see Sumer region. *258* -- 2. ancient city, N of Larsa, in this region. *258*

Laghman : valley in Bactria, in present-day NE Afghanistan, W of the Kunar valley, in C Asia. *266*

Lahore : city W of Sangala, in ancient Bactria, present-day Punjab, near the center of Pakistan, in C Asia. *266*

Laistrugonia : mythical land of the giant Laistrugonoi, perhaps on the island of Corsica, at the N edge of the Tyrrhenian Sea, in W Europe. *269*

Laitas : inland town in CW of the island of Sicily, in W Mediterranean Sea, W Europe. *234*

Lake : mythological unnamed lake. *268*

Lakedaimon : area around the city of Sparta, in C Lakonia, SE Peloponnesos. *198*

Lakedaimonia : see Sparta. *198*

Lakonia : 1. region in the SE of the Peloponnesos, bordering on Arkadia and Argolis to the N, the Mirtóön Sea to the E, the Gulf of Lakonia to the S and Messenia to the W. *190, 192, 196, 198 & 202*; – 2. gulf of the Mediterranean Sea, in SE Peloponnesos *198*; -- 3. ancient isthmus in the S of Lakonia, opposite the island of Kuthera. *198*

Lamia : town of E Malis, S of the Gulf of Malis and W of Thermopulai, in C mainland Greece. *214*

Lamos : 1. river flowing E from the E summit of the Helikon mountain range in SW Boiotia, then S until it joins the river Termessos as a tributary, in SE mainland Greece. *212* -- 2. river of CS Anatolia, present-day CS Turkey, flowing SE from the W Taurus mountains, across Cilicia, as E border of Tracheia, into the Mediterranean Sea. *256*

Lampedusa : island of the Libyan Sea, opposite Syrtis Minor, in CN Africa. *244*

Lampeia : city of SE Elis, NE of Olumpia, in NW Peloponnesos. *194*

Lamponion : Aiolian town at the N of the entrance into the gulf of Edremit, in E Mysia, NW Asia Minor. *250*

Lampsakos : city of Hellespontine, on the SE end of the Strait of Hellespontos (Dardanelles), opposite Gallipoli, in NW Asia Minor, present-day NW Turkey. *250*

Lamptras : town in CS Attika, E of the Humettos mountain range, in SE mainland Greece. *208*

Lamtah : see Leptis Minor. *244*

Lankia : spring at Pellana in NE Lakonia, SE Peloponnesos. *198*

Laodikeia : 1. city in the Lukos valley, between Hierapolis and Kolossai, in Caria, CW Asia Minor, present-day CW Turkey. *254*; --2. city of N Phoenicia, present-day Lebanon, opposite the N island of Cyprus, in NE Mediterranean Sea, W Asia. *256*

Laodikion : city in SW Arkadia, probably in the uncertain area of Oresthis, in N Peloponnesos. *192*

Laphustios : mountain W of Lake Kopais, S of Lebadea, in C Boiotia, SE mainland Greece. *212*

Lapithos : 1. mount in SW Arkadia, S of the Alpheios river, near the border with Elis, in CW Peloponnesos. *192*; -- 2. city in CN of the island of Cyprus, on the coast of the E Mediterranean Sea, in W Asia. *256*

Lappa : ancient village, a short distance from Rithumna to the NE, in the NW of the island of Crete, C Mediterranean Sea. *204*

Larissa : 1. lake in CN Thessalia, N and W of the river Peneios, in NE mainland Greece. *220*; -- 2. town on the S shore of this lake. *220*; -- 3. mount SW of ancient Argos, next to mount Aspis, in CW Argolis, NE Peloponnesos. *202*; -- 4. city on this mount, below Argos. *202*; -- 5. Aiolian town on the coast of the NE Aegean Sea, near the border between Troas to the N and Mysia to the S, in NW Asia Minor, present-day NW Turkey. *250*

Larisos : river on the border between SW Achaia and N Elis, in NW Peloponnesos, flowing NW into the Ionian Sea. *194 & 200*

Larnaka : city on the W side of the Gulf of Larnax, in SE of the island of Cyprus, W Asia. *256*

Larnax : gulf in the SE of the island of Cyprus, in W Asia. *256*

Larsa : ancient city of Sumer, modern Tell Sankarah, SE of Erech, in present-day S Iraq, W Asia. *258*

Larumna : city in NE Boiotia, on the coast of Gulf Oropos, in CE mainland Greece. *212*

Las : seaport city on the W side of the Gulf of Lakonia, N of Arainon, in CW Lakonia, SE Peloponnesos. *198*

Las Bela : see Alexandria-in-Oreitidae. *264*

Lasea : see Lassaia. *206*

Lasithi : region around the Gulf of Megambellou, in E of the island of Crete, CS Mediterranean Sea. *206*

Lassaia : town, biblical Lasea identified with Fair Havens, later called Alassa, in the CS of the island of Crete, on the Libyan Sea, in C Mediterranean Sea. *206*

Latium : region of CW Italy on the Tyrrhenian Sea, including Rome, in W Europe. *238*

Latmos : 1. mountain range, probably same as Phthires, along the coast of Caria, in SW Asia Minor, present-day SW Turkey, W Asia. *254*; -- 2. gulf on the S side of this mountain range. *254*; -- 3. city on this gulf, S of Miletos. *254*

Lato : ancient site, identified with the modern town of Agios Nikolaos, W of the gulf of Megambellou, in NE of the island of Crete, CS Mediterranean Sea. *206*

Laurion : 1. mountain site of mines in SE Attika, N of cape Sunion, in SE mainland Greece. *208*; -- 2. port city on the nearby coast of the Aegean Sea. *208*

Laus : town on the W of the boot of S Italy, in W Europe. *238*

Lavka : high peak, see White Mountains. *204*

Leaia : tribal land, adjacent to the Agrianes, S of Triballi, CN Macedonia, NE mainland Greece. *224*

Lebanon : 1. modern country, ancient Phoenicia, on the NE coast of the Mediterranean Sea, bordering on Turkey, Syria and Israel, in W Asia. *188, 246 & 256*; -- 2. mountain range parallel to the NE Mediterranean Sea, from N Syria along the length of Lebanon. *256*

Lebadea : city W of Lake Kopais, S of the river Herkune, in C Boiotia, SE mainland Greece. *212*

Lebedos : Ionian city, W of Lydia, S of Teos, in CW Asia Minor, present-day CW Turkey, off the coast of the Aegean Sea. *254*

Lebena : harbor city, SE of Phaistos, on the CS coast of the island of Crete, facing the Libyan Sea, in C Mediterranean Sea. *206*

Lechaion : 1. one of the two ports of NW Argolis, servicing Korinthos, facing W, at the E end of the Gulf of Korinthos, in NE Peloponnesos. *202*; 2. town at this port. *202*

Ledon : town in C Phokis, N of Daulis, in CS mainland Greece. *214*

Lefkadia : village of C Macedonia, possible site of ancient Mieza, N of Beroia, in NE mainland Greece. *224*

Lefkandi : ancient town S of Eretria, in the CW of the island of Euboia, in W Aegean Sea, E of mainland Greece. *228*

Leibethra : town of Pieria, in CS Macedonia, N of Mount Olumpos, in NE mainland Greece. *224*

Leimone : see Elone. *220*

Leipsudrion : village in CN Attika, SW of Dekeleia, in SE mainland Greece. *210*

Lektos : 1. town at the foot of Mount Olumpos, near Enienae, in CN Thessalia, NE mainland Greece. *220*; -- 2. Homeric promontory in Troas, SW of Mount Ida, opposite N Lesbos island in the NE Aegean Sea, in NW Asia Minor, present-day NW Turkey. *250*

Lekuthos : isthmus adjacent to Torone, in the S of the C peninsula Sithonia of the Chalkidike, in NE mainland Greece. *228*

Lelantine : plain in C of the island of Euboia, in the Aegean Sea, E of mainland Greece. *228*

Lemnos : Greek island of the Thracian Sporades, in NE Aegean Sea, facing the entrance to the Hellespontos (Dardamelles), in present-day NW Turkey. *190 & 228*

Leninabad : see Eschate. *262*

Leon : inland fortified town, in the NE of the island of Sicily, W Mediterranean Sea, W Europe. *236*

Leontes : see Litani river. *258*

Leontini : town on the SE end of the island of Sicily, W of Xiphonia, in W Mediterranean Sea, W Europe. *236*

Leontion : town in NW Achaia, N Peloponnesos, near the entrance to the Gulf of Korinthos. *200*

Lepreon : Minyan town of S Triphulia, in S Elis, N of the river Minueios, in CW Peloponnesos. *194*

Lepte : promontory of Paphlagonia, in CS of the Euxine (Black) Sea, in Asia Minor, present-day Turkey. *252*

Leptis Magna : harbor city of Tripolitania, modern Labda in present-day Libya, E of Tripoli, in NW Africa, along the Mediterranean Sea. *244*

Leptis Minor : city of Tunisia, modern Lamtah, on the S Mediterranean coast, in CN Africa. *244*

Lera : cave near the town of Akrotiri, in the NW end of the Island of Crete, CS Mediterranean Sea. *204*

Lerna : city in SW Argolis, on the NW side of the Gulf of Argolis, S of the river Erasinos, in NE Peloponnesos. *202*

Leros : island of the N Dodekanesoi, N of Kalumnos, in SE Aegean Sea. *230*

Lesbos : Aiolian island in NE Aegean Sea, opposite the gulf of Adramuttion in Aiolis, NW Asia Minor, present-day NW Turkey. *190, 228 & 250*

Lessa : town in the CN of the peninsula of Argolis, N of mount Titthion, in C Argolis, NE Peloponnesos. *202*

Lêtopolis : town in N Egypt, at the SW entrance to the Nile Delta, opposite Heliopolis on the E side, N of Cairo, in NE Africa. *242*

Letrini : inland city of SW Elis, between Pheia and Duspontion, in NW Peloponnesos. *194*

Leukae : 1. city in the SE of Lakonia, opposite the N end of the Gulf of Lakonia, in SE Peloponnesos. *198*; -- 2. island in the NW of the Euxine (Black) Sea, at the mouth of the Danube (Ister) delta, in Romania, SE Europe. *240*

Leukas : 1. white island of the E Ionian Sea, N of the island of Kephallenia, perhaps the same as Dulichion, off the coast of N Akarnania, in SW mainland Greece. *216*; -- 2. city on the NE side of this island. *216*; -- 3. isthmus on which the city stood, in N Akarnania, NW mainland Greece. *216*

Leukasia : river of N Messenia, tributary of the river Elektra, in SW Peloponnesos. *196*

Leukatas : 1. cape on the island of Leukas, in the E Ionian Sea, off the coast of W Akarnania, in CW mainland Greece. *216*; -- 2. mythological cape, probably somewhere at the S tip of the heel of Italy, in W Europe. *269*

Leukimme : cape at the S end of the island of Kerkura (Corfu), in the NE Ionian Sea, opposite NW Thesprotis, in NW mainland Greece. *218*

Leukonion : city, probably on the island of Chios, exact location unknown, in CE Agean Sea. *230*

Leuktra : 1. city of the SW plain of Boiotia, in SE mainland Greece. *212*; -- 2. city of CW Lakonia, on the W coast of the Gulf of Lakonia, in SE Peloponnesos. *198*

Leukuanias : river of CE Elis, flowing SW and merging with the Alpheios river, in CW Peloponnesos. *194*

Levantine : sea at the E end of the Mediterranean Sea, surrounded by Turkey to the N, Phoenicia and Palestine to the E and Egypt to the S, in W Asia. *258*

Levka : harbor town on the NW coast of the island of Cyprus, in E Mediterranean Sea. *256*

Liatovouni : site of a cemetery, near the border with Illyria (Albania), in NW Epeiros, NW mainland Greece. *218*

Libya : 1. country in NE Africa, on the S Mediterranean coast, W of Egypt & Sudan, E of Tunisia & Algeria and N of Niger & Chad. *188 & 244*; -- 2. in Antiquity, identified with all Africa. *187 & 244*

Libyan : 1. sea, also called Cyrenic Sea for its E part, in the CS of the larger Mediterranean Sea, between Libya in NE Africa to the S and the island of Crete to the N. *204 & 244*; -- 2. desert of Kyrenaica, in present-day E Libya, NE Africa. *244*

Liger : river, modern Loire, flowing from CS France, first N, then W into the Atlantic Ocean, in W Europe. *232*

Liguria : 1. sea of the NW Mediterranean Sea, bordered by S France, Monaco and NW Italy to the N and E, with the island of Corsica to the S, in W Europe. *232*; -- 2. region of MW Italy, on the Ligurian Sea. *232 & 238*

Likodhimon : mountain of S Messenia, in SW Peloponnesos. *196*

Lilaia : ancient town, near the source of the river Kephisos, in NW Phokis, CS mainland Greece. *214*

Lilybaeum : 1. cape at the W end of the island of Sicily, in W Mediterranean Sea, W Europe. *234*; -- 2. seaport city, modern Marsala, at the foot of this cape. *234*

Limassol : town in CS of the island of Cyprus, near Amathus, in the NE Mediterranean Sea, in W Asia. *256*

Limenas : see Thasos. *228*

Limera : ancient site, modern Momenvasia, next to the SE Lakonian Epidauros, in SE Peloponnesos, along the Mirtóön Sea. *198*

Limnai : city of CE Messenia, E of Thuria, in SW Peloponnesos. *196*

Limnaia : 1. town in SE Thrace, at the NE Aegean Sea, along the N side of the Hellespontos (Dardanelles), in present-day NW Turkey, SE Europe. *226*; -- 2. town at the SE end of the Gulf of Ambrakia, in NW Aitolia, CW mainland Greece. *216*

Lindii : site of the citadel of Gela, on the SE of the island of Sicily, in W Mediterranean Sea, W Europe. *236*

Lindos : city on the CE side of the island of Rhodes, in the S Dodekanesoi, SE Aegean Sea. *230*

Linguetta : cape in NW Epeiros, stretching into the Adriatic Sea, opposite SE Italy, making the Strait of Otranto the narrowest passage between the Adriatic Sea in the N and the Ionian Sea in the S, in C Europe. *218 & 240*

Lipari : small Aiolian island N of NE island of Sicily and W of SW Italy, in SE Tyrrhenian Sea, W Europe. *238*

Lipsoi : island of the Dodekanesoi, N of Leros island, in SE Aegean Sea. *230*

Lisos harbor town, W of Sougia, both servicing the inland city of Eluros, in the SW of the island of Crete, C Mediterranean Sea. *204*

Lissa : see Vis. *218*

Lissos : city on the coast where the river Drilon meets the SE Adriatic Sea, in W ancient Illyria, present-day Albania, W Balkans, SE Europe. *218*

Litani : river, also called Leontes, flowing SW through Coele Syria, between the Lebanon and Anti-Lebanon mountains, into the Mediterranean Sea, in W Asia. *258*

Lithaios : river flowing N and joining river Peneios in the plain of C Thessalia, N mainland Greece. *220*

Lithares : town N of Thebes, in SE Boiotia, SE mainland Greece. *212*

Lithino : cape in the SE of the Gulf of Mesara, CS of the island of Crete, CS Mediterranean Sea. *204*

Lithuania : country of E Europe, N of Poland, on the Baltic Sea. *188*

Little Prespa : see Prespa. *224*

Lixus : 1. river of NW Morocco, flowing from the Atlas mountains into the Atlantic Ocean, in NW Africa. *244*; -- 2. town of present-day W Morocco, at the mouth of the Lixus river. *244*

Locri : city on E side of the S tip of Italy, along the Ionian Sea, in W Europe. *238*

Loire : see Liger. *232*

Lokris : two regions separated by Phokis, 1. NE region of CE mainland Greece, referred to as Opuntian Lokris, from Halai in NE Boiotia to Thermopulai in the N and between Phokis and Malis in the SW and the Gulf of Oropos in the NE. *190, 212 & 214*; -- 2. S region of CS mainland Greece, referred to as Ozolian Lokris, above the Gulf of Korinthos and surrounded by Aitolia, Doris and Phokis. *190 & 214*

Long Walls : 1. between Athens and Phaleron (Peiraia), in Attika, SE mainland Greece. *208*; -- 2. between Argos and Epidauros, in C Argolis, NE Peloponnesos. *202*; -- 3. between Megara and Nisaea, in Megaris, in SE mainland Greece. *210*; -- 4. between Patrai and Achaian Rhion, in NW Achaia, N Peloponnesos. *200*

Lophis : river S of Lake Kopais and N of the Valley of Muses, in CS Boiotia, SE mainland Greece. *212*

Loralei : modern city, E of Ziarat-Gali-Chah, on an ancient site in Carmenia, present-day SW Pakistan, C Asia. *266*

Loruma : seaport city on the W tip of Doris, in SW Asia Minor, present-day SW Turkey, opposite the island of Sumi of the Dodekanesoi, in SE Aegean Sea. *254*

Loudhias : river of E Macedonia, flowing S of the Tripotamos river, in opposite direction, into the Gulf of Thermaikos, in NW Aegean Sea, NE mainland Greece. *224*

Loukou : site near Astros, exact location uncertain, in SW Argolis, CE Peloponnesos. *202*

Louros : river of C Epeiros, one of the tributaries of the river Peneios in Thessalia, N mainland Greece. *218*

Loutraki : town of NW Argolis, NW of the city of Korinthos, near the E end of the Gulf of Korinthos, exact location uncertain, in NE peloponnesos. *202*

Loutsa : town N of Brauron, in CE Attika, near the Gulf of Petalion, in SE mainland Greece. *208*

Lucania : region of SW Italy, modern Basilicata, in W Europe. *238*

Luchnidos : town of modern Macedonia, on the shore of Lake Luchnites, on the border with Epeiros, in NE mainland Greece. *21*8 *& 224*

Luchnites : lake of N ancient Macedonia, modern Ochrid, on the border with Epeiros, in present-day Macedonia, SE of Bosnia. in NE mainland Greece. *224*

Luginos : plain N of Mount Haemos, in N Thrace, NE mainland Greece, present-day Romania, E Europe. *226*

Lukaion : Hesiodic mountain, running EW from SW Arkadia to SE Elis, in the Theisoa territory, near the border with N Messenia, in SW Peloponnesos. *192*

Lukavettos : see Anchesmos. *208*

Lukestos : town in the C of the island of Crete, CS Mediterranean Sea. *206*

Lukoa : town SE of Mainalos, in SE Arkadia, SE Peloponnesos. *192*

Lukone : mountain in CW Argolis, W of Mount Larisa and the city of Argos, in NE Peloponnesos. *202*

Lukos : 1. river of Scythia, flowing through present-day Romania, into the Gulf of Maeotis (Azov), off the N Euxine (Black) Sea, in E Europe. *248*; -- 2. river of C Lydia, tributary of the Maeander river, in CW Asia Minor, CW Turkey. *254*; -- 3. valley along this river. *254*; -- 4. river of N Mesopotamia, flowing S as a tributary of the Great Zab river, in present-day N Iraq, W Asia. *258*

Lukosura : town in SW Arkadia, SW of Megalopolis, near the border with Messenia, in CS Peloponnesos. *192*

Luktas : sacred mount, E of Arkhanes, in CN of the island of Crete, CS Mediterranean Sea. *206*

Luktos : town near the cave of Skoteino, in the CN of the island of Crete, CS Mediterranean Sea. *206*

Lukuria : town in CS Arkadia, N of Mount Oruxis, in CE Peloponnesos. *192*

Luni : Town of S Etruria, in C Italy, W Europe. *238*

Lunkestis : 1. tribal area of CW Macedonia, in CN mainland Greece. *224*; -- 2. town in this area. *224*

Lunkos : area of NW Macedonia, exact location uncertain, in N mainland Greece. *224*

Lurkea : city in the NW of Argolis, on the N bank of the river Inachos, in NE Peloponnesos. *202*

Lurnessos : ancient town of SW Troas, N of Pedassos, in NW Asia Minor, present-day NW Turkey. *250*

Lusi : town on the W edge of the Aroanios mountain range, in CN Arkadia, CN Peloponnesos. *192*

Lusia : village in C Attika, NE of the Bay of Eleusis, SE mainland Greece. *210*

Lusimacheia : town of Troas, S of the Hellespontos, in NW Asia Minor, present-day NW Turkey. *250*

Lusimachia : city W of Kardia, in the Chersonesos, S Thrace, present-day European Turkey. *226*

Lusios : see Gortunios. *192*
Lut : one of the hottest deserts, SE of the Kavir desert, in present-day CE Iran, near the border with Afghanistan, in C Asia. *260*
Luttos : site E of Luktos, in the CN of the island of Crete, CS Mediterranean Sea. *206*
Luxor : see Egyptian Thebes. *242*
Lycaonia : area of S Anatolia, N of Pamphylia and W of Cappadocia, in present-day CS Turkey, W Asia. *252 & 256*
Lycia : 1. region of SW Asia Minor, along the coast of the NE Mediterranean Sea, surrounded by Caria to the W, Pamphylia to the E and the Taurus Mountains to the N. *254*; -- 2. ancient area around Zeleia in NW Troas, NW Asia Minor, present-day NW Turkey. *250*
Lydia : region of CW Asia Minor, with the Homeric name of Maeonia, in the valleys of the Hermos and Kaustros rivers, in present-day CW Turkey. *190, 250 & 254*
Lykopolis : city of C Egypt, modern Asyût, on the W bank of the Nile river, N of Akhmim, in NE Africa. *242*
Lysimeleia : marsh, probably W of Siracusa, on the E side of the island of Sicily, in W Mediterranean Sea, W Europe. *236*

M

Macedonia : 1. ancient region, Homeric Paionia or Pannonia, referred to as Greek Macedonia, with variable borders presented here as follows: Thessalia and the Aegean Sea in the S, Epeiros and Illyria in the W, Kosovo and Serbia in the N and the Strumon river basin separating it from Thrace in the E, modern Bulgaria, in NE mainland Greece. *190, 218, 220, 224, 226, 228 & 240*; -- 2. modern Macedonia, N of Greece and S of Serbia, E of Albania and W of Bulgaria, in the Balkans, E Europe. *188 & 224*
Macella : inland town in NW of the island of Sicily, exact location uncertain, in W Mediterranean Sea, W Europe. *234*
Macetia : peninsula, ancient Makai and Meka, modern Masandam, SW of the Strait of Hormuz, in ancient Arabia, present-day site of the countries of Dubai in N, Abu Dhabi in CW, Emirates in SW and N Oman in E, in W Asia. *246 & 264*
Mactorium : inland city on the SE side of the island of Sicily, above Gela, in W Mediterranean Sea, W Europe. *236*
Madraki : port city on the island of Kos, in the Dodekanesoi, SE Aegean Sea. *230*

Maeander : river, also called Menderez, flowing first in a W direction from the Phrygian plateau of Anatolia, in W Asia Minor, then SW between Lydia and Caria, and into the Ikarian gulf of the Aegean Sea, NW of Miletos, in present-day SW Turkey. *252 & 254*; -- 2 Little Maeander, see Kaustros river. *254*

Maeonia : see Lydia. *250 & 254*

Maeotis : sea E of the Crimea, modern Azov, a N arm of the Euxine (Black) Sea, in SE Europe. *248*

Magarsos : city in Cilicia, W of the Gulf of Issos, in present-day CE Turkey, W Asia. *256*

Magasa : village near Sitia, in the NE of the island of Crete, C Mediterranean Sea. *206*

Magna Graecia : Greece and her colonies, especially those of Asia Minor, the islands of the Aegean Sea, S Italy and Sicily. *190, 234-238*

Magnesia : 1. Ionian city of N Lydia, inland E of Smyrna (Izmir), S of Hermos river, near Mount Sipulos, in CW Asia Minor, present-day CW Turkey. *250*; -- 2. coastal city in SW Lydia, SE of Ephesos, near the estuary of the Maeander river, in present-day CW Turkey, W Asia. *254*; -- 3. area from Mount Olumpos in the N and the Gulf of Volos in the S of Thessalia, along the Aegean Sea, in NE mainland Greece. *220*; -- 4. peninsula in the S of this area, enclosing the E side of the Gulf of Volos and the N of the island of Euboia. *220*

Mago : desert in ancient Drangiana, SE of the desert of Lut, in present-day C Afghanistan, C Asia. *260*

Maiden Well : see Parthenos Phreatia. *210*

Mainake : ancient town of Iberia, in present-day S Spain, near Malaca, along the Mediterranean Sea, in W Europe. *232*

Mainalos : 1. town in SE Arkadia, NW of Lukoa, in NE Peloponnesos. *192*; -- 2. Hesiodic town of Lycia, near the mountains, N of Xanthos, in SW Asia Minor, present-day SW Turkey. *254*

Mainland Greece : the upper half of Ancient Greece, upper part of Continental Greece, N of the Gulf of Korinthos that separates it from the Peloponnesos in the S. *187, 188 & 208-226*

Maira : city of CE Arkadia, NW of Melangea, W of Mount Alesion, in CE Peloponnesos. *192*

Majorca : island in W Mediterranean Sea, between Spain and Sardinia, in W Europe. *232*

Makai : see Macetia. *264*

Makaria : town, modern Kalamata, in the E plain irrigated by the river Pamisos, in NE Messenia, N of the Gulf of Messenia, in SW Peloponnesos. *196*

Makistos : Minyan town of Triphulia, near Aipu, exact location unknown, in S Elis, CW Peloponnesos. *194*

Makrãn : 1. see Baluchistan. *264*; -- 2. mountain range in E Baluchistan. *264*

Makrobia : region in the S of Kush (Sudan), CE Africa. *244*

Malaca : town of the S of Iberia (Spain), along the Mediterranean Sea, E of the Strait of Gibraltar, in W Europe. *232*

Malakand : 1. area in NW Pakistan, in the foorhills of the Himalayas, S of the Swat valley, in C Asia. *262*; -- 2. town in the SW of this area. *262*; -- 3. pass to the Swat valley to the N. *262*

Malan : city on the shore of the Arabian Sea, near Cocala, in present-day S Pakistan, C Asia. *264*

Malea : 1. cape in NE Argolis, at the end of the Gulf of Korinthos, between NE Argolis in NE Peloponnesos and SW Megaris in SE mainland Greece. *202*; -- 2. peninsula of SE Lakonia, also called Mani, on the Mirtóön Sea, in SE Peloponnesos. *198*; -- 3. cape at the S tip of this peninsula. ; -- 4. city in Arkadia, probably between CS Kromi and Megalopolis, in C Peloponnesos. *192*;-- 5. cape at the SE end of the island of Lesbos, at Mytilene, in CE Aegean Sea. *228*

Maletya : town in SE Hittite territory, present-day CE Turkey, W Asia. *248*

Mali : country of NW Africa, S of Algeria, between Mauritania and Niger. *188 & 244*

Malia : town on the NE coast of the island of Crete, C Mediterranean Sea. *206*

Malis : 1. region in C mainland Greece, surrounded by Ainis, Phthiotis, Opuntian Lokris, Doris and Aitolia. *190, 214 & 222*; -- 2. gulf on the NE corner of the region of Malis, above Thermopulai, in CE mainland Greece. *214*

Malla : town, NW of Kirva, in the SE of the island of Crete, C Mediterranean Sea. *206*

Malli : 1.area E of the Hydaspes river, in Bactria, present-day N India, C Asia. *266*; -- 2. city in the S of this region. *266*

Mallus : town in Cilicia, N of Magarsos, in the NE corner of the Mediterranean Sea, in present-day SE Turkey, W Asia. *256*

Malta : see Melite. *244*

Maltepe : town of CS Thrace, along the Maritsa river, in NE mainland Greece, present-day NW Turkey, SE Europe. *226*

Malthi : village in N Messenia, exact location uncertain, in SW Peloponnesos. *196*

Mand : see Sitaces river. *264*

Mandra : village in Elis, exact location unknown, in W Peloponnesos. *194*

Mani : see Malea. *198*

Manika : town on the CW coast of the island of Euboia, N of Chalkis, facing Boiotia on mainland Greece. *228*

Manisa : inland town of Lydia, near Callatabos, NE of Smyrna (Izmir), in CW Asia Minor, present-day CW Turkey. *250*

Mantineia : city in SE Arkadia, N of modern Tripolis, in CE Peloponnesos. *192*

Mantua : Etruscan town of CN Italy, in W Europe. *238*

Maracanda : city of ancient Sogdiana, modern Samarkand, in present-day S Uzbekistan, N of the border with Tahkistan, C Asia. *262*

Marathon : 1. Plain in NE Attika. *210*; -- 2. Bay of the Gulf of Petalion, separating this plain from the island of Euboia. *210*; -- 3. Town on the E side of the plain, facing the Bay. *210*

Marathousa : small Ionian island, somewhere near the island of Chios, in CE Aegean Sea, opposite Klazomenae, on the CW coast of Asia Minor. *230*

Marathus : city of Phoenicia, present-day Lebanon, on the coast of the NE Mediterranean Sea, S of Arados, in W Asia. *256*

Mardia : tribal area S of the Caspian Sea, between Cadusia in the W and Hyrcania in the E, in present-day N Iran, W Asia. *260*

Marea : town on the NE side of Libya, on the border with Egypt, in NE Africa. *244*

Mareotis : lake adjacent to Alexandria, in NW Egypt, NE Africa. *242*

Margiana : city of W Bactria, in present-day Turkmenistan, C Asia. *260*

Margiane : area in W Bactria, also called Margush, N of Areia and SW of Sogdiana, in present-day SW Afghanistan and SE Turkmenistan, C Asia. *246 & 260*

Margush : 1. see Margiane area. *260*; -- 2, river, also called Epardus, modern Murgab, mostly in Bactria, NW Afghanistan, flowing from the Parapamisadai mountains, in E of Herat, through the area of Margiane , into the Caspian Sea, C Asia. *262*; -- 3. city along this river, near Merv. *260*

Mari : city of ancient Syria, modern NE Syria, on the NW bank of the Euphrates river, in W Asia. *258*

Mariandyni : tribal area of Paphlagonia, in the CS of the Euxine (Black) Sea, present-day NW Turkey, W Asia. *252*

Marios : city NW of Gluppia, in CE Lakonia, SE Peloponnesos. *198*

Maris : river flowing SW from the Carpathian mountains of Romania, across Transylvania, into the Tisza river. In E Europe. *240*

Maritsa : river, also called Hebros, flowing from the Haemos mountains of E Thrace, through present-day Bulgaria and NW Turkey, along the border with Greece, and discharging into the Aegean Sea, near Ainos, N of the Hellespontos, in NE mainland Greece. *226*

Marmara : 1. see Propontis. *188, 190, 226, 240, 250 & 252*; -- 2. see Prokonessos. *250*; -- 3. strait separating the island of Rhodes, in the SE Aegean Sea, from the region of Doris, in SW Asia Minor, present-day SW Turkey. *230*

Marmariani : town of SE Thessalia, on the Magnesia peninsula, NE side of mainland Greece, near the coast of the NW Aegean Sea. *220*

Maroneia : city on the S coast of Thrace, along the N Aegean Sea, in NE mainland Greece,. *226*

Marsala : see Lilybaeum. *234*

Marseille : see Massalia. *232*

Marsi : region of C Italy, SE of Rome, in W Europe. *238*

Marsyas : river of Caria, flowing from the S as a tributary of the Maeander river, in SW Asia Minor, present-day SW Turkey. *254*

Masandam : see Macetia. *246 & 264*

Masat : town NE of Hattusa, in CN of the Hittite territories, present-day CNTurkey, W Asia. *248*

Mases : city on the SW side of the peninsula of Argolis, S of Didumi, in SE Argolis, NE Peloponnesos. *202*

Massaga : city in NW India, S of the valley of Kashmir, C Asia. *266*

Massagetai : tribal land located in NW Sogdiana, E of the Caspian Sea and SE of the Aral Sea, in present-day Uzbekistan, C Asia. *262*

Massalia : seaport city of the NW Mediterranean Sea, modern Marseille, in the SW of France, W Europe. *232*

Matala : seaport town on SE side of the plain of Mesara, servicing the cities of Phaistos and Gortus, on the CS coast of the island of Crete, C Mediterranean Sea. *206*

Matapan : see Tainaron. *198*

Matauros : town on the W side of the S tip of Italy, S of Medna, along the Tyrrherian Sea, in W Europe. *238*

Mathia : mount in CE of the peninsula of Sphakteria, in SW Messenia, SW Peloponnesos. *196*

Mathura : town E of the Ganges river, in present-day NE India, C Asia. *266*

Matiene : area of N Media, S of Armenia, in present-day NW Iran, W Asia. *248*

Matruh : see Paraitonion. *242*

Mauritania : 1. ancient region of NW Africa, present-day Morocco and Algeria. *187 & 244*; -- 2. modern country on the Atlantic Ocean, S of Morocco and Algeria, N of Senegal and NW of Mali. *188 & 244*

Maurya : region centered on the junction of the Son and Ganges rivers at Patna, covering the N and C of India, in C Asia. *266*

Mavromati : see Messene. *196*

Mavrovouni : mountain range of Magnesia, S of mount Ossa, in E Thessalia, NE mainland Greece. *220*

Mazaka : town of E Phrygia, ancient Hittite Territories, S of the Euxine (Black) Sea, in present-day NE Turkey, W Asia. *248*

Mazarakata : site on the island of Kephallenia, exact location uncertain, in the Ionian Sea, near the entrance to the Gulf of Patraikos, in SW mainland Greece. *216*

Mazar- e- Sharif : modern city on an ancient site in Arcia, present-day NW Afghanistan, C Asia. *262*

Medeon : 1. port city at the top E side of the Bay of Antikura, opposite the city of Antikura, on the N side of the Gulf of Korinthos, in CS phokis, CS mainland Greece. *214*; -- 2. town of N Akarnania, in SW mainland Greece. *216*

Media : region between N Mesopotamia on the W side, Parthia and Carmania on the E side, S of the Caspian Sea and N of Susiana, mostly ancient NW Persia and modern Iran, in W Asia. *246, 258 & 260*

Media Atropatene : region between Armenia and the Caspian Sea, in present-day Azerbaijan, W Asia. *258*

Medinet Habu : site opposite Thebes, on the W bank of the Nile river, in C Egypt, NE Africa. *242*

Mediterranean : large sea surrounded by Europe, W Asia and N Africa, made of four basins from E to W, Levantine, Ionian, Tyrrhenian and Algerian, connected at Gibraltar with the Atlantic Ocean. *187, 188, 190, 204, 232, 236, 242, 244, 246, 254 & 256*

Medna : town on the W side of the S tip of Italy, S of Hipponion, along the Tyrrherian Sea, in W Europe. *238*

Megalo Kastelli : cemetery on a hill near Thebes, in S Boiotia, SE mainland Greece. *212*

Megalopolis : 1. major city in CS Arkadia, on the river Helisson, in C Peloponnesos. *192*; -- 2. city in NE Messenia, near the borders with Arkadia to the N and Lakonia to the E, near Athenaion in NW Lakonia, CS Peloponnesos. *196*

Megambellou : large gulf, known also as Mirabellou, on the NE side of the island of Crete, in CS Mediterranean Sea. *206*

Meganissi : see Taphos. *216*

Meganitas : river in CN Achaia, flowing N into the Gulf of Korinthos, W of Aigion, in CN Peloponnesos. *200*

Megara : seaport city of SE Megaris, NE of the Saronic Gulf, in SE mainland Greece. *210*

Megara Hyblaea : coastal town on the SE side of the island of Sicily, N of Siracusa, in W Mediterranean Sea, W Europe. *236*

Megaris : region of the Isthmus of Korinthos, between Korinthia to the SW, the Saronic Gulf to the S, Attika to the E, Boiotia to the N and the Gulf of Korinthos to the W, also border between Peloponnesos and mainland Greece. *190, 210 & 212*

Megiste : thirtheenth island added to the Dodekanesoi, also calleld Kastellorizon, opposite the coast of Caria, E of Rhodes, in SE Aegean Sea. *230*

Meilichos : river in W Achaia, flowing W into the Gulf of Patraikos, N of Patrai, in NW Peloponnesos. *200*

Meka : see Macetia. *264*

Mekuberna : town in NW peninsula Sithonia of the Chalkidike, in the N Aegean Sea, NE mainland Greece. *228*

Melainiai : town in SW Arkadia, NW of Buphagion, in C Peloponnesos. *192*

Melangea : city of CE Arkadia, NE of Mantineia, W of Mount Alesion, in CE Peloponnesos. *192*

Melas : gulf of the NE Aegean Sea, in S Thrace, into which the river Maritsa discharges and the city of Ainos is located, in NW Turkey, SE Europe. *226*

Meles : Homeric river of Lydia, flowing from Mount Erymanthos, past Smyrna, into the CE Aegean Sea in Asia Minor, present-day CW Turkey. *254*

Meliboia : Homeric seaport city of NE Thessalia, on the coast of the Aegean Sea, in NE mainland Greece. *220*

Melissa : town on the coast of the Atlantic Ocean, in modern Morocco, NW Africa. *244*

Melite : 1. town W of the Kephisos river, SW of Athens, to the W, in CW Attika, SE mainland Greece. *208*; -- 2.small lake N of the city of Oiniadai, in SW Akarnania, SW mainland Greece. *216*; -- 3. island, modern Malta, belonging to a group of islands S of the larger island Sicily, in W Mediterranean Sea, W Europe. *244*

Melitia : town in the C of Achaia Phthiotis, CE mainland Greece. *222*

Melos : island in the SW of the Cyclades, CW Aegean Sea. *230*

Memphis : city on the W bank of the Nile river, S of the opening of the delta, S of Cairo, in N Egypt, NE Africa. *242*

Menae : inland city on the SE side of the island of Sicily, exact location uncertain, in W Mediterranean Sea, W Europe. *236*

Menares : palace site at the NE end of the island of Crete, in C Mediterranean Sea. *206*

Mende : town in the S of the W peninsula Kassandra of the Chalkidike, along the Aegean Sea, in NE mainland Greece. *228*

Menderez : 1. see Maeander river. *252 & 254*; -- 2. see Scamander river. *250 & 269*

Mendes : town E of the C of the Nile Delta, on the Mediterranean Sea, in N Egypt, NE Africa. *242*

Mene : island in lake Tritonis, in S Tunisia, CN Africa. *244*

Menelaion : site NE of Sparta, in C Lakonia, CS Peloponnesos. *198*
Menidi : inland town in CN Attika, SE mainland Greece. *210*
Meninx : island of the Libyan Sea, near the coast of Syrtis Minor (Gabes), in CN Africa. *244*
Merenda : see Murrhinos. *208*
Meroë : city of Kush, S of Egypt, on the E bank of the Nile river, in NE Africa. *244*
Meropis : town at the E end of the island of Kos, in SE Aegean Sea. *230*
Mersa Matruh : 1. region in NW Egypt, along the SE coast of the Mediterranean Sea, in NE Africa. *242*; -- 2. see Paraitonion. *242*
Mersin : coastal town of Cilicia, in the NE corner of the Mediterranean Sea, W of Tarsus, in present-day SE Turkey, W Asia. *256*
Merv : 1. oasis in W Bactria , present-day S Turkmenistan, C Asia. *260*; -- 2. town, near Alexandria-in-Margiane, in this oasis. *260*
Mesara : 1. gulf on the Libyan Sea, in the CS of the island of Crete, in C Mediterranean Sea. *204*; -- 2. plain where Phaistos and other cities are located, E of this gulf. *204*
Mesembria : town of NE Thrace, in the Danube river delta, on the W shore of the Euxine (Black) Sea, in present-day Romania, SE Europe. *226*
Meshed : modern city in Khorãzãn, ancient Parthia, present-day NE Iran, W Asia. *260*
Mesolongion : see Kaludon. *216*
Mesopotamia : ancient region of SW Asia, irrigated by the Tigris and Euphrates rivers flowing in SE direction, mostly in present-day Iraq, W Asia. *246 & 258*
Messana : see Zankle. *236*
Messapia : area of Calabria and Apulia, in the SE heel of Italy, W Europe. *238*
Messapios : mountain in CE Boiotia, NE of Mount Hupatos, in SE mainland Greece. *212*
Messe : Homeric city in SW Lakonia, on the E coast of the Gulf of Messenia, in SE Peloponnesos. *198*
Messeis : fountain near Argos, in Argolis, NE Peloponnesos. *202*
Messene : city of C Messenia, modern Mavromati, N of the Gulf of Messenia, on the S slope of Mount Ithome, in SW Peloponnesos. *196*
Messenia : 1. region of the SW Peloponnesos, between the Ionian Sea to the W, the Mediterranean Sea to the S, Lakonia to the E, and Arkadia and Elis to the N. *190, 192, 194, 196 & 198*; -- 2. gulf of the SE Ionian Sea, ancient Koroni, between Messenia and Lakonia, in SW Peloponnesos. *196 & 198*

Messina : strait at the S tip of Italy, separating it from the island of Sicily, in W Mediterranean Sea, W Europe, in mythology referred to as Charybdis and Scylla . *236 & 238*

Mesta : see Nestos. *226*

Metapontion : town at the NW side of the gulf of Taranto, W of Taras, in S Italy, W Europe. *238*

Methana : 1. peninsula of CE Argolis, into the Saronic Gulf, in NE Peloponnesos. *202*; -- 2. isthmus connecting it with Troizen, in CE Argolis. *200*; -- 3. city N of the isthmus and on the W side of this peninsula. *202*

Methone : 1. seaport on the SE coast of Macedonia, on the NW side of the gulf of Thermai, in NW Aegean Sea. *224*;-- 2. harbor town of SW Messenia, also known as Modon, on the coast of the Ionian Sea, in SW Peloponnesos. *196*

Methudrion : city in C Arkadia, SW of Numphasia, in CE Peloponnesos. *192*

Methumna : coastal town on the N side of the island of Lesbos, in NE Aegeab Sea, W of Aiolis, in present-day NW Turkey. *228*

Metropolis : town probably in amphilochia, NW Aitolia, E of the Gulf of Ambrakia, in SW mainland Greece. *216*

Midea : town of CW Argolis, N of Tiruns, in NE Peloponnesos. *202*

Mideia : akropolis on the town of Aspledon, in CN Boiotia, SE mainland Greece. *212*

Midius : ancient river near the Hellespontos area of Phrygia, course unknown, in NW Asia Minor, present-day NW Turkey. *252*

Mieza : see Lefkadia. *224*

Mikalitsi : site of a cemetery in SW Epeiros, N of Preveza, in SW mainland Greece. *218*

Mikinae : see Mukenae. *202*

Mikrolimani : see Munuchia harbor. *206*

Mila : ancient town of CW Akarnania, contiguous to the promontory of Aktion, in CW mainland Greece. *216*

Miletos : 1. town in the NE of the island of Crete, C Mediterranean Sea. *206*; -- 2. Ionian city of Caria, on the coast of the Aegean Sea, standing on an isthmus, at the mouth of the Maeander river, on the Ikarian Gulf, in SW Asia Minor, present-day SW Turkey. *254*

Mimas : peninsula in W Lydia, CW Asia Minor, opposite the island of Chios, in CE Aegean Sea. *250 & 254*

Minoa : 1. cape on the SE side of Lakonia, into the Mirtoön Sea, in SE Peloponnesos. *198*; -- 2. peninsula extending from S Megaris into the Saronic Gulf, toward the island of Salamis, in SE mainland Greece. *210*; -- 3. ancient islet, now submerged, between this peninsula and the island of Salamis. *210*; -- 4.

town on the island of Amorgos of the Cyclades, in CW Aegean Sea. *230*; -- 5. see Herakleia Minoa. *234*

Minthe : mount in NE Elis, part of the Erumanthos mountain range, E of Sandy Pulos, in SW Peloponnesos. *194*

Minuae : 1.name of a tribe, also known as Mynians, located in an area around Orchomenos, in CN Boiotia, SE mainland Greece. *212*; -- 2. the same tribe migrated later to Triphulia, SE Elis, CW Peloponnesos. *194*

Minueios : river flowing from the Parrhasios mountain range in SW Arkadia, E through S Elis and NW Messenia, into the Ionian Sea near Arene, in CW Peloponnesos. *194 & 196*

Minyans : see Minuae. *212*

Mirabellou : see Megambellou. *206*

Mirmekion : town on S end of Sea of Maeotis (Azov), W of the Strait connecting it to the Euxine (Black) Sea, in SE Europe. *206*

Mirtóön : sea along the E coast of the Peloponnesos, S of the Gulf of Argolis, an arm of the Mediterranean Sea. *198*

Mitropolis : site of a palace in CS of the island of Crete, in C Mediterranean Sea. *206*

Mitrovika : see Sirmium. *240*

Mochlos : 1. seaport city at the NE side of the gulf Megambellou at the NE end of the island of Crete, in C Mediterranean Sea. *206*; -- 2. island just off the coast, opposite the city. *206*

Modaeoi : town between Kissamos and Kudonia, in the NW of the island of Crete, C Mediterranean Sea. *204*

Modon : see Methone. *196*

Moeris : lake W of the Nile river, in N Egypt, NE Africa. *242*

Moldova : small country located between Romania and Ukraine, near the NW Euxine (Black) Sea, in E Europe. *188 & 240*

Molossia : area of N Epeiros, E of Chaonia and W of Orestis, in NW mainland Greece. *218*

Molossis : area from Hellopia in SW Illyria to the border with Epeiros, near the Adriatic Sea, in NW mainland Greece. *218*

Molukria : area of SW Ozolian Lokris, N of the Strait of Rhion, in SW mainland Greece. *214*

Molukrion : city in W Ozolian Lokris, N of the Gulf of Korinthos, N of Rhion, probably near Naupaktos, in CS mainland Greece. *214*

Momemphis : site along the Nile river, exact location uncertain, in Egypt, NE Africa. *242*

Monastiraki : site of a palace in CW of the island of Crete, in C Mediterranean Sea. *204*

Monemvasia : see Epidauros Limera. *198*

Mongolia : country of CN Asia, N of China and S of Russia. *188 & 246*

Montenegro : small country adjacent to Serbia, in the C of the N Balkan Peninsula, surrounded by Croatia and Bosnia to the W, Hungary to the N, Romania and Bulgaria to the E, and Albania and Macedonia to the S, in SE Europe. *240*

Morava : river of Moravia, flowing S from Slovakia, into E Austria where it joins the Danube river, in E Europe. *240*

Moravia : region straddling the border between present-day Czech Republic and Slovakia, covering ancient Bohemia and S Silesia, in the Balkans, E Europe. *240*

Morgantina : inland town in the CE of the island of Sicily, in W Mediterranean Sea, W Europe. *236*

Morocco : country at the W end of N Africa, part of ancient W Mauritania, between the Atlantic Ocean and Algeria. *188 & 244*

Morphou : bay on the NW coast of the Island of Cyprus, at the E end of the Mediterranean Sea, in W Asia. *256*

Mosarna : city, in ancient CS Gedrosia, on the N coast of the Arabian Sea, in present-day S Pakistan, C Asia. *264*

Moschaton : modern name of a village on an ancient site E of Peiraios, in CW Attika, SE mainland Greece. *208*

Mosul : city of Assyria, on the W bank of the Tigris river, in N Mesopotamia, present-day N Iraq, W Asia. *258*

Mosynoëci : area of W Armenia, near the coast of the SE end of the Euxine (Black) Sea, in W Asia. *248*

Motya : coastal town on the W side of the island of Sicily, in W Mediterranean Sea, W Europe. *234*

Motyum : inland town in the CS of the island of Sicily, in W Mediterranean Sea, W Europe. *234*

Mouliana : village in the NE of the island of Crete, near the E shore of the Gulf of Megambellou, in CS Mediterranean Sea. *206*

Mouriatadha : town in CW Messenia, N of Pulos, in the SW Peloponnesos. *196*

Mudraya : region in the NE of Egypt, along the Mediterranean Sea, in NE Africa. *242*

Mugdonia : tribal area of SE Macedonia, in the N of the Chalkidike peninsula, extending NE as far as SW Thrace, in NE mainland Greece. *224*

Mukale : 1. mountain in CW Caria, SW Asia Minor, present-day SW Turkey. *254*; – 2. Ionian city below this mountain, near the estuary of the Maeander river, opposite the island of Samos, in SE Aegean Sea. *254*

Mukalessos : Homeric city of CE Boiotia, SW of Aulis, in SE mainland Greece. *212*

Mukenae : ancient city, next to modern Mikinae, N of Tiruns, in NW Argolis, NE Peloponnesos. *202*

Mukonos : island on the E side of the Cyclades, N of Delos, in the CW Aegean Sea. *230*

Mulasa : inland town of Caria in SE Asia Minor, present-day Turkey. *254*

Mulla : river of S Pakistan, ancient Tomerus, modern Hingol, flowing from the Kalāt highlands, through present-day C Pakistan and Baluchistan, and emptying like a torrent into the Arabian Sea, in C Asia. *262 & 264*

Mundos : city of SW Caria, near Halikarnassos, on the Bodrum Peninsula of SW Asia Minor, present-day SW Turkey. *254*

Munuchia : 1. one of three harbors, modern Mikrolimani, on the E side of the peninsula of Peiraios, N of Zea, in CW Attika, SE mainland Greece. *208*; -- 2. hill behind the harbor. *208*; -- 3. town on this harbor. *208*

Muonessos : Ionian town of CW Lydia, on the coast of the CE Aegean Sea, S of Teos, in CW Asia Minor, present-day Turkey. *254*

Muonia : town in CE Ozolian Lokris, S of Amphissa, in CS mainland Greece. *214*

Muos : town of SW Lydia, E of Magnesia, in SW Asia Minor, near the mouth of the Maeander river, on the SE coast of the Aegean Sea. *254*

Murgab : see Margush river. *260 & 262*

Murina : island in CN Aegean Sea, SW of Lemnos island. *228*

Murine : grave, see Batieia. *250*

Murkinos : town at the S end of the lake Kerkinitis, along the Strumon river, in SW Thrace, NE mainland Greece. *228*

Murleia : see Kelainae for Apameia Murleia. *254*

Muros : Ionian city of Caria, on the coast of the Aegean Sea, between Miletos to the S and Priene to the N, in SW Asia Minor, present-day SW Turkey. *254*

Murrhinos : town in CS Attika, modern Merenda, NE of Prospalta, in SE mainland Greece. *208*

Mursini : coastal town in the CE side of the Gulf of Megambellou, in the NE of the island of Crete, C Mediterranean Sea. *206*

Mursinos : Homeric city, S of the city of Buprasion in NW Elis and Cape Araxos in W Achaia, on the Ionian Sea, in NW Peloponnesos. *194*

Murtina : see Antalya. *256*

Murtos : town near the SE coast of E island of Crete, in C Mediterranean Sea. *206*

Musaeon : inland city in SE Achaia, W of the river Suthas, in NE Peloponnesos. *200*

Muses : 1. hill on the W side of the Akropolis of Athens, in C Attika, SE mainland Greece. *208*; -- 2. valley in CS Boiotia, S of Lake Kopais, in SE mainland Greece. *212*

Mut : Modern city, S of Koropissos, at the foot of the Taurus mountains, in S Cilicia, present-day CS Turkey, W Asia. *256*

Mutika : see Komaros. *218*

Mutilene : major city on the E side of the island of Lesbos, in NE Aegean Sea. *228*

Myecphoris : island, opposite Bubastis, in the CE Delta of the Nile river, N Egypt, NE Africa. *242*

Mylai : town in the NE of the island of Sicily, along the S Tyrrhenian Sea, opposite the Aiolian islands, in W Europe. *236*

Myriandros : town probably on the E coast of the Gulf of Issos, S of Iskenderon, in E Cilicia, present-day SE Turkey, W Asia. *256*

Mysia : region of Asia Minor, on the coast of the NE Aegean Sea, S of Troas and N of Lydia, in present-day NW Turkey. *190 & 250*

N

Nabatea : region equivalent to present-day Jordan, inland from the E end of the Mediterranean Sea, in W Asia. *258*

Nafpaktos : see Naupaktos. *216*

Nafplion : see Nauplia. *202*

Nagidos : town of Pamphylia on the N coast of the Mediterranean Sea, in CS present-day Turkey, W Asia. *256*

Naousa : village in C Macedonia, near Lefkadia, in NE mainland Greece. *224*

Naparis : one of five rivers flowing from the Carpathian mountains, between the Pyretus and Tiarantus rivers, into the Danube river, in Scythia, present-day Romania, E Europe. *240*

Napata : town of Kush (Nubia), S of Egypt, on the W bank of the Nile river, in NE Africa. *244*

Naples : 1. see Neapolis Bay. *238*; -- 2. see Neapolis city. *238*

Narbo : coastal town at the NW Mediterranean Sea, in present-day SW France, W Europe. *232*

Nari : river of ancient Gedrosia, from the mountains E of Quetta, joining the Bolãn river in the Kachi plain, S Pakistan, C Asia. *264*

Naro : ancient river, modern Neretva, in NW Illyria, present-day Croatia, along the NE side of the Adriatic Sea, in CS Europe. *218*

Narthakios : mountain of S Thessalia, SE of Pharsalos, near the border with Phthiotis, in NE mainland Greece. *220*

Nasamones : inland area of C Libya, in NE Africa. *244*

Natho : city in the center of the Delta of the Nile River, exact location uncertain, in N Egypt, NE Africa. *242*

Naukratis : city on the W branch of the Delta of the Nile river, SE of Alexandria, in NW Egypt, NE Africa. *242*

Naupaktos : town in SE Aitolia, near the W entrance of the Gulf of Korinthos, on the N side, in CW mainland Greece. *216*

Nauplia : seaport city, also called Nafplion, on the NE shore of the Gulf of Argolis, SE of Tiruns, in SW Argolis, NE Peloponnesos. *202*

Nautaca : city in C Sogdiana, present-day N Pakistan, C Asia. *262*

Navarino : 1. gulf in SW Messenia, on the coast of the Ionian Sea, in SW Peloponnesos, between the island of Sphakteria and the cities of Pulos and Palaiokastro. *196*;-- 2. town off the natural harbor created by the Bay. *196*

Naxos : 1. the largest island of the Cyclades, in the SE, E of Paros, in the C Aegean Sea. *230*; -- 2. port city on the W coast of this island. *230*; -- 3. coastal town on the NE side of the island of Sicily, in W Mediterranean Sea, W Europe. *236*

Nea Anchialos : see Thebes in Phthiotis. *222*

Nea Ionia : site of a cemetery in W Magnesia, SE Thessalia, NE of the Gulf of Volos, in N mainland Greece. *220*

Nea Makri : settlement in the Plain of Marathon, in NE Attika, SE mainland Greece. *210*

Neandreia : town of SW Troas, S of Sigeion, in NW Asia Minor, present-day NW Turkey. *250*

Nea Nikomedia : city in CE Macedonia, in the NW of the Chalkidike peninsula, in NE mainland Greece. *224*

Neapolis :1. bay, modern Naples, on the W side of S Italy, along the Tyrrherian Sea, in W Europe. *238*; -- 2 seaport city, modern Naples, on this bay. *238* ; -- 3. seaport city, modern Kavala, on the CN coast of the Aegean Sea, E of the Chalkidike peninsula, in SW Thrace, NE mainland Greece. *226*; -- 4. mine in NW Lakonia, near Sparta, in SE Peloponnesos. *198*

Nebrodes : mountains in the NE of the island of Sicily, in the W Mediterranean Sea, W Europe. *236*

Neda : river flowing EW from SW Arkadia, along the border with N Messenia, then on the border between Messenia and Elis, into the Ionian Sea, near Aulon, in CW Peloponnesos. *194 & 196*

Neetum : city on the SE side of the island of Sicily, in W Mediterranean Sea, W Europe. *236*

Negev : desert of S Palestine, present-day S Israel, between Egypt and Jordan, in W Asia. *258*

Negotino : see Antigoneia. *224*

Neion : see Neriton. *216*

Nemea : 1. ancient city of NW Argolis, SW of Korinthos, in NE Peloponnesos. *202*; -- 2. ancient river, now a dry bed, flowing N, past W of the city, toward the Gulf of Korinthos. *202*

Nepal : country on the W side of the Himalaya mountains between India and Tibet, in CS Asia. *246 & 266*

Nera : island in the Bay of Eleusis in NW Attika, N of the Saronic Gulf, in SE mainland Greece. *210*

Neretva : see Naro. *218*

Nerikos : Homeric city on the E side of the island of Leukas, in CE Ionian Sea, off the W coast of Akarnania, in CW mainland Greece. *216*

Neris : town in SW Argolis, at the S end of the mountainous area of Thureatis, in CE Peloponnesos. *202*

Neriton : mountain, also called Neion, on the island of Ithaka, in CE Ionian Sea. *216*

Nessos : Hesiodic river, so called after the legendary centaur, probably identical with the Euenos river of Thessalia and Aitolia, in C mainland Greece. *216 & 220*

Nestane : city in CS Arkadia, W of Mount Artemision of CW Argolis, near the border, in NE Peloponnesos. *192*

Nestor : 1. kingdom of Nestor, on the coast of the Ionian Sea, around Pulos, in SW Messenia, SW Peloponnesos. *196*;-- 2. cave in this kingdom, at Palaiokastro, N of the Bay of Navarino. *196*;-- 3. see Epano Englianos about the palace. *196*

Nestos : river, also called Mesta, flowing S from the Rhodope mountain range, through Thrace, present-day Bulgaria, and NE Greece, into the CN Aegean Sea. *226*

Nicaea : 1. city in the Pontos region, also known as Iznik, on the S shore of lake Iznik, in present-day NW Turkey, W Asia. *252*; -- 2. see Alexandria-in-Caucasus. *262*; -- 3. see Alexandria-Nicaea. *266*

Nicephorum : town probably S of Thapsacus, on the Euphrates river, in NW Mesopotamia, present-day N Syria, in W Asia. *258*

Nichoria : town in S Messenia, on the W coast of the Gulf of Messenia, in SW Peloponnesos. *196*

Nidri : town on the E side of the island of Leukas in the Ionian Sea, off the coast of Akarnania, in CW mainland Greece. *216*

Niger : country of N Africa, surrounded by Algeria, Chad, Nigeria and Mali. *188 & 244*

Nigeria : country of N Africa, S of Niger. *188 & 244*

Nigrita : city E of the Chalkidike peninsula, near the border between Macedonia and Thrace, in NE mainland Greece. *226*

Nikisiani : city near Neapolis, E of the Chalkidike peninsula, on the border between Macedonia and Thrace, in NE mainland Greece. *226*

Nikomedia : see Chalkedon. *252*
Nikopolis : city in Akarnania, N of the Gulf of Ambrakia, SW mainland Greece. *218*
Nile : river of NE Africa, with the Homeric name of Aiguptos, flowing from Ethiopia, through Sudan and the length of Egypt, into the Mediterranean Sea. *187, 242 & 244*
Nineveh : major city of Assyria on the E bank of the Tigris river, present-day Mosul in N Iraq, in W Asia. *258*
Ninoi : village of NE Attika, SW of Marathon, in SE mainland Greece. *210*
Nirou Khani : seaport city, E of Herakleion, in the CN of the island of Crete, in C Mediterranean Sea. *206*
Nisa : 1. Homeric sacred town in E Boiotia, exact location uncertain, in SE mainland Greece. *212*; -- 2. town of Parthia, also called Parthaunisa, E of the Caspian Sea, in present-day Turkmenistan, C Asia. *260*
Nisaia : 1. seaport city of SE Megaris, on the W side of the Saronic Gulf, in SE mainland Greec. *219*; -- 2. peninsula on the SW side of th Bay of Eleusis. *210*; -- 3. island in the SW bay of Eleusis, S of this peninsula. *210*; -- 4. plain in W Media (Persia), along the Zagros mountains, in present-day NW Iran, C Asia. *260*
Nisibis : town of the area of Thura, in N Mesopotamia, between the Euphrates and Tigris rivers, in present-day N Iraq, W Asia. *258*
Nisos : island of the E Cyclades, modern Mikonos, E of Delos, in CW Aegean Sea. *230*
Nisuros : island of the Dodekanesoi, NW of Rhodes, in SE Aegean Sea. *230*
Nola : town in SW Italy, E of Neapolis, in W Europe. *238*
Nomia : mountain range in the NE corner of Messenia, on the border with SW Arkadia, in CS Peloponnesos. *192 & 196*
Nonakris : city of NE Arkadia where, according to legend, the river Stux surfaces, in CN Peloponnesos. *192*
Nora : coastal town, at the S end of the island of Chardan (Sardinia), in the Tyrrhenian Sea, W Europe. *232*
Norsuntepe : city on the N border of the Hittite territories, in present-day NE Turkey, W Asia. *248*
North : sea between the island of Britain and the N mainland of W Europe. *232*
Notion : Aiolian city of Lydia, N of Ephesos, on the coast of the Aegean Sea in the CW Asia Minor, present-day CW Turkey. *254*
Nubia : see Kush. *244*
Nudion : Minyan town in Triphulia, exact location unknown, in S Elis, CW Peloponnesos. *194*

Numidia : region of NW Africa, corresponding to present-day E Algeria and Tunisia. *244*

Numphaion : 1. seaport city, at the tip of SE Lakonia, on the SE coast of the Gulf of Lakonia, in SE Peloponnesos. *198*; -- 2. town of the Crimea, along the N Euxine (Black) Sea, S of the Sea of Maeotis, in SE Europe. *248*

Numphasia : city in CE Arkadia, W of Mount Phalanthos, in CE Peloponnesos. *192*

Nusa : 1. mythological site in Thrace, N of the Aegean Sea, in NE mainland Greece. *269*; -- 2. mythological valley of goddess Demeter, somewhere in Greece. *269*; -- 3. Mythological mountain where god Dionysus was born, somewhere in Asia. *269*; -- 4. mythological city founded by god Dionysus in Bactria, imagined to be in NW India, C Asia. *269*; -- 5. Homeric mountain on the island of Euboia, in CW Aegean Sea. *228*; -- 6. mound in the E delta of the Nile river in Egypt, near the SE end of the Mediterranean Sea, in NE Africa. *242*; -- 7. mountain in Nubia, S of Egypt, NE Africa. *244*

Nuzu : city of Assyria, E of the Tigris river, S of Arraphka (Kirkuk), in present-day N Iraq, W Asia. *258*

O

Oarus : river of Scythia, flowing through present-day Romania, before entering the Gulf of Maeotis (Azov), off the N Euxine (Black) Sea, in E Europe. *248*

Oaxos : 1. river flowing N from Mount Ida, by the ancient village of Axos, into the Sea of Crete, in CN of the island of Crete, CS Mediterranean Sea. *204*; -- 2. see Axos. *204*

Obia : town on the NW coast of the Euxine (Black) Sea, near Odessa, in Thrace, present-day Ukraine, SE Europe. *240*

Ocean : 1. see Okeanos/ Mythological Underworld. *268*; -- 2. see Okeanos/ Mythological World. *269*

Ocha : mount at the S tip of the island of Euboia, in CW Aegean Sea. *228*

Ochrid : see Luchnites. *224*

Odessa : city of NE Thrace, in present-day S Ukraine, at the NW end of the Euxine (Black) Sea, in SE Europe. *240*

Odessos : city, also called Varna, on the CW coast of the Euxine (Black) Sea, in E Thrace, present-day Bulgaria, SE Europe. *226 & 240*

Odomantia : tribal area of SW Thrace, N of Edonia, in NE mainland Greece. *226*

Odrusia : area in the C of Thrace, reaching to the Euxine (Black) Sea in the E and mostly surrounded on three other sides by mountains, the Rhodope in the S, the Skombros in the W and the Haemos in the N, in present-day Bulgaria, SE Europe. *226*

Oea : city on the coast of the CS Mediterranean Sea, modern Tripoli, in present-day NW Libya, CN Africa. *244*

Oëroë : 1. river in S Boiotia, flowing E from N of Mount Kithairon, into the Saronic Gulf, in SE mainland Greece. *212*; -- 2. plain along this river. *212*

Ogugia : Hesiodic island, probably modern Gozo, NW of Malta and S of Sicily, in the W Mediterranean Sea, W Europe. *244*

Ogulia : 1. Hesiodic portion of the Mediterranean Sea between the Peloponnesos and the island of Crete. *204*; --2. island, off the NW of the island of Crete, near Grambousa, in C Mediterranean Sea. *204*

Oianthea : city in the SE of Ozolian Lokris, on the SW side of the Bay of Krisa, N of the Gulf of Korinthos, in CS mainland Greece. *214*

Oichaleis : seaport city of CW island of Euboia, in CW Aegean Sea, opposite Aulis in CE mainland Greece, on the E side of the Strait of Euripos, N of Chalkis, in CW Euboia. *228*

Oichalia : 1. city in the N of the island of Euboia, exact location uncertain, in CW Aegean Sea. *228*; -- 2. city of NE Messenia, SE of Andania, in SW Peloponnesos. *196*; -- 3. see Eurution. *220*

Oineon : see Oinoë, in Ozolian Lokris. *214*

Oiniadai : seaport city in S Akarnania, in the Delta of the river Acheloos into the Ionian Sea, N of the entrance to the Gulf of Patroklos, in SW mainland Greece. *216*

Oinoë : 1. town in CW Argolis, on the river Charadros, in NE Peloponnesos. *202*; -- 2. town of NE Attika, on the river Charadra, SE of Aphidna, in SE mainland Greece. *210*; -- 3. town of NW Attika, W of Eleutherae, in SE mainland Greece. *210*; -- 4. town in Elis, exact location unknown, NW Peloponnesos. *194*;-- 5. town on the island of Ikaria, in CE Aegean Sea. *230*; -- 6. town in Korinthia, near the Gulf of Korinthos, in CS mainland Greece. *202*; -- 7. town in SW Ozolian Lokris, also called Oineon, on the NW shore of the Gulf of Korinthos, in CE mainland Greece. *214*; -- 8. town in Kastoria, W Macedonia, in CN mainland Greece. *224*; -- 9. city of Phrygia, on the SE shore of the Euxine (Black) Sea, E of Thermiscyra, in present-day NW Turkey, W Asia. *248*

Oinophuta : town of SE Boiotia, SW of Tanagra, in SE mainland Greece. *212*

Oinussai : 1. islands S of SW Messenia, in SE Ionian Sea, off SW Peloponnesos. *196*; -- 2. islets of the Aegean Sea, between the island of Chios and the mainland of Ionia, in CW Asia Minor, present-day CW Turkey. *230*

Oisume : town, also called Emathia, on the CN coast of the Aegean Sea, E of the Chalkidike peninsula, in SW Thrace, NE mainland Greece. *226*

Oita : 1. mount near Cape Kenaion, at the N end of the island of Euboia, in CW Aegean Sea. *228*; -- 2. mountain in NW Phokis, NW of Mount Parnassos, in CS mainland Greece. *214*; -- 3. tribal area with a mount, in E Malis, S of Thermopulai, opposite Cape Kenaion, in CE mainland Greece. *214*

Oitulos : Homeric city in the CW of the W peninsula of Lakonia, near the Gulf of Messenia, in SE Peloponnesos. *198*

Okalea : Homeric city In CW Boiotia, near Haliartos, in SE mainland Greece. *212*

Okeanos : 1. large bodies of water, ancient and present, called Ocean surrounding the land of the earth. *188 & 266*; -- 2. mythical river, modernized in Ocean, surrounding the Underworld. *268*; -- 3. mythical river, modernized in Ocean, surrounding the world. *269*

Olba : city of Tracheia, in W Cilicia, at the estuary of the Lamos river, on the NE Mediterranean Sea, in SE Anatolia, present-day SE Turkey. *256*

Olbia : 1. town, also known as Borystenes, in SW Scythia, present-day S Ukraine, at the NW end of the Euxine (Black) Sea, in SE Europe. *248*; -- 2. seaport town in NE of the island of Sardinia, in the Tyrrhenian Sea, W Europe. *232*

Olen : 1. Homeric rocky mound, probably modern Skollis, on the NW border of Elis, in NW Peloponnesos. *194*; -- 2. town in CW Achaia, near Elis, exact location uncertain, in NW Peloponnesos. *200*; -- 3. Homeric city in SW Aitolia, exact location uncertain, between the rivers Acheloos and Euenos, in CS mainland Greece. *216*

Olenos : 1. Homeric city of Aitolia, near Pleuron, in SW mainland Greece. *216*; -- 2. city of NW Achaia, near the S shore of the Gulf of Patraikos, E of Dume, in NW Peloponnesos. *200*

Olizon : Homeric seaport city on the E coast of Thessalia, facing the NW side of the Gulf of Thermai, in NW Aegean Sea, in NW Mainland Greece. *220*

Olmeios : spring at the foot of Mount Helikon in Boiotia, SE mainland Greece. *212*

Oloösson : town in NE Thessalia, in the area of Perrhaibia, N of modern Elassòn, in CN mainland Greece. *220*

Olophixos : city on the CE coast of the peninsula Akti, in
   EChalkidike, on the NW of the Aegean Sea, in NE mainland
   Greece. *228*
Olous : town at the E end of the island of Crete, now almost
   completely submerged, near Agios Nikolaos, in C Mediterranean
   Sea. *206*
Olpai : town of Amphilochia, probably on the CE coast of the Gulf
   of Ambrakia, in NW Aitolia, SW mainland Greece. *216*
Olumpia : major inland city in SE Elis, where the Alpheios and
   Kladeos rivers meet, SE of Herakleia, in NW Peloponnesos. *194*
Olumpos : 1. high mountain, Homeric Oulumpos, astride the
   border of NE Thessalia and S Macedonia, in NE mainland
   Greece, near the Gulf of Thermaikos in NW Aegean Sea. *220*; --2.
   mountain range of Phrygia, along the SE Sea of Propontis
   (Marmara), in NW Asia Minor, present-day NW Turkey. *252*; -- 3.
   mountain peak in the CN of the Troödos range, ancient
   Chionistra, near the W end of the island of Cyprus, at the NE end
   of the Mediterranean Sea. *256*
Olunthos : town on the N side of the Gulf of Kassandra, in the
   Chalkidike, NE of Potidaia, in NE Aegean Sea, NE mainland
   Greece. *224 & 228*
Oman : 1. gulf S of the Strait of Hormuz, in the NW Arabian Sea, W
   Asia. *264*; -- 2.country of the S Arabian peninsula, along the
   Arabian Sea, and surrounded on land by Yemen, Saudi Arabia
   and the Emirates, in W Asia. *188, 246 & 264*
Ombos : village in S Egypt, on the W bank of the Nile river, S of
   Coptos and the road to the Red Sea, in NE Africa. *242*
Omphace : inland town in the CS of the island of Sicily, in W
   Mediterranean Sea, W Europe. *234*
Omphale : inland city near the CS of the island of Sicily, in W
   Mediterranean Sea, W Europe. *234*
Omphis : town in the C Nile Delta, exact location uncertain, in N
   Egypt, NE Africa. *242*
Ôn : see Heliopolis. *242*
Onchestos : 1. Homeric town in a grove of the Tenerion Plain, in
   C Boiotia, on the S shore of Lake Kopais, NW of Thebes, in SE
   mainland Greece. *212*; -- 2. river flowing N from NE Phthiotis,
   across C Thessalia, along the hills of Kunoskephalai, into the
   Peneios river, in NE mainland Greece. *220 & 222*
Oneion : mount in Korinthia, probably S of Korinthos and W of the
   N Saronic Gulf, in SE mainland Greece. *202*
Onochonos : river flowing N from Phthiotis and joining the river
   Peneios in the plain of Thessalia, N mainland Greece. *220 & 222*
Onugnathos : cape in SE Lakonia, into the SE Gulf of Lakonia, in
   SE Peloponnesos. *198*

Ophis : river flowing N from Mount Pelagos, in SE Arkadia, past Mantineia, toward the Gulf of Korinthos, in NE Peloponnesos. *192*

Opiene : 1. area of N India, E of the Hydaspes river, in C India. *266*; -- 2. see Alexandria-in-Opiene. *266*

Opis : town of Babylonia on the Tigris river, in present-day S Iraq, W Asia. *258*

Opoeis : Homeric city, also called Opos, on the coast of SE Opuntian Lokris, S of Kunos, near the Gulf of Oropos, in CE mainland Greece. *214*

Opuntian : see Lokris. *190, 212 & 214*

Opos : 1. town in N Elis, on the bank of the Peneios river, exact location unknown, in NW Peloponnesos. *194*; -- 2. see Opoeis. *214*

Orbellos : mountain of E Thrace, in NE mainland Greece, modern Pirin mountain, in present-day SW Bulgaria, SE Europe. *226*

Orchomenos : 1. major city of Minuae, in CN Boiotia, on the NW shore of lake Kopais, in SE mainland Greece. *212*; 2. city of CN Arkadia, W of Mount Trachu, NW of Mantineia, in CN Peloponnesos. *192*

Ordessus : one of five rivers flowing from the Carpathian mountains, between the Pyretus and Tiarantus rivers, into the Danube river, in Scythia, present-day Romania, E Europe. *240*

Oreitidae : 1. area in the region of Sangada, present-day SE Pakistan, C Asia. *264*; -- 2. see Alexandria-in-Oreitidae. *264*

Oreitis : area in E Gedrosia, present-day SW Pakistan, C Asia. *264*

Oreos : see Histiaia. *228*

Oresthasion : town in SE Arkadia, between SE of Haimoniae and SW of Asea, in CS Peloponnesos. *192*

Oresthis : area, probably in CS Arkadia, C Peloponnesos. *192*

Orestia : town of NW Aitolia, N of Amphilochian Argos, E of the Gulf of Ambrakia, in SW mainland Greece. *216*

Orestis : area in N Epeiros, near the border with SW Illyria, E of Chaonia, in N mainland Greece. *218*

Orfanou : see Pieria gulf. *224 & 228*

Orion : town in the NW of the island of Crete, near Rithumna, in C Mediterranean Sea. *204*

Ormara : city, in ancient S Gedrosia, E of Bagisara, on the N coast of the Arabian Sea, in present-day S Pakistan, C Asia. *264*

Ormenion : Homeric city in S Thessalia, exact location uncertain, CN mainland Greece. *220*

Orneiae : Homeric city of NW Argolis, SW of Arantia, in NE Peloponnesos. *202*

Oroatis : river of Persia, also called Diz river, flowing S from Elam
(Susiana), through present-day SW Iran, into the Persian Gulf, in
W Asia. *258*

Orobatis : village near the Khyber Pass, in Bactria, present-day NE
Afghanistan, C Asia. *262*

Orobiae : town in the NW of the island of Euboia, on the Gulf of
Oropos, opposite Opuntian Lokris, in CE mainland Greece. *228*

Orontes : river, also called Axios, flowing N from Coele Syria
between the Lebanon and Anti-Lebanon mountains through
Syria and SE Turkey into the Mediterranean Sea, in W Asia. *256*

Oropos : 1. gulf between Opuntian Lokris and Boiotia to the W
and the N island of Euboia to the E, in SE mainland Greece.*212,
214, 222 & 228*; -- 2. town in NE Boiotia, exact location
uncertain, along this Gulf. *212*; -- 3. city in the territory
Amphiareion, near the E border between N Attika and S Boiotia,
near the Gulf of Petalion, in SE mainland Greece. *210*

Orracia : small island, off the coast of S Carmania, in SE Persian
Gulf, C Asia. *264*

Orsinos : river of Caria, flowing N and joining the Maeander river
as a tributary, in SW Asia Minor, present-day SW Turkey. *254*

Orthe : town in CE Thessalia, on the edge of the plain, near
Kedros, in CN mainland Greece. *220*

Ortugia : 1. mythical island, perhaps the island of Delos, in the
Cyclades, CW Aegean Sea. *230 & 269*; -- 2. island adjacent to SE
of Siracusa on the SE of the island of Sicily, in the W Mediterranean Sea, W Europe. *236*

Oruxis : mountain in NE Arkadia, SE of the river Ladonas, in NE
Peloponnesos. *192*

Osca : city of CN Iberia (Spain), modern Huesca, S of the Pyrenaei
mountain range, in W Europe. *232*

Oskios : river flowing N from the Rhodope mountains of Thrace,
in present-day Bulgaria, through Romania, into the Danube river
as a tributary, in SE Europe. *226*

Osmanaga : lagoon in SW Messenia, SW Peloponnesos, E of the
Bay of Voidokoilia and N of the Bay of Navarino. *196*

Osmaniye : town of SW Urartu, in E Cilicia, E of Toprakkale, in
present-day SE Turkey, W Asia. *256*

Ossa : mountain, later called Kissavos, forming a range with
Mount Pelion, separated from Mount Olumpos to the N by the
Vale of Tempe, on the NE side of Thessalia, in NE mainland
Greece, along the Aegean Sea. *220*

Ostia : seaport on the Tyrrhenian Sea, SW of Rome, in CW Italy, W
Europe. *238*

Osuna : inland city of Iberia, present-day S Spain, halfway
between Hispalis and Malaca, in W Europe. *232*

Othris : mountain range from CS Thessalia, S through N Achaia Phthiotis, then E toward N island of Euboia, in CE mainland Greece. *220*

Otranto : strait at the narrowest point between SE Italy and N Epeiros, present-day Albania, separating the Adriatic Sea in the N from the Ionian Sea in the S, in W Europe. *238*

Otzaki : ancient site in CN Thessalia, famous for its pottery style, N of the Gulf of Volos, in N mainland Greece. *220*

Ouxioi : tribal land in Susiana, between Elam and Persis, in present-day CW Iran, W Asia. *264*

Oxus : river of CN Asia, modern Amu Darya, flowing NW from the Hindu Kush, through Bactria, along the SW border of Uzbekistan with Turkmenistan, into the Aral Sea. *187, 260 & 262*

Oxydracae : tribal land located in N India, SE of the Hydraotes river and NE of the region of Malli, in C Asia. *266*

Oxyrhynchos : town in C Egypt, near the W bank of the Nile river, S of Herakleopolis, in NE Africa. *242*

Ozolian : see Lokris. *190 & 214*

P

Pachinus : harbor town at the SE tip of the island of Sicily, in W Mediterranean Sea. W Europe. *236*

Pactolos : river flowing from Mount Sardene, in Lydia, past Sardis down in the plain, then joining the river Hermos, before entering the Aegean Sea, near Smyrna, in present day CW Turkey, W Asia. *252*

Paeania : village of CS Attika, in the hills of Mount Humettos, N of Sphettos, in SE mainland Greece. *208*

Paesos : Homeric city of Troas, N of Troy, in present-day NW Turkey, W Asia. *250*

Paestum : see Poseidonia. *238*

Pagai : seaport at the SE end of the Gulf of Korinthos, in Megaris, SE mainland Greece. *210*

Pagasitikos : see Pagassai. *220 & 222*

Pagassai : 1. gulf shared by E Achaia Phthiotis and SE Thessalia, also known as Volos, modern Pagasitikos, in CN mainland Greece, N of the island of Euboia, in CW Aegean Sea. *220 & 222*; -- 2. seaport city, also called Volos, archaeological site called Pelromagula, perhaps the same as Iolkos or Dimini, N of this Gulf, in SE Thessalia. *220*

Paghman : city in ancient Bactria, near Alexandria-Kapisu, in present-day NE Afghanistan, C Asia. *262*

Paionia : 1. see Greek Macedonia. *224* -- 2. tribal area in CE Macedonia, N of the Chalkidike, between the rivers Axios and Strumon, near Thrace, in NE mainland Greece, covering modern Macedonia and a portion of Bulgaria, in E Europe. *224*

Pakistan : modern country of CS Asia, bordering the Arabian Sea to the S and stretching as far N as the Hindu Kush, E of Iran & Afghanistan and W of India & China, in C Asia. *188, 246, 260, 262, 264 & 266*

Palaia : ancient part of the city of Volos at the N end of the Gulf of Volos (Pagassai) in NE mainland Greece. *220*

Palaiokastro : 1. seaport city on the W side of the Bay of Herakleion, CN coast of the island of Crete, in C Mediterranean Sea. *206*; -- 2. hill (akropolis) in C Pellana, in C Lakonia, SE Peloponnesos. *198*; -- 3. site in Messenia, N of the Bay of Navarino, in SW Peloponnesos. *196*; -- 4. seaport on the S coast of the island of Cyprus, in NE Mediterranan Sea, W Asia. *256*

Palaiopolis : town on the W coast of island of Andros, in the N Cyclades, CW Aegean Sea. *230*

Palaira : town in NW Akarnania, N of Sollion, in SW mainland Greece. *216*

Pale : town on the W coast of the island of Kephallenia in the Ionian Sea, opposite W Akarnania, in CW mainland Greece. *216*

Paleochoria : site somewhere in Messenia, SW Peloponnesos. *196*

Palermo : see Panormos. *234*

Palestine : region covering both sides of the Jordan river, surrounded by the N Litani river and mount Hermon in the N, Syria in the E, the Negev desert in the S and the Mediterranean Sea in the W, at some ancient time a part of Greater Syria, W Asia. *246 & 258*

Palestrina : see Praeneste. *238*

Palice : inland city on the SE side of the island of Sicily, exact location uncertain, in W Mediterranean Sea, W Europe. *236*

Palimbothra : see Patna. *266*

Pallacopas : canal in Sumer, along the W bank of the Euphrates river, from Babylon through the marshlands of present-day S Iraq, into the N Persian Gulf, in W Asia. *258*

Pallantion : city of SE Arkadia, N of Mount Boreos, in CE Peloponnesos. *192*

Pallene : 1. town E of Athens, near N Mount Humettos, in C Attika, SE mainland Greece. *208*; -- 2. see Kassandra. *228*

Palmyra : city in N Syria, on the W bank of the Euphrates river, in W Asia. *258*

Paluka : town on the NE coast of the island of Salamis, in N
Saronic Gulf, SE mainland Greece. *208*

Pamisos : 1. river of CS Messenia, carrying S the flow of the river
Elektra from the N of Messenia, into the CN end of the Gulf of
Messenia, in SW Peloponnesos. *196*;-- 2. river flowing N as
tributary joining the river Peneios in the plain of Thessalia, in N
mainland Greece. *220*

Pamphylia : region of CS Anatolia, present-day CS Turkey,
between Lycia to the W and Cilicia to the E, S of Pisidia and N of
Gulf of Antalya, along the NE Mediterranean Sea, in W Asia. *256*

Pan : cave NW of Marathon, in NE Attika, SE mainland Greece. *210*

Panachaikon : mountains separating CS Achaia from NW Arkadia,
in CN Peloponnesos. *200*

Panagurishte : town of NW Thrace, in Ancient NE mainland
Greece, present-day Romania, SE Europe. *226*

Panakton : town of NW Attika, NE of Eleutherae, in SE mainland
Greece. *210*

Panayia Gourtsouli : see Ptolis. *192*

Pangaion : mount E of Amphipolis in SW Thrace, E of the
Chalkidike peninsula, near the coast of the Aegean Sea, in NE
mainland Greece. *226*

Panhellenios : mountain on the E side of the island of Aegina, in
the Saronic Gulf, SE mainland Greece. *208*

Panj : river of Margiane, flowing SW from the Hindu Kush, joining
the Cophen river N of Kabul, in Afghanistan, C Asia. *262*

Panjnad : river formed by the confluence of five rivers of the
Punjab, namely Hydaspes, Acesines, Hydraotes, Zaradros and
Hyphasis, all flowing SW and emptying into the Indus river, in C
Asia. *266*

Panjshir : valley N of the Khawak pass through the Hindu Kush
mountain, in Bactria, present-day N Pakistan, C Asia. *262*

Pannonia : see Greek Macedonia. *224*

Panopeios : 1. see Phanotis. *214*; -- 2. see Kume. *250*

Panopolis : see Chemmis. *242*

Panormos : 1. city in CN Achaia, near the SW shore of the Gulf of
Korinthos, E of Bolina, in CN Peloponnesos. *200*; -- 2. ancient
city of Epeiros, in Molossia, NW mainland Greece. *218*; -- 3.
Ionian town on the E coast of the SE Aegean Sea, N of the Gulf of
Iasos, in present-day SW Turkey, SW Asia Minor. *254*; -- 4. village
in the CN of the island of Crete, W of Eleutherna, in CS Medi-
terranean Sea. *206*; -- 5. coastal town, modern Palermo, on the
NW side of the island of Sicily, on the coast of the S Tyrrhenian
Sea, in W Europe. *234*.

Pantacyas : river at the E end of the island of Sicily, possibly N of
Siracusa, in W Mediterranean Sea, W Europe. *236*

Pantelleria : small island of the W Mediterranean Sea, S of Sicily and E of Tunisia, between W Europe and N Africa. *244*

Pantikapaion : 1. branch of the delta of the Danube river, discharging into the Euxine (Black) Sea, in Scythia, present-day Romania, SE Europe. *240*; -- 2. city in the N Crimea, also known as Kerch, S of the Sea of Maeotis (Azov), in S Ukraine, SE Europe. *248*

Paphlagonia : region CS of the Euxine (Black) Sea, surrounded by Bithynia in the W, Pontos in the E and Galatia in the S, in N Anatolia, present-day NW Turkey, W Asia. *252*

Paphos : two towns on the SW coast of the island of Cyprus, at the E end of the Mediterranean Sea, in W Asia: 1. S of the other, *256*; -- 2. N of the other. *256*

Papoura : ancient site on the CS coast of the island of Crete, in C Mediterranean Sea. *204*

Paprëmis : city at the opening of the C Nile Delta, near Memphis, in N Egypt, NE Africa. *242*

Parachoathras : high mountains, modern Elburz, S of the Caspian Sea and N of Tehrãn, in N Media, present-day N Iran, W Asia. *260*

Paraetanece : city of Media, S of Tehrãn, in the area of present-day Ispahan, CW Iran, W Asia. *260*

Paraitonion : town, modern Mersa Matruh, on the coast of the Mediterranean Sea, in NW Egypt, NE Africa. *242*

Paralia : area in S Attika, SE mainland Greece. *208*

Parapamisadai : 1. area of C Asia, between Bactria to the N, Gandhãra to the E, Anachosia to the S and Parthia to the W, in present-day NE Afghanistan, C Asia. *246 & 262*; -- 2. mountains in this region. *262*

Parapamisus : large mountain range, called Caucasus by the ancient Greeks, present-day Hindu Kush, in Bactria, stretching N-SW in present-day N Pakistan and N into W Afghanistan, C Asia. *187, 246, 262 & 266*

Parapotamii : 1. ancient river, in NE Phokis, tributary of the river Kephisos, in CS mainland Greece. *214*; -- 2. town at the confluence of this river and the river Kephisos. *214*

Parauaea : area of C Epeiros, S of Molossia, in NW mainland Greece. *218*

Pareitacae : area of E Sogdiana, present-day S Kazakhstan, in C Asia. *262*

Parga : ancient site on the W coast of Epeiros, along the Ionian Sea, in NW mainland Greece. *218*

Parion : city of Hellespontine, at the SE end of the Hellespontos (Dardanelles), in NW Asia Minor, present-day NW Turkey. *250*

Parma : Etruscan town of CN Italy, in W Europe. *238*

Parnassos : 1. mountain in CW Phokis, providing its S slope to Delphi, in CS mainland Greece. *214*; -- 2. small wooded valley in the foothills of this mountain. *214*

Parnes : mount in CN Attika, source of the Charadros river, in SE mainland Greece. *210*

Parnon : mountain range extending NS from SW Argolis to CN Lakonia, in SE Peloponnesos. *198 & 202*

Paroikia : town in the NW of the island of Paros, in the Cyclades, CW Aegean Sea. *230*

Paropus : inland town in the CS of the island of Sicily, exact location uncertain, in W Mediterranean Sea, W Europe. *234*

Paros : island in CS of the Cyclades, famous for its white marble, W of Naxos, in CW Aegean Sea. *230*

Parrhasia : 1. area in the SW of Arkadia, CN Peloponnesos. *192*; -- 2. city in this area, W of Megalopolis. *192*

Parrhasios : mountain range in CS Arkadia, source of the river Alpheios, in CS Peloponnesos. *192*

Parthaunisa : see Nisa. *260*

Partheneios : 1. mountain range, running NS along the border between SW Argolis and CE Arkadia, in NE Peloponnesos. *202*; -- 2. river of SE Elis, flowing SW between the rivers Harpenites to the N and Leukuanias to the S, into the Alpheios river, in CW Peloponnesos. *194* ; -- 3. river separating W Paphlagonia from E Bithynia, flowing N into the Euxine (Black) Sea, in NW Anatolia, present-day NW Turkey, in W Asia. *252*

Parthenos Phreatia : fountain. now known as Maiden Well, N of the Bay of Eleusis, in NW Attika, SE mainland Greece. *210*

Parthia : region S of the Caspian Sea and NE of the Desert of Kavir, in E Media, also called Parthyaea, mainly the area of Khorāsān, in NE Iran, including at its largest expansion present-day Turkmenistan, Afghanistan and N Pakistan, in W and C Asia. *246 & 260*

Parthyaea : see Parthia. *260*

Pasalimani : 1. small island in SW of the Sea of Propontis (Marmara), in present-day NW Turkey, W Asia. *250*; -- 2. ancient site a short distance from Sounion, up the E coast of Attika, in SE mainland Greece *208*; -- 3. see Zea. *208*

Pasargadai : city S of the region of Anshan in Persis, N of Persepolis, in present-day SW Iran, W Asia. *264*

Pasitigris : river of Babylonia, S Mesopotamia, flowing SW from the Zagros Mountains, into the Tigris river near the N end of the Persian Gulf, in present-day S Iraq, W Asia. *258*

Patalene : region of SW India, along the Arabian Sea, in C Asia. *266*

Patara : seaport city of W Lycia, opposite the island of Rhodes, in SW Asia Minor, present-day SW Turkey. *254*

Patmos : island of the NW Dodekanesoi, near Lipsoi, in SE Aegean Sea. *230*

Patna : city, ancient Greek name Palimbothra, at the junction of the Ganges, Gandak and Son rivers, in CE India, C Asia, *266*

Patrai : seaport city in NW Achaia, modern Patras, on the E side of the Gulf of Patraikos, at the S end of the Long Walls, in NW Peloponnesos. *200*

Patraikos : gulf of the CE Ionian Sea, leading to the W entrance of the Gulf of Korinthos, S of Aitolia and N of Achaia, in SW mainland Greece. *200 & 216*

Patras : see Patrai. *200*

Patroklos : island of the CW Aegean Sea, off the SW end of Attika, in SE mainland Greece. *208*

Pattaia : town on the border between Gedrosia and Patalene, at the head of the Indus river delta into the Arabian Sea, in SW India, CS Asia. *266*

Paus : town in NW Arkadia, on the W side of the river Soron, in NE Peloponnesos. *192*

Pautalia : town in NE Macedonia, W of Mount Dunax, in N mainland Greece. *224*

Pavlopetri : submerged city of SE Peloponnesos, off the coast of the peninsula Malea in the Mirtóön Sea. *198*

Paximadhia : small island S of the CW of the island of Crete, in C Mediterranean Sea. *204*

Paxos : one of the Ionian islands, S of Kerkura (Corfu), off the coast of Epeiros, in NW mainland Greece. *218*

Payas : river flowing W from the Amanos mountains, in E Cilicia, past Pinaros, into the E side of the Gulf of Issos, in present-day E Turkey, W Asia. *256*

Pedaion : Homeric city in Troas, NW Asia Minor, present-day NW Turkey. *250*

Pedasos : 1. city of SW Messenia, near Pulos, in SW Peloponnesos. *196*; -- 2. city on the border between S Troas and NW Mysia, at the entrance of the Gulf of Edremit, facing the N of the island of Lesbos, in NW Asia Minor, present-day NW Turkey. *250*

Pediaios : river on the island of Cyprus, flowing N from the mountains in C Cyprus, then E, past Salamis, toward the Mediterranean Sea, in W Asia. *256*

Pedion : mountain range in CW Arkadia, N of the city of Heraia and S of the river Tithoa, in C Peloponnesos. *192*

Pefkakia : promontory at the N harbor of Demetrias, N of the Gulf of Volos, in SE Thessalia, NE mainland Greece. *220*

Peiraios : 1. seaport city of W Attika, known as Piraeus, with three harbors on the Saronic Gulf, SW of Athens, in SE mainland Greece. *208*; 2. peninsula harboring the seaport. *208*

Peirene : area of Korinthia, S of Akrokorinthos, at the SE end of the Gulf of Korinthos, in NW Argolis, NE Peloponnesos. *202*

Peiros : 1. river flowing NW from the E Erumanthos mountain of SW Achaia, into the Gulf of Patraikos, in NW Peloponnesos. *200*; -- 2. see Acheloos river. *216 & 220*

Pelagonia : tribal area from E Illyria to CS Macedonia, N of Epeiros, in the Balkans, ancient NW mainland Greece, present-day Macedonia, E Europe. *224*

Pelagos : mountainous area in SE Arkadia, W of Mount Partheneios, S of Skope, in CE Peloponnesos. *192*

Pele : small Ionian island, somewhere near the island of Chios, in CE Aegean Sea, opposite Klazomenae, on the CW coast of Asia Minor. *230*

Pelinna : town in N Thessalia, exact location uncertain, in CN mainland Greece. *220*

Pelion : 1. mountain range of Magnesia, in SE Thessalia, from NE of the Gulf of Volos in the S to Mount Ossa in the N, in NE mainland Greece. *220*; -- 2. town in CS Illyria, present-day Albania, near Macedonia, in NW mainland Greece. *218*

Pella : 1. city in CS Macedonia, ancient Bounomos, originally on the N coast of the Gulf of Thermaikos, NW Aegean Sea, but present-day inland, NW of the gulf, in NE mainland Greece. *224*; -- 2. city in Samaria, ancient Palestine, present-day N Jordan, S of Gadara, on the E side of the Jordan river, in W Asia. *258*

Pellana : town with cemetery N of Sparta, in NE Lakonia, SE Peloponnesos. *198*

Pellanis : spring at Pellana, in NE Lakonia, SE Peloponnesos. *198*

Pellene : inland town in E Achaia, near the border with Argolis, E of the river Krios and S of the Gulf of Korinthos, in NE Peloponnesos. *200*

Peloponnesos : region shaped as a peninsula, the S half of Greece, S of the Gulfs of Patroklos & Korinthos, the Ionian Sea to the W, the Saronic Gulf & Mirtóön Sea to the E, and the Mediterranean Sea to the S. *190- 202*

Pelops : isles in the Saronic Gulf, between the island of Aigina and the E coast of the peninsula of Argolis, in SE mainland Greece. *202*

Pelorus : cape at the NE end of the island of Sicily, on the Strait of Messina, separating it from S Italy, in W Europe. *236*

Pelos : island in SW of the Cyclades, E of Melos, in the Aegean Sea. *230*

Pelromagula : see Pagassai. *220*

Pelusion : town, modern Port Said, on the SE coast of the Mediterranean Sea, on the E side of the Nile Delta, in N Egypt, N of the Sinai Peninsula, in NE Africa. *242*

Peneios : 1. major river flowing from the Pindos mountains of E Epeiros, with many tributaries through the plain of Thessalia, past Larissa, to a gorge at the vale of Tempe, between Mounts Olumpos and Ossa, into the Gulf of Thermai in W Aegean Sea, N mainland Greece. *218 & 220*; -- 2. lake formed by the river Peneios before the Vale of Tempe. *220*; -- 3. river of N Elis in NW Peloponnesos, flowing W from Mount Erumanthos, past the cities of Pulos and Elis, into the Ionian Sea. *194*;-- 4. plain where the city of Elis is located in N region of Elis. *194*

Pentelikon : mountain, also called Brilessos, E of Acharnae, in CE Attika, in SE mainland Greece. *210*

Peparethos : island of the Thessalian Sporades, in CW Aegean Sea. *228*

Pephnos : seaport city of CW Lakonia, on the CE coast of the Gulf of Lakonia, in SE Peloponnesos. *198*

Perachora : 1. harbor opposite the city of Korinthos, on the NW side of the Bay of Salamis, in SW Megaris, CS mainland Greece. *210*; -- 2. city at this harbor. *210*

Peraithea : town S of river Elaphos and E of Megalopolis, in SE Arkadia, C Peloponnesos. *192*

Perati : harbor town in SE Attika, along the Aegean Sea, near Laurion, in SE mainland Greece. *208*

Perea : area of ancient Palestine, on the E side of the Jordan river, in present day C Jordan, W Asia. *258*

Pereia : town of SE Thessalia, probably in Magnesia, in NE mainland Greece. *220*

Perga : see Antalya. *256*

Pergamon : city of Mysia, modern Bergama, a short distance inland from the coast of the Aegean Sea, along the Kaikos river, in NW Asia Minor, present-day NW Turkey. *250*

Pergamos : 1. town in the S of the peninsula Akrotiri, between Kudonia and Aptera, in NW island of Crete, C Mediterranean Sea. *204*; -- 2. hill used as citadel in the city of Troy, in present-day NW Turkey, W Asia. *250*

Perinthos : town of E Thrace, on the CN shore of the Sea of Propontis, in present-day NW Turkey, SE Europe. *226*

Periphlegeton : branch of the mythological river Stux, tributary of the river Acheron, in Hades. *268*

Peristeria : inland town in NW Messenia, NW of Messene, in SW Peloponnesos. *196*

Perivolia : town in SW Arkadia, between Bassai to the N and Phigalia to the W, in C Peloponnesos. *192*

Perkote : Homeric city of Troas, NE of Troy, in present-day NW Turkey, W Asia. *250*

Permessos : spring at the foot of Mount Helikon in Boiotia, SE mainland Greece. *212*

Perrhaibia : territory of N Thessalia, E of the Peneios river, in C mainland Greece. *220*

Persepolis : city in the S region of Persis, S of Pasargadai, in Persia, present-day S Iran, W Asia. *264*

Persia : see Media and Iran. *260*

Persian : 1. gulf as an arm of the Arabian Sea, in Antiquity called Red Sea, between SW Iran on the E side, and Iraq, Kuwait and Arabia on the W side, in W Asia. *188, 246, 258 & 264*; -- 2. gates like a narrow pass in Persis, W of Ardakan, in present-day S Iran, W Asia. *264*

Persis : area in SW Persia, bordering the E side of the Persian Gulf, in present-day S Iran. *246, 260 & 264*

Perusia : Etruscan town in CE Italy, W Europe. *238*

Peshãwar : 1. valley of ancient Bactria, also referred to as Khyber area, S of the Khyber Pass, in present-day NW Pakistan, C Asia. *262*; -- 2. city in this area. *262*

Petalion : gulf separating SE Boiotia and NE Attika from the S of the island of Euboia, in CW Aegean Sea. *210, 212 & 222*

Peteon : Homeric town of W Boiotia, near Thebes, in CS mainland Greece. *212*

Petra : 1. town of Nabatea, biblical Sela, in present-day SW Jordan, W Asia, N of the Gulf of Aqaba. *258*; -- 2. town on the Rhegion region, at the SW tip of Italy, exact location unknown. *238*; -- 3. town of CW Thrace, W of Razlog, in present-day Bulgaria, E Europe. *226*

Petralona : cave in SE Macedonia, near Salonika, in N mainland Greece. *224*

Petrosaka : town in CE Arkadia, SE of Mount Phalanthos and N of Mount Mainalos, in C Peloponnesos. *192*

Petrovouni : hill of S Aitolia, near the W entrance to the Gulf of Patraikos where Pleuron was once located, in SW mainland Greece. *216*

Peuce : city of NE Thrace, N of the Danube river, in NE mainland Greece, present-day Romania, E Europe. *226*

Peucelaotis : city near the Khyber Pass, in present-day NW India, C Asia. *266*

Phaeacia : see Phaiekia. *269*

Phaedrias : city in SW Arkadia, E of the border with Messenia, in CS Peloponnesos. *192*

Phagres : city on the coast of the CN Aegean Sea, E of the Chalkidike Peninsulas, in SW Thrace, NE mainland Greece. *226*

Phaia : port city of CW Elis, in CW Peloponnesos, N of Mount Ichthos and W of Letrini, opposite the island of Zakinthos, in the Ionian Sea. *194*

Phaiekia : Mythical land, also spelled Phaeacia and called Skeria, perhaps the island of Crete, in C Mediterranean Sea. *269*

Phaistos : town and palace site in the SW of the island of Crete, near the gulf of Mesara, in C Mediterranean Sea. *204*

Phakion : town in C Thessalia, N of Pharsalos, in NE mainland Greece. *220*

Phalaisia : town in CS Arkadia, E of the river Karnion, in SE Peloponnesos. *192*

Phalanna : 1. town in CN Thessalia, NE of Larissa, NW mainland Greece. *220*; -- 2. town on the W side of the island of Crete, exact location uncertain, in C Mediterranean Sea. *204*

Phalanthos : mountain range running NS between Anemosa to the E and Methudrion to the W, in C Arkadia, C Peloponnesos. *192*

Phalarium : coastal town in the CS side of the island of Sicily, in W Mediterranean Sea, W Europe. *234*

Phalaros : river in SW Boiotia, flowing from Mount Helikon, NE into Lake Kopais, in SE mainland Greece. *212*

Phalasarna : port town, probably on the Grambousa peninsula, in the NW of the island of Crete, exact location uncertain, in C Mediterranean Sea. *204*

Phaleron : 1. bay E of Peiraia, on the NE side of the Saronic Gulf, in SE mainland Greece. *208*; -- 2. seaport town on this Bay, in SW Attika. *208*

Phanagoria : town on S Sea of Maeotis, E of the Strait of Kerch, connecting it to the Euxine (Black) Sea, in SE Europe. *248*

Phanai : cape at the S tip of the island of Chios, in CE Aegean Sea. *230*

Phanotis : town, also called Panopeios, W of Cheronia, in C Phokis, CS mainland Greece. *214*

Pharai : 1. inland city of SW Achaia, S of the river Peiros, in NW Peloponnesos. *200*; -- 2. city near the NE corner of the Gulf of Messenia, in SE Messenia, SW Peloponnesos. *196*

Pharbaetus : town in the C Nile Delta, N Egypt, NE Africa. *242*

Pharis : Homeric city of Lakedaimon, in C Lakonia, exact location unknown, in SW Peloponnesos. *198*

Pharmakoussai : small islands in the Bay of Eleusis in NW Attika, N of the Bay of Salamis in the N Saronic Gulf. *210*

Pharos : island in the E Mediterranean Sea, near the W Delta of the Nile river, presently a peninsula at Alexandria, in NW Egypt, NE Africa. *242*

Pharsalos : city in the C plain ot Thessalia, along river Aridanos, in N mainland Greece. *220*

Phaselis : city of SE Lycia, on the N coast of the E Mediterranean Sea, in SW Asia Minor, present-day SW Turkey. *256*

Phasis : 1. river, ancient Arkturos in Scythia, also called Rioni river, flowing SW from the Caucasus mountains, into the CE Euxine (Black) Sea, in present-day Georgia, SE Europe. *248*; -- 2. town, near modern Poti and also called Poti at one time, on the coast of the E Euxine (Black) Sea, S of the mouth of this river. *248*

Phelloe : inland city of SE Achaia, SE of Aigeira, in NE Peloponnesos. *200*

Pheneos : town in NE Arkadia, W of Mount Kullene, in NE Peloponnesos. *192*

Pherai : 1. city of SE Thessalia, near the border with Achaia Phthiotis, identified with modern Velestinon, In NE mainland Greece. *220*; -- 2. city of SW Messenia, near Pulos, in SW Peloponnesos. *196*

Pherusa : ancient city of SE Megaris, near Nisaia, on the W side of the Saronic Gulf, in SE mainland Greece. *210*

Phigalia : city in SW Arkadia, N of the river Neda and the border with Messenia, in CS Peloponnesos. *192*

Phikios : mount in SE Thessalia, near the border with Phthiotis, in NE mainland Greece. *220*

Philai : town on the bank of the Nile river, S of the island of Elephantine, in S Egypt, NE Africa. *242*

Philippi : see Krenides. *226*

Philippopolis : 1. inland town of CW Thrace, modern Plovdiv, along the Maritsa river, in present-day Bulgaria, SE Europe. *226*; -- 2. see Thebes in Phthiotis. *222*

Philister : seaport of SW Illyria, in NW mainland Greece, facing the heel of S Italy across the S Adriatic Sea. *218*

Philistia : SW portion of ancient Palestine occupied by the Philistines, NE of Egypt, in W Asia. *258*

Phintias : town in the CS side of the island of Sicily, near the coast of W Mediterranean Sea, in W Europe. *234*

Phla : island in lake Tritonis, S Tunisia, CN Africa. *244*

Phlegra : mythical land of the Giants, probably a plain near a volcanic mountain, such as Mount Aetna in Sicily, W Europe. *236 & 269*

Phlios : town of NW Argolis, N of Keleae, in NE Peloponnesos. *202*

Phlua : inlandtown NE of Athens, in C Attika, SE mainland Greece. *210*

Phoenicia : region at the E end of the Mediterranean Sea, covering modern Lebanon, NW Syria and N Israel, in W Asia. *256*

Phoenikos : 1. harbor city in CS Messenia, in SW Peloponnesos, opposite the Oinussai islands. **196**;-- 2. harbor city in the W peninsula Mimas, opposite the island of Chios, in W Lydia, CW Asia Minor, present-day CW Turkey. **254**

Phoenix : river in CN Achaia, flowing W of river Meganitas, N into the Gulf of Korinthos, in CN Peloponnesos. **200**

Phokaia : city of N Ionia, in CW Asia Minor, N of the estuary of the Hermos (Gediz) river, on a promontory above the Gulf of Candath (Izmir), in the CE Aegean Sea. **250**

Phokis : region along the N shore of the Gulf of Korinthos, surrounded by Lokris, Doris and Boiotia, in CS mainland Greece. **190, 212 & 214**

Pholoë : 1. city in CW Arkadia, NE of Olumpia in Elis, CN Peloponnesos. **192**; -- 2. mountain in CE Elis, near the border with Arkadia, in NW Peloponnesos. **194**

Phorbantia : small island W of the island of Sicily, in W Mediterranean Sea, W Europe. **234**

Phrearrhioi : village in CS Attika, in SE mainland Greece. **208**

Phrikonis : see Kume. **250**

Phrixae : Minyan town in the SE of Elis, E of Olumpia and S of the Alpheios river, in CW Peloponnesos. **194**

Phrukos : site of a fort in Elis, exact location unknown, in NW Peloponnesos. **194**

Phrygia : region of CW Asia Minor, S of the Sea of Propontis (Marmara), E of Troas and N of Mysia, at one time extending E to S of the Euxine (Black) Sea, in present-day NW Turkey. **190, 248, 250 & 252**

Phthia : see the city of Phthiotis. **222**

Phthiotis : 1. region SE of Thessalia and N of Malis and Opuntian Lokris, also called Achaia Phthiotis, in E mainland Greece. **190, 214, 218, 220 & 228**;-- 2. city in this region, also called Homeric Phthia, on the border with Thessalia to the N. **222**

Phthires : see Latmos mountain range. **254**

Phulake : Homeric town, also called Protesilaos, in NE Achaia Phthiotis, NW of Almuros, in NE mainland Greece. **222**

Phulakopi : Town in the N of the island of Melos, in the SW Cyclades, C Aegean Sea. **230**

Phule : fortified village on a rolling slope of Mount Parnes, in CN Attika, near the border with Boiotia, in SE mainland Greece. **210**

Phuska : site probably located in SE Macedonia, NE mainland Greece. **224**

Phutia : town probably located in C Akarnania, SW mainland Greece. **216**

Picedo : town at the SW entrance to the Gulf of Taranto, in S Italy, W Europe. **238**

Picene : region in the Apennine mountains, SE Umbria, NE Italy, W Europe. *238*

Pieria : 1. hills near Eleutherae, in NW Attika, SE mainland Greece. *210*; -- 2. tribal area of CS Macedonia, NE of Thessalia, around Mount Olumpos and the city of Dion, in NE mainland Greece. *224*; -- 3. gulf, modern Orfanou, in NW Aegean Sea, NE of the Chalkidike, in SE Macedonia, NE mainland Greece. *224 & 228*; -- 4. sacred fountain in the area of this gulf. *224*; -- 5. area in the N of Phoenicia, along the NE coast of the Mediterranean Sea, in present-day NW Syria, W Asia. *256*

Pierion : town located somewhere in S Thessalia, NE mainland Greece. *220*

Pillars of Herakles : ancient name for the headlands on either side of the Strait of Gibraltar, one side at Gibraltar in SW Spain and the other at Spanish Ceuta in NW Africa. *187 & 232*

Piloros : town on the peninsula Sithonia of the C Chalkidike, N of Ampelos, in the N Aegean Sea, NE mainland Greece. *228*

Pinaros : town of E Cilicia, SE of Issos, near the NE coast of the Gulf of Issos, in present-day SE Turkey, W Asia. *256*

Pindos : 1. mountain range running NS from E Epeiros, near the border with Thessalia, across Thessalis into Macedonia, in CN mainland Greece. *218, 220 & 224*; -- 2. river flowing WE through Doris and Phokis, and becoming tributary of the Kephisos river, in CS mainland Greece. *214*; -- 3. one of a group of four cities, with Boion, Kitinion and Erineos, in the valley of the Pindos river, in Doris, CS mainland Greece. *214*

Piraeus : see Peiraios. *208*

Pirene : spring at the foot of Mount Helikon in Boiotia, source of stream flowing SW through Phokis, into the Gulf of Korinthos, in CS mainland Greece. *212*

Pirin : see Orbellos. *226*

Pir Sarai : 1. ancient, see Aornos mountain. *262*; -- 2. modern, see Aornos city. *266*

Pisa : 1. area straddling the border between SE Elis and CW Arkadia, N of the river Alpheios, in NW Peloponnesos. *192 & 194*; -- 2. town of SE Elis, between Olumpia to the W and Harpina to the E, in NW Peloponnesos. *194*

Pisae : Etruscan town of NE Italy, in W Europe. *238*

Pisidia : region of CS Turkey, at the W end of the Taurus Mountain range, N of Lycia and Pamphilia, and S of Phrygia, in W Asia. *256*

Pitane : Aiolian town, in W Lydia, on the NW coast of Asia Minor, along the Aegean Sea. *250*

Pithekoussai : small island of the Tyrrhenian Sea, near the entrance to the Bay of Naples, in SW Italy, W Europe. *238*

Pitiussa : island off the SW coast of the peninsula of Argolis, in the N Mirtóön Sea, NE Peloponnesos. *200*

Pitsa : town in E Achaia, S of the Gulf of Korinthos, near the border with Argolis, W of Sikuon, in NE Peloponnesos. *200*

Pitueia : town of Troas, on the S side of the Hellespontos, where it reaches the Sea of Propontis (Marmara), in NW Asia Minor, present-day NW Turkey. *250*

Plagktas : Homeric cliffs, Clashing Rocks, near Scylla and Charybdis, between NE Sicily and S Italy, in W Europe. *236*

Plakios : mountain of Mysia, above Thebe, in NW Asia Minor, present-day NW Turkey. *250*

Plataia : 1. area in SW Boiotia, on the N side of Mount Kithairon, in SE mainland Greece. *212*; -- 2. city in this area, overlooking the plain of the river Oëroë. *212*; -- 3. island of CS Mediterranean Sea, off the coast of Kyrenaika, in CN Africa. *244*

Platanias : 1. see Iardanos river. *204*; -- 2. city in the S of the Gulf of Khanion, at the mouth of this river, W of Khania, in the NW of the island of Crete, CS Mediterranean Sea. *204*

Platanios : river in NE Boiotia, flowing along the border with Opuntian Lokris, into the Gulf of Oropos, in CE mainland Greece. *212*

Plataniston : 1. river of SW Arkadia, tributary of the Helisson river, in CS Peloponnesos. *192*; -- 2. cape at the N end of the island of Kuthera, in the S Mirtóön Sea, S of Lakonia, in SE Peloponnesos. *198*

Platanos : village a short distance SW of Kisamos, in the NW of the island of Crete, C Mediterranean Sea. *204*

Plate : small island off the coast of Kyrenaica, facing Aziris, in NE Africa. *244*

Plati : town on the plain of Lasithi, S of the Gulf of Megambellou, in CE of the island of Crete, C Mediterranean Sea. *206*

Pleistos : river flowing W through the vale S of Delphi, in CW Phokis, into the Gulf of Krisa, in CS mainland Greece. *214*

Plemmyrium : 1. promontory at the SE corner of the harbor of Siracusa, in SE of the island of Sicily, W Mediterranean Sea, W Europe. *236*; -- 2. site of a nearby settlement and forts. *236*

Pleuron : city in SW Aitolia, at the W entrance of the Gulf of Patraikos, first occupying two hills, Guphtokastro and Petrovouni, then moved successively NE to the plain and to a site on Mount Arakunthos, in SW mainland Greece. *216*

Plovdiv : see Philippopolis. *226*

Pnyx : hill on the W side of the Akropolis in Athens, C Attika, SE mainland Greece. *208*

Po : see Eridanos river. *248*

Polichne : 1. city of C Messenia, between Dorion and Andania, in
  SW Peloponnesos. *196*; -- 2. town near Klazomenae, exact
  location unknown, in Lydia, CW Asia Minor, opposite the island
  of Chios, in CE Aegean Sea. *254*
Poland : country of W Europe, on the Baltic Sea, surrounded by
  Lithuania, Belarus, Ukraine, Hungary, Slovakia and Germany.
  188
Polis : 1. town on the W side of Akarnania, on the coast of the
  Ionian Sea, opposite Ithaka, in SW mainland Greece. *216*; -- 2.
  coastal city in the NW of the island of Cyprus, NE Mediterranean
  Sea, W Asia. *256*
Poluchna : town S of the Gulf of Khanion, W of the city of Khania,
  in NW island of Crete, C Mediterranean Sea. *204*
Poludora : see Spercheios. *214, 220 & 222*
Polurrenia : town in the NW of the island of Crete, near Kissamos,
  exact location uncertain, in C Mediterranean Sea. *204*
Polytimelus : river in N Sogdiana, modern Zarafshan, flowing
  from the mountains of present-day Tajikistan, into S Uzbekistan,
  past Samarkand and Bukhara, emptying in the desert before
  reaching the Oxus river, in C Asia. *262*
Pontinos : mountain W of Lerna, in SW Argolis, NE Peloponnesos.
  202
Pontos : 1. region of NW Asia Minor, S of the E Euxine (Black) Sea,
  E of Paphlagonia, present-day NW Turkey, W Asia. *252*; -- 2. see
  Euxine Sea. *252*
Poros : island in the NW Saronic Gulf, facing the Argolis
  peninsula, in NE Peloponnesos. *202*
Porti : site in the CS of the island of Crete, in C Mediterranean
  Sea. *206*
Porto Kayio : see Psamathos. *198*
Portomandri : harbor on the S side of the promontory of Agios
  Nikolaos, at Thorikos, opposite the harbor Frankolimani, in SE
  Attika, SE mainland Greece. *208*
Portugal : modern country along the Atlantic Ocean to the W and
  S, and Spain to the E and N, in SW Europe. *188 & 232*
Port Said : see Pelusion. *242*
Poseideïon : ancient city at the mouth of the Orontes river, on the
  coast of the NE Mediterranean Sea, in present-day Turkey, W
  Asia. *256*
Poseidon : site of a sanctuary on the coast of the NW Saronic Gulf,
  in NE Argolis, NE Peloponnesos. *202*
Poseidonia : town of Lucania, Roman Paestum, on the coast of
  the Tyrrherian Sea, S of Neapolis, in SW Italy, W Europe. *238*

Potamos : city in the SE of Attika, between Prasiai to the N and Thorikos to the S, near the coast of CW Aegean Sea, in SE mainland Greece. *208*

Poti : see Phasis city. *248*

Potidaia : seaport city, also called Kassandreia, on the isthmus at the top of the W peninsula Kassandra, in the Chalkidike, SE Macedonia, NE mainland Greece. *228*

Potidania : ancient city of Aitolia, exact location unknown, in C mainland Greece. *216*

Potniai : town S of Thebes, in CS Boiotia, SE mainland Greece. *212*

Praeneste : city of the Latium in C Italy, modern Palestrina, a short distance SE of Rome, in W Europe. *238*

Praisos : village E of the Gulf of Megambellou, at the CE end of the island of Crete, in C Mediterranean Sea. *206*

Praktios : Homeric city of Hellespontine, NE of Perkote, in NW Asia Minor, present-day NW Turkey, W Asia. *250*

Prasiai : 1. city in the SE of Attika, S of Stiria, in SE mainland Greece, on the coast of CW Aegean Sea. *208*; -- 2. seaport city on the coast of the Mirtóön Sea, in NE Lakonia, SE Peloponnesos. *198*

Prasias : see Kerkinitis. *226*

Prespa : two lakes of ancient W Macedonia, 1. Great (Megale) Prespa shared by present-day Greece, Albania and Macedonia. *224*; -- 2. Little (Mikra) Prespa, to the S, in SW Macedonia, NE mainland Greece. *224*

Preveza : modern city N of the entrance to the Gulf of Ambrakia, off the Ionian See, near the border between SW Epeiros and Akarna-nia, in SW mainland Greece. *218*

Priansos : town on a mountaintop, next to Gortus, in the CS of the island of Crete, C Mediterranean Sea. *204*

Priapos : town of Hellespontine, at the SW end of the Sea of Propontis (Marmara), in NW of present-day Turkey, W Asia. *250*

Priene : Ionian town on the coast of the Aegean Sea, now pushed inland by alluvion, S of the estuary of the river Maeander (Menderez) of Lydia, in present-day CW Turkey, W Asia. *254*

Prinias : 1. village in C of the island of Crete, in C Mediterranean Sea. *206*; -- 2. site at the E end of the island of Crete, exact location uncertain, in C Mediterranean Sea. *206*

Priniatiko : seaport city on the SW shore of the Gulf of Megambellou, at the E end of the island of Crete, in C Mediterranean Sea. *206*

Prino : town on the NW coast of the island of Thasos, in CN Aegean Sea. *228*

Prinos : town in CW Argolis, N of mount Artemision, in NE Peloponnesos. *202*

Probalinthos : town of CE Attika, between Mount Pentelikon to the W and the Gulf of Petalion to the E, in SE mainland Greece. *210*

Prodromos : village N of Trikala, in CW Thessalia, N mainland Greece. *220*

Prokonnesos : largest island in the W side of the Sea of Propontis (Marmara), in NW Asia Minor, present-day NW Turkey. *250*

Pronnai : town on the E coast of the island of Kephallenia in the Ionian Sea, W of Akarnania, in CW mainland Greece. *216*

Prophthasia : area of W Drangiana, modern Farah, in C Afghanistan, C Asia. *260*

Propontis : small sea, modern Marmara, connected with the Euxine (Black) Sea by the Bosporos and with the Aegean Sea by the Hellespontos (Dardanelles), in present-day NW Turkey, W Asia. *190, 226, 240, 250 & 252*

Pros : mount in the SW of the peninsula of Argolis, S of mount Thornax, in SE Argolis, NE Peloponnesos. *202*

Proschion : city NE of Pleuron, in SW Aitolia, SW mainland Greece. *216*

Prosopitis : island in the Delta of the Nile river, exact location unknown, in N Egypt, NE Africa. *242*

Prospalta : town in CS Attika, SW of Murrhinos, in SE mainland Greece. *208*

Prosumna : site beneath the sanctuary of Hera (Heraion), SE of Mukenae, in CN Argolis, NE Peloponnesos. *202*

Prote : desert island in the SE Ionian Sea, off the coast of CW Messenia, N of Pulos, in SW Peloponnesos. *196*

Protesilaos : see Phulake. *222*

Prusa : town of Phrygia, modern Bursa, inland S of the SE end of the Sea of Propontis, in NW Asia Minor, present-day NW Turkey. *252*

Psamathos : ancient port city of SW Lakonia, modern Porto Kayio, N of the cape of Tainaron, on the SW coast of the Gulf of Lakonia, in SE Peloponnesos. *198*

Pseira : small island near the NE coast of the island of Crete, at the entrance to the Gulf of Megambellou, in C Mediterranean Sea. *206*

Psiloneron : town on the SW coast of the Gulf of Khanion, in NW island of Crete, C Mediterranean Sea. *204*

Psiloritis : peek, see Ida. *204*

Psophis : city in NW Arkadia, at the juncture of the rivers Erimanthos and Aroanios, in CN Peloponnesos. *192*

Psuchro : town with sacred cave, W of Agios Nikolaos, in CE of the island of Crete, in C Mediterranean Sea. *206*

Psuria : small island in C Aegean Sea, NE of the island of Chios, opposite Mimas in CW Asia Minor. *230*

Psuttaleia : small island E of the island of Salamis, in N Saronic Gulf. *208*

Pteleon : 1. Homeric territory in SE Thessalia, on the border with Achaia Phthiotis, in CE mainland Greece. *220*; -- 2. site of a fort in E Ionia, somewhere in the vicinity of Eruthrae, in CW Asia Minor, present-day CW Turkey. *254*

Pteleos : 1. city in the territory of Pteleon, in SE Thessalia, on the border with Achaia Phthiotis, CE mainland Greece. *220*; -- 2. city in Nestor's kingdom, near Pulos, in SW Messenia, SW Peloponnesos. *196*

Pteria : city of N Cappadocia, exact location uncertain, in NE Asia Minor, present-day CN Turkey. *252*

Ptoion : 1. mount in NE Boiotia, between the city of Gla and the Gulf of Oropos, in SE mainland Greece. *212*; -- 2. town on this mount. *212*

Ptolemais : coastal town of Kyrenaica in NE Africa, along the Mediterranean Sea. *244*

Ptolis : ancient city, modern Panayia Gourtsouli, on a hill N of Mantineia, in CS Arkadia, C Peloponnesos. *192*

Ptous : mountain range running from E of Lake Kopais, in C Boiotia, into E Phokis, in SE mainland Greece. *212*

Ptuchia : islet E of the island of Kerkura, in NE Ionian Sea. *218*

Pudna : town on the E coast of Thessalia, on the NW side of the gulf of Thermai, in NW Aegean Sea, NE mainland Greece. *220*

Pugela : town of Caria, NW of Miletos, in SW Asia Minor, present-day SW Turkey, on the coast of the Aegean Sea. *254*

Puglia : see Apulia. *238*

Puknos : river, modern Kiliaris, flowing from the White mountains, N through the region, past Armenoi, into the Bay of Souda, in NW of the island of Crete, into the Sea of Crete, C Mediterranean Sea. *204*

Pulene : Homeric city of Aitolia, near Pleuron, in SW mainland Greece. *216*

Pulos : 1. major city of Nestor's kingdom, on the NW side of the Peninsula of Sphakteria, on the SW coast of Messenia, in SW Peloponnesos. *196*;-- 2. city in CN Elis, also known as Sandy Pulos, where the river Ladon becomes tributary of the river Peneios, in NW Peloponnesos. *194*

Pulvar : see Araxes/Persian. *264*

Punjab : region in Bactria, present-day NE Pakistan, covering the area between the Indus river to the W and the Zaradros river to the E, in C Asia. *266*

Pura : 1. region of NE Gedrosia, N of the Gulf of Oman, in present-day SE Iran, W Asia. *264*; -- 2. town in this region.

Purali : see Arabis. *264*

Puramos : river, also called Saros, modern Ceyhan (Seyhan) Nehri, flowing S from the E Taurus mountain range of Cilicia, present-day SE Turkey, past Mallus, into the Gulf of Issos, into the NE Mediterranean Sea. *256*

Purasos : Homeric city in NE Achaia Phthiotis, near the border with Thessalia, NE mainland Greece. *222*

Puratta : see Euphrates river. *248 & 258*

Purgos : 1. Minyan town in the W of Elis, near Kakovatos, in CW Peloponnesos. *194*;-- 2. several locations identified only by a palace (*purgos*), such as at CN of the island of Crete, in C Mediterranean Sea. *206*

Purrha : town in C of the island of Lesbos, in NE Aegean Sea. *228*

Purrichos : city in the CW peninsula of Lakonia, in SE Peloponnesos. *198*

Puthion : city in N Thessalia, territory of Perrhaibia, **N** of the Peneios river, in C mainland Greece. *220*

Putho : see Delphi. *214*

Pyan : river of Bactria, flowing NW from the Himalayas, S of the Waksh river, in N Afghanistan, into the Oxus river as a tributary, in C Asia. *262*

Pyrenaei : mountain range separating SW Gaul (France) from N Iberia (Spain), modern Pyrenees, in W Europe. *232*

Pyretus : one of five rivers flowing from the Carpathian mountains, most to the E, into the Danube river, in Scythia, present-day Romania, E Europe. *240*

Pyrgi : coastal town in SW Etruria, in C Italy, W Europe. *238*

Pythopolis : inland city of N Caria, also called Antioch on the Maeander, on the S bank of this river, at the confluence with the Orsinos river, in W Asia Minor, present-day W Turkey. *254*

Pyxous : coastal town of SW Italy, along the Tyrrhenian Sea, in W Europe. *238*

Q

Qabes : see Gabes Gulf. *244*

Qandahãr : see Kandahãr (Alexandria-in-Arachosia). *262*

Qasiyun : mountains, S of Damascus, in Syria, W Asia. *258*

Qasr Ibrim : town in S Egypt, on the W bank of the Nile river, in NE Africa. *244*

Qatar : small country occupying a peninsula with Bahrain on the W coast of the Persian Gulf, next to E Saudi Arabia, in SW Asia. *246 & 264*

Qift : town on the E bank of the Nile river, N of Thebes, in C Egypt, NE Africa. *242*

Qom : see Kum. *260*

Qomsheh : city of Media, modern Shahreza, SW of Isfahan, in present-day NW Iran, W Asia. *260*

Qonduz : see Konduz. *262*

Quetta : city in Bactria, present-day SW Pakistan, near the border with SE Afghanistan, in C Asia. *262*

Qulzum : town at the N end of the Gulf of Suez, between NE Egypt and the Sinai peninsula, in NE Africa. *242*

R

Rachi : see Kouphia. *218*

Rafah : see Raphia. *242*

Rai : see Rhagae. *260*

Rakshastal : lake of SW Tibet, in the Himalaya mountains, CN Asia. *266*

Rambacia : 1. area in E Gedrosia, W of the Indus river and N of the Arabian Sea, in C Asia. *264*; -- 2. see Alexandria-at-Rambacia. *264*

Ramsës : see Avaris. *242*

Rankos : town, S of Herakleion, near the CN coast of the island of Crete, in C Mediterranean Sea. *206*

Raphia : city most S of Syria, also known as Rafah, on the boundaries with Palestine and Egypt, in W Asia. *242*

Raphina : town in NE Attika, on the coast E of the Plain of Marathon, in SE mainland Greece. *210*

Ras Shamra : see Ugarit. *256*

Rãvi : see Hydraotes river. *266*

Razlog : town of CW Thrace, on the Nestos river, E of Petra, in present-day Bulgaria, E Europe. *226*

Red : 1. sea as a narrow body of water between NE Africa and W Arabia, also known as Egyptian Sea, connected with the Arabian Sea by the Gulf of Aden. *187, 188, 242, 244, 246, & 264*; -- 2. see Persian Gulf. *264*; -- 3. mythological isle, see Erutheia. *268*

Reggio di Calabria : see Rhegion. *238*

Rezinea : town, near Knossos, near the CN coast of the island of Crete, in C Mediterranean Sea. *206*

Rhaeteai : town SW of Gortus, in SW Arkadia, C Peloponnesos. *192*

Rhagae : ancient town of W Hyrcania, modern Rai, now absorbed by the modern Therãn, separated to the N from the Caspian Sea by the Parachoatras (Elburz) mountains, in present-day N Iran, W Asia. *260*

Rhaidestos : see Bisanthe. *226*

Rhamnos : town of NE Attika, N of Marathon, on the coast of the Gulf of Petalion, in SE mainland Greece. *210*

Rharos : plain N of the Bay of Eleusis, in NW Attika, opposite the island of Salamis, in SE mainland Greece. *210*

Rhegion : city, modern Reggio di Calabria, at the SW tip of Italy, opposite NE Sicily across the Strait of Messina, in W Europe. *236 & 238*

Rheithron : harbor city, N of Mount Neriton, on the E coast of the island of Ithaka, in CE Ionian Sea, off mainland Akarnania. *217*

Rheiti : town of NW Attika, also known as the Brooks, W of mount Aigaleos, in NE mainland Greece. *210*

Rheitos : town, probably of SE Korinthia, in CN Argolis, on the NW Saronic Gulf, in NE Peloponnesos. *202*

Rhekaios : city of SE Macedonia, on CN of the Gulf of Thermai, at the mouth of the river Charadros, in NE mainland Greece. *224*

Rheneia : 1. small island SW of the island of Aigina, in the Saronic Gulf, in SE mainland Greece. *208*; -- 2. small island of the Cyclades, next to Delos, in CW Aegean Sea. *230*

Rhesos : river in Bithynia, flowing N into the SW Euxine (Black) Sea, in NW Asia Minor, present-day NW Turkey. *250*

Rhine : river of W Europe, flowing from the Swiss Alps, N through Germany and W through Holland, into the North Sea. *232*

Rhinocolura : town on the Mediterranean coast at the border between Gaza and NE Egypt, in NE Africa. *242*

Rhion : 1. city on a promontory in NW Achaia, N of Patrai, on the Gulf of Patraikos, in NE Peloponnesos. *200*; -- 2. city on a promontory across the gulf from Achaian Rhion, referred to as Molukrian Rhion, in SW Ozolian Lokris, SW mainland Greece. *214*; -- 3. strait between the two cities of Rhion, connecting the Gulf of Patraikos and the Gulf of Korinthos, in N Peloponnesos. *214*

Rhipe : Homeric city in Arkadia, exact location unknown, in CN peloponnesos. *192*

Rhitsona : site of a cemetery near Thebes, in CS Boiotia, SE mainland Greece. *212*

Rhitumna : city of CN Crete, on the gulf of Almirou, off the Sea of Crete, in CS Mediterranean Sea. *204*

Rhodes : 1. major island of the Dodekanesoi, in SE Aegean Sea, facing the S shore of Doris across the Strait of Marmara, in SW Asia Minor. *190, 230 & 254*;-- 2. city at the N end of this island. *230*

Rhodios : river in Troas, exact location unknown, in NW Asia Minor, present-day NW Turkey. *250*

Rhodope : mountain range of W Thrace, N of CN Aegean Sea, running WE between the rivers Nestos and Maritsa, in NE mainland Greece, present-day Bulgaria, E Europe. *226*

Rhoeteum : town of Troas, on the S side of the entrance to the Hellespontos, in NE Asia Minor, present-day NE Turkey. *250*

Rhone : river flowing S from SW Switzerland, through France, into the Mediterranean Sea W of Massalia (Marseille), in W Europe. *232*

Rhundakos : river flowing W through Hellespontine, E of the Granikos river, in NW Asia Minor, into NE Aegean Sea. *250*

Rhupes : ancient city of CN Achaia, W of Aigion, near the coast of the Gulf of Korinthos, in CN Peloponnesos. *200*

Rhution : seaport on the CS of the island of Crete, in C Mediterranean Sea. *206*

Rioni : see Phasis river. *248*

Rithumna : Mycenaean town, just S of Rhitumna, on the Almirou Gulf, in CN Crete, C Mediterranean Sea. *204*

Rodopou : 1. peninsula between the gulfs of Kissamos to the W and Khanion to the E , in the NW island of Crete, C Mediterranean Sea. *202*; -- 2. town in the CS of this peninsula. *204*

Rogozen : city in NW Thrace, in NE mainland Greece, present-day N Bulgaria, E Europe. *226*

Rohri : see Alexandria-at-Rohri. *266*

Rokka : see Keraia. *204*

Romania : country NW of the Black Sea, surrounded by Moldova, Ukraine, Hungary, Serbia and Bulgaria, in SE Europe. *188, 226 & 240*

Rome : major city of the Latium, in C Italy, W Europe. *238*

Rosetta : 1. W branch of the Nile Delta, also called Canobia, in NW Egypt, NE Africa. *242*; -- 2. site, also called Canobia, at the mouth of this branch. *242*

Routsi : town SE of Pulos in SW Messenia, SW Peloponnesos. *196*

Rupei : site in SW Thrace, W of the Nestos river, in NE mainland Greece, present-day Bulgaria, E Europe. *226*

Russia : largest country of E Europe from the Arctic Ocean in the N. the Pacific Ocean in the E, China, Mongolia, Kazakhstan and the Caspian Sea in the S, the Black Sea, Ukraine, Belarus, Lithuania, Latvia, Estonia and Finland in the W. *188, 246 & 248*

Rutio : town in the C of the island of Crete, exact location uncertain, C Mediterranean Sea. *204*

S

Sabina : region of the Apennine mountains, between Latium and Umbria, in CE Italy, W Europe. *238*

Sacae : tribal land located N of ancient Sogdiana, E of the Jaxartes river, in modern Tajikistan, CN Asia. *262*

Sagalassus : city of Pisidia, near the Eurymedon river, in CS Asia Minor, present-day SW Turkey. *256*

Sahara : immense desert dotted with oases, covering from the Atlantic Ocean to the Nile river in Egypt. N Africa. *244*

Sais : town on the NW side of the Nile delta, along the Canobic branch, in N Egypt, NE Africa. *242*

Sakovouni : ancient settlement on a hill, in the plain of Alkimedon, CE Arkadia, CN Peloponnesos. *192*

Salamis : 1. island in N Saronic Gulf, between Attika and Argolis, in SE mainland Greece. *208 & 210*; -- 2. seaport city on the E side of this island. *208 & 210*; -- 3. bay in the NE Saronic Gulf, also called Eleusis, in NW Attika, SE mainland Greece. *210*; -- 4. ancient city in the NE of the island of Cyprus, E Mediterranean Sea, SW Asia. *256*

Salang : pass between Kabul to the S and Mazar-e-Sharif to the NW of Afghanistan, in C Asia. *262*

Salerno : gulf on the SW side of Italy, on the Tyrrhenian Sea, S of the Gulf of Neapolis, in W Europe. *238*

Saliagos : site in the N of the island of Naxos, in the Cyclades, CW Aegean Sea. *230*

Salmonia : inland town of N Elis, S of Opos, exact location unknown, in NW Peloponnesos. *194*

Salmudessos : town on the SW coast of the Euxine (Black) Sea, in E Thrace, present-day Bulgaria, E Europe. *226*

Salonika : 1. bay at the NE of the Gulf of Thermai, W of the peninsula Kassandra of the Chalkidike. *224*; -- 2. seaport city, also called Thessaloniki and Therme, at the head of this bay, in S Macedonia, NE mainland Greece. *224*; -- 3. see Chalkidike. *224 & 228*

Salt : 1. lake N of the Bay of Marathon, in NE Attika, SE mainland Greece. *210*; -- 2. see Kavir desert. *260*

Samaria : 1. area of C ancient Palestine, in present-day N Israel, at the E end of the Mediterranean Sea. *258*; -- 2. city in this area. *258*; -- 3. river flowing S from Mount Ida, into the Libyan Sea, on the NW of the Gulf of Mesara, in CS of the island of Crete, CS Mediterranean Sea. *204*

Samarkand : 1. area in W Sogdiana, present-day S Uzbekistan, E of the Caspian Sea, in C Asia. *262*; -- 2. city, see Maracanda. *262*

Same : 1. see Kephallenia. *216*; -- 2. city on the CN coast of the island of Kephallenia, in the CE Ionian Sea, facing the Gulf of Patraikos, in CW mainland Greece. *216*

Saminthos : town of CW Argolis, somewhere in the plain near Argos, in NE Peloponnesos. *202*

Samos : 1. the nearest of the Aegean islands to the coast of Asia Minor, present-day NW Turkey. *190, 230 & 254*; -- 2. city on the E side of this island. *230*; -- 3. narrow strait separating this island from the coastal mainland of Ionia. *230*

Samosata : city of NW Mesopotamia, on the W bank of the Euphrates river, in present-day SE Turkey, W Asia. *258*

Samothrace : Homeric island of the Thracian Sporades, between the islands of Thasos and Imbros, in NE Aegean Sea. *228*

Samsun : see Amisos. *252*

San al- Hajar al- Qibliyah : see Tanis. *242*

Sandios : hill S of the Maeander river and Ephesos, in SW Lydia, SW Asia Minor, present-day SW Turkey. *254*

Sandy : desert in C Baluchistan, present-day SW Pakistan, C Asia. *264*

Sandy Pulos : see Pulos in Elis. *194*

Sane : town in the N of the peninsula Kassandra, W Chalkidike, along the NW Aegean Sea, in NE mainland Greece. *228*

San Filippo d'Argiro : see Agurion. *236*

Sangada ; ancient region of present-day SE Pakistan, C Asia. *246, 264 & 266*

Sangala : ancient city of Bactria (Punjab), in N India, between the Hydraotes river to the W and the Hyphasis river to the E, the areas Kathaei to the N and Oxydracae to the S, in C Asia. *266*

Sangarios : river of Bithynia, flowing N into the W Euxine (Black) Sea, in NW Asia Minor, present-day NW Turkey. *252*

Sānghar : 1. area of ancient Sangada, in present-day SE Pakistan, near the border with India, in C Asia. *266*; -- 2. city in this area. *266*

Sanglākh : mountain range in Bactria, present-day W of the Hindu Kush and NW of Kabul, CN Afghanistan, C Asia. *262*

Santorini : see Thera. *230*

Sapaei : tribal land of SW Thrace, located on the E side of Mount Pangaion, in NE mainland Greece. *226*

Sar : mountain range of the N Balkan Peninsula, from S Kosovo and NW Macedonia in the NE, to Epeiros, modern Albania, in the SW, in E Europe. *224*

Sardar : see Caspian Gates. *260*

Sardene : mountain range in C Lydia, in CW Asia Minor, present-day CW Turkey. *252*

Sardika : city of W Thrace, modern Sofia, in NE mainland Greece, present-day CW Bulgaria, SE Europe. *226 & 240*

Sardinia : see Chardan. *188 & 232*

Sardis : city of Lydia, inland E of Smyrna, in the plain at the foot of Mount Tmolos, in CN Asia Minor, present-day W Turkey. *252*

Sari : see Zadracarta. *260*

Saria : small island of the Rhodian Dodekanesoi, N of Krapathos, in SE Aegean Sea. *230*

Sarmatia : tribal region located N of Apsilaean Scythia, in present-day Ukraine and S Russia, NE of the Euxine (Black) Sea, in E Europe. *248*

Sarnia : city of W Triphulia, SE Elis, in CW Peloponnesos, near the coast of the Ionian Sea. *194*

Saronic : gulf of the Aegean Sea , also called Gulf of Aigina, between Attika of SE mainland Greece and Argolis of the NE Peloponnesos. *190, 202 & 208*

Saros : see Puramos. *256*

Sarpedon : mythical island of the Gorgons. *269*

Sarte : town on the SW of the peninsula Sithonia of the C Chalkidike, in the N Aegean Sea, NE mainland Greece. *228*

Saryekshan : town in SW Armenia, present-day E Turkey, W Asia. *248*

Satmiois : river flowing from the S Ida mountain range, through Troas, past Pedasos, into the Aegean Sea, in NW Asia Minor, present-day NW Turkey. *250*

Sattagydia : mountainous region of W Baluchistan, straddling the border between present-day Iran and Pakistan, in C Asia. *260*

Satyrion : town at the NE end of the gulf of Taranto, S of Taras, in S Italy, W Europe. *238*

Saudi Arabia : country of W Asia, between the Red Sea to the W, Iraq, Jordan, Syria and Iraq to the N, the Persian Gulf to the E, and Yemen and Oman to the S. *188, 246 & 264*

Sauromatai : tribal area of Scythia, N of the Tanais river, in present-day S Ukraine, SE Europe. *248*

Sava : river flowing SE from the Alps, through Croatia and Serbia and into the Danube River as its tributary, in SE Europe. *240*

Savnob : see Aornos city. *262*

Scamander : mythical river in Troas, also called Xanthos by the Gods and Menderez by the Greeks, flowing from Mount Ida, through the plain below Troy, into the Hellespontos, S of Troy, in NW Asia Minor, present-day NW Turkey. *250 & 269*

Scheria : see Phaiekia. *269*

Schoinias : coastal site in NE Attika, S of Marathon, on the Gulf of Petalion, in SE mainland Greece. *210*

Scilly : see Cassiterides. *232*

Scoglio del Tonno : town of S Italy, on the NE side of the Gulf of Taranto, in W Europe. *238*

Scylax : river of Paphlagonia, flowing N from the center of the circle made by the river Halys, into the Euxine (Black) Sea, in CN Turkey, W Asia. *252*

Scylla : in mythology, this rock refers with Charybdis to the Strait of Messina, between NE Sicily and SW Italy, in W Europe. *236*

Scythia : ancient region from NW to N of the Euxine (Black) Sea, covering present-day E Romania, Moldova, S Ukraine, Georgia, Ukraine, Kazakhstan and SW Russia where it was called Apsilaean Scythia, at one time all the territory between the Euxine and Caspian seas, in E Europe and W Asia. *187, 240 & 248*

Sebennytos : town along a C branch of the Nile Delta, N Egypt, NE Africa. *242*

Sefid Rud : see Amardus. *260*

Segesta : inland town at the NW end of the island of Sicily, at the foot of mount Eryx, in W Mediterranean Sea, W Europe. *234*

Sehwan : see Sindimanao. *264*

Seistan : area N of Baluchistan, covering present-day SW Afghanistan and SE Iran, in C Asia. *262*

Sela : see Petra. *258*

Selas : river of CW Messenia, flowing S from mount Aigaleos, first S, then W into the Ionian Sea, N of Pulos, In SW Peloponnesos. *196*

Selemnos : river of CN Achaia, flowing W along the river Bolinaios, N into the Gulf of Korinthos, near Argura, in CN Peloponnesos. *200*

Selge : city of Pisidia, in CS Asia Minor, present-day CS Turkey. *256*

Selinos : 1. city in CN Lakonia, NW of Geronthrae, in SE Peloponnesos. *198*; -- 2. river in C Achaia, flowing from the mountains near Triteia in the S to the Gulf of Korinthos, near Helike in the N, in CN Peloponnesos. *200*; -- 3. coastal town on the SW side of the island of Sicily, SE of Motya, in W Mediterranean Sea, W Europe. *234*

Sellana : city in CN Lakonia, along the river Tanaos, in SE Peloponnesos. *198*

Sellasia : city N of Sparta, in NW Lakonia, SE Peloponnesos. *198*

Selleis : 1. river of N Elis, flowing from Mount Pholoë, S of the river Ladon of Elis, into the CE Ionian Sea, in NW Peloponnesos. *194*;-- 2. river in E Achaia, flowing by Sikuon in Argolis, into the Gulf of Korinthos, in CN Peloponnesos. *200*; -- 3. river of Troas, flowing NE of Troy, into the Hellespontos, in NW Asia Minor, present-day NW Turkey. *250*

Selumbria : city of E Thrace, on the N shore of the Sea of Propontis, in NE mainland Greece, present-day NW Turkey, SE Europe. *240*

Senegal : country of NW Africa, on the Atlantic Ocean, S of Mauritania and N of Guinea. *188 & 244*

Senir : see Hermon. *258*

Seraglio : ancient port city at the E end of the island of Kos, in SE Aegean Sea. *230*

Serbia : country in the C of the N Balkan Peninsula, surrounded by Croatia and Bosnia to the W, Hungary to the N, Romania and Bulgaria to the E, and Albania and Macedonia to the S, in SE Europe. *188, 218, 224 & 240*

Serbonis : lake that turned into a bog in the NE Delta of the Nile river, in NE Egypt, NE Africa. *242*

Seriphos : island of CW Cyclades in the CW Aegean Sea. *230*

Sermule : town N of the peninsula Sithonia of the C Chalkidike, in CN Aegean Sea, NE mainland Greece. *228*

Servia : site in E Macedonia, near the coast of the Aegean Sea, exact location uncertain, in SE Europe. *224*

Sesamos : town of Paphlagonia, also called Amastris, at the CS of the Euxine (Black) Sea, in present-day NW Turkey, W Asia. *252*

Sesklo : village of SE Thessalia, near Dimini, N of the Gulf of Volos, N mainland Greece. *220*

Sestos : city of Hellespontine, in Troas, on the CS of the Strait of Hellespontos, in NW Asia Minor, present-day NW Turkey. *250*

Setaia : site next to Praisos, in the CE end of the island of Crete, C Mediterranean Sea. *206*

Seuthopolis : town of C Thrace, in present-day Romania, SE Europe. *226*

Sevaste : city near Dion, on the NW side of the peninsula Akti, in the Chalkidike, NW Aegean Sea, NE mainland Greece. *228*

Sevilla : see Hispalis. *232*

Sexi : town of S Iberia (Spain), E of Malaca, along the Mediterranean Sea, in SW Europe. *232*

Seyhan Nehri : see Puramos river. *256*

Shahbat : see Kyrene. *244*

Shahreza : see Qomsheh. *260*

Shankhar : see Babylon. *258*

Shahrud : modern city of NE Iran, also called Emānshar and perhaps Hekatompulos, SE of the Caspian Sea and N of the desert of Kavir, in W Asia. *260*

Sher- Dahan : pass between Kandahār to the S and Kabul to the N, in E Afghanistan, C Asia. *262*

Shipka : mountain pass in Thrace, NE mainland Greece, between modern C Bulgaria and NW Turkey, E Europe. *226*

Shiraz : city in C Persis, N of the Persian Gulf, present-day S Iran, W Asia. *264*

Shortugai : city in S Bactria, present-day NE Afghanistan, near the border with Tajikistan, in C Asia. *262*

Sialek : see Caspian Gates. *260*

Sibi : 1. area of mountains and plains in ancient Gedrosia, present-day N Baluchistan, between the Sulaiman and Brahui mountain ranges, in S Pakistan, C Asia. *264*; -- 2. town in the C of this area, in the NE of the Kachhi plain, E of the Nari river. *264*

Sicania : region covering the W side of the island of Sicily, W Mediterranean Sea, W Europe. *234*

Sicilian : sea of the W Mediterranean Sea, S of Italy and E of the island of Sicily, in W Europe. *236*

Sicily : large island, originally called Trinacria, separated from the SW tip of Italy by the Strait of Messina, between the Tyrrherian Sea to the N and the Mediterranean Sea to the S and W, in W Europe. *187, 188, 238. & 244*

Siculia : region covering the E side of the island of Sicily, in W Mediterranean Sea, W Europe. *236*

Side : 1. city on the SE coast of Lakonia, on the Mirtóön Sea, N of Cape Malea, in SE Peloponnesos. *198*; -- 2. town of Pamphylia, on the N coast of the E Mediterranean Sea, E of Eurymedon, in CS present-day Turkey, W Asia. *256*

Sidon : seaport of Phoenicia, at the E end of the Mediterranean Sea, N of Tyre, in present-day S Lebanon, W Asia. *258*

Sidoussa : site of a fort in E Ionia, somewhere in the vicinity of Eruthrae, in CW Asia Minor, present-day CW Turkey. *254*

Sidra : long gulf of the S Mediterranean Sea, also called Sirte or Syrtis Major, carved out of the coast of Libya, in NE Africa. *244*

Sigeion : see Alexandria-in-Troas. *250*

Sikanos : river of Iberia (Spain), flowing E into the Mediterranean Sea, in W Europe. *232*

Sikinos : island of SW Cyclades, between Siphnos and Melos, in SW Aegean Sea. *230*

Sikiona : see Vasiliko. *200*

Sikuon : town in NW Argolis, S of the Gulf of Korinthos and NW of the city of Korintho, in NE Peloponnesos. *202*

Silë : fortress town in N Egypt, in the NE Nile Delta, on the Suez Canal, NE of Bubastis, in NE Africa. *242*

Silesia : region straddling the border between present-day SW Poland and NE Czech Republic, in SE Europe. *240*

Sillyum : city near the coast of NE Mediterranean Sea, NW of Side, in Pamphylia, SW Asia Minor, present-day SW Turkey. *256*

Simeto : river flowing W and ending in wetlands on the W slopes of Mount Aetna, in CE of the island of Sicily, W Mediterranean Sea, W Europe. *236*

Simois : river of Troas, flowing from the Ida mountain range and with the Scamander encircling Troy before emptying into the NE Aegean Sea, in NW Asia Minor, present-day NW Turkey. *250*

Sinai : peninsula, mostly rough desert, also known as Aiguptos, between Suez gulf & canal to the W and gulf of Aqaba & Negev desert to the E, in NE Egypt, NE Africa. *242, 246 & 258*

Sind : modern area in the region of Sangada, present-day SE Pakistan, crossed by the Indus river, C Asia. *264 & 266*

Sindimanao : city, modern Sehwan, in Sagada, present-day SE Pakistan, NW of the Thar Desert and N of the Arabis river, in C Asia. *264*

Sindos : site of a cemetery, near Phthiotic Thebes, in CN mainland Greece. *222*

Singitikos : gulf in the Chalkidike, modern Agion Oros, between the peninsulas of Sithonia in C and Akti in E, in NW Aegean Sea. *228*

Singos : town on CE of the peninsula Sithonia of the C Chalkidike, in the N Aegean Sea, NE mainland Greece. *228*

Sinope : port city of Paphlagonia, on the CS of the Euxine (Black) Sea, W of Amisos, flanked to the S by mountains of Anatolia, in present-day NW Turkey, W Asia. *252*

Sintia : tribal area in CW Thrace, between the rivers Strumon and Nestos, in NE mainland Greece. *226*

Siphae : see Delion. *212*

Siphnos : island of CW Cyclades, S of Seriphos, in CW Aegean Sea. *230*

Sipulos : mount in N Ionia, NE of Smyrna, in W Asia Minor, present-day W Turkey. *250*

Siracusa : 1. city, also known as Syracuse, on the SE coast of the island of Sicily, in W Mediterranean Sea. *236*; -- 2. harbor of this city. *236*

Sirai : town in NW Arkadia, between Psophis to the NW and Paus to the SE, in CN Peloponnesos. *192*

Sirion : see Hermon. *258*

Siris : 1. town C Macedonia, exact location uncertain, N mainland Greece. *224*; -- 2. town on the NW side of the Gulf of Taranto, in CS Italy, W Europe. *238*

Sirmium : city on the W bank of the Sava river, modern Sremska Mitrovica, in Serbia, E Europe. *240*

Sirte : gulf, see Sidra. *244*; -- 2. town, modern Surt, on the SW side of this gulf. *244*

Sisaea : town in the CW of the island of Crete, in the region around Rhitumna, exact location uncertain, in C Mediterranean Sea. *204*

Sistan : swampish area of Baluchistan, tribal land of the Ariaspi, in present-day SE Iran, on the border with Pakistan, in W Asia. *260 & 264*

Sitaces : see Granis river. *260*

Sitagroi : site in SW Thrace, NW of Dikili Tash, in NE mainland Greece. *226*

Sithonia : the C finger of the peninsula Chalkidike, extending S into the NW Agean Sea. *228*

Sitia : harbor city, NE of the Gulf of Megambellou, on the Sea of Crete, in NE of the island of Crete, CS Mediterranean Sea. *206*

Siwa : 1. oasis of the E Libyan desert, in the NW of Egypt, NE Africa. *242*; -- 2. see Ammonium city. *242*

Siwalik : mountain range, S of the Kashmir-Jammu region, in N India, C Asia. *266*

Skandia : city in the C of the island of Kuthera, in the S Mirtóön Sea, at the entrance to the Gulf of Lakonia, near the peninsula Malea, in SE Peloponnesos. *198*

Skardos : mountain of the W Balkan Peninsula, in ancient W Illyria, present-day Albania, near the E Adriatic Sea, in E Europe. *218*

Skarphe : Homeric town of Opuntian Lokris, near Thermopulai, on the coast along the Gulf of Oropos, in CE mainland Greece. *214*

Skepsis : inland town in SW Phrygia, in NW Asia Minor, present-day NW Turkey. *250*

Skiathos : 1. mountain range in NE Arkadia, running NS, S of Mount Kullene, in CN Peloponnesos. *192*; -- 2. island of the Thessalian Sporades, between SE Pherai in NE mainland Greece and the island of Ikos in CW Aegean Sea. *228*

Skidros : coastal town of SW Italy, along the Tyrrhenian Sea, in W Europe. *238*

Skillos : city of N Triphulia, CS Elis, S of Mount Tupaios, in NW Peloponnesos. *194*

Skione : town in the S of the W peninsula Kassandra of the Chalkidike, along the Aegean Sea, in NE mainland Greece. *228*

Skiritis : area of N Lakonia, N of Sparta, in CS Peloponnesos. *198*

Skirtos : stream flowing through Edessa, in CS Macedonia, NE
mainland Greece. *234*
Skollis :see Olen. *194*
Skolos : 1. Homeric city, in the mountainous area N of Eruthrae,
in SE Boiotia, SE mainland Greece. *212*; -- 2. Homeric city of W
Boiotia, at the foot of the Kithairon mountain, in SW mainland
Greece. *212*; -- 3. town somewhere in the Chalkidike territory,
NE mainland Greece. *228*
Skombros : mount on the border between NE Macedonia and CW
Thrace, source of the river Strumon, in NE mainland Greece. *224*
Skope : town in SE Arkadia, S of Mantineia, in CE Peloponnesos.
192
Skopelos : island of the Thessalian Sporades, in CW Aegean Sea.
228
Skordiski : Tribal land located in N Illyria, near the coast of NE
Adriatic Sea, in present-day Croatia, E Europe. *218*
Skoteino : sacred cave E of Herakleion, in the CN of the island of
Crete, in C Mediterranean Sea. *206*
Skotussa : town of C Thessalia, SE of Kranon, in NE mainland
Greece. *220*
Skoubris : site of a cemetery near Xeropolis, on SW Euboia, along
the Gulf of Petalion, in SE mainland Greece. *228*
Skudra : equivalent to the S portion of Thrace, N of the Sea of
Propontis (Marmara), in present-day NW Turkey, SE Europe. *226*
Skullaion : cape at the SE end of the peninsula of Argolis, on the
W entrance to the Saronic Gulf, in SE Argolis, CE Peloponnesos.
202
Skupi : city located between the Dardani and the Paeoni tribes, in
W Macedonia, N mainland Greece. *224*
Skuros : island of the Thessalian Sporades, off the coast of N
Euboia, in CW Aegean Sea. *228*
Slovakia : country of the Balkans, in SE Europe, N of Hungary, S of
Poland, W of Ukraine and E of Austria & Czech Repulic *188 &
240*
Slovenia : country most to the NW of the Balkans,surrounded by
Italy, Austria, Hungary and Croatia, in SE Europe. *188 & 240*
Smeneous : town, probably on the E side of the island of Sicily,
exact location unknown, in W Mediterranean Sea, W Europe. *236*
Smenos : river in SW Lakonia, flowing SE from the S Teügetos
mountain range, into the Gulf of Lakonia, near Las, in SE Pelo-
ponnesos. *198*
Sminthe : city of Troas, W of mount Ida, near Lurnessos, in
present-day NW Turkey, W Asia. *250*
Smirtoula : village of SW Epeiros, near the modern city of Nikopolis, N of the Gulf of Ambrakia, in SW mainland Greece. *218*

Smoljan : city of E Thrace, high on the SE side of the Rhodope mountains, on the Cherna river, in S Bulgaria, E Europe. *226*

Smyrna : 1. bay of the Aegean Sea, extending the Gulf of Candath to the SE, S of the estuary of the Hermos river and N of the Kaustros river, in Lydia, CW Asia Minor, present-day CW Turkey. *254*; -- 2. Ionian city, modern Izmir, at the E end of this bay. *254*

Sochi : city in NW Syria, along the Karasu river, S of the Amanos Mountain range, in W Asia. *258*

Sofia : see Sardika. *226 & 240*

Sogda : see Alexandria-at-Rohri. *266*

Sogdia : see Sogdiana. *262*

Sogdiana : 1. ancient region, also referred to as Sogdia, covering N Pakistan and parts of the bordering countries to the N, in C Asia. *246 & 262*; -- 2. steep rock in the S of this region. *262*

Soli : 1. ancient seaport of Cilicia, present-day SE Turkey, near Mersin and the estuary of the Lamos river, along the NE Mediterranean Sea, in W Asia. *256*; -- 2. ancient city on the Bay of Morphou, on the NW coast of the island of Cyprus, in E Mediterranean Sea. *256*

Sollion : city on a cape in NW Akarnania, SE of the isthmus leading to the island of Leukas, in CW mainland Greece. *216*

Soloeis : 1. seaport city in NW Sicily, SE of Panormos, on S Tyrrhenian Sea, W Europe. *234*; -- 2. cape in Libya, in NE Africa. *244*

Solontum : town in the CN of the island of Sicily, on the coast of the S Tyrrhenian Sea, in W Europe. *234*

Soluma : Homeric mountain range in E Lycia, near Pamphylia, in present-day CS Turkey, W Asia. *254*

Somalia : country on the E horn of Africa. *188 & 246*

Son : river flowing N from C India, toward the Ganges river it joins as its tributary near Patna, in C Asia. *266*

Soron : river in CN Arkadia, flowing EW and becoming a tributary of the river Ladon in Elis, CE Peloponnesos. *192*

Soros : mound in NE Attika, SW of the Bay of Marathon, off the Gulf of Petalion, in SE mainland Greece. *210*

Sotera : town in SW of the island of Cyprus, at the E end of the Mediterranean Sea, in W Asia. *256*

Souda : 1. bay between the Akrotiri peninsula and Cape Drapano, in NW island of Crete, CS Mediterranean Sea. *204*; -- 2. small island in this bay. *204*

Sougia : harbor town, on the Cyrenic Sea, E of Lisos, both servicing the inland city of Eluros, in the SW of the island of Crete, CS Mediterranean Sea. *204*

Souphli : site of a cemetery, in the E Thessalian plain, near the coast of the NW Aegean Sea, in N mainland Greece. *220*

Soureza : site in the Agrileza valley, N of Sounion, in S Attika, SE mainland Greece. *208*

Spain : country of SW Europe, on the Iberian Peninsula, N and E of Portugal, in SW Europe. *188, 232 & 244*

Sparta : major city of CW Lakonia, also called Lakedaimon, W of the river Eurotas, in SE Peloponnesos. *198*

Spartalos : town N of the W peninsula Kassandra of the Chalkidike, in NW Aegean Sea, S Macedonia, NE mainland Greece. *224 & 228*

Spasinou : town near the estuary of the Euphrates and Tigris rivers into the Persian Gulf, in present-day S Iraq, W Asia. *258*

Spercheios : river, also called Homeric Poludora, flowing from the mountains of Thessalia through Achaia Phthiotis and Malis, into the Gulf of Malis, W of Thermopulai, in CE mainland Greece. *214, 220 & 222*

Spetsoi : islands of the Saronic Sporades, E of the Troizen territory, in SE Argolis, NE Peloponnesos. *202*

Sphaeria : island of the Sporades in the E Saronic Gulf, off the coast of Troizen, in SW of the peninsula of Argolis, in NE Peloponnesos. *202*

Sphakteria : 1. peninsula in SW Messenia, between the Ionian Sea and the Gulf of Messenia, in SW Peloponnesos. *196*; -- 2. island in SW Messenia, between the Ionian Sea and the Gulf of Navarino, S of Pulos, in SW Peloponnesos. *196*

Sphettos : village in CS Attika, in the hills of Mount Humettos, S of Paeania, in SE mainland Greece. *208*

Sphinx : mountain SE of Lake Kopais, in CS Boiotia, SE mainland Greece. *212*

Spilia : site probably in Magnesia, exact location uncertain, on the CE side of mainland Greece. *220*

Spina : seaport of NE Italy, on the Adriatic Sea, in W Europe. *238*

Spiraeon : coastal town on the NW side of the Saronic Gulf, S of Kenchreai, in NE Argolis, NE Peloponnesos. 202

Sporades : 1. Thessalian islands, in CW Aegean Sea, near the N end of the island of Euboia. *228*; -- 2. Thracian islands of the NE Aegean Sea, S of Thrace in NE mainland Greece. *228*; -- 3. Saronic Gulf islands, W of Attika, in SE mainland Greece. *208*; -- 4. islands of the SE Aegean Sea, also called Dodekanesoi. *230*

Sremska Mitrovica : see Sirmium. *240*

Stageiros : city in SE Macedonia, N of the Chalkidike E Peninsula Akti, on the coast of the Aegean Sea, in NE mainland Greece. *224*

Stagnone : island in a lagoon, N of Lilybaeum (Marsala), at the W end of the island of Sicily, in W Mediterranean Sea, W Europe. *234*

Stavromenos : site in CN of the island of Crete, near Eleutherna, N of Mount Ida, in C Mediterranean Sea. *206*

Stavros : 1. town on the W corner of the peninsula Akrotiri, on the shore of the Gulf of Khanion, in NW island of Crete, C Mediterranean Sea. *204*; -- 2. mountain on the N side of the town. *204*

Stenukleros : plain in NE Messenia, SE of the river Amphitos, in SW Peloponnesos. *196*

Steppe : the migratory route made of large plains of grassland and mountain ranges, stretching from modern Hungary in E Europe, through CN Asia, as far as NE China, accommodating many nomadic tribes, such as the Scythians and the Parthians. *246*

Stiboates : river, modern Chesmeh-i-Ali, flowing NW in NW Iran, past Hekatompulos, through Hyrcania, into the Caspian Sea, W Asia. *260*

Stiria : city in the SE of Attika, N of Prasiai, in SE mainland Greece, on the coast of CW Aegean Sea. *208*

Stiris : town in SE Phokis, NE of Medeon, in CS mainland Greece. *214*

Stobi : town in C Macedonia, S of Bulazoia, near the Axios river, in N mainland Greece. *224*

Stratia : Homeric river in Arkadia, exact location unknown, in CN Peloponnesos. *192*

Stratos : town in S Akarnania, on hills above the Acheloos river, near the border with Aitolia, in SW mainland Greece. *216*

Strepsa : inland town located somewhere in Bottike, N of the Chalkidike, in SE Macedonia, NE mainland Greece. *224*

Strongule : small Aiolian island N of NE island of Sicily and W of SW Italy, in SE Tyrrhenian Sea, W Europe. *238*

Strophades : see Echinades. *216*

Strumon : river flowing between Macedonia and Thrace, from Mount Skombros, through present-day Bulgaria and NE Greece, into the N Aegean Sea, SW of Kavala, in NE mainland Greece. *224 & 226*

Struthos : cape on the SW side of the peninsula Argolis, NW of Mases, in CS Argolis, NE Peloponnesos. *202*

Stulari : village in S Elis, exact location unknown, in CW Peloponnesos. *194*

Stumphalis : ancient lake at the foot of Mount Chaon, source of the Erasinos river, S of Argos, in CW Argolis, NE Peloponnesos. *202*

Stumphalos : town in NE Arkadia, S of Mount Kullene, in NE Peloponnesos. *192*

Sturia : town at the SE end of the island of Euboia, in CW Aegean Sea. *228*

Stux : 1.mythological river, tributary of Acheron in Hades. *268*; --
2. according to legend, this mythological river surfacing on the
W side of Nonakris in CN Arkadia, CN Peloponnesos. *192*

Subota : town of SW Epeiros, exact location uncertain, in NW
mainland Greece. *218*

Subrita : site in the CN of the island of Crete, C Mediterranean
Sea. *206*

Sudan : see Kush. *188, 244 & 246*

Suez : 1. gulf extending as a NW arm of the Red Sea, between
Egypt and the Sinai Peninsula, in NE Africa. *242*; -- 2. city at the
N end of this gulf. *242*; -- 3. canal stretching N from this gulf to
the SE Mediterranean Sea, in NE Africa. *242*

Sukas : see Tell Sukas. *256*

Sulaimãn : mountain range in ancient N Gedrosia, running NS in C
Pakistan, between Baluchistan to the W and the Indus river to
the E, in C Asia. *262 & 264*

Sulcis : coastal town, N of Nora, at the S end of the island of
Chardan (Sardinia), in the N Tyrrhenian Sea, W Europe. *232*

Sumbola : town in SE Arkadia, near the border with Lakonia, in SE
Peloponnesos. *192*

Sume : island of the Dodekanesoi, N of the island of Rhodes, in
Aegean Sea. *230 & 254*

Sumer : most ancient S region of Mesopotamia, later known as
Lagash and Babylonia, along the Euphrates river, in present-day
S Iraq, W Asia. *258*

Sumetia : town in the mountainous area S of Lukoa, in SE Arkadia,
CE Peloponnesos. *192*

Sunion : 1. cape at the S tip of Attika. *208*; -- 2. city on this cape,
in SE mainland Greece. *208*

Surie : Homeric island of mythology, near Ortugia, either Delos in
the Cyclades, CW Aegean Sea, or SE of Siracusa, off the island
of Sicily, in W Mediterranean Sea. *269*

Suros : island in the C of the Cyclades, NW of Delos, in the
Aegean Sea. *230*

Surt : 1, see Sirte city. *244*; -- 2. see Sidra gulf. *244*

Susa : ancient city of Elam, in the SW of Media (Persia), at the foot
of the S Zagros mountain range, along the Eulaeus river, in
present-day SW Iran, W Asia. *258 & 260*

Susia : city of E Parthia, NE of Meshed, in present-day NE Iran, C
Asia. *260*

Susiana : see Elam. *258 & 260*

Suthas : river flowing SN along the border between NW Argolis
and E Achaia, into the Gulf of Korinthos, near Aristonautae, in
CN Peloponnesos. *200 & 202*

Sutlej : see Zaradros river. *266*

Suto : town in N Egypt, NW Nile Delta, between Canopus and Xois, in NE Africa. *242*

Suva : town in the NW of the island of Crete, exact location uncertain, C Mediterranean Sea. *204*

Suvritos : town, near Rithumna, exact location uncertain, in the CN of the island of Crete, C Mediterranean Sea. *204*

Sveshtari : town of C Thrace, in NE mainland Greece, present-day E Bulgaria, SE Europe. *226*

Swat : 1. see Choaspes river, in Afghanistan, C Asia. *262*; -- 2. see Choaspes valley. *262*

Switzerland: country of W Europe, surrounded by France, Italy, Austria and Germany. *188*

Sybaris : town, later renamed Thurii, on the SW side of the Gulf of Taranto, in CS Italy, W Europe. *238*; -- 2. river by this town, discharging where the gulf becomes the Ionian Sea. *238*

Syca : city near the SE end of the island of Sicily, NW of Siracusa, in W Mediterranean Sea. *236*

Syene : see Aswan. *242*

Symaethus : river flowing SE from the Aetna mountains, into the Sicilian Sea near Catana, in the NE of the island of Sicily, W Mediterranean Sea. *236*

Symplegades : see Kuaneia. *250 & 269*

Syracuse : see Siracusa, city and harbor. *236*

Syrdarya : 1. area of ancient Chorasmia, SE of the Aral Sea, in present-day N Uzbekistan, CN Asia. *260*; -- 2. city in the SW of this region. *260*; -- 3. see Jaxartes river. *260*

Syrgis : river of Scythia, flowing from the Carpathian mountains, through present-day Romania, before entering the Gulf of Maeotis (Azov) in S Ukraine, off the N Euxine (Black) Sea, in E Europe. *248*

Syria : 1. in ancient times, general region beyond the E end of the Mediteranean Sea, including Palestine to the W & S and Coele Syria to the NE, in W Asia. *256 & 258*; -- 2. in modern times, country covering mostly ancient Coele Syria, S of E Turkey, W of Iraq, N of Jordan and E of Lebanon & Israel *188 & 246*

Syrtis Major : see Sidra. *244*

Syrtis Minor : see Gabes. *244*

T

Tacompso : island in the Nile river, near the border between Egypt and Nubia (Sudan), in NE Africa. *244*

Tadzen : river in Turkmenistan, continuation of the Harirûd river of Afghanistan, flowing NW into the Kara Kum desert, E of the Caspian Sea, in C Asia. *260*

Tadzhikistan : see Tajikistan. *262*

Tagus : river of Iberia, flowing W from E Spain, across Portugal, into the Atlantic Ocean, in W Europe. *232*

Tahtali : mountain range rising N of Tarsus, in Cilicia, in present-day SE Turkey, W Asia. *256*

Tainaron : 1. cape in SW Lakonia, modern Matapan, at the S tip of the Malea (Mani) Peninsula, in SE Peloponnesos. *198*; 2, seaport city, modern Kaparisso, at the foot of this cape. *198*

Tajikistan : country of ancient Sogdiana, also known as Tadzhikistan, surrounded by Uzbekistan, China and Afghanistan, in CN Asia. *188, 246 & 266*

Taleton : mountain in CW Lakonia, S of Sparta, in SE Peloponnesos. *198*

Talioti : see Asine. *202*

Tall Bastah : see Bubastis. *242*

Talmena : seaport city of Gedrosia, on the coast of the Arabian Sea, in present-day SW Pakistan, C Asia. *264*

Tamassos : town in CN of the island of Cyprus, in the NE Mediterranean Sea, W Asia. *256*

Tamnus : mountains of C Lydia, in C Asia Minor, present-day CW Turkey. *250*

Tamunae : city of Eretria, in C of the island of Euboia, E of the N end of the Gulf of Petalion, in CW Aegean Sea. *228*

Tanagra : city in SE Boiotia, on the N bank of the Asopos river, in SE mainland Greece. *212*

Tanais : 1. river of Scythia, modern Don river, in present-day S Russia, SE Europe, flowing SW and joining the Danube river as a branch of the delta, in present-day Romania, before entering the Gulf of Maeotis (Azov), off the N Euxine (Black) Sea. *187 & 248*; -- 2. ancient city at the NE end of the Sea of Maeotis, on the W bank of the Tanais river, in SE Europe. *248*; -- 3. see Caspian Sea. *248 & 260*

Tanaos : river flowing N from mount Parnon, in CN Lakonia, through Thureatis in SW Argolis, into the Bay of Thurea, in CE Peloponnesos. *198 & 202*

Tangier : see Tingis. *244*

Tanis : major city of N Egypt. modern San al-Hajar al-Qibliyah, biblical Zoan, in the NE Delta of the Nile river, halfway between Mendez and Pelusion, in NE Africa. *242*

Tanos : town, near Kudonia, exact location uncertain, in the NW of the island of Crete, C Mediterranean Sea. *204*

Taoke : city on the coast of NE Persian Gulf, W of Shiraz, In Persis, present-day S Iran, W Asia. *264*

Tapacae : city of Syrtis Minor, at the Gulf of Gabes in W Libya, on the N African coast of the Libyan Sea, in C Mediterranean Sea. *244*

Taphos : Homeric island, modern Meganissi, probably near the island of Ithaka, in the Ionian Sea, off Akarnania, on the SW coast of mainland Greece. *216*

Tapsus : 1. peninsula of the SE coast of Sicily, N of Siracusa, in W Europe. *236*; -- 2. city on this peninsula. *236*

Tapuria : tribal area, between Mardia in the W and Hyrcania in the E, S of the Caspian Sea, in present-day N Iran, W Asia. *260*

Taranto : 1. large gulf of the Ionian Sea, forming the arch of the boot of SE Italy, in W Europe. *238*; -- 2. city of Apulia, on the N side of this gulf. *238*

Taras : seaport city at the NE end of the gulf of Taranto, in SE Italy, W Europe. *238*

Tarne : Aiolian city of Mysia in NW Asia Minor, on the coast of the Aegean Sea, facing the island of Lesbos. *250*

Tarphe : Homeric city of Opuntian Lokris, on the Gulf of Oropos, in CE mainland Greece. *214*

Tarquinii : Etruscan town in Etruria, CW Italy, W Europe. *238*

Tarra : town on a hill overlooking the Libyan Sea, on the W bank of the Samaria river Gorge, NW of the Gulf of Mesara. in CS of the island of Crete, C Mediterranean Sea. *204*

Tarraco : town in NE Iberia (Spain), along the Mediterranean Sea, in W Europe. *232*

Tarsus : city of Cilicia near the NE corner of the Mediterranean Sea, in present-day SE Turkey, W Asia. *256*

Tartaria : ancient site, modern Turda, in Transylvania, C Romania, SE Europe. *240*

Tartaros : abyss at the bottom of Hades, in the Underworld. *268*

Tartessos : town of SW Iberia (Spain), on a bend near the mouth of the river Quadalquivir, in W Europe. *232*

Tash : see Dikili. *226*

Tashkurghan : see Khulm. *262*

Tatarevo : town of CW Thrace, along the Maritsa river, in present-day Bulgaria, SE Europe. *226*

Taucheira : coastal town of Libya, modern Tocra, in CN Africa, along the Mediterranean Sea. *244*

Taulantii : tribal land located in SW Illyria, present-day Albania, along the SE coast of the Adriatic Sea, in NW Ancient Greece. *218*

Taurica : see Crimea. *248*

Tauromenium : coastal town on the NE side of the island of Sicily, in W Mediterranean Sea, W Europe. *236*

Taurus : mountain range from Pisidia in present-day CS Turkey, W Asia, running E around Cilicia, along the NE Mediterranean Sea, then curving in a NE direction until it reaches NE Syria where the Euphrates river finds its source. *187 & 256*

Taxila : major city of ancient Bactria, in the area of Gandhāra, E of the Indus river, at the juncture of trade routes, in present-day NW India, C Asia. *266*

Taygetus : see Teügetos. *198*

Tearos : river with hot and cold springs, in SE Europe, N of the Bosporos, flowing through Thrace and joining the Agrianes and the Maritsa rivers before reaching the NE Aegean Sea, near Ainos. *226*

Tegea : 1. city of SE Arkadia, SE of modern Tripolis, in CE Peloponnesos. *192*;-- 2. town, near Kissamos, in the NW of the island of Crete, C Mediterranean Sea. *204*

Tegura : town in NW Boiotia, near Orchomenos, in CE mainland Greece. *212*

Tehrān : see Rhagae. *260*

Teichioussa : Ionian town near the coast of the SE Aegean Sea, between Miletos to the N and Iasos to the S, in Caria, SW Asia Minor, present-day SW Turkey. *254*

Teikhos : town in NW Elis, near the city of Elis, in NW Peloponnesos. *194*

Tejend : river flowing from CW Afghanistan, S of the Margush river, across NE Iran, into the Caspian Sea, in C Asia. *260*

Tekirdag : see Bisanthe. *226*

Tel Aviv : see Joppa (Jaffa). *258*

Teleboa : ancient area of Pelasgians, probably in Akarnania, in SW mainland Greece, opposite the island of Taphos, in the E Ionian Sea. *216*

Telepulos : mythical port city of the Laistrugonoi, perhaps on the island of Corsica, in the Tyrrhenian Sea, W Europe. *269*

Tell Acana : see Alalakh. *256*

Tell el- Amarna : see Amarna. *242*

Tell Sankarah : see Larsa. *258*

Tell Sukas : seaport at the NE end of the Mediterranean Sea, S of Ugarit, in S Phoenicia, present-day NW Syria, W Asia. *256*

Telmessos : town, modern Fethiye, in W Lycia, NE of the island of Rhodes, on the coast of the E Mediterranean Sea, in SW Asia Minor, present-day SW Turkey. *254*

Tembi : see Tempe. *220*

Temenion : city near the N end of the Gulf of Argolis, W of Tiruns, in CW Argolis, NE Peloponnesos. *202*

Temese : Homeric site, perhaps on the island of Cyprus, in E Mediterranean Sea, W Asia. *256*

Temnos : Aiolian town, in W Lydia, on the NW coast of Asia Minor, along the Aegean Sea. *250*

Tempe : 1. vale of NE Thessalia, modern Tembi, between S Mount Olumpos and N Mount Ossa, in N mainland Greece. *220*; -- 2. gorge through which the waters of the river Peneios of Thessalia flow to the Gulf of Thermai, in NW Aegean Sea. *220*

Tenea : town in NW Argolis, NE of mount Tretos, in NE Peloponnesos. *202*

Tenedos : Aiolian island in NE Aegean Sea, opposite Aiolis of Anatolia, in NW Asia Minor, present-day NW Turkey. *228 & 250*

Tenerion : plain in CS Boiotia, S of the Sphinx mountain, in SE mainland Greece. *212*

Tenos : island of the NE Cyclades, S of Andros, in CW Aegean Sea. *230*

Teos : town of Ionia, SE of Eruthrae, in CW Asia Minor, on the E coast of the Aegean Sea, in present-day CW Turkey. *254*

Tereia : mountain in Troas, NE of Troy, near the S shore of the Hellespontos, in NW Asia Minor, present-day NW Turkey. *250*

Terias : small river in the SE of the island of Sicily, flowing E into the Sicilian Sea, N of Siracusa, W Europe. *236*

Terina : coastal town on the W side of the boot of S Italy, along the Tyrrhenian Sea in W Europe. *238*

Terinaea : gulf probably on the E side of S Italy, S of the Gulf of Taranto, in W Europe. *238*

Termessos : 1. river in SW Boiotia, receiving the discharge of the river Lamos and flowing W into a small lake, S of Thisbe, in SE mainland Greece. *212*; -- 2. city of Pisidia, in CS Asia Minor, present-day CS Turkey. *256*

Termez : city of Bactria, along the Oxus river, in present-day N Afghanistan, C Asia. *262*

Termita : town in S Sogdiana, present-day S Kazakhstan, in C Asia. *262*

Termitito : town on the W side of the Gulf of Taranto, in CS Italy, W Europe. *238*

Teügetos : mountain range, running NS on the W side of Lakonia, in SE Peloponnesos. *198*

Teumesos : city of CE Boiotia, NE of Thebes, in SE mainland Greece. *212*

Teuthis : town in SW Arkadia, E of the river Gortunios, in C Peloponnesos. *192*

Teuthrania : 1. Homeric city of Troas, very near and sometimes taken for Troy, in NW Asia Minor, present-day NW Turkey. *250*; -- 2. area of Mysia, N of the Hermos river, in CW Asia Minor, present-day CW Turkey. *250*

Teuthrone : port city on the CW side of the Gulf of Lakonia, in Lakonia, SE Peloponnesos. *198*

Teutloussa : small island of the Dodekanesoi, N of the island of Rhodes, in the SE Aegean Sea. *230*

Thal : small desert in the Punjab, on the E side of the Indus river, in NE Pakistan, C Asia. *266*

Thalamae : city in the SW Teügetos mountain range of C Lakonia, in SE Peloponnesos. *198*

Thamiskia : city of E Macedonia, near Kalindoea, on the S side of Lake Bolbe in Mugdonia, N of the Chalkidike, in NE mainland Greece. *224*

Thapsacus : town, also called Jerabius, on the W bank of the Euphrates river, in NW Mesopotamia, present-day N Syria, in W Asia. *258*

Thapsus : 1. town of Tripolitania, in present-day NE Tunisia, in CN Africa. *244*; -- 2. small peninsula at the SE end of the island of Sicily, N of Siracusa, wih an isthmus connecting it to the island, in the Sicilian Sea, W Europe. *236*; -- 3. coastal town on this peninsula. *236*

Thar : desert In CW India, along the border with Pakistan, in C Asia. *266*

Tharros : coastal town, on the CW side of the island of Sardinia, in the Tyrrhenian Sea, W Europe. *232*

Thasopoula : small island near the island of Thasos, in N Aegean Sea. *228*

Thasos : 1. island of the Thracian Sporades, in NE Aegean Sea , adjacent to the Delta of the Nestos river, near the coast between Macedonia and Thrace. *190 & 228*;-- 2. town, also called Limenas, on this island. *228*

Thaumakia : Homeric city of E Thessalia, in CE mainland Greece, near the W coast of the Aegean Sea. *220*

Thebe : inland Homeric town of Mysia, at the foot of Mount Plakios, therefore also referred to as Hupoplakia like its surrounding plain, in W Asia Minor, present-day NW Turkey. *250*

Thebes : 1. major city, modern Thivai, on the SE plain of Boiotia, with Upper and Lower areas, in the SE of mainland Greece. *212*; -- 2. town in NE Achaia Phthiotis, renamed Nea Anchialos and later Philippopolis, on the NW shore of the Gulf of Pagassai, in NE mainland Greece. *222*; -- 3. town of Mysia, at the foot of mount Plakios, on a plain called Hupoplakia, in NW Asia Minor, present-day NW Turkey. *250*; -- 4. ancient city on both sides of the Nile river in S Egypt, present-day site of Luxor and Karnak, in NE Africa. *242*

Theganussa : island of the Mediterranean Sea, S of the Cape Akritas, in S Messenia, SW Peloponnesos. *196*

Theisoa : 1. town in CW Arkadia, E of the river Gortunios and N of Teuthis, in C Peloponnesos. *192*; -- 2. city of SW Arkadia, SE of Aliphera and NW of mount Lukaion, in C Peloponnesos. *192*

Thelpusa : city in NW Arkadia, E of the river Ladon, in CN Peloponnesos. *196*

Theodosia : port city on the E side of the Crimea, modern Kaffa, extending into the N Euxine (Black) Sea, in SE Europe. *248*

Theopetra : cave of Thessalia, S of Kalambaka, in N mainland Greece. *220*

Theotokou : town at the SE tip of Thessalia, between the Gulf Pagassai and the Aegean Sea, on the peninsula Magnesia, in NE mainland Greece. *220*

Thera : island most to the S of the Cyclades in the E Aegean Sea, destroyed by a volcanic eruption, renamed Santorini. *230*

Therapne : site of a shrine on the ridge S of Menelaion, SE of Sparta and E of the river Eurotas, in CW Lakonia, SE Peloponnesos. *198*

Thermai : 1. ancient name of the modern Gulf of Thermaikos, in NW Aegean Sea, between Thessalia to the W, Macedonia to the N and the peninsula Kassandra of the W Chalkidike to the E, in NE mainland Greece. *220, 224 & 228*; -- 2. city near the NE coast of this Gulf. *224*; -- 3. town on the CN side of the island of Sicily, on the coast of the S Tyrrhenian Sea, in W Europe. *234*; -- 4. town on the N coast of the island of Ikaria, in CS Aegean Sea. *230*

Thermaikos : see Thermai. *220 & 224*

Therme : see Salonika city. *224*

Thermi : city on the E side of the island of Lesbos, in NE Aegean Sea. *228*

Thermiscyra : city of Phrygia, on the SE shore of the Euxine (Black) Sea, E of Amisos, in N Turkey, W Asia. *248*

Thermodon : river of Phrygia, flowing N into the CS of the Euxine (Black) Sea, near Amisos, present-day NW Turkey, W Asia. *252*

Thermon : inland settlement in C Aitolia, in SW mainland Greece. *216*

Thermopulai : 1. pass on the border of Malis with Opuntian Lokris, between the Kallidromon mountain and the Gulf of

Oropos, in CE mainland Greece. *214*; -- 2. city near this pass, on the coast along this Gulf, W of the NE island of Euboia. *214*

Thespiai : town in the S plain of Boiotia, SE of Mount Helikon and N of Leuktra, in SE mainland Greece. *212*

Thespios : river flowing through NE Boiotia, into the Gulf of Oropos, in SE mainland Greece. *212*

Thesprotis : Homeric territory of W Epeiros, S of the river Thuamis, in NW mainland Greece, opposite the S part of the island of Kerkira (Corfu), in the Ionian Sea. *218*

Thessalia : 1. lowland region in NE mainland Greece, surrounded by mountains: the Khasia and Kambunion Mountains separating it in the N from Macedonia, Mount Olumpos in the N & E from Macedonia and the Gulf of Thermai, Mounts Othros, Pelion and Ossa in the E & S from Achaia Phthiotis and the Aegean Sea, and the Pindos Mountains in the W from Epeiros. *190, 218, 220, 222, 224 & 228*; -- 2. plain in the C of this region. *220*

Thessaloniki : 1. see Salonika city. *224*; -- 2. see Chalkidike. *224 & 228*

Thinis : town in S Egypt, on the W bank of the Nile river, N of Abudos, in NE Africa. *242*

Thisbe : Homeric city of SW Boiotia, SE of Mount Helikon, in SE mainland Greece. *212*

Thius : river in CS Arkadia, E of Kromi, in CS Peloponnesos. *192*

Thivai : see Thebes in Boiotia. *212*

Thmuis : town in the C Nile Delta, N Egypt, NE Africa. *242*

Thoenis : town in CS Arkadia, NW of Megalopolis, in CS Peloponnesos. *192*

Thorikos : port town, at the promontory of Agios Nikolaos, separating the two harbors Frankolimani and Portomandri. In SE Attika, SE mainland Greece. *208*

Thornax : mount in the SW of the peninsula of Argolis, in SE Argolis, NE Peloponnesos. *202*

Thospitis : see Van Lake. *248*

Thouria : settlement in C Messenia, W of Kalamata, SW Peloponnesos. *196*

Thrace : region E of the Balkan peninsula, NE Ancient Greece, between the Danube river to the N, the Euxine (Black) sea and the Sea of Propontis (Marmara) to the E, the Aegean sea to the S and, to the W, variable between the Axios (Vardar) and the Strumon river basins, mostly present-day Bulgaria and NW Turkey. *190, 224, 228 & 240*

Thria : 1. plain in NW Attika, N and E of Eleusis, in SE mainland Greece. *210*; -- 2. city on this plain, E of Eleusis. *210*

Thrimakia : mythical island of god Helios, probably off the coast of Lakonia, in SE Peloponnesos. *269*

Thrimbokambos : town on the SW coast of the island of Crete, in C Mediterranean Sea. *204*

Thronion : Homeric town of Opuntian Lokris, near Thermopulai, on the coast along the Gulf of Oropos, in CE mainland Greece. *214*

Thruoëssa : see Thruon. *196*

Thruon : Homeric city, also called Thruoëssa, in SW Messenia, near Pulos in Nestor's Kingdom, in SW Peloponnesos. *196*

Thuamis : river, also known as Kalamas, flowing S and W from N Epeiros, between the areas of Kestrine in the N and Thesprotis in the S, into the NE Ionian Sea, near modern Igoumenitsa, in NW mainland Greece, opposite the S end of the island of Kerkura (Corfu). *218*

Thuamos : mountain range running from SW Epeiros, along the border with Akarnania, to the E of the S end of the Gulf of Ambrakia, in SW mainland Greece. *216 & 218*

Thumbre : Homeric city in Troas, near Troy, along the Scamander river, in NW Asia Minor, present-day NW Turkey. *250*

Thura : ancient region of N Mesopotamia, in present-day Iraq, W Asia. *258*

Thurea : 1. bay in SE of the Gulf of Argolis, in Thureatis, SW Argolis, NE Peloponnesos. *202*; -- 2. city, also called Kunuria, W of this bay. *202*

Thureatis : mountainous strip along the W shore of the Gulf of Argolis, from Astros to the S of the Gulf, in SW Argolis, NE Peloponnesos. *202*

Thuria : city in CE Messenia, N of the Gulf of Messenia, in SW Peloponnesos. *196*

Thurides : cape in SW Lakonia, on the SE side of the Gulf of Messenia, in SE Peloponnesos. *198*

Thurii : see city of Sybaris . *238*

Thurmeidai : village N of Peiraios, in CW Attika, SE mainland Greece. *208*

Thussos : city on the CW side of the peninsula Akti, in E Chalkidike, on the Gulf Agion Oros, in NW Aegean Sea, NE mainland Greece. *228*

Thynias : islet in the SW of the Euxine (Black) Sea, opposite Calpe, in NW Asia Minor, present-day NW turkey. *252*

Thyssagetai : area of Scythia, N of the Caspian Sea, in present-day Kazakhstan, NW Asia. *248*

Tiarantus : one of five rivers flowing from the Carpathian mountains, most to the W, into the Danube river, in Scythia, present-day Romania, E Europe. *240*

Tibareni : tribal area in Pontos, S of the E Euxine (Black) Sea, in C Anatolia, present-day CN Turkey, W Asia. *252*

Tiber : river of C Italy flowing SW from the Apennine mountains, past Rome, to the Tyrrhenian Sea, in W Europe. *238*

Tibet : region of CN Asia, N of the Himalaya mountains. *266*

Tibisis : river, modern Timis, flowing S from the S Carpathian mountains, across Romania, into the Danube river, in N Serbia, SE Europe. *240*

Tibur : city in CW Italy, modern Tivoli, W of Rome, in W Europe. *238*

Tichion : ancient city of Aitolia, exact location unknown, in C mainland Greece. *216*

Tigres : mythical river of the Peloponnesos, later called Harpus, course unknown. *269*

Tigris : river flowing from the E Taurus mountains of present-day E Turkey, SE through Mesopotamia, E of the Euphrates river, through modern N Syria and the length of Iraq, to end in the S marshes and the Persian Gulf, in W Asia. The Tigris and Euphrates rivers may have remained separate to the S end until the fourth century BCE. *187 & 258*

Tilos : island of the Dodekanesoi, NW of Rhodes, in SE Aegean Sea. *230*

Tilphusios : mountain SE of Lake Kopais, between the rivers Phalaros and Lophis, in SW Boiotia, SE mainland Greece. *212*

Timis : see Tibisis. *240*

Tin : islands, probably England and Ireland, so called because of the copper and tin mines, off the coast of Continental W Europe. *232*

Tingis : town on the SW coast of the Strait of Gibraltar, modern Tangier, on the Atlantic Ocean, in present-day NW Morocco, NW Africa. *244*

Tios : town in SW of the Euxine (Black) Sea, in NW Asia Minor, present-day NW Turkey. *252*

Tipha : port city in CS Boiotia, on the NE end of the Gulf of Korinthos, in SE mainland Greece. *212*

Tirana : major city of Albania, in ancient SW Illyria, E Europe. *218*

Tiruns : city near the NE end of the Gulf of Argolis, on the shore in Antiquity, now inland because of the sediments from the river Inachos, in CW Argolis, NE Peloponnesos. *202*

Tisza : river of the Balkans, flowing W from the Carpathian mountains, then S into E Hungary and Serbia where it joins the Danube river, in SE Europe. *240*

Titan : mountain in S Thessalia, in NE mainland Greece. *220*

Titane : town in NW Argolis, W of the river Asopos, in CN Peloponnesos. *202*

Titarisios : tributary joining the river Peneios in the plain of Thessalia, in N mainland Greece. *220*

Tithorea : town NW of Ledon, in C Phokis, CS mainland Greece. *214*

Tithronion : ancient city in N Phokis, NE of Amphikaea, in CS mainland Greece. *214*

Titthion : mountain in CE Argolis, CE of the peninsula of Argolis, W of Epidauros, in NE Peloponnesos. *202*

Tivoli : see Tibur. *238*

Tmolos : mount in the C of Maeonia (Lydia), E of Mount Sipulos, above the valley of the Hermos river, near Smyrna, on the coast of the Aegean Sea, in CW Asia Minor, present-day CW Turkey. *250*

Tocra : see Taucheira. *244*

Tombos : town in S Egypt, on the E bank of the Nile river, at the third Cataract, in NE Africa. *244*

Tomerus : see Mulla river. *262 & 264*

Tomis : port city, modern Constanta, on the W Euxine (Black) Sea, in present-day E Romania, E Europe. *226 & 240*

Tonsos : city of Thrace, in NE mainland Greece, modern Yambol, on the Tundja river, near the coast of the Euxine (Black) Sea, in present-day SE Bulgaria, E Europe. *226*

Toprakkale : town of SW Urartu, in E Cilicia, SW of lake Van, in present-day NE Turkey, W Asia. *256*

Torone : town in the SW of the peninsula Sithonia of the C Chalkidike, on a promontory above the seaport open to the N Aegean Sea, in NE mainland Greece. *228*

Toscana : region in the C of Italy, N of Etruria, in W Europe. *238*

Toumba : 1. town probably in Magnesia, SE Thessalia, NE mainland Greece. *220*; -- 2. site of a cemetery near Xeropolis, on the SW of the island of Euboia, along the Gulf of Petalion, E of mainland Greece. *228*

Tourliditsa : village with tholos tombs, in Messenia, SW Peloponnesos. *196*

Tracheia : area of Cilicia, along the NE Mediterranean Sea, between the Lamos and Calycadnus rivers, in SE Anatolia, present-day SE Turkey, W Asia. *256*

Trachis : 1. Homeric city in N Malis, between the Sperkeios and Asopos rivers, near Thermopulai, in NE mainland Greece. *214*; -- 2. area around this city. *214*

Trachu : mountain in NE Arkadia, E of Orchomenos, in NE Peloponnesos. *192*

Tragana : village of SW Messenia, near the coast of the Ionian Sea, S of Pulos, in SW Peloponnesos. *196*

Tragia : small island in the SE Aegean Sea, S of Samos, opposite Miletos, in SW Asia Minor, present-day SW Turkey. *230*

Transylvania : region in C Romania, plateau N of the Alps, in E Europe. *240*

Traostalos : village near the SE coast of the island of Crete, in C Mediterranan sea. *206*

Trapani : see Drepanon. *234*

Trapezos : 1. town in SW Arkadia, E of Mount Lukaion, in CS Peloponnesos. *192*;-- 2. town of N Armenia, on the coast of the SE end of the Euxine (Black) Sea, in W Asia. *248*

Trasimene : lake in N Umbria, C Italy, W Europe. *238*

Trebeniste : town in CE Illyria, NW of lake Luknites of Macedonia, in N mainland Greece. *218*

Tretos : mountain N of Mukenae, in NW Argolis, NE Peloponnesos. *202*

Trianda : Ancient city on a cape in the N of the island of Rhodes, in SE Aegean Sea. *230*

Triballi : tribal land in the N of Macedonia, S of the Danube river, in present-day Serbia, E Europe. *224*

Trieste : 1. gulf in the NE corner of Italy, in CS Europe. *238*; -- 2. seaport city on this gulf. *238*

Trikala : city SW of Larissa, on the Lithaios river, in C Thessalia, NE mainland Greece. *220*

Trikhonis : lake, SE of Agrinion, in SW Aitolia, SW mainland Greece. *216*

Trikka : town of CW Thessalia, E of the E Pindos mountain range, in CN mainland Greece. *220*

Trikolini : town in C Arkadia, N of Megalopolis, in CS Peloponnesos. *192*

Trikorithos : town of NE Attika, S of Rhamnos, near the coast of the Gulf of Petalion, in SE mainland Greece. *210*

Trikrana : small island, S of the peninsula of Argolis, in the Mirtóön Sea, NE Peloponnesos. *202*

Trinacria : original name of Sicily, referring to its triangular shape within three promontories: Lilybaeum in the W, Pelorus in the NE and Plemmyrium in the SE. *234*

Trinasos : group of three small islands, in the NW side of the Gulf of Lakonia, in SE Peloponnesos. *198*

Triopion : 1. cape at the W end of the peninsula Bubassos, opposite the island of Sumi, in SW Caria, Asia Minor, present-day SW Turkey. *254*; -- 2. town on this cape. *254*

Triphulia : territory astride the land of the Minyans who migrated from Boiotia to S Elis and N Messenia, between the Ionian Sea to the W and Arkadia to the E, in CW Peloponnesos. *194*

Tripoatis : city of E Macedonia, near Kalindoea, on the SE side of Lake Bolbe in Mugdonia, N of the Chalkidike, in NE mainland Greece. *224*

Tripodiskos : city W of the Bay of Salamis, E of Mount Geraneia, in Megaris, CS mainland Greece. *210*

Tripoli : see Oea. *244*

Tripolis : modern city of SE Arkadia, founded to replace the three ancient cities of Tegea, Mantineia and Pallantion, in C Peloponnesos. *192*

Tripolitania : region of present-day NW Libya and Tunisia, in CN Africa. *244*

Tripotamos : river of C Macedonia, tributary of the Aliakmon river, in NE mainland Greece. *224*

Triteia : city of CS Achaia, near the border with Arkadia, in CN Peloponnesos. *200*

Trito : Hesiodic mythical river on whose banks Zeus gave birth to goddess Athena. *269*

Tritonis : ancient lake in S Tunisia, CN Africa. *244*

Troas : region bordering on the S side of the Hellespontos (Dardanelles), in NW Asia Minor, present day NW Turkey. *190 & 230*

Trogilos : city probably on the SE coast of the island of Sicily, in W Mediterranean Sea, W Europe. *236*

Troitilum : coastal town, probably on the CE side of the island of Sicily, N of Siracusa, in W Mediterranean Sea, W Europe. *236*

Troizen : 1. territory in the SE of the peninsula of Argolis, in SE Argolis, NE Peloponnesos, along the W side of the Saronic Gulf. *202*; -- 2. city in this territory. *202*

Troödos : mountain range in the CW of the island of Cyprus, in E Mediterranean Sea. *256*

Troy : major city, the Homeric Ilios, on a promontory overlooking the Hellespontos, in Troas, NW Asia Minor, present-day NW Turkey. *250*

Tsangli : 1. site of important ceramic work, SE of Larissa, in CN Thessalia, N mainland Greece. *220*; -- 2. settlement in N Caria in C Asia Minor, between Ephesos and Miletos, in CW Turkey. *254*

Tsangon : pass in S Illyria, from W Macedonia to the E Adriatic Sea, in NW mainland Greece. *218*

Tsopani- Rachi : tumulus for burial in Messenia, SW Peloponnesos. *196*

Tsoungiza : settlement on a hill, SE of Mount Apesas, below ancient Nemea, in NW Argolis, NE Peloponnesos. *202*

Tulcea : see Aigussos. *226 & 240*

Tulissos : town in CN of the island of Crete, SW of Knossos, in C Mediterranean Sea. *206*

Tundja : river of SE Thrace, tributary of the Maritsa river from the W side, near Uskudama, in present-day E Bulgaria, E Europe. *226*

Tunis : 1. gulf of the Mediterranean Sea, on the CN coast of Africa, in Tunisia. *244*; -- 2. see Carthage. *244*

Tunisia : country of CN Africa, between Algeria and Libya, on the Mediterranean Sea. *188 & 244*

Tunka : see Tundja. *226*

Tupaios : mountain S of Olumpia, in SE Elis, NW Peloponnesos. *194*

Tupanaei : see Aipu. *194*

Tuphaoneos : mount in SE Thessalia, N of Phthiotic Thebes, in NE mainland Greece. *220*

Turda : see Tartaria. *240*

Turkey : country mostly in W Asia, with a small portion of the SE Balkan peninsula and Chersonesos in the NW pertaining to SE Europe, covering the overlapping region of ancient Asia Minor, Anatolia and the ancient Hittite territories, E of the Aegean Sea, S of the Euxine (Black) Sea, N of E Mediterranean Sea, Syria and Iraq, W of NW Iran and Azerbaijan. *188, 226, 230, 240, 246, 248, 252 & 256*

Turkmenistan : modern country of ancient Hyrcania, bordering on Kazakhstan to the N, Uzbekistan the to the NE, Iran & Afghanistan to the S and the Caspian Sea to the W, in CN Asia. *188, 246, 248, 260 & 262*

Turrha : inland city of Ionia, on the N bank of the Kaustros river, in present-day CW Turkey, W Asia. *254*

Tuthoa : river in CW Arkadia, tributary of the river Ladonas, in C Peloponnesos. *192*

Tyana : city N of Tarsus, in Cilicia, present-day CS Turkey, W Asia. *256*

Tyndaris : town in the NE of the island of Sicily, along the S Tyrrhenian Sea, in W Europe. *236*

Tyras : 1. N branch of the delta of the Danube river discharging into the Euxine (Black) Sea, in S Scythia, present-day Romania, SE Europe. *240*; -- 2. town along the estuary of this river. *240*

Tyre : seaport on the E coast of the Mediterranean sea, S of Sidon, in ancient Phoenicia, present-day S Lebanon, W Asia. *258*

Tyritake : town of the Crimea, along the N Euxine (Black) Sea, S of the Sea of Maeotis (Azov), in SE Europe. *248*

Tyrrhenia : 1. sea as an arm of the Mediterranean Sea, between Italy to the E, and the islands of Corsica, Sardinia and Sicily to the Strait of Messina where it connects with the Ionian Sea to the S. *188, 234, 236 & 238*; -- 2. see Etruria. *238*

U

Udyana : region at the W end of the Himalaya mountain range and E of Badakhshan, in C Asia. *266*

Ugarit : seaport city of Phoenicia, modern Ras Shamra, on a mound overlooking the NE Mediterranean Sea, in present-day NW Syria, W Asia. *256*

Ukraine : country of SE Europe, ancient Scythia, N of the Euxine (Black) Sea, between Russia to the E, Belarus to the N, and Poland, Slovakia, Romania and Moldova to the W. *188, 240, 246 & 248*

Ullais : town of Babylonia on the W bank of the Euphrates river, in S Mesopotamia, present-day S Iraq, W Asia. *258*

Ulu Burun : town on Cape Gelidonya, overlooking the Mediterranean Sea, in S Pampylia, present-day Turkey, SW Asia Minor. *256*

Umbria : region of CE Italy extending from the Tiber river to the Adriatic sea, in W Europe. *238*

Underworld : 1. see Hades. *268*; -- 2. lake in this mythical Underworld. *268*

Upati : town in the mountains of Ainis, C mainland Greece. *214*

Ural : mountain range from the Arctic Ocean in the N, through C Russia to N Kazakhstan in the S, in E Europe. *248*

Urartu : area of E Anatolia, in present-day NE Turkey, from S Armenia in the N to Kurdistan of N Iraq in the S, SE of the Euxine (Black) Sea and SW of Scythia, in W Asia. *248*

Urfa : see Edessa. *258*

Urmia : 1. inland lake in SE Urartu, S of the Caucasus Mountains, E of lake Van, in E Anatolia, present-day NW Iran, W Asia. *258*; -- 2. city on the W side of this lake. *258*

Urtakos : town, near Thrumbokambos, exact location uncertain, in the NW of the island of Crete, C Mediterranean Sea. *204*

Uruk : city, also called Erech, NW of Ur, in ancient Sumer, on the W bank of the Euphrates river, in S Mesopotamia, later part of W Parthia, W Asia. *258*

Uskudama : city, later called Adrianople and presently Edirne, in CS Thrace, W of the Euxine (Black) Sea, in present-day European Turkey, near the borders with Greece and Bulgaria. *226*

Ustica : island of the S Tyrrhenian Sea, NW of Palermo, in SW Sicily, W Europe. *234 & 238*

Utica : city on the N coast of Africa, near present-day Tunis in Tunisia, N of Carthage. *244*

Uzbekistan : modern country of ancient Chorasmia, between the Amu Darya (Oxus) and Syrdarya (Jaxartes) rivers, in of CN Asia, bordering on Kazakhstan to the NE & NW, Tahkistan to the S & SE, Afghanistan to the S and Turkmenistan to the SW, in CN Asia. *188, 246, 248, 260 & 262*

V

Vahlika : see Bactra. *262*

Vai : coastal town, opposite the island of Elassa, at the NE tip of the island of Crete, CS Mediterranean Sea. *206*

Van : 1. lake in C Urartu, also known as Thospitis and Arsissa, S of the Caucasus Mountains, in present-day SE Turkey, in W Asia. *248*; -- 2. city on the E shore of this lake. *248*

Vapheio : town in CW Lakonia, SE of Sparta, in CS Peloponnesos. *198*

Vardar : see Axios river. *224*

Varna : see Odessos. *240*

Vasiliki : town in the E of the island of Crete, in C Mediterranean Sea. *206*

Vasiliko : town in NE Achaia, also called Sikiona, near the border with Argolis, W of Sikuon in Argolis, S of the Gulf of Korinthos, in NE Peloponnesos. *200*

Vathia : town on the SE coast of the island of Salamis, in N Saronic Gulf, SE mainland Greece. *208*

Vatupetro : site S of Archanes, near the C of the island of Crete, in C Mediterranean Sea. *206*

Vedea : river of N Thrace, present-day Romania, flowing S into the Danube river as a tributary, in SE Europe. *226*

Veii : town of S Etruria, N of Rome, in C Italy, W Europe. *238*

Velatouri : hill (akropolis) in C of Thorikos, in SE Attika, SE mainland Greece. *208*

Velestinon : see Pherai. *220*

Venice : 1. gulf in the NE Adriatic Sea, W of the peninsula of Istria, in NE Italy, C Europe. *238*; -- 2. see Altinum. *238*

Vergina : town of SE Macedonia, in NE mainland Greece, also known as Aigai, on the Aliakmon river, W of the Gulf of Thermai, in NW Aegean Sea. *224*

Vermion : mountain of the CS Macedonia, in NE mainland Greece. *224*

Vesuvius : volcanic mountain near the Bay of Neapolis, in S Italy, W Europe. *238*

Vetulonia : Etruscan town in Etruria, CE Italy, W Europe, facing the island of Elba in the N Tyrrhenian Sea. *238*

Viannos : site NE of Arvi, in SE of the island of Crete, C Mediterranean Sea. *206*

Vigla : town on a hill overlooking the town of Torone, in the SW of the C peninsula Sithonia of the Chalkidike, in NE mainland Greece. *228*

Vinca : ancient area near the Danube river, from NE Serbia to its S border with the Republic of Macedonia, in SE Europe. *240*

Vis : island of the archipelago in NE Adriatic Sea, also called Lissa, along the coast of Dalmatia, in ancient W Illyria, E Europe. *218*

Visentium : Etruscan town in Etruria, C Italy, W Europe. *238*

Vistritsa : see Aliakmon river. *224*

Vitsa : site of a cemetery, N of Ioannina, in CN Epeiros, NW mainland Greece. *218*

Vivara : town of SW Italy, on the gulf of Salerno, in W Europe. *238*

Vlachopoulo : village with tholos tombs in Messenia, exact location unknown, SW Peloponnesos. *196*

Vlichada : cave at Diros, on the Mani Peninsula, in SE Lakonia, SW Peloponnesos. *198*

Vlorë : bay of the E Adriatic Sea, in NW Epeiros, on the border with Illyria, present-day Albania, in NW mainland Greece. *218*

Vodomatis : Mount N of lake Ioaninna, in CN Epeiros, NW mainland Greece. *218*

Voidhokoilia : 1. bay of SW Messenia, in the Ionian Sea, W of the Osmanaga lagoon, in SW Peloponnesos. *196*; -- 2. site with tholos tombs, on the shore of the same bay, N of Pulos, in SW Messenia, SW Peloponnesos. *196*

Voidomatis : river of Epeiros, flowing N from the Pindos mountains into the Aoos river, at Konitsa, in NW mainland Greece. *218*

Volaterrae : Etruscan town in CE Italy, W Europe. *238*

Volga : river of Russia, flowing SE from the hills NW of Moscow, into the Caspian Sea, in E Europe. *248*

Volomandra : funerary site of an Archaic kouros in Attika, exact location unknown, in SE mainland Greece. *208*

Volos : 1. see Gulf of Pagassai. *220 & 222*; -- 2. town, ancient Pagassai. *220*

Volturnum : city on the SW side of S Italy, N of Neapolis, along the Tyrrhenian Sea, in W Europe. *238*

Vouliagmeni : lake E of Perachora, in SW Megaris, NE Peloponnesos. *210*

Vounous : town on CN island of Cyprus, in E Mediterranean Sea, W Asia. *256*

Vourvoura : city in NE Lakonia, exact location unknown, in C Peloponnesos. *198*

Vrakhori : see Agrinion. *216*
Vranesi : town in NE Phokis, C mainland Greece. *214*
Vratsa : town of NW Thrace, along the Oskios river, in present-day Bulgaria, SE Europe. *228*
Vrokastro : town in the SW corner of Gulf of Megambellou, near the E end of the island of Crete, in C Mediterranean Sea. *206*
Vrusinas : town probably near Rhitumna, on the N side of the CW of the island of Crete, in C Mediterranean Sea. *204*
Vulci : Etruscan town in Etruria, C Italy, W Europe. *238*
Vurgunda : town at the N end of the island of Krapathos, between the islands of Crete and Rhodes in C Mediterranean Sea. *230*

W

Waksh : river of Bactria, flowing NW from the Himalayas, N of the Pyan river, into the Pyan river as a tributary, in S Tajikistan, C Asia. *262*
Walachia : area in S Transylvania, C Romania, SE Europe. *240*
Watar : city of Gedrosia, on the coast of the Arabian Sea, in present-day SW Pakistan, C Asia. *264*
Waziristan : mountainous region of Bactria, in NW Pakistan, along the Afghanistan border, in C Asia. *266*
West Bank : modern territory populated mostly by Arabs, on the W side of the Jordan river, within Israel, in W Asia. *258*
White : 1. mountain range, also known as Lavka, covering the CW of the island of Crete, in C Mediterranean Sea. *204*; -- 2. mythical island of Achilles' burial, perhaps Leukas, in the Ionian Sea. *269*
Wular : lake in the Jammu area, source of the Hydraotes and Hydaspes rivers, in NE Pakistan, C Asia. *266*

X

Xanthos : 1. river flowing from the Taurus Mountains, through Lycia, into the Gulf of Antalya in Pamphylia, NE Mediterranean Sea, in W Asia. *254*; -- 2. city near the mouth of this river. *254*; -- 3. see Scamander. *250 & 269*

Xeropolis : site SE of Lefkandi, on the C island of Euboia, along the Gulf of Petalion, E of mainland Greece. *228*

Xerovrusi : village in E Elis, exact location unknown, in CW Peloponnesos. *194*

Xiphonia : 1. coastal promontory on the CE side of the island of Sicily, in W Mediterranean Sea, W Europe. *236*; -- 2. harbor city, S of this promontory. *236*

Xois : city in the CN of the Nile Delta, N Egypt, between Sais and Sebennytos, in NE Africa. *242*

Xuthia : inland town in the CE of the island of Sicily, in W Mediterranean Sea, W Europe. *236*

Y

Yambol : see Tonsos. *226*

Yemen : country on the Gulf of Aden, S of Saudi Arabia and W of Oman, in W Asia. *188 & 246*

Yesil : river of Phrygia, ancient Iris river, flowing into the S Euxine (Black) Sea, in present-day NW Turkey, W Asia. *252*

Z

Zab : 1. river called Great Zab, to the N of the Lesser Zab, in Mesopotamia, flowing W from the Zagros mountains into the Tigris river, in present-day C Iraq, W Asia. *258*; -- 2. river called Lesser Zab, to the S of the Great Zab. *258*

Zabatos : river flowing from the W slopes of the Caucasus mountains, through Armenia, into the E Euxine (Black) Sea, in CN Anatolia, Present-day CN Turkey, W Asia. *248*

Zadrakarta : city of Hyrcania, near the SE coast of the Caspian Sea, probably modern Sari, in present-day N Iran, C Asia. *260*

Zagros : mountain range between the length of Iran to the E, and Turkey and Iraq to the W, down to the Persian Gulf, W Asia. *258, 260 & 264*

Zahedan : city between the S of two deserts, Lut to the W and Mago to the E, in present-day C Afghanistan, C Asia. *260*

Zakinthos : 1. island of the CE Ionian Sea, S of the island of Kephallenia, off the coast of Elis, on the NW side of the Peloponnesos. *194*; -- 2. major city on the CE of this island. *194*

Zakros : city with a palace on a small bay, at the CE end of the island of Crete, in C Mediterranean Sea. *206*

Zankle : town, also called Messana, on NE island of Sicily, opposite the S tip of Italy across the Strait of Messina, in W Mediterranean Sea, W Europe. *236*

Zaradros : river, also called Hesidros, modern Sutlej, flowing from lake Rakshastal of SW Tibet, through the Himalaya gorges, into NE Pakistan and the Punjab where it meets with the Hyphasis (Beãs) river and other rivers on the way to the Indus river, in C Asia. *266*

Zarafshan : 1. city in mining area, ancient Sogdiana, present-day Uzbekistan, C Asia. *262*; -- 2. see Polytimelus river. *262*

Zaranj : town in the area of Zranka, at the point where three regions of C Asia meet, namely Parthia, Bactria and Gedrosia, in present-day Pakistan. *262*

Zarax : seaport city in SE Lakonia, on the Mirtóön Sea, N of Epidauros Limera, in SE Peloponnesos. *198*

Zariaspa : see Bactria. *260 & 262*

Zea : 1. harbor on the E side of the peninsula of Peiraia, modern Pasalimani, in SW Attika, SE mainland Greece. *208*; -- 2. town on this harbor. *208*

Zeleia : town in NW Troas, S of the Strait of Hellespontos (Dardanelles), in NW Asia Minor, present-day NW Turkey. *250*

Zeugma : city of NW Syria, on the W bank of the N Euphrates river, in W Asia. *258*

Zeus Ammon : see Ammonium city. *242*

Ziãrat : 1. city known as Ziãrat-e-shah-Maqsûd, in the Peshãwar area, NE of Quetta, in present-day NW Pakistan, C Asia. *266*; -- 2. city known as Ziãrat-Gali-Chah, in Baluchistan, W of Sandy Desert, SW Pakistan, C Asia. *264*

Zoan : city in the NE Nile Delta, in NE Egypt, NE Africa. *242*

Zone : port city on the NE coast of the Aegean Sea, W of the mouth of river Maritsa, in CS Thrace,NW Turkey, SE Europe. *226*

Zoster : cape on the E coast of the C Saronic Gulf, in SW Attika, SE mainland Greece. *208*

Zou : palace site at the NE end of the island of Crete, in C Mediterranean Sea. *206*

Zranka : area between Areia and Baluchistan, N of the Arabian Sea, in present-day S Pakistan, C Asia. *246 & 262*

ATLAS

FOREWORD

The use of numbering instead of naming the places is necessary because of the crowded condition on most of the maps.

Signs are used to indicate the nature of each place, except on a few general maps:

simple number for a city or site (except p. 189)

square for ancient region or area

parenthesis for modern country (except p. 189)

triangle for mountain or cave

circle and grayish tone for river or sea

underline for island or peninsula

The reference at the end of every entry in the Lexicon is to the page of the list where the direction and number indicate the place on the following map of the Atlas.

The references to directions North, South, East, West and Center are abbreviated in the Atlas also: N, S, E, W and C.

All the maps were developed by the author with the assistance of a multiplicity of sources whose contribution was adapted to the special purpose of this Lexicon and Atlas.

Boundaries of regions and location of certain places, especially rivers, are flexible, the first for political and military reasons, the second for reasons of nature. High times are preferred, for example the Classical Period for Greece and the time of Alexander the Great for Central Asia.

In order to avoid every confusion, abbreviations appear occasionally next to the name of places by using the first two letters, except for island = il (isthmus = is) and cove = cv (country = co).

ANCIENT GREEK WORLD

For the Ancient Greeks, the earth was a flat oval sphere, longer from west to east than from north to south, and surrounded by a huge ocean, as Aristotle attested in his *Meteorology* of about 350 BCE (354b, 23-25 and 362b, 19-23, in Loeb Classical Library, vol. 397). Besides Hellas, the Greek world encompassed the lands of Southern Europe, Lybia (for North Africa) and Egypt, and West and Central Asia.

AFRICA SW1
Aegean SW2
Aithiopia SE3
Arabia SE4
Arabian/sea SE5
Aral Sea NE6
ASIA E7
Atlas/mt SW8
Ausonia NW23
Caspian Sea NE9
Caucasus/
   mt CE10
Celtic/re NW11
Crete SW12
Danube/ri NW13
Desert S14

Egypt SE15
Euphrates SE16
EUROPE W17
Euxine Sea C18
Greece CW19
Hellas CW19
Iberia CW20
India CE21
Indus/ri CE22
Italy NW23
Jaxartes/ri NE24
LIBYA SW1
Mauritania SW25
Mediterranean Sea
   CW26

Nile/ri SE27
OCEON Around28
Okeanos 28
Oxus NE29
Parapamisus/mt
   CE30
Persia SE31
Pillars of Herakles
   SW32
Red Sea SE33
Scythia NE34
Sicily CW35
Tanais/ri NE36
Taurus/mt CE37
Tigris SE38
Tin NW39

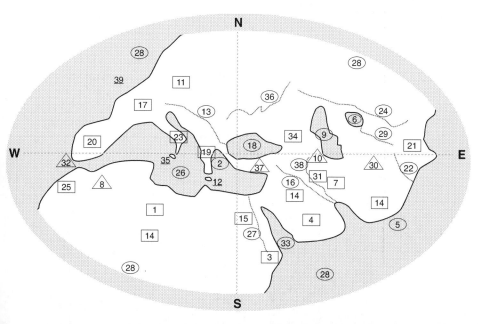

RELATED MODERN WORLD

Abu Dhabi SE33
Aden SE1
Adriatic NW2
Aegean NW3
Afghanistan CE4
Africa SW 5
Albania NW22
Algeria SW7
Alps NW8
Arabian SE9
Aral NE10
Armenia NE11
Asia E12
Atlantic NW13
Atlas SW14
Austria NW15
Azerbaijan NE16
Bahrain SE17
Belarus NW18
Belgium NW19
Bengal SE20
Black CN21
Bosnia NW22
Britain NW23
Bulgaria NW24
Caspian NE25
Caucasus NE26
Chad SW27
China NE28
Corsica NW29
Crete CW30
Croatia NW22
Cyprus C31
Czech Republic
  NW32
Djibouti SE 37
Dubai SE33
Egypt SW34
Emirates SE35

English NW36
Eritrea SE 37
Ethiopia SE37
Europe NW38
France NW39
Germany NW40
Greece NW41
Guinea SW42
Herzegovina
  NW22
Holland NW43
Hungary NW44
India SE45
Ionian NW46
Iran CE47
Iraq CE48
Ireland NW49
Israel C50
Italy NW51
Jordan C52
Kashmir NE53
Kazakhstan
  NE54
Kosovo NW22
Kyrgystan NE55
Lebanon CN56
Libya SW57
Lithuania NW58
Macedonia NW59
Mali SW60
Marmara NW61
Mauritania SW62
Mediterranean
  NW63
Moldova NW64
Mongolia NE65
Montenegro
  NW22
Morocco CW66

Netherlands
  NW43
Niger SW67
Nigeria SW68
Oman/co SE69
Oman/gu SE70
Pakistan SE71
Persian SE72
Poland NW73
Portugal NW74
Red CS75
Romania NW76
Russia NE77
Sardinia NW78
Saudi Arabia
  SE79
Senegal SW80
Serbia NW22
Sicily NW82
Slovakia NW83
Slovenia NW22
Somalia SE 37
Spain NW85
Sudan CS86
Switzerland
  NW87
Syria NE88
Tajikistan NE89
Tunisia CW90
Turkey CN91
Turkmenistan
  NE92
Tyrrhenian
  NW93
Ukraine NW94
Uzbekistan NE95
Yemen SE96

RELATED MODERN WORLD

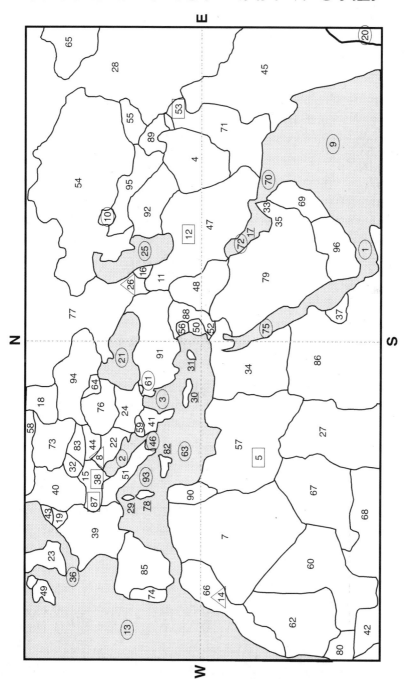

ANCIENT GREECE and AEGEAN REGION

Achaia/Peloponnesos CW1
Achaia Phthiotis NW51
Adriatic NW2
Aegean Sea NE3
Aigaion NE3
Ainis NW4
Aiolis NE5
Aitolia NW6
Akarnania NW7
Anatolia NE8
Argolis SW9
Arkadia SW10
Asia Minor CE11
Attika CW12
Black NE24
Boiotia CW13
Caria SE14
Chalkidike NW15
Chios CE16
Crete SE17
Cyclades SE18
Doris/Asia SE19
Doris/Greece: NW20
Elis SW21
Epeiros NW22
Euboia CN23
Euxine NE24
GREECE W25
Hellas W25
Hellespontos NE26
Illyria NW27
Ionia CE28

Ionian Sea CW29
Kephallenia CW30
Kerkura NW31
Korinthia CW32
Korinthos CW33
Kos SE34
Kuthera SW35
Lakonia SW36
Lemnos NE37
Lesbos NE38
Lokris/Opuntian NW39
Lokris/Ozolian NW40
Lydia NE41
Macedonia NW42
Malis NW43
Marmara NE52
Mediterranean CS44
Megaris CW45
Messenia SW46
Mysia NE47
Peloponnesos SW48
Phokis NW49
Phrygia NE50
Phthiotis NW51
Propontis NE52
Rhodes SE53
Samos SE54
Saronic Gulf SW55
Thasos CN56
Thessalia NW57
Thrace NE58
Troas NE59

ANCIENT GREECE AND AEGEAN REGION

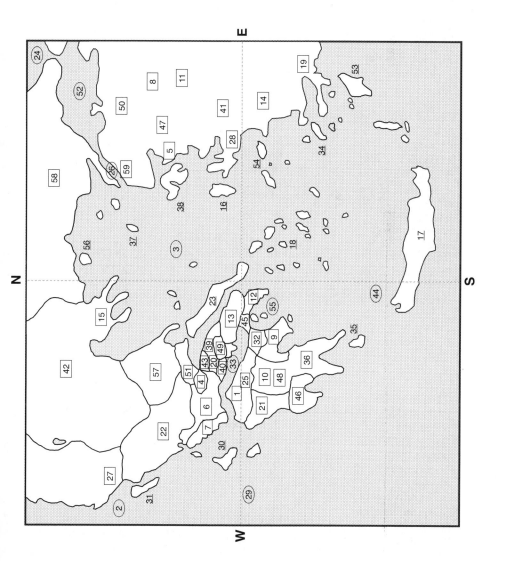

ARKADIA
Achaia N1
Akakeson SW2
Alea NE3
Alesion CE4
Alipheira SW5
Alkimedon SE6
Alpheios SW7
Amilos NE8
Anchisia CE9
Andritsaina SW10
Anemosa CE11
Aphrodisia NW12
Argolis NE13
Aroanios/ci
  NW14
Aroanios/mt
  NW15
Aroanios/ri
  NW16
Arsen NW17
Asea SE18
Azania NW19
Bassai SW20
Belemina CS21
Boreos SE22
Brenthe SW23
Buphagion SW24
Buraikos CN25
Daseae SW26
Despoina SW27
Dipaia SE28
Elaios SW29
Elaphos SE30
Elis SW31
Enispe ?
Garates SE32
Gathea CS33
Gatheatas CS34
Gortunios SW35
Gortus SW36
Gourtsouli CE102
Haimoniae CS37
Helisson/ci SE38
Helisson/ri SE39
Heraia SW40
Hupsos CS41

Kaphuae NE42
Karnion CS43
Keladon SW44
Kleitor CN45
Klenies NE46
Klimax NE 47
Klitoria CW48
Knakalos NE49
Kotiliusa SW50
Krathis NE51
Kretea SW52
Kromi CS53
Kullene NE54
Kunaitha CN55
Kupsela SW56
Ladonas CW57
Lakonia SE58
Laodikion SW59
Lapithos SW60
Lukaion SW61
Lukoa SE62
Lukosura SW63
Lukuria NE64
Lusi NW65
Lusios SW35
Mainalos SE66
Maira CE67
Malea CS68
Mantineia SE69
Megalopolis
  CS70
Melainiai SW71
Melangea SE72
Messenia SW73
Methudrion C74
Nestane SE75
Nomia SW76
Nonakris NE77
Numphasia CE78
Ophis E79
Orchomenos
  NE80
Oresthasion
  SE81
Oresthis ?
Oruxis NE82
Pallantion SE83

Panayia Gourt-
  souli CE102
Parrhasia/ar
  SW84
Parrhasia/ci
  SW85
Parrhasios CS86
Paus NW87
Pedion CW88
Pelagos SE89
Peraithea SE90
Perivolia SW91
Petrosaka CE92
Phaedrias SW93
Phalaisia CS94
Phalanthos C95
Pheneos NE96
Phigalia SW97
Pholoë CW98
Pisa CW99
Plat1niston SW100
Psophis NW101
Ptolis CE102
Rhaeteai SW103
Rhipe ?
Sakovouni SE104
Sirai NW105
Skiathos NE106
Skope SE107
Soron NW108
Stratia ?
Stumphalos NE109
Stux NE110
Sumbola SE111
Sumetia SE112
Tegea SE113
Teuthis SW114
Theisoa SW115
Theisoa SW116
Thelpusa NW117
Thius CS118
Thoenis CS119
Trachu NE120
Trapezos SW121
Trikolini CS122
Tripolis SE 123
Tuthoa CW124

ARKADIA

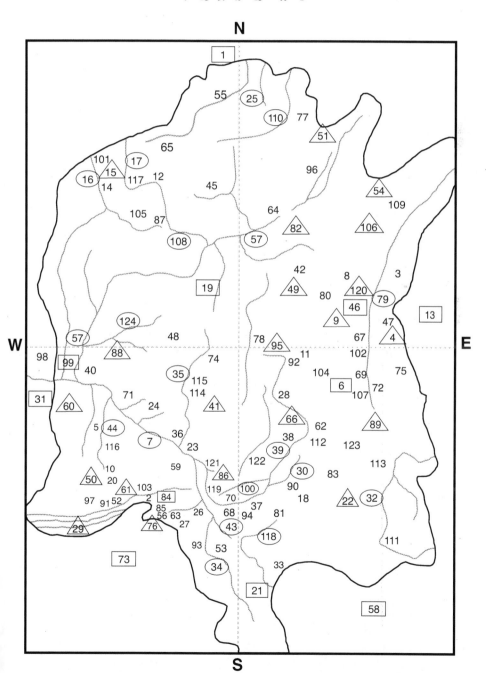

ELIS

Achaia NE1
Agios Dhimitrios SE2
Agios Ilias NW3
Agrapidochori NE4
Aipu SE5
Akidos SE26
Akroterion NW6
Alesion SW7
Alpheios SE8
Anigros SE9
Arethusa SE10
Arkadia CE11
Aulon SE12
Bouprasion/ar CN13
Bouprasion/ci CN14
Dhimitrios SE2
Diagon SE15
Dumaion CN16
Duspontion SE17
Elis/ci CN18
Epion SE19
Erumanthos/mt NE20
Erumanthos/ri SE21
Harpina SE22
Harpinates SE23
Herakleia SE24
Hurmine NW25
Iardanos SE26
Ichthos CS27
Ilias NW3
Ionian Sea SW28
Kakovatos CW29
Kaman ?
Kladeos SE30
Korax SE31
Krounoi SE32
Kullene NW33
Ladon NE34
Lampeia SE35
Larisos NE36
Lepreon SE37

Letrini CS38
Leukuanias SE39
Makistos SE40
Mandra ?
Messenia SE41
Minthe NE42
Minuae SE43
Minueios SE44
Mursinos CN45
Mynian SE43
Neda SE46
Nudion SE47
Oinoë ?
Olen CN48
Olumpia SE49
Opos NE50
Partheneios SE51
Peneios/pl NE52
Peneios/ri NE53
Phaia CS54
Pholoë CE55
Phrixae SE56
Phrukos ?
Pisa/ar SE57
Pisa/ci SE58
Pulos NE59
Purgos SE60
Salmonia NE61
Sandy Pulos NE59
Sarnia SE62
SelleisNE63
Skillos SE64
Skollis CN48
Stulari SE65
Teikhos CN66
Triphulia SE67
Tupaios SE68
Tupanei SE5
Xerovrusi SE69
Zakinthos/ci NW70
Zakinthos/il NW71

ELIS

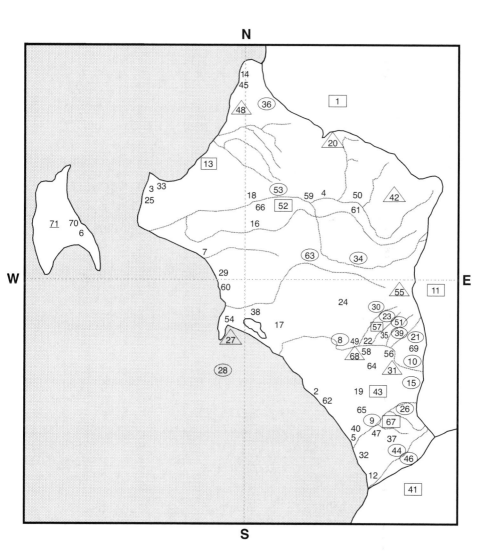

MESSENIA
Abia SE1
Aigaleos NW2
Aipu Box3
Aithaia CE4
Akovitika Box5
Akritas SW6
Amphia NE7
Amphigeneia Box8
Amphitos NE9
Andania NE10
Aphrodisia NW11
Arene NW12
Argupheia NW13
Arkadia NE14
Asine CS15
Balura CN16
Bias CS17
Charadros NE18
Charakopid SW19
Choerios SE20
Dara C21
Dardanos NW22
Divari ?
Dorion NW23
Eira CN24
Elektra CN25
Elis NW26
Enope Box27
Epano Englianos
  Box28
Eua CN29
Gerenon Box30
Geresia Box31
Helos Box32
Hire Box33
Ire SE1
Ithome CN34
Kalamai NE35
Kalamata CE36

Kambos C37
Kaphirio CS38
Kardamule Box39
Kissos ?
Kolonides CS40
Korone CS41
Koroni/ci CS15
Koroni/Gu SE57
Koruphasion/ca
  Box42
Koruphasion/ci
  Box43
Koukounara NE44
Kuparisseis/ar
  NW45
Kuparisseis/ci
  NW46
Kuparisseis/ri
  NW47
Kuparission NW48
Lakonia SE49
Leukasia NW50
Likodhimon SW51
Limnai NE52
Makaria CE36
Malthi NW53
Mathia SW54
Mavromati CN55
Megalopolis NE56
Messene CN55
Messenia/gu SE57
Methone SW58
Minueios NW59
Modon SW58
Mouriatadha
  CW60
Navarino/ci Box61
Navarino/bay
  Box62
Neda NW63
Nestor/ar Box64

Nestor/cv Box65
Nestor/pa Box28
Nichoria CS66
Nomia CN67
Oichalia NE68
Oinussai SW69
Osmanaga Box70
Palaiokastro Box65
Paleochoria ?
Pamisos NE71
Pedasos Box72
Peristeria NW73
Pharai CE74
Pherai Box75
Phoenikos SW76
Polichne CN77
Prote CW78
Pteleos Box79
Pulos SW & Box80
Routsi Box81
Selas CW82
Sphakteria/il
  Box83
Sphakteria/pe
  Box84
Stenukleros NE85
Theganussa SE86
Thouria C87
Thruoëssa Box88
Thruon Box88
Thuria NE89
Tourliditsa ?
Tragana SW90
Tsopani-Rachi ?
Vlachopoulo ?
Voidhokoilia/bay
  Box91
Voidhokoilia/si
  Box92

MESSENIA

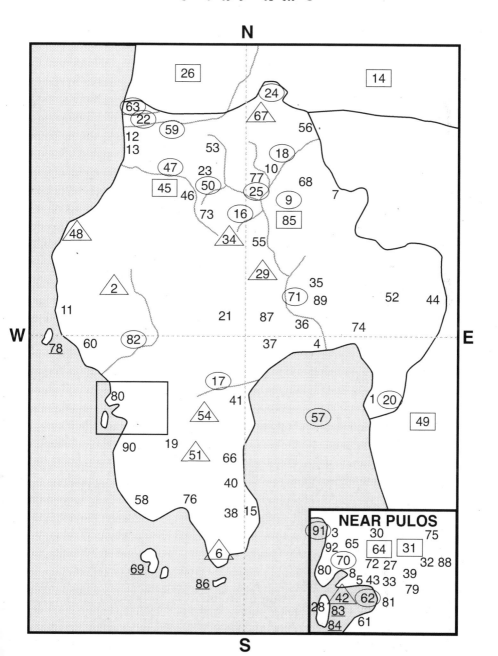

LAKONIA

Achilles' Harbor
  SW1
Aegiae SW2
Akra SE3
Akriae CE4
Alagonia NW5
Alepotrupa SE6
Amuklai NW7
Aphrodisia ?
Arainon SW8
Argolis NE9
Arkadia NW10
Arkines ?
Asia SW11
Asopios SE12
Asopos SE13
Athenaion NW14
Augeiae CN15
Belemina NW16
Boeai SE17
Brasiai NE18
Bruseia NW19
Choerios NW20
Diros SE21
Elaphonisos
  SE22
Epidauros Limera
  SE23
Epidelion SE24
Eurotas/ri NW25
Eurotas/va NW26
Gerenia NW27
Geronthrae
  CN28
Gluppia NE29
Gutheion SW30
Helos CE31
Hippola SW32
Huperteleaton
  SE33
Kaiadas NW34
Kainepolis SW35
Kalathios NW36

Kaparisso SW37
Kardamule NW38
Karuai NW39
Kastri Box40
Kayo SW78
Koturta ?
Kranae SW41
Krokeae/ci NW42
Krokeae/qu
  NW43
Kuphanta NE44
Kuprianon NW45
Kuthera/ci
  Box46
Kuthera/il Box47
Laas NW48
Lakedaimon
  NW49
Lakedaimonia
  NW50
Lakonia/gu CS51
Lakonia/is SE52
Lankia NW53
Las SW54
Leukae CE55
Leuktra CW56
Limera SE23
Malea SE57
Mani SE57
Marios NE58
Matapan SW59
Menelaion NW60
Messe SW61
Messenia/gu
  SW62
Messenia/re
  NW63
Minoa SE64
Mirtóön NE65
Monemvasia
  SE23
Neapolis NW66
Numphaion SE67
Oitulos SW68

Onugnathos
  SE69
Palaiokastro
  NW70
Parnon CN 71
Pavlopetri SE72
Pellana NW73
Pellanis NW74
Pephnos CW75
Pharis NW76
Plataniston
  Box77
Porto Kayio
  SW78
Prasiai NE79
Psamathos SW78
Purrichos SW80
Selinos CN 81
Sellana CN82
Sellasia NW83
Side SE84
Skandia Box85
Skiritis NW86
Smenos SW87
Sparta NW50
Tainaron/ca
  SW59
Tainaron/ci
  SW37
Taleton NW88
Tanaos CN89
Taygetus NW90
Teügetos NW90
Teuthrone SW91
Thalamae CW92
Therapne NW93
Thurides SW94
Trinasos CS95
Vapheio NW96
Vlichada SE97
Vourvoura NE98
Zarax CE99

LAKONIA

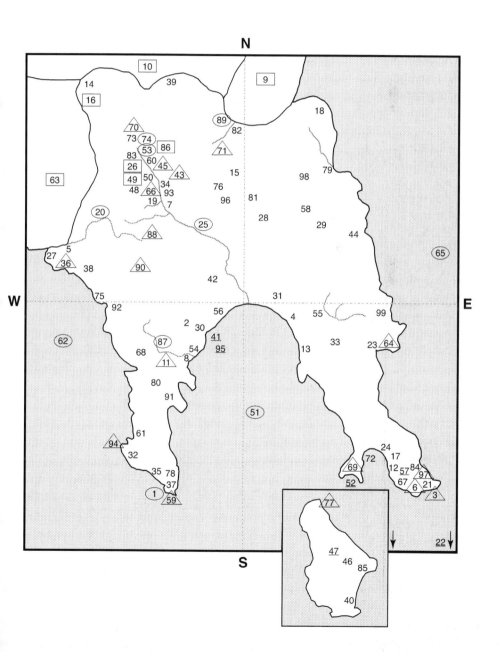

ACHAIA/ PELOPONNESOS

Aigai NE1
Aigeira NE2
Aigialos CE3
Aigion NE4
Aigira CE5
Araxos NW6
Arethurea SE7
Argolis SE8
Argura NW9
Aristonautae SE10
Arkadia SE11
Athenaion NW12
Bolina NW13
Bolinaeos NW14
Bouga SW15
Bura NE16
Buraikos CE17
Charadros NW18
Chelidoria SE19
Donussa NE20
Drepanon NW21
Dume NW22
Elis SW23
Erineos CN24
Erumanthos SW25
Glaukos NW26
Helike/ci NE27
Helike/la NE28
Hule SE29
Huperesia NE2
Ionian Sea W30
Kallithea CW31
Katharevousa NE4
Kerunia NE32

Kerunites CE33
Kiata SE34
Kirrha CE35
Korinthos/gu NE36
Krathis CE37
Krios SE38
Laechon NE39
Larisos SW40
Leontion NW41
Long Walls NW42
Meganitas CN43
Meilichos NW44
Musaeon SE45
Olen CW46
Olenos CW47
Panachaikon SW48
Panormos NW49
Patrai NW50
Patraikos NW51
Patras NW50
Peiros SW52
Pellene SE53
Pharai SW54
Phelloe SE55
Phoenix CN56
Pitsa SE57
Rhion NW58
Rhupes CN59
Selemnos NW60
Selinos NE61
Selleis SE62
Sikionia SE63
Suthas SE64
Triteia SW65
Vasiliko SE63

ACHAIA IN PELOPONNESOS

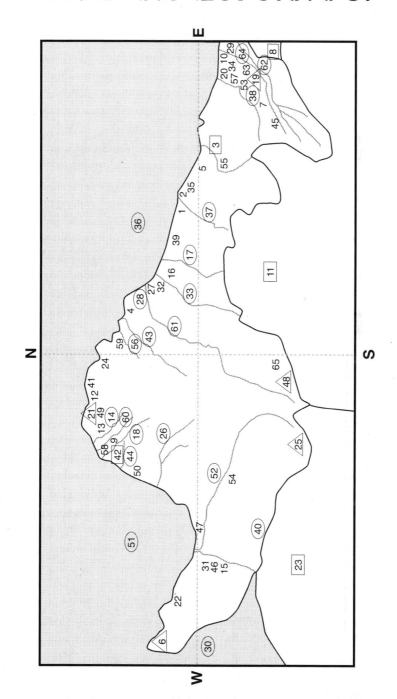

ARGOLIS (ARGOLID)

Abas CN1
Achaia NW2
Aigion Box3
Akraia NW4
Akrokorintos NW5
Anigraia SW6
Anthene SW22
Aperopia SE7
Apesas NW8
Arachnaeos CN1
Arantia NW9
Argolis/gu SW10
Argolis/pe SE11
Argos/ci CW & Box12
Argos/gu SW10
Aristerai SE13
Arkadia CW14
Artemision CW15
Asine SW16
Askulepios CS17
Asopos NW18
Aspis Box19
Asterion NW20
Astros SW21
Athene SW22
Berbati Box23
Bukephala SE24
Buporthmos SE25
Chaon SW26
Charadros CW & Box27
Cheimarros SW28
Chersonesos CN29
Corinth NW72
Daphni NW30
Deiras Box31
Dendra CW32
Didumi SE33
Dine SW34
Eilei SE35
Eionae SE36
Ephura NW72
Epidauros CE37
Erasinos Box38
Eua SW39
Euboia NW40
Franchthi SW41
Garates SW42
Geraneia NE43
Gonoëssa Box44
Halieis SE45
Helisson NW46

Hellenikon SW39
Heraion/ca CE47
Heraion/ci NW48
Hermione SE49
Honikas Box50
Hudra SE51
Hudrea SE52
Hullikos SE53
Hupereia Box54
Husiai SW55
Inachos/ci NW56
Inachos/ri NW57
Iria CS58
Kalauria SE59
Kastro CS60
Kekruphalia CE61
Keleae NW62
Kelenderis SE63
Kenchreai SW64
Kenchreai CN65
Kleonae NW66
Klimax NW67
Koluergia SE68
Korakou NW69
Korinthia NW70
Korinthos/bay NW71
Korinthos/ci NW72
Korinthos/gu NW73
Korinthos/is CN74
Koruphon SE75
Kranidhion SW76
Krisae/bay NW71
Krisae/gu NW73
Kromion NE77
Kunortion CS78
Kunouria SW79
Kunuria SW135
Lakonia SW80
Larissa/ci Box81
Larissa/mt Box82
Lechaion/ci NW83
Lechaion/po NW84
Lerna SW85
Lessa CE86
Long Walls CW87
Loukou SW88
Loutraki NW89
Lukone SW90
Lurkea NW91
Malea CN92
Mases SE93
Messeis Box94
Methana/ci CE95
Methana/is SE96
Methana/pe CE97

Midea CW98
Mikinae NW99
Mukenae NW99
Nafplion SW100
Nauplia SW100
Nemea/ci NW101
Nemea/ri NW102
Neris SW103
Oinoë/Argolis CW104
Oinoë/Korinthia NW105
Oneion NW106
Orneiae NW107
Parnon SW108
Partheneios SW109
Peirene NW110
Pelops CE111
Phlios/ci NW112
Pitiussa SE113
Pontinos SW114
Poros NE115
Poseidon CN116
Prinos CW117
Pros SE118
Prosumna Box119
Rheitos CN120
Saminthos Box121
Saronic NE122
Sikuon NW123
Skullaion SE124
Spetsoi SE125
Sphaeria SE126
Spiraeon NE127
Struthos SE128
Stumphalis CW129
Suthas NW130
Talioti SW16
Tanaos SW131
Temenion Box132
Tenea NW133
Thornax SE134
Thurea/ci SW135
Thurea/ba SW136
Thureatis SW137
Tiruns Box138
Titane NW139
Titthion CE140
Tretos NW141
Trikrana SE142
Troizen/ar SE143
Troizen/ci SE144
Tsoungiza NW145

ARGOLIS (ARGOLID)

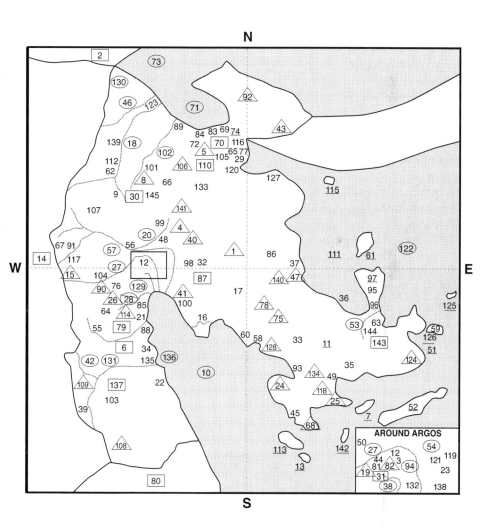

CRETE WEST (KRETE/ KANDIA)

Agia Triada SE1
Akrotiri/ci NW2
Akrotiri/pe NW3
Allana CW4
Almirou NE5
Anopolis SW6
Antikuthera NW7
Aptera NW8
Aradaena/ci SW9
Aradaena/ri
  SW10
Arkades SE11
Arkoudiotissa
  CN14
Armenoi NW15
Arsinoë NE16
Axos CE17
Crete/sea N18
Cyrenic S19
Drapano CN21
Elafonissi SW22
Elearchos SE23
Elthuna NE24
Eluros SW25
Falassarua NW26
Gaudos SW27
Gonies NE28
Gortus SE29
Grambousa/il
  NW30
Grambousa/pe
  NW31
Herronisos
  NW44
Iardanos NW32
Ida/ca SE33
Ida/mt SE34
Idhi SE34

Inatos SE35
Kamares SE36
Kamilari SE37
Kandia/sea N18
Katri NW38
Kephali SE39
Keraia NW40
Khania NW41
Khanion NW42
Khrusoskalitissa
  SW43
Kiliaris NW77
Kissamos/ci
  NW44
Kissamos/gu
  NW45
Kolumbari NW46
Kommos SE47
Kourtes SE48
Kudonia NW49
Lappa NE50
Lavka CW51
Lera NW52
Libyan S19
Lisos SW53
Lithino SE54
Mediterranean
  N55
Mesara/gu SE56
Mesara/pl SE57
Modaeoi NW58
Monastiraki
  CE59
Oaxos/ci CE17
Oaxos/ri NE60
Ogulia/il NW61
Ogulia/sea NW
  62
Orion NE63
Papoura SE64
Paximadhia SE65

Pergamos NW66
Phaistos SE67
Phalanna CW68
Phalasarna NW69
Platanias/ci
  NW70
Platanias/ri
  NW32
Platanos NW72
Poluchna NW73
Polurrenia NW74
Priansos SE75
Psiloneron NW76
Psiloritis SE34
Puknos NW77
Rhitumna NE78
Rithumna NE78
Rodopou/ci
  NW79
Rodopou/pe
  NW80
Rokka NW40
Rutio CE81
Samaria SE82
Sisaea NE83
Souda/bay CN84
Souda/il CN85
Sougia SW86
Stavros/ci NW87
Stavros/mt
  NW88
Suva NW89
Suvritos NE90
Tanos NW91
Tarra SE92
Tegea NW93
Thrimbokambos
  SW94
Urtakos SW95
Vrusinas NE96
White CW51

CRETE (KANDIA) WEST

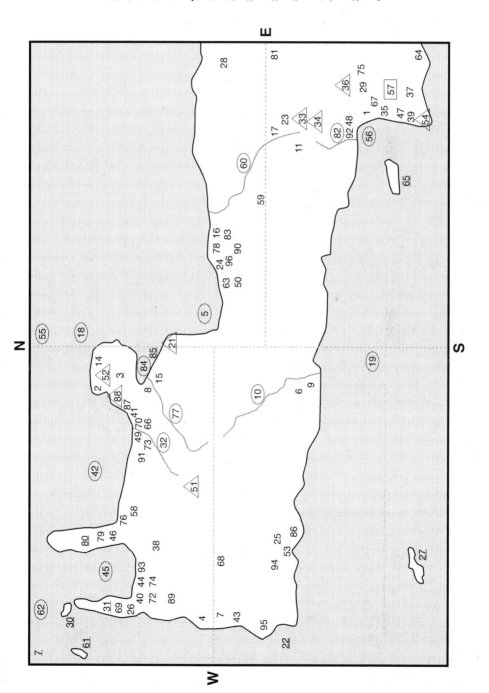

CRETE EAST (KRETE/ KANDIA)

Agios Nikolaos CE1
Aina CW2
Alassa SW49
Amnisos NW3
Ano CE4
Apollonia NW18
Archanes NW5
Arkolochori/ca NW6
Arkolochori/vi NW7
Arvi SW8
Christos NW9
Crete/sea N10
Dia/ci NW11
Dia/il NW12
Dikte SE13
Dragmos CE14
Dreros NE15
Eileithuia NW16
Elassa NE17
Eleutherna NW18
Erganos CW19
Eronos CE20
Ertaea NW21
Etiani SE22
Fair Havens SW49
Foinikia NW23
Gaidhouronisi CS24
Gazi NW25
Gianisadhes NE26
Giophurakia NW27
Gournia SE28
Gupsades SW29

Herakleion/bay NW30
Herakleion/ci NW31
Hersonissos NW32
Hieraputna SE33
Istron SE34
Itanos NE35
Iteia CE36
Juktas NW37
Kandia/sea N10
Kanli Kastelli CW2
Karphi C38
Katsambas NW39
Kavousi CE40
Kavrochori NW41
Kephala SE42
Khani NW70
Kirva SE33
Knossos NW43
Kolokithia NE44
Kophinas SW45
Koumasa SW46
Kouphonisi/il SE47
Kouphonisi/ci SE48
Lassaia SW49
Lasea SW49
Lasithi SE50
Lato CE1
Lebena SW52
Lukestos CW53
Luktas NW54
Luktos NW55
Luttos NW56
Magasa NE57
Malia NW58
Malla SE59
Matala SW60
Megambellou NE63

Menares CE61
Miletos CN62
Mirabellou NE63
Mitropolis SW64
Mochlos/il NE65
Mochlos/ci CE66
Mouliana CE67
Mursini CE68
Murtos SE69
Nirou Khani NW70
Olous NE71
Palaiokastro NW72
Panormos NW73
Plati SE74
Porti SW75
Praisos CE76
Prinias/si SE77
Prinias/vi CW78
Priniatiko SE79
Pseira NE80
Psuchro C81
Purgos SW82
Rankos NW83
Rezinea NW84
Rhution SW85
Setaia SE86
Sitia NE87
Skoteino NW88
Stavromenos NW89
Subrita NW90
Traostalos SE91
Tulissos NW92
Vai NE93
Vasiliki SE94
Vatupetro NW95
Viannos SW96
Vrokastro SE97
Zakros CE98
Zou CE99

CRETE (KANDIA) EAST

ATTIKA SOUTH

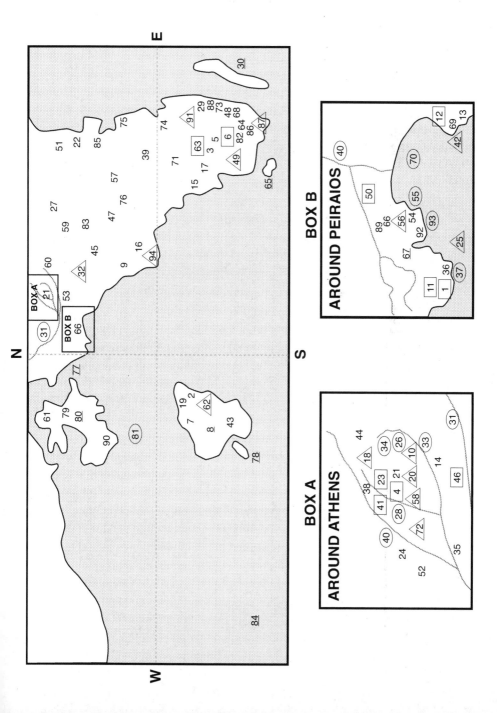

BOX B

AROUND PEIRAIOS

BOX A

AROUND ATHENS

ATTIKA
NORTH
Acharnae SE1
Agrieliki SE2
Aigaleos CS3
Alope SW4
Amphiareion
  NE5
Aphidna CE7
Araphen SE8
Askitario SE9
ATTIKA E10
Boiotia N11
Brilessos SE53
Brooks CS63
Charadra/ci
  CE12
Charadra/ri
  CE13
Cholarges SE14
Dekeleia CE15
Elefsina SW16
Eleusis/ba SW16
Eleusis/ci SW17
Eleutherae CW18
Gargettos SE20
Guphtokastro
  CW21
Herakleion SE22
Ikarion SE23
Kallichoros CS24
Kato Suli SE25
Kaza NW26
Kephisia SE27
Kephisos SE28
Kephisos CS 29
Kithairon CW30
Korinthia SW31
Korinthos/gu
  SW32
Korudallos/ar
  CS33

Korudallos/ci
  SE34
Krisae SW32
Kunosura/ci
  SE35
Kunosura/pe
  SE36
Leipsudrion SE37
Lusia CS38
Maiden Well
  CS52
Marathon/ci
  SE39
Marathon/bay
  SE40
Marathon/pl
  SE41
Menidi SE42
Nea Makri SE43
Nera SW44
Ninoi SE45
Oinoë CE46
Oinoë CW47
Oropos NE48
Pan SE49
Panakton NW50
Parnes NE51
Parthenos
  Phreatia CS52
Pentelikon SE53
Petalion SE54
Pharmakoussai
  SW55
Phlua SE56
Phule C57
Pieria CW58
Probalinthos
  SE59
Raphina SE60
Rhamnos NE61
Rharos SW62
Rheiti CS63

Salamis/bay
  SW16
Salamis/ci SW17
Salamis/il SW64
Salt SE65
Schoinias SE66
Soros SE67
Thria/ci CS68
Thria/pl CS69
Trikorithos CE70

MEGARIS
Agios Kosmas
  SW71
Aigosthena
  CW72
Budoron SW73
Diolkos SW74
Dunamene SW75
Enualios SW76
Geraneia SW77
Isthmia SW78
Isthmos SW79
Kosmas SW71
Kura Vrusi SW78
Long Walls SW80
Megara SW81
MEGARIS SW82
Minoa/il SW83
Minoa/pe SW84
Nisaia/ci SW85
Nisaia/il SW86
Nisaia/pe SW87
Pagai SW88
Perachora/ci
  SW89
Perachora/ha
  SW90
Pherusa SW91
Tripodiskos
  SW92
Vouliagmeni
  SW93

ATTIKA NORTH AND MEGARIS

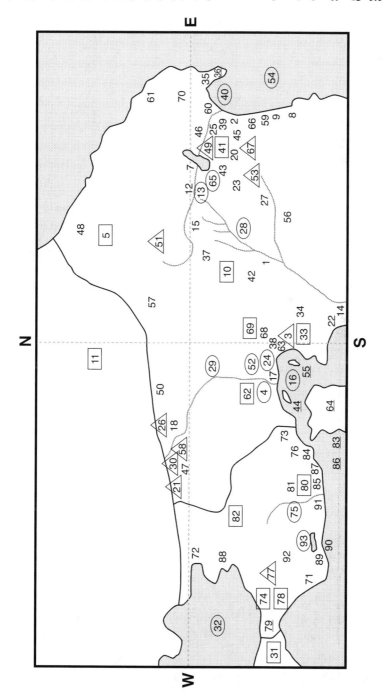

BOIOTIA (KADMEIA)

Abantes NE20
Aganippe SW1
Aigai NE2
Akraiphia CN3
Akraiphnion CW4
Alalkomenae CW5
Anthedon NE6
Apollo C7
Arne NW13
Askra SW8
Asopos SE9
Aspledon NW10
Attika SE11
Aulis CE12
Chaironeia NW13
Chantsa NW14
Delion SE15
Druoskephalae CS16
Eilesion SE17
Eleon SE18
Eruthrae SE19
Eteonos ?
Euboia NE20
Euripos NE21
Eutresis SE22
Gla/ci NW23
Gla/il NW24
Glechon NW25
Glisas CE26
Graia SE27
Halai/ci NW28
Halai/si SE29
Haliartos SW30
Harma CE31
Helikon SW32
Herkune NW33
Hippokrene SW1

Horse's Spring SW1
Hudria SE34
Hulika C35
Hupatos CE36
Huria SE37
Husiai SE38
Ilesion SE17
Ismenos SE39
Kabeiri SW40
Kadmea SE41
Kastri SE42
Kephisos NW43
Keressos SW44
Kithairon SE45
Kopae NW46
Kopais NW47
Korinthos/gu SW48
Koroneia CW49
Korsea NW50
Kreusis SW51
Krisae SW48
Kurtone NW52
Lamos SW53
Laphustios CW54
Larumna CN55
Lebadea NW56
Leuktra SW57
Lithares CS58
Lokris Opuntian NW59
Lophis SW60
Megalo Kastelli SE61
Megaris SW62
Messapios NE63
Mideia NW64
Minuae NW65
Minyans NW65
Mukalessos CE66
Muses SW67

Nisa CE68
Oëroë/pl SW69
Oëroë/ri SW70
Oinophuta SE71
Okalea SW72
Olmeios SW73
Onchestos SW74
Opuntian NW59
Orchomenos NW75
Oropos/ci NE76
Oropos/gu NE77
Permessos SW78
Petalion SE79
Peteon CS80
Phalaros SW81
Phokis SW82
Pirene SW83
Plataia/ar SE84
Plataia.ci SE85
Platanios NW86
Potniai CS87
Ptoion/ci NE88
Ptoion/mt NE89
Ptous CN90
Rhitsona CS91
Siphae SE15
Skolos/SE SE92
Skolos/SE 93
Sphynx SW94
Tanagra SE95
Tegura NW96
Tenerion SW97
Termessos SW98
Teumesos SE99
Thebes CS100
Thespiai SW101
Thespios NE102
Thisbe SW103
Thivai CS100
Tilphusios SW104
Tipha SW105

BOIOTIA (KADMEIA)

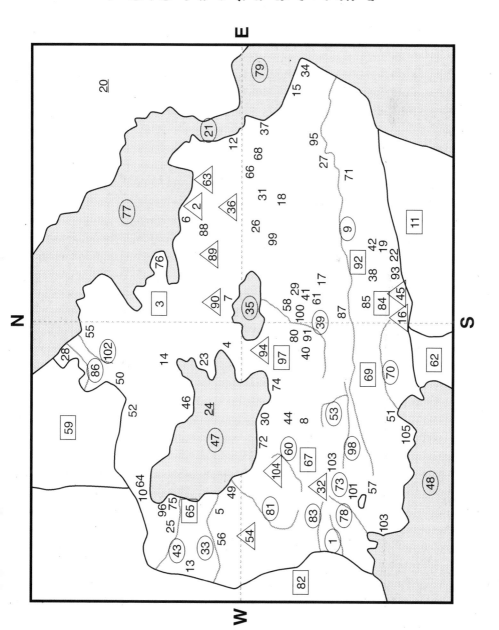

PHOKIS
Abae CE1
Ambrosos SE2
Amphikaea NE3
Amphiklea NE3
Anemoreia SE4
Antikura/ci SE5
Antikura/bay SE6
Boiotia SE8
Bulis SE9
Charadra CN10
Cheronia SE11
Cleft Way SE12
Daulis CE13
Delphi CS14
Drumaia NE15
Druopis CN16
Elatea NE17
Erochos NE18
Hua/ar NE19
Hua/ci NE20
Huampolis/ar
   NE19
Huampolis/ci NE20
Hupata CN21
Kalapodi NE22
Kastalia SE23
Kave C24
Kephisos NE25
Kirphis SE26
Kirrha SW27
Korinthos/bay
   CS30
Korinthos/gu CS28
Krisa/ci CS29
Krisa/bay SW30
Kuparissos SE31
Ledon CE32
Lilaia CN33
Medeon SE34
Oita/mt NW35
Panopeios SE36
Parapotamii/ci
   SE37

Parapotamii/ri
   CE38
Parnassos/mt C39
Parnassos/va CE40
Phanotis SE36
Phokis CE41
Pleistos CS42
Putho CS14
Stiris SE43
Tithorea NE44
Tithronion NE45
Vranesi NE46

LOKRIS/ OPUNTIAN
Alope NE47
Atalanta NE48
Athena NE49
Augeiae NE50
Bessa NE51
Boagrios NE52
Elatae NE53
Elatheia NE53
Kalliaros NE54
Knemis NE55
Kunos NE56
Lokris/Opuntian
   NE57
Opoeis NE58
Opos NE58
Oropos NE59
Skarphe NE60
Tarphe NE61
Thronion NE62

LOKRIS OZOLIAN
Amphissa CW63
Antikura SW64
Eupalion SW65
Lokris/Ozolian
   CW66
Molukria SW67

Molukrion SW 68
Muonia CW69
Oianthea SW70
Oineon SW71
Oinoë SW71
Rhion/ci SW72
Rhion/st SW73

DORIS
Boion NW74
Doris NW75
Erineos NW76
Kitinion NW77
Pindos/ci NW78
Pindos/ri NW79

MALIS
Anthela CN80
Antikura NW81
Asopos NW82
Herakleia NW83
Kallidromon CN84
Lamia CN85
Malis/gu CN86
Malis/re NW87
Oita NW88
Poludora NW89
Spercheios NW89
Thermopulai/ci
   CN90
Thermopulai/pa
   CN84
Trachis/ar CN91
Trachis/ci CN92

AINIS
Ainis NW93
Aitolia W94
Epeiros NW95
Phtiotis NW96
Upati NW97

PHOKIS, LOKRIS, DORIS, MALIS, AINIS

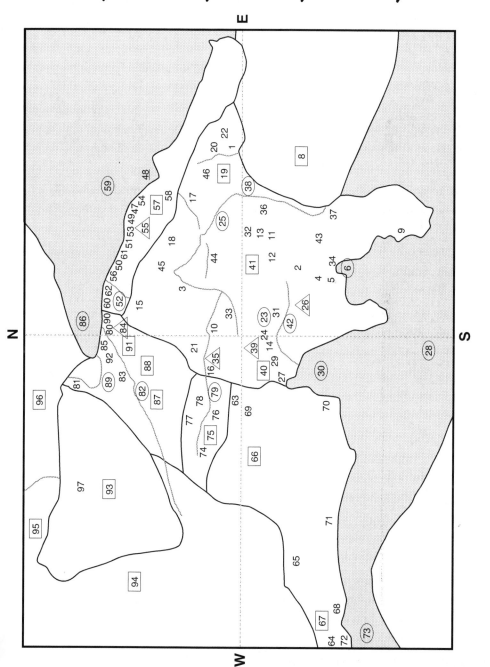

AITOLIA
Achaia SE 1
Agrinion CE2
Aigition SE3
Ainis NE4
Aitolia E5
Alos ?
Ambrakia/ar
  NW6
Ambrakia/ci
  NW7
Ambrakia/gu
  NW8
Amphilochia
  CN9
Arakuntos/mt
  SE10
Arakuntos/pl
  SE11
Ardeskos ?
Argos CN12
Arta NW8
Avenos SE17
Bura SE13
Chalkis SE14
Driopia NE15
Epeiros NE16
Euenos SE17
Guphtokastro
  SE29
Kaludon SE18
Kaludonia SE19
Krenae NE20
Krokule ?
Limnaia CN21
Mesolongion
  SE18
Metropolis CN22
Nafpaktos SE23
Naupaktos SE23

Nessos SE17
Olen SE24
Olenos SE25
Olpai CN26
Orestia CN27
Patraikos SE28
Petrovouni SE29
Pleuron SE29
Potidania ?
Proschion SE30
Pulene SE31
Thermon CE32
Thuamos CN33
Tichion ?
Trikhonis SE34
Vrakhori CE2

AKARNANIA
& ISLANDS
Acheloos E35
Agraia CN36
Aigilips SW37
Aitos CS38
Akarnania W39
Aktion NW40
Aluzia CS41
Anaktorion
  NW42
Anapos SE43
Aspropotamos
  E35
Astakos CW44
Asteris/ci NW45
Asteris/il NW46
Chrusovitsa ?
Dulichion NW59
Echinades SW47
Echinae SW48
Eliomenos NW49
Iaphos NW50

Ionian W51
Ithaka SW52
Kephallenia
  SW53
Koronta NE54
Kranae SW55
Kreine CS56
Krokuleia NW57
Leukas/ci NW58
Leukas/il NW59
Leukas/is NW60
Leukatas NW61
Mazarakata
  SW62
Medeon NW63
Meganissi CW79
Melite CS64
Mila NW65
Neion SW66
Nerikos NW67
Neriton SW66
Nidri NW68
Oiniadai CS69
Palaira NW70
Pale SW71
Peiros E35
Phutia CN72
Polis CS73
Pronnai SW74
Rheithron SW75
Same/ci SW76
Same/il SW53
Sollion NW77
Stratos SE78
Strophades
  SW47
Taphos CW79
Teleboa CW80

AITOLIA, AKARNANIA AND ISLANDS

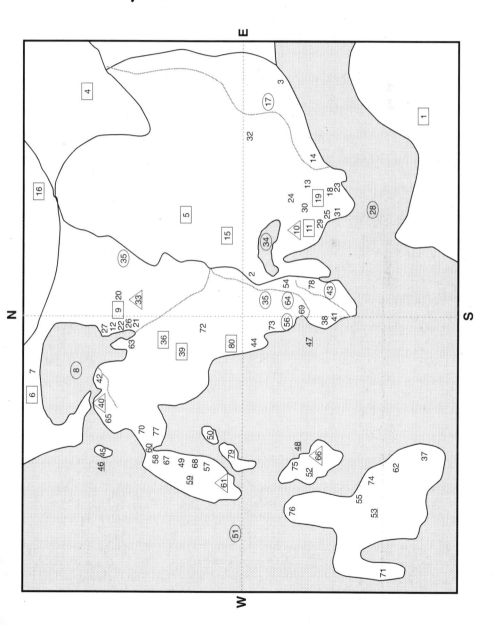

EPEIROS

Abantes SW1
Acheron SW2
Acherusia/ci SW3
Acherusia/la
  SW4
Adriatic NW5
Aias SE6
Aitolia SE7
Akarnania SE8
Akrokeraunia
  CW9
Antigoneia SW10
Aoos SE6
Apollonia SW11
Arta SE12
Asprochaliko
  SE13
Atintania SW14
Chaonia SW15
Chimerion SW16
Choanes SW17
Corcyra SW35
Corfu SW35
Dassaretis SE18
Dodona SW19
Dolopia SW20
EPEIROS S21
Ephura SW22
Hullaikos SW23
Idomene SE24
Igoumenitsa
  SW25
Ioannina/ci
  SW26
Ioannina/la
  SW27
Ionian/il SW28
Ionian/sea SW29
Ionic SW30
Istone SW31
Kalamas SW64
Kassope CS32

Kastritsa SW33
Kerkura/ci SW34
Kerkura/il SW35
Kestrine SW36
Klithi SW37
Kokkinopulos
  SE38
Komaros SW39
Konitsa SE40
Kouphia Rachi
  SE41
Ladochori SW42
Leukimme SW43
Liatovouni CW44
Linguetta SW45
Louros SE46
Mikalitsi SW47
Molossia SW48
Mutika SW39
Nikopolis CS49
Orestis CS50
Panormos
  SW51
Parauaea SW52
Parga SW53
Paxos SW54
Peneios SE55
Phthiotis SE56
Pindos SE57
Preveza SW58
Ptuchia SW59
Rachi SE41
Smirtoula CS60
Subota SW61
Thesprotis SW62
Thessalia SE63
Thuamis SW64
Thuamos CS65
Vitsa SW66
Vlorë CW67
Vodomatis SW68
Voidomatis SE69

ILLYRIA

Albania NW71
Antariatae NW72
Ardiaei NW73
Autariatae NW74
Bosnia NE75
Croatia NW76
Dalmatia NW77
Dardania CN78
Drilon CN79
Durrachion
  NW80
Enchelea NW81
Eordaikos C82
Epidamnos/ci
  NW80
Hellopia CW91
Herakleia CE83
Herzegovina
  NE75
ILLYRIA CN84
Korcë C85
Koritsa C85
Labeati NW86
Lissa NW87
Lissos NW88
Luchnidos CE89
Macedonia E90
Molossis CW91
Naro N92
Neretva N92
Pelion NE93
Philister NW94
Serbia NE95
Skardos NE96
Skordiski NW97
Taulantii NW98
Tirana NW99
Trebeniste
  NE100
Tsangon CE101
Vis NW87

ƐPƐIROS AND ILLYRIA

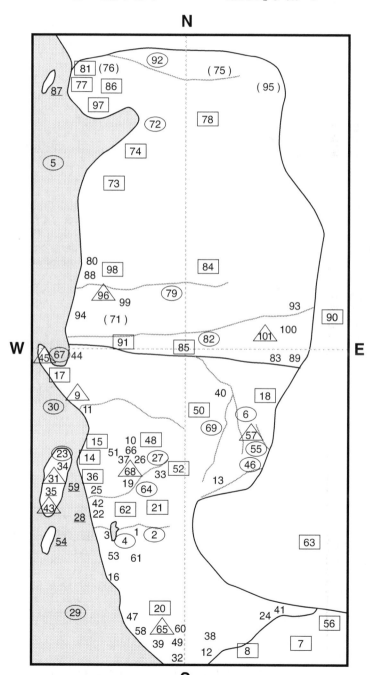

THESSALIA

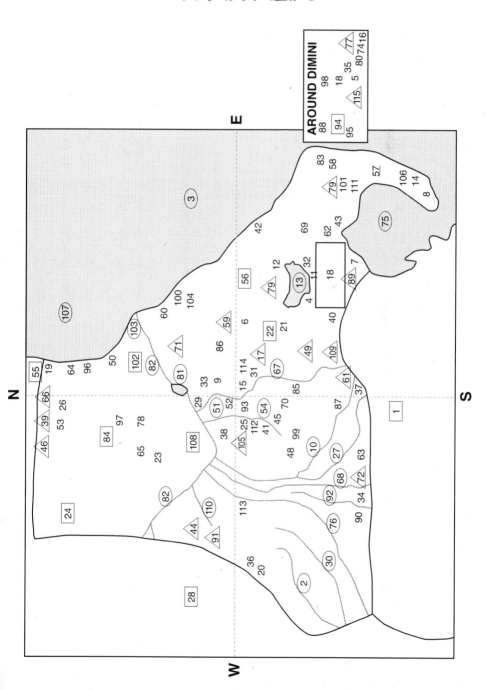

AROUND DIMINI

ACHAIA
PHTHIOTIS

Achilles NE1
Ainis SW2
Almuros NE3
Alos NE10
Antron NE4
Echinos SE5
Enipeos CN6
Epeiros NW7
Euboia SE8
Gritsa SE9
Halos NE10
Hellas NE1
Hupereia SE11
Malis CS12
Melitia SE13
Nea Anchialos NE23

Onchestos NE14
Onochonos NW15
Oropos SE16
Pagasitikos NE17
Pagassai/gu NE17
Philippopolis NE23
Phthia NE18
Phthiotis/ci NE18
Phulake NE19
Poludora NW22
Protesilaos NE19
Purasos CN20
Sindos NE21
Spercheios NW22
Thebes NE23
Thessalia CN24
Volos/gu NE17

ACHAIA PHTHIOTIS

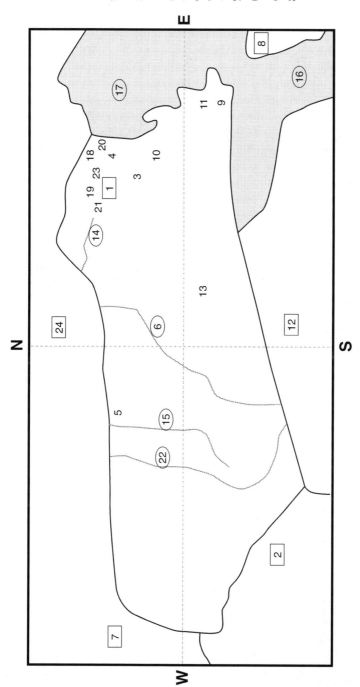

MACEDONIA
(PAIONIA / PANNONIA)

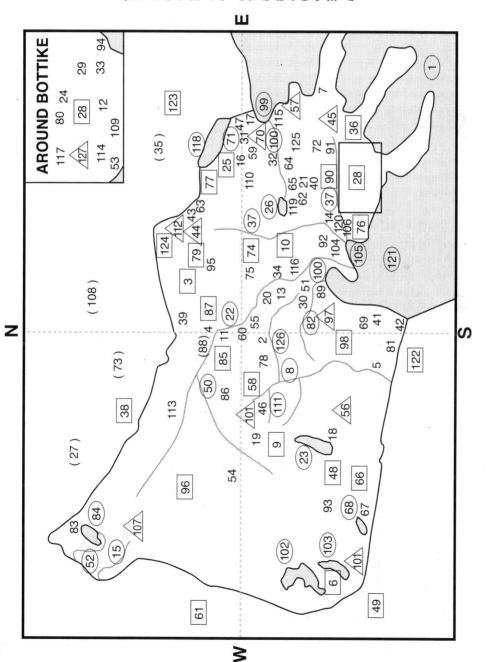

THRACE

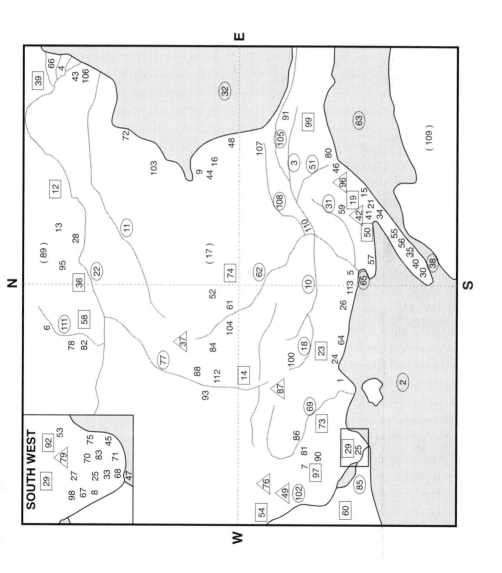

AEGEAN SEA NORTH

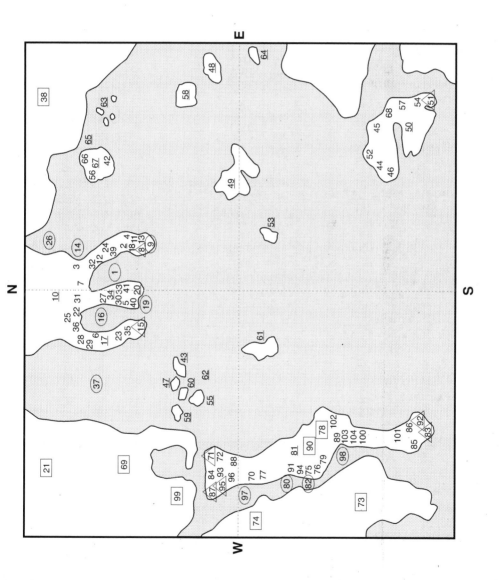

AEGEAN SEA
SOUTH

CYCLADES
Agia Irini NW1
Aigiale SE2
Akrotiri CS3
Amorgos CS4
Anaphe SE5
Andros/ci NW6
Andros/il NW7
Arkesine CS8
Chalandriani
  NW9
Cyclades NW10
Delos NW11
Grotta C12
Hermoupolis
  NW13
Inopos NW14
Ios CS15
Iria CS16
Kalandriani
  NW17
Kea NW18
Keos NW19
Kephala NW20
Keros CS21
Korthion NW22
Kuaneia SW23
Kunthos NW24
Kuthnos NW25
Melos SW26
Minoa CS27
Mukonos CN28
Naxos/ci CS29
Naxos/Il CS30
Nisos CN28
Ortugia NW11
Palaiopolis NW31
Paroikia CW32

Paros CW33
Pelos SW34
Phulakopi SW35
Rheneia CN36
Saliagos C37
Santorini CS43
Seriphos CW38
Sikinos SW39
Siphnos SW40
Suros NW41
Tenos NW42
Thera CS43

ISLANDS
Amphiareion
  NE44
Asia Minor E45
Astupalaia/ca
  SE46
Astupalaia/il
  SE47
Ataburion SE48
Bolissos NE49
Chios/ci NE50
Chios/il NE51
Delphinion NE52
Dhikaios SE53
Dodekanesoi
  SE54
Drumoussa NE55
Emborio NE56
Heraion NE57
Ialusos SE58
Ikaria NE59
Kaludnae CE60
Kalumnos SE61
Kameiros SE62
Kardamule NE63
Karpathos CS64
Kasos SE65
Kastellorizon
  SE78

Kephalos SE66
Khalki SE67
Kos/ci SE68
Kos/il SE69
Krapathos CS64
Lade NE70
Leros CE71
Leukonion NE72
Lindos SE73
Lipsoi CE74
Madraki SE75
Marathousa
  NE76
Marmara SE77
Megiste SE78
Meropis SE79
Nisuros CS80
Oinoë NE81
Oinussai NE82
Patmos CE83
Pele NE84
Phanai NE85
Psuria NE86
Rhodes/ci SE87
Rhodes/il SE88
Samos/ci NE89
Samos/il NE90
Samos/st NE91
Saria CS92
Seraglio SE93
Sporades/Dode-
  kanesoi SE54
Sume SE94
Teutloussa SE95
Thermai NE96
Tilos SE97
Tragia NE98
Trianda SE99
Turkey E45
Vurgunda CS100

AEGEAN SEA SOUTH

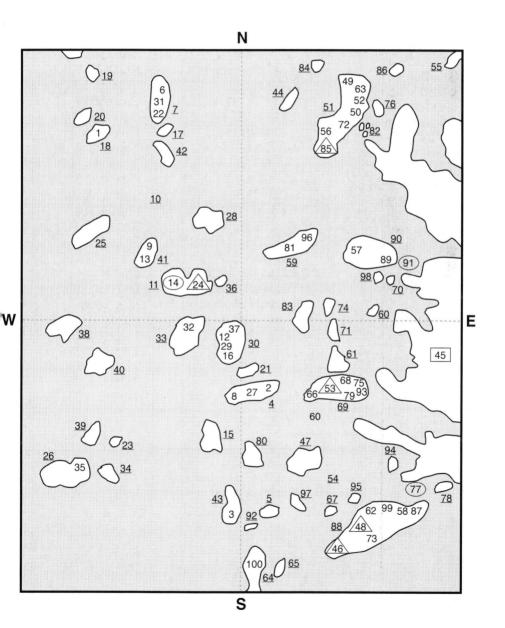

EUROPE
WEST

Abdera SW1
Abula SW2
Adra SW1
Agatha SE3
Agylla SE4
Alalia SE5
Albion NE6
Aléria SE5
Alesia SE7
Algeria SE8
Almeria/ci SW9
Almeria/gu
  SW10
Almunécar SW61
Alps SE11
Andalusia SW12
Antigori SE13
Atlantic CW14
Baleares SE15
Black NE16
Bonifacio SE17
Britain NE6
Cadiz/ci SW31
Cadiz/gu SW18
Calpe SW34
Caralis SE19
Carmona SW20
Cassiterides
  NW21
Ceuta SW2

Chardan SE22
Charente SE23
Corsica SE24
Cotinusa SW25
Douro SW26
Duero SW26
Emporion SE27
England NE6
France NE28
Gadira SW25
Garumna SE29
Gaul SE30
Gedeira SW31
Genoa SE32
Germany NE33
Gibraltar/pe
  SW34
Gibraltar/st
  SW35
Gironde SE29
Guadalquivir
  SW36
Guadiana SW37
Hispalis SW38
Huelva SW39
Huesca SE54
Iberia SW40
Ierne NW41
Ireland NW41
Liger NE42
Liguria/re SE43
Liguria/sea SE44

Loire NE42
Mainake SW45
Majorca SE46
Malaca SW47
Marseille SE48
Massalia SE48
Mediterranean
  CS49
Narbo SE50
Nora SE51
North NE52
Olbia SE53
Osca SE54
Osuna SW55
Pillars SW56
Portugal SW57
Pyrenaei SE58
Pyrenees SE58
Rhine NE59
Rhone SE60
Sardinia SE22
Scilly NW21
Sevilla SW38
Sexi SW61
Sikanos SW62
Spain SW63
Sulcis SE64
Tagus SW65
Tarraco SE66
Tartessos SW67
Tharros SE68
Tin NE & NW69

€UROP€ W€ST

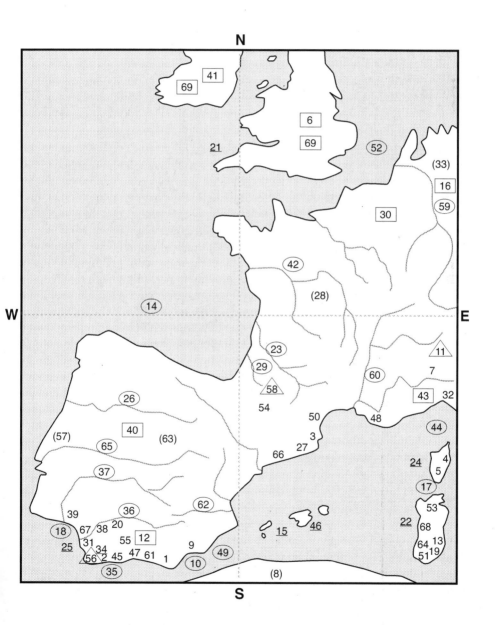

SICILY WEST

Aegithallos NW1
Aegusa NW2
Agrigento SE3
Akragas/ci SE3
Akragas/ri SE4
Camicus SE5
Cephaloedium NE6
Crimissus CS7
Drago SE21
Drepanon NW8
Egesta NW9
Elumi NW10
Entella NE11
Eryx/ci NW12
Eryx/mt NW13
Halicus SE14
Herakleia Minoa SE15
Himera NE17
Himeras NE18
Hippana NE19
Hyccara CN20
Hypsas SE21
Inycum SE22
Laitas NE23
Lilybaeum/ca NW24

Lilybaeum/ci NW25
Macella NW26
Marsala NW25
Minoa SE15
Motya NW27
Motyum SE28
Omphace SE29
Omphale SE30
Palermo NE31
Panormos NE31
Paropus SE32
Phalarium SE33
Phintias SE34
Phorbantia NW35
Segesta NW36
Selinos SW37
Sicania C38
Soloeis NE39
Solontum NE40
Stagnone NW41
Thermai NE42
Trapani NW8
Trinacria C43
Tyrrhenian N44
Ustica NE45

SICILY WEST

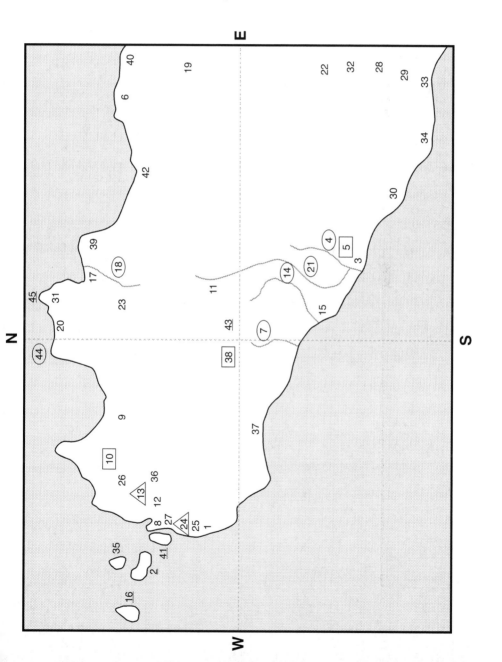

SICILY EAST

Abacaenum NE1
Acesines NE2
Acradina SE3
Acrae SW4
Adrano CN34
Aetna/ci CN5
Aetna/mt NE6
Agatha NE7
Agathurnum NE7
Agurion NW8
Aluntium NE9
Ameselum NW10
Anapos SE11
Apollonia NE12
Arethusa SE13
Assinaros SE14
Assorus NW15
Bricinniae SW16
Cacyparis SE17
Cacyrum SE18
Camarina SW19
Catana CE20
Catania CE20
Centuripa CN21
Charybdis NE54
Daskon SE23
Echetia CS24
Engyum NW25
Enna NW26
Epipolae SE27
Erineos SE28
Euboia CS29
Euryelus SE30
Galeria CW31
Gela SW32
Gelas SW33

Geleatis NE40
Hadranon CN34
Halaesa NE35
Heloros SE36
Heraei SW37
Herbessus SW38
Herbita NW39
Hybla Geleatis
  NE40
Hyblaea SE52
Ietae SE41
Inessa CN5
Italy NE42
Kaleakte NE43
Kallipolis NE44
Kasmenai SW45
Labdalum SE46
Leon NW47
Leontini SE48
Lindii SW32
Lysimeleia SE49
Mactorium SW50
Mediterranean
  SW51
Megara Hyblaea
  SE52
Menae SW53
Messana NE89
Messina NE54
Morgantina SW55
Mylai NE56
Naxos NE57
Nebrodes NE58
Neetum SE59
Ortugia SE60
Pachinus SE61
Palice CS62
Pantacyas SE63

Pelorus NE64
Phlegra NE65
Plagktas NE66
Plemmyrium/ca
  SE67
Plemmyrium/si
  SE68
Reggio di Calabria
  NE69
Rhegion NE69
San Filippo
  d'Argiro NW8
Scylla NE54
Sicilian NE70
Siculia C71
Simeto NW72
Siracusa/ci SE76
Siracusa/ha SE77
Smeneous NE73
Syca SE74
Symaethus CN75
Syracuse/ci SE76
Syracuse/ha SE77
Tapsus/ci SE78
Tapsus/pe SE79
Tauromenium
  NE80
Terias SE81
Trogilos SE82
Troitilum SE83
Tyndaris CN84
Tyrrhenian N85
Xiphonia/ca SE86
Xiphonia/ci SE87
Xuthia NW88
Zankle NE89

SICILY EAST

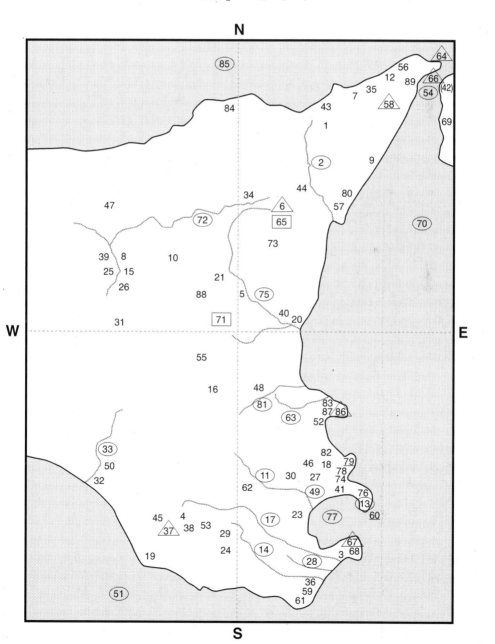

N

85

64
56
12
43   7   35   89   66
84   (42)
1   58   54
69
2   9
47   34   80
72   6   57
65
70
73
39 8   10
25 15
26
21
88   5   75
31   40
20
W   E
55
16   48
81
63   83
87 86
52
33   82
50   46 18   79
32   62   30 27   78 74
11   49 41 76
45 4   17   23   77   13
37 38 53   29   60
24   14   67
19   28   3   68
36
51   59
61

S

ITALY
(Ausonia)

ITALY

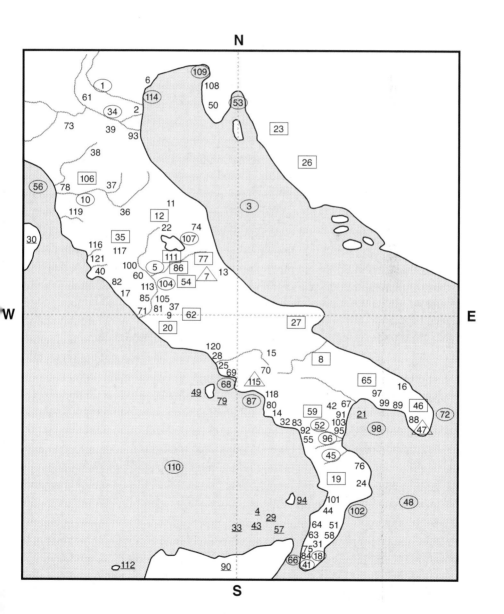

€UROP€ SOUTH€AST

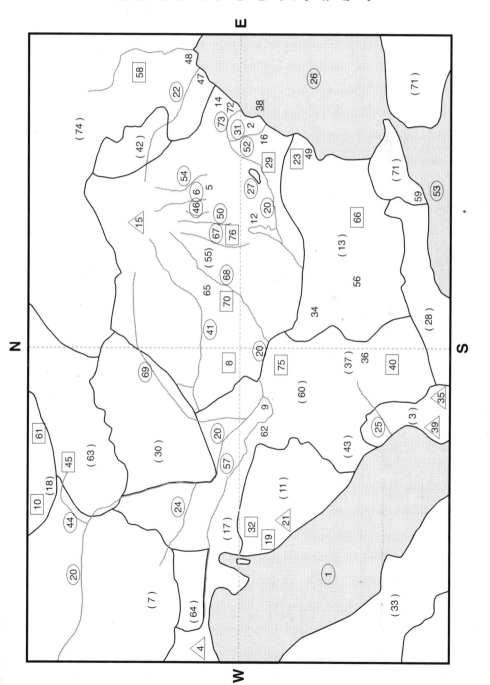

EGYPT NORTH

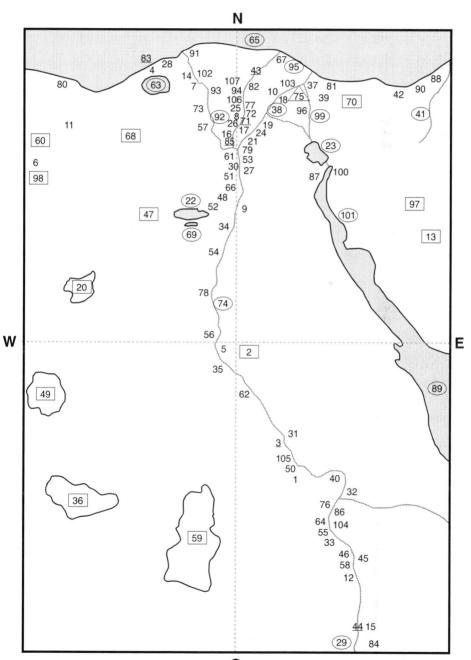

EGYPT SOUTH and AFRICA NORTH

EGYPT SOUTH AND AFRICA NORTH

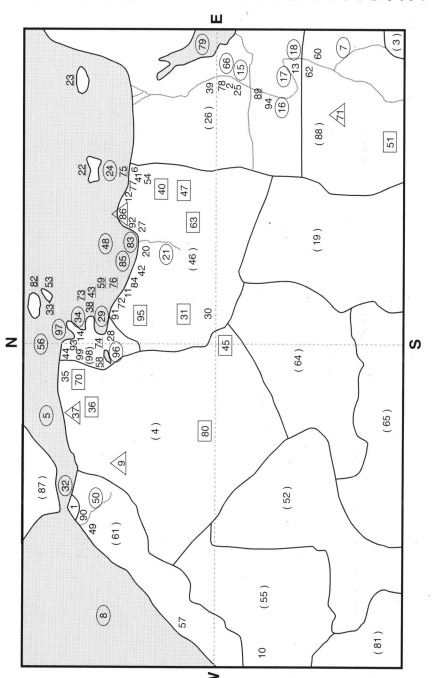

ASIA
WEST & CENTRAL

MODERN
Abu Dhabi CS1
Afghanistan NE2
Arabian SE3
Aral NW4
Armenia NW5
Azerbaijan NW6
Bengal SE7
Black NW8
Caspian NW9
China NE10
Crimea NW11
Cyprus NW12
Djibouti SW 17
Dubai CS13
Egypt SW14
Emirates CS15
Eritrea SW16
Ethiopia SW17
Georgia NW18
Hindu Kush NE19
India SE20
Iran CW21
Iraq CW22
Israel CW23
Jordan SW24
Kazakhstan NE25
Kuwait SW26
Kyrgystan NE27
Lebanon NW28
Masandam CS1, 13, 15 & 32
Mediterranean CW29
Mongolia NE30
Nepal SE31
Oman CS32
Pakistan SE33
Persian SW34
Qatar SW35
Red SW36

Russia NW37
Saudi Arabia SW38
Sinai SW39
Somalia SW 17
Sudan SW40
Syria NW41
Tajikistan NE42
Turkey NW43
Turkmenistan CN44
Ukraine NW45
Uzbekistan NE46
Yemen SW47

ANCIENT
Anatolia NW48
Arachosia CE49
Areia CE50
Asia Minor NW51
Bactria NE52
Baluchistan SE53
Cadusia NW54
Carmania CS55
Dahae NW56
Drangiana SE57
Euxine NW8
Gandhãra NE58
Gedrosia SE59
Hyrcania NW60
Israel SW23
Khorãzãn NE61
Macetia CS1, 13, 15 & 32
Margiane NE62
Media NW63
Mesopotamia CW64
Palestine CW65
Parapamisadai NE66
Parapamisus NE19
Parthia CN67
Persis SW68
Sangada SE69
Sogdiana NE70
Steppe CN71
Zranke SE72

ASIA WEST AND CENTRAL

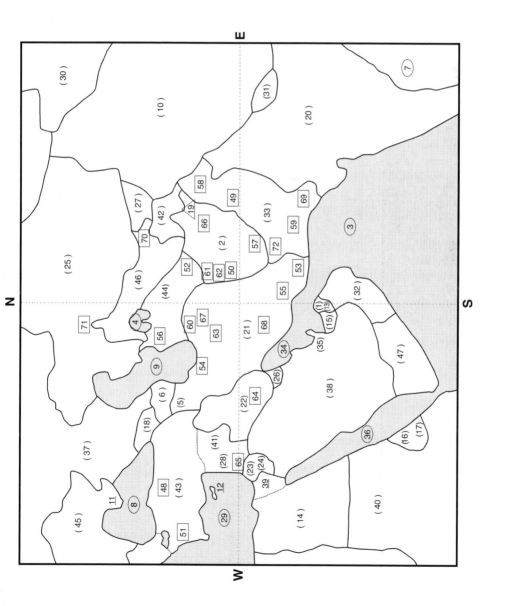

EUROPE EAST AND ASIA WEST

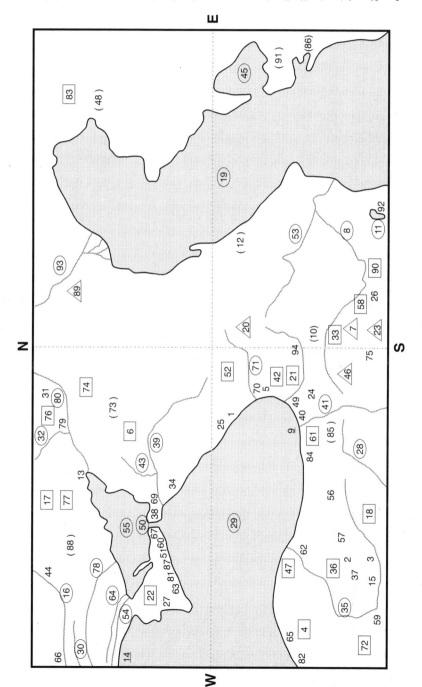

ANATOLIA NORTHWEST 1

ANATOLIA NORTHWEST 1

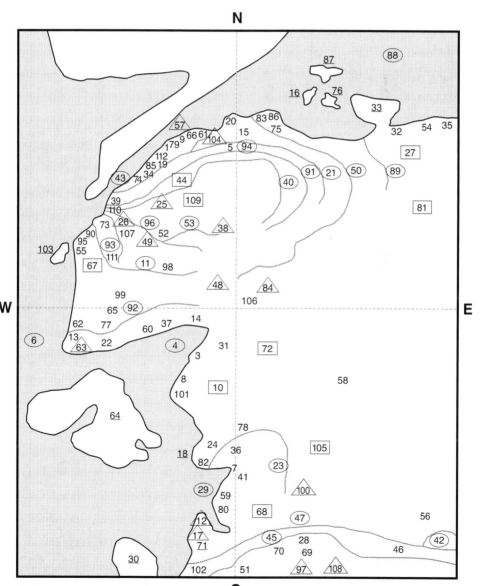

ANATOLIA NORTHWEST 2

Aigialos NE1
Alube NE2
Amastris NE3
Amisos NE4
Ancyra NE5
Arzawa SW6
ASIA MINOR C7
Assesus SW8
Bathymasi NW9
Bebryces NW10
BITHYNIA CN11
Bithynion NE12
Black N26
Bolu NE12
Bosporos NW13
Bursa NW55
Busantion NW14
Calpe CN15
CAPPADOCIA
  SE16
Chalkedon NW17
Chalybes NE18
Chios NW19
Comana NE20
Constantinople
  NW14
Cromna/ci NE21
Cromna/ri NE22
Demonesi NW23
Enete NE24
Eruthini NE25
Euenos ?

Euxine N26
Fraktin SE27
GALATIA NE28
Gediz SW33
Gordion NE29
Halizonia SE30
Halys NE31
Herakleia NE32
Hermos SW33
Hyllus SW34
Ipsos SW35
Iris NE67
Issedones ?
Istanbul NW14
Iznik/ar NW36
Iznik/ci CN47
Iznik/la CN37
Karaoglan
  NW38
Karasu NE39
Keiros CN40
Kizil NE31
Kuthoros/ci
  NE41
Kuthoros/mt
  NE42
Lepte NE43
Lycaonia CS44
Maeander SW45
Mariandyni NE46

Marmara NW54
Menderez SW45
Midius ?
Nicaea CN47
Nikomedia NW17
Olumpos NW48
Pactolos SW49
PAPHLAGONIA
  NE50
Partheneios
  NE51
PHRYGIA CN52
Pontos/ar NE53
Pontos/sea N26
Propontis NW54
Prusa NW55
Pteria SE56
Samsun NE4
Sangarios NE57
Sardene SW58
Sardis SW59
Scylax NE60
Sesamos NE3
Sinope NE61
Thermodon
  NE62
Thynias CN63
Tibareni NE64
Tios NW65
TURKEY C66
Yesil NE67

ANATOLIA NORTHWEST 2

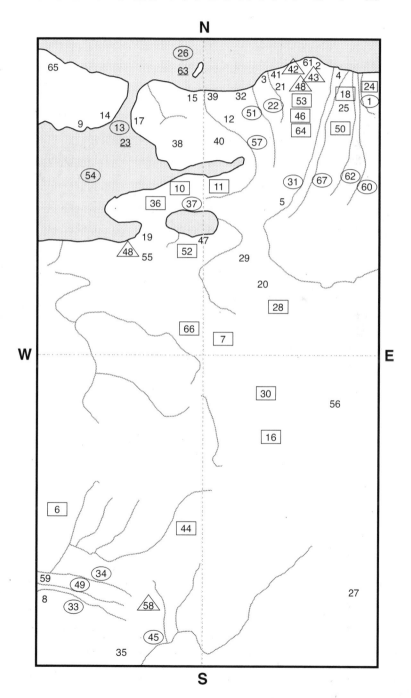

ANATOLIA SOUTHWEST

Abasa NW1
Aegean W2
Aisageia NW3
Alinda NW4
Antioch NW82
Apameia Murleia
 NE35
Arae NW5
Bambyce NE6
Battus SE7
Bodrum/ci SW8
Bodrum/pe SW9
Branchidai CW13
Bubassos SW10
CARIA NW11
Comlekci SE12
Denizli NE6
Diduma CW13
Dina NW14
Dinar NE35
Dindymus NE15
Dirmil CS16
DORIS SE17
Embatum NW18
Ephesos NW19
Eruthrae NW20
Fethiye CW92
Gediz NW24
Glauke NW21
Halikarnassos
 SW22
Hasarlik SE23
Hermos NW24
Hierapolis NE6
Hyparna SE25
Iasos/ci CW26
Iasos/gu SW27
Iduma CS28
Ikaria NW29
IONIA NW30
Izmir NW88
Kalumnos SW31

Karuanda SW32
Kaunos SE33
Kaustros NW34
Kelainae NE35
Kerameikos
 CS36
Keramos SW37
Klaros NW38
Klazomenae
 NW39
Knidos SW40
Kolophon NW41
Kolossai NE42
Komlekci SE43
Korudallos SE44
Korukos NW45
Kos SW46
Lade NW47
Laodikeia NE48
Latmos/ci NW49
Latmos/gu
 NW50
Latmos/mt
 NW51
Lebedos NW52
Loruma SW53
Lukos/ri NE54
Lukos/va NE55
LYCIA SE56
LYDIA CN57
Maeander NW58
Maeander/Little
 NW34
Maeonia CN57
Magnesia NW59
Mainalos SE60
Marsyas NW61
Mediterranean
 S62
Meles NW63
Menderez NW58
Miletos NW64

Mimas NW65
Mukale/ci NW66
Mukale/mt
 NW67
Mulasa CW68
Mundos SW69
Muonessos
 NW70
Muos NW71
Murleia NE35
Muros NW72
Notion NW73
Orsinos NE74
Panormos CW75
Patara CS76
Phoenikos NW77
Phthires NW51
Polichne NW78
Priene NW79
Pteleon NW80
Pugela NW81
Pythopolis NW82
Rhodes CS83
Samos NW84
Sandios NW85
Sidoussa NW86
Smyrna/bay
 NW87
Smyrna/ci NW88
Soluma SE89
Sume SW90
Teichioussa
 NW91
Telmessos SE92
Teos NW93
Triopion/ci SW94
Triopion/ca
 SW95
Tsangli NW96
Turrha NW97
Xanthos/ci SE98
Xanthos/ri SE99

ANATOLIA SOUTHWEST

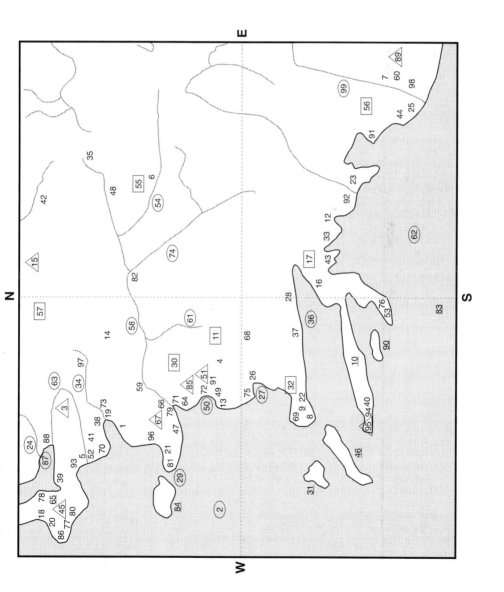

ANATOLIA SOUTHEAST, CYPRUS, SYRIA & LEBANON

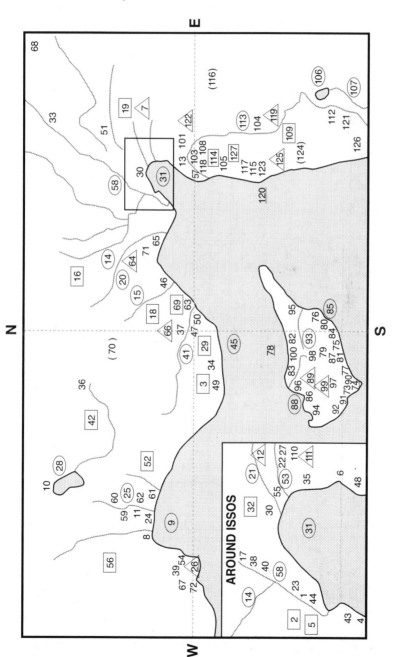

ASIA SW

ASIA SOUTHWEST

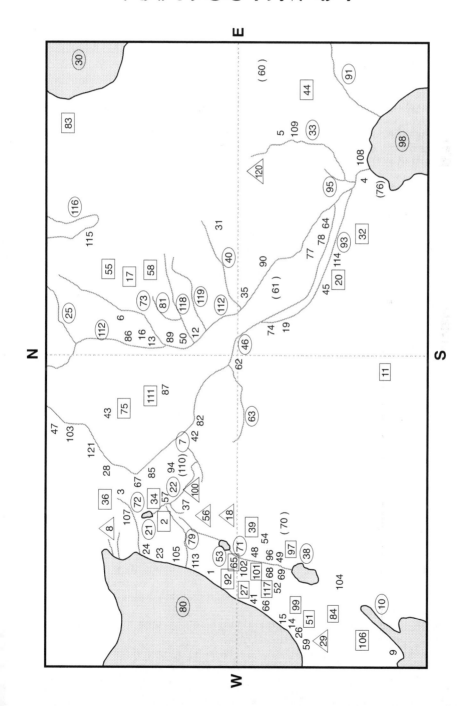

ASIA CENTER WEST

Abivard CS28
Aces SW1
Afghanistan SE2
Agbatana SW3
Alexandria-in-Areia SE4
Alexandria-in-Margiane SE5
Alexandria-in-Prophthasia SE6
Amardus SW7
Amu Darya NE66
Anshan/ar SW8
Anshan/ci SW9
Aral NW10
Areia SE11
Ariaspi SE74
Artacoana SE12
Aspadana SW40
Atok SW13
Bactria C14
Bagistane SW15
Behistun SW16
Bhagasthena SW16
Bisitun SW16
Cadusia SW17
Caspian/gate SW18
Caspian/sea CW19
Cheshmeh-i-Ali SW75
Choarene/ar SE20
Choarene/ci SE21
Chorasmia CN22
Cissia SW23
Comisene SE24
Cossaea SW25
Dahae nW26
Damghan SW27
Dara CS28
Darya NE66
Ecbatana SW3
Elam SW29
Elburz SW68
Emāmshar CS72
Epardus CE60

Esfahan SW40
Farah/ar SE30
Farah/ci SE31
Farah/ri SE32
Gazaca SW33
Gorgān SW34
Hamadan SW3
Hangmatana SW3
Harirûd/ri SE35
Harirûd/va SE36
Hekatompulos CS28 or 72
Herat/ar SE37
Herat/ci SE4
Hyrcania/re SW38
Hyrcania/sea CW19
Iran SW39
Isfahan SW40
Jaxartes NE41
Kara-Bogaz NW42
Kara Kum SW43
Kashan SW44
Kavir CS45
Kazakhstan NE46
Kerman SW47
Khanates NE48
Khash/ci SE49
Khash/ri SE50
Khorāsān SW51
Khwarezm CN22
Kizil Kum NE52
Kum SW53
Lut SE54
Mago SE55
Mardia SW56
Margiana CW57
Margiane SE58
Margush/ar SE58
Margush/ci SE59
Margush/ri CE60
Media SW39
Merv/ci SE61
Merv/oa SE62
Meshed CS63
Murgab CE60

Nisa SE64
Nisaia SW65
Oxus NE66
Pakistan SE67
Parachoathras SW68
Paraetanece SW69
Parthaunisa SE64
Parthia SE70
Parthyaea SE70
Persia SW39
Prophthasia SE30
Qom SW53
Qomsheh SW71
Rai SW82
Rhagae SW82
Salt CS45
Sardar SW18
Sari SW86
Sattagydia SE73
Sefid Rud SW7
Shahreza SW71
Shahrud CS72
Sialek SW18
Sistan SE74
Stiboates CS75
Susa SW76
Susia SE77
Susiana SW29
Syrdaria/ar NE78
Syrdaria/ci NE79
Syrdaria/ri NE41
Tadzen CS80
Tanais CW19
Tapuria SW81
Tehrān SW82
Tejend SE83
Turkmenistan CW84
Uzbekistan NE85
Zadrakarta SW86
Zagros SW87
Zahedan SE88
Zariaspa C14

ASIA CENTER WEST

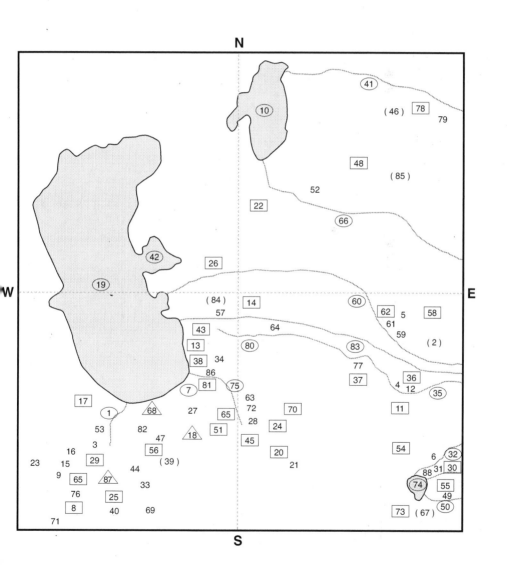

N

W   E

S

ASIA CENTER

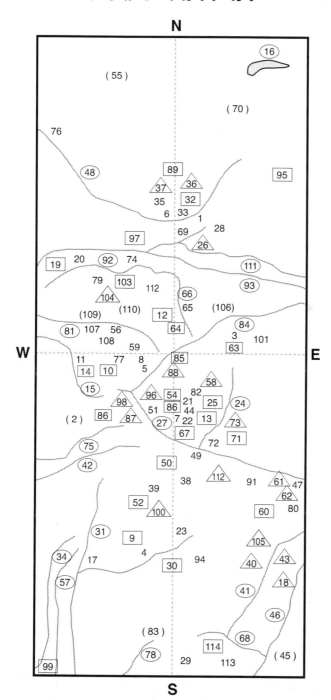

ASIA CENTER SOUTH

Abu Dhabi SW1
Alexander's
  Harbor CE2
Alexandria-in-
  Carmania CW3
Alexandria-in-
  Oreitidae NE4
Alexandria-at-
  Rambacia NE5
Anamis CS6
Apostana SW7
Arabian SE8
Arabis NE9
Araxes NW10
Ardakan NW11
Ariaspi NE81
Badis CS12
Bagia CE13
Bagisara SE14
Baluchistan SE15
Bam CN16
Bolān CE17
Brahui/ar NE18
Brahui/mt NE19
Canate.SE20
Carmana C21
Carmania CN22
Cocala SE23
Cophas SE24
Dagaseira SE25
Dubai SW26
Emirates SW27
Erymandrus
  NE28
Farah NE29
Firdawsi CW30
Gedrosia NE31
Gerrha SW32
Gogana SW33
Granis NW34

Gulashkird CW3
Gwadar SE35
Gwatar SE36
Harmozia/ar
  CW37
Harmozia/ci
  SW38
Helmand NE28
Hieratis CW39
Hingol NE54
Hormuz/ci SW40
Hormuz/il SW41
Hormuz/st SW42
Ila CS43
India NE44
Indus NE45
Iran NW46
Kachi CE47
Kalat/ar NE48
Kalat/ci NE49
Karachi CE2
Las Bela NE4
Macetia SW50
Makai SW50
Makran/re SE15
Makran/mt CE51
Malan SE52
Mand NW34
Masandam SW50
Meka SW50
Mosarna CE53
Mulla NE54
Nari NE55
Oman/co CS56
Oman/gu CS57
Oreitidae/ar
  NE58
Oreitidae/ci NE4
Oreitis NE59
Ormara CE60

Orracia SW61
Ouxioi NW62
Pakistan NE63
Pasargadai NW64
Persepolis NW65
Persian/ga NW66
Persian/gu SW67
Persis CW68
Pulvar NW10
Pura/ar NW69
Pura/ci NW70
Purali NE9
Qatar SW71
Rambacia/ar
  NE72
Rambacia/ci NE5
Red SW67
Sandy CE73
Sangada NE74
Saudi Arabia
  SW75
Sehwan NE80
Shiraz CW76
Sibi/ar NE77
Sibi/ci NE78
Sind NE79
Sindimanao
  NE80
Sistan NE81
Sitaces NW34
Sulaimān NE82
Talmena CE83
Taoke CW84
Tomerus NE54
Watar SE85
Zagros NW86
Ziārat-Gali-Chah
  CE87

ASIA CENTER SOUTH

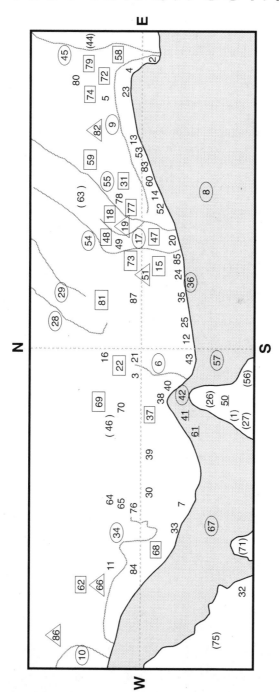

ASIA CENTER EAST

Abisares NW1
Acesines NW2
Afghanistan NW3
Alexandria-in-
    India SW4
Alexandria-Nicaea
    NW5
Alexandria-in-
    Opiene CW6
Alexandria-at-
    Rohri SW7
Aornos/mt NW8
Arachosia SW9
Arigaeum NW10
Aspasii NW11
Assaceni NW12
Attock NW13
Bactria NW14
Badakhshan NW15
Barce SE16
Bazira NW17
Beãs C34
Bukephala NW18
Buner/ar NW19
Buner/ri NW20
Caucasus NW31
Charsadda NW21
Chenãb NW2
China NE22
Erannoboas SE23
Gandak SE24
Gandhãra NW25
Ganges SE26
Glausae NW27
Gumal NW28
Guraei NW29

Hesidros NE85
Himalayas NE30
Hindu Kush NW31
Hydaspes NW32
Hydraotes CN33
Hyphasis C34
India SE35
Indus N & SW37
Islamabad NW38
Jammu/ar NW39
Jhelum/ar NW40
Jhelum/ci NW41
Jhelum/ri NW32
Jumma NE42
Kamalia NW43
Kaoshan NW44
Kashmir NW45
Kathaei CN46
Kunar NW47
Kunlun NE48
Kush NW31
Kyrgyzstan NW49
Laghman NW50
Lahore CN51
Loralei SW52
Malli/ar CW53
Malli/ci SW54
Massaga NW55
Mathura SE56
Maurya SE57
Nepal SE58
Nicaea NW5
Opiene/ar CW59
Opiene/ci CW6
Oxydracae CN60
Pakistan SW61

Palimbothra SE64
Panjnad SW62
Parapamisus
    NW31
Patalene CS63
Patna SE64
Pattaia SW65
Peucelaotis SW66
Pir Sarai SW8
Punjab NW67
Rakshastal NE68
Rãvi CN33
Rohri SW7
Sangada SW69
Sangala CN70
Sãnghar/ar SW71
Sãnghar/ci SW72
Sind SW74
Siwalik NW75
Sogda SW7
Son SE76
Sutlej NE85
Tajikistan NW77
Taxila NW78
Thal CW79
Thar CS80
Tibet NE81
Udyana NW82
Waziristan NW83
Wular NW84
Zaradros NE85
Ziarat-e-Shah-
    Maqsûd CW86

ASIA CENTER EAST

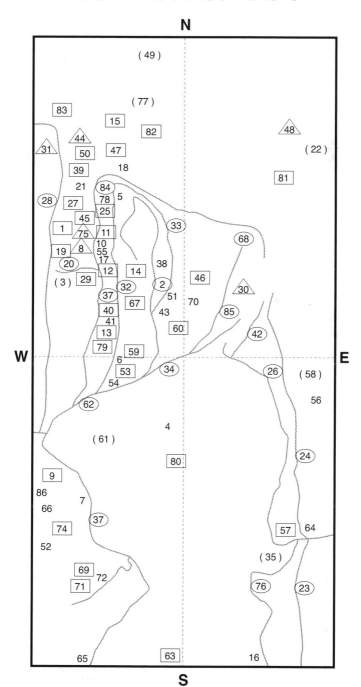

UNDERWORLD MYTHOLOGY

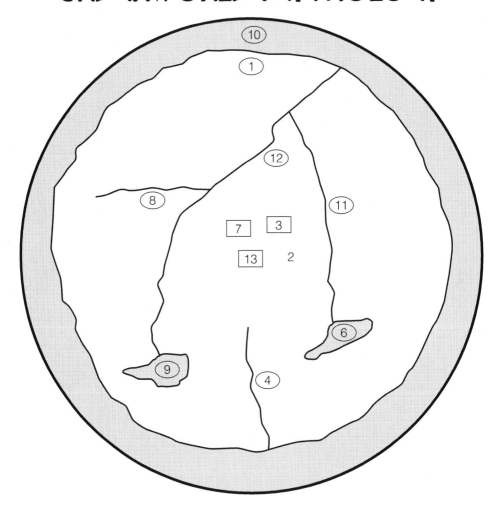

Acheron 1   Konkutos 8
Arima 2   Lake 9
Elysian Fields 3   Ocean 10
Erebos 4   Okeanos 10
Erutheia 5   Periphlegeton 11
Frogs 6   Red 12
Hades 7   Stux 13
Kokutos 8   Tartaros 14

WORLD MYTHOLOGY

All lcations are uncertain

Aiaia
Aigaios
Amphirho
Antemoessa
Antimacheia
Apeire
Arimaspia
Artakia
Astupalaia
Atlantis
Biblis
Charybdis
Cyclops
Dhiktaion
Erumanthos
Harpus
Hupereia
Ida
Kikonos
Kimmeria
Kirke
Kuaneia
Laistrugonia
Leukatas

Menderez
Nusa/Asia
Nusa/Greece
Nusa/India
Nusa/Thrace
Ocean
Okeanos
Ortugia
Phaeacia
Phaiekia
Phlegra
Sarpedon
Scamander
Scylla
Skeria
Surie
Symplegades
Telepulos
Thrimakia
Tigres
Trito
White
Xanthos

*　　　*　　　*

INDEX OF MAPS

INDEX OF ENTRIES

FOREWORD

The categories of places will be listed as follows:

1. Cities, towns, villages, sites, settlements
2 Islands, peninsulas, isthmuses
3. Mountains, hills, rocks, caves, mines, quarries, promontories, capes, plateaus, passes
4. Regions, areas, territories, valleys, plains, oases, deserts, countries
5. Rivers, streams, springs, fountains, deltas, straits, canals
6. Seas, gulfs, bays, harbors, ports, inlets, lakes, marshes, oceans

Four major groups will divide each of these categories of places:

A. Greece, Crete and Aegean Islands
B. Europe
C. Asia
D. Africa

The following abbreviations will be used, when appropriate:

ar : area
ca : cave
ci : city
cn : country
co : coast
de : desert
gu : gulf

ha : harbor
il : island
in : inland
is : isthmus
la : lake
pa : pass
pe : peninsula

pr : promontory
re : region
ro : rock
ri : river
si : site

Mythological places will be referred to at the end.

1. CITIES, TOWNS, VILLAGES, SITES, SETTLEMENTS

A. Greece, Crete, Aegean Islands

Abantes
Abia
Abae
Acharnae
Acherusia
Aegiae
Agea
Agia Irini
Agia Marina
Agios Nikolaos
Agia Triada/
  Crete
Agia Triada/
  Greece
Agios Dhimitrios
Agios Ilias
Agios Kosmas
Agios Nikolaos
Agora
Agrapidochori
Agrileza
Agrinion
Aiane
Aigai/Achaia
Aigai/Euboia
Aigai/Macedonia
Aigeira
Aigiale
Aigialos
Aigilips
Aigina
Aigion/Achaia
Aigion/Argolis
Aigira
Aigition
Aigosthena
Aigussos
Aina
Ainos
Aipeia

Aipu
Aisume
Aithaea
Aitos
Aixone
Akakesum
Akanthos
Akovitika
Akraiphnion
Akriae
Akrothoi
Akroterion
Akrotiri/Crete
Akrotiri/Thera
Alalkomenae
Alassa
Alexandropolis
Aliki
Alimos
Alipheira
Allana
Almuros
Alope
Alopeoe
Alos/Aitolia
Alos/Phthiotis
Alus
Aluzia
Ambrakia
Ambrosos
Amilos
Amnisos
Ampelos
Amphanae
Amphia
Amphigeneia
Amphikaea
Amphiklea
Amphipolis
Amphissa

Amphitrope
Amudon
Amuklai
Amuros
Anaguros
Anaktorion
Anantia
Anaphlustos
Anavusos
Andania
Andritsaina
Anemoreia
Ano
Anopolis
Anthedon
Antheia
Anthela
Anthemos
Anthene
Anthili
Antigoneia/
  Epeiros
Antigoneia/
  Macedonia
Antikura/Lokris
Antikura/Malis
Antikura/Phokis
Antissa
Antron
Aphaia
Aphetae
Aphidna
Aphrodisia/
  Arkadia
Aphrodisia/
  Lakonia
Aphrodisia/
  Messenia
Aphutis
Apollonia/Crete

Apollonia/
  Epeiros
Aspledon
Apollonia/
  Macedonia
Apollonia/Thrace
Aradaena
Arainon
Arantia
Araphen
Arcenices
Archanes
Arethurea
Arethusa
Argilos
Argissa
Argos/Aitolia
Argos/Argolis
Argupheia
Argura
Aristonautae
Arkades
Arkesine
Arkines
Arkolochori
Arkoudiotissa
Arktonnessos
Armenoi
Arne/Boiotia
Arne/Chalkidike
Arnisa
Aroanos
Arobanes
Arsinoë
Arta
Artemision
Arvi
Asea
Asine/Argolis
Asine/Messenia
Askitario
Askra
Askulepios
Asopios
Asopos

Aspledon
Asprochaliko
Assa
Astakos
Asterion
Asteris
Astibos
Astros
Atalante
Athena
Athenaion/
  Achaia
Athenaion/
  Lakonia
Athene
Athens
Augeiai/Lakonia
Augeiai/Lokris
Aulis
Aulon/
  Macedonia
Aulon/Messenia
Axos
Babura
Bassai
Berbati
Beroia/
  Macedonia
Beroia/Thrace
Bessa
Bisanthe
Boeai
Boibe
Boion
Bolina
Bolissos
Bottiaia
Boudeion
Bouga
Bounomos
Bouprasion
Branichevo
Brasiai
Brauron
Bromion

Brea
Brenthe
Bromiskos
Brooks
Bruseia
Budoron
Bulazoia
Bulis
Buphagion
Buprasion
Bura/Achaia
Bura/Calydonia
Calliarus
Capija
Chaironeia
Chalandriani
Chalkis/Aitolia
Chalkis/Euboia
Chantsa
Charadra/Attika
Charadra/Phokis
Charakopid
Cheronia
Chersonese
Chimerion
Choerea
Cholarges
Christo
Chrusovitsa
Cleft Way
Copae
Corinth
Daphni
Daphni/Attika
Daphni/
  Chalkidike
Daphni/Lokris
Dara
Dardanos
Daseae
Daulis
Deipnias
Dekeleia
Delion
Delphi

Delphinion
Demetrias
Demir Kapija
Dendra
Derveni
Despoina
Dia
Didimi
Didumi
Dikaia/
   Macedonia
Dikaia/Thrace
Dikili Tash
Dimini
Dine
Diolkos
Dion/NW Chalk
Dion/SW Chalk
Dion/Euboia
Dion/Thessalia
Dipaia
Diros
Divari
Doberos
Dodona
Dolopia
Donussa
Dorion
Dotion
Drabeskos
Dragmos
Dreros
Drumaia
Druopis
Dumaion
Dume
Durrachion
Duspontion
Echelidai
Edessa
Eetionea
Eilei
Eilesion
Eion
Eionae

Eiresiai
Elaia
Elaios
Elassòn
Elatae
Elatea
Elatheia
Elearchos
Elefsina
Eleon
Eleusis
Eleutherai
Eleutherna
Elis
Ellomenos
Elone
Elthuna
Elumi
Eluros
Emathia
Emborio
Enienae
Enispe
Ennea Hodoi
Enope
Enualios
Epano Englianos
Ephura/Korinthia
Ephura/
   Thesprotia
Epidauros/
   Argolis
Epidauros/
   Lakonia
Epidelion
Epion
Erchia
Eresos
Eretria
Erganos
Erineos/Achaia
Erineos/Doris
Erochos
Eronos
Ertaea

Eruthrae
Eteonos
Etiani
Etone
Eua
Eupalion
Europos
Eurution
Eutresis
Fair Havens
Falassarua
Foinikia
Frankolimani
Galepsos
Gargettos
Gathaea
Gazi
Geraistos
Gerenia
Gerenon
Geresia
Geronthrae
Gigonos
Giophurakia
Gla
Glaphurai
Glechon
Glisas
Gluppia
Gonies
Gonoëssa
Gordaia
Gortunia
Gortus
Gournia
Gourtsouli
Graia
Gritsa
Grotta
Gupsades
Gurtone
Gutheion
Haimoniae
Halai/Oropos
Halai/Thebes

Haliartos
Halieis
Halos
Harma
Harpina
Helike
Helisson
Hellenikon
Helos/Lakonia
Helos/Messenia
Heraia
Heraion
Herakleia/Elis
Herakleia/Illyria
Herakleia/
   Trachis
Herakleion
Hermione
Hermoupolis
Herronisos
Hieraputna
Himeraion
Hippola
Hire
Histiaia
Honikas
Hormuz
Hua
Huampolis
Hudria
Hule
Hupata/Ainis
Hupata/Phokis
Hupata/
   Thessalia
Huperesia
Huperteleaton
Huria/Boiotia
Huria/Thessalia
Hurmine
Husiai/Argolis
Husiai/Boiotia
Ialusos
Idomene/Epeiros
Idomene/Thrace

Ieraputna
Igoumenitsa
Ikarion
Ikos
Ilesion
Ilias
Inakhos
Inatos
Ioannina
Iolkos
Ire
Iria/Argolis
Iria/Naxos
Ismaros
Isthmia
Istron
Isvoria
Itanos
Iteia
Ithome
Iton
Juktas
Kabeiri
Kabesos
Kadmea
Kaenepolis
Kaiadas
Kakovatos
Kalamai
Kalamata
Kalambaka
Kalapodi
Kalauria
Kalindoea
Kalliaros
Kallithea/Achaia
Kallithea/Attika
Kaludon
Kamakaea
Kaman
Kambos
Kameiros
Kamilari
Kanli Kastelli
Katharevousa

Kantharos
Kapakli
Kaparisso
Kaphirio
Kaphuae
Karamoti
Kardamule/
   Chios
Kardamule/
   Lakonia
Kardamule/
   Messenia
Kardia
Karditsa
Karphi
Karuai
Karustos
Kassope
Kasthanaia
Kastoria
Kastraki
Kastri/Boiotia
Kastri/Kythera
Kastritsa
Katakolou
Katerini
Kato Suli
Katri
Katsambas
Kavala
Kave
Kavousi
Kavrochori
Kayio
Kedros
Kelames
Keleae
Kelenderis
Keletron
Kenchreai/inland
Kenchreai/port
Kenoskephalai
Kephala
Kephale
Kephali

Kephalos
Kephisia
Keraia
Keressos
Kerinthos
Kerkura
Kerunia
Khani
Khania
Kiata
Kirrha/Achaia
Kirrha/Phokis
Kirva
Kissamos
Kissos
Kithira
Kitinion
Kleitor
Kleonae/Argolis
Kleonae/
  Chalkidike
Klimax
Klithi
Klitoria
Knossos
Kokkinopulos
Kolonides
Kolonna
Kolumbari
Komaros
Kommos
Konitsa
Kopae
Kopanos
Kophinas
Koprinka
Korakou
Korinthos
Korone
Koroneia
Koroni
Korthion
Korudallos
Koruphasion
Koronta

Korsea
Koruphasion
Kos
Koturta
Koukounara
Koumasa
Kouphia Rachi
Kouphonisi
Kourtes
Kranae/Ionian
Kranae/Lakonian
Kranon
Krenae
Krenides
Kreston
Kretea
Kreusis
Krisa
Kritsina
Krokeae
Krokuleia
Kromi
Kromion
Kropia
Kunaitha
Kunuria
Kupsela
Kurrhos
Kurtone
Kranidhion
Kranae
Krannon
Krenides
Krisa
Krokule
Krounoi
Krusoskalitissa
Kudonia
Kunaitha
Kullene
Kunos
Kunoskephalai
Kunossema
Kunosura
Kuparisseis

Kuparissos/
  Messenia
Kuparissos/
  Phokis
Kuphanta
Kuphos
Kura Vrusi
Kurrhos
Kuthera
Laas
Ladochori
Laechon
Lakedaimonia
Lamia
Lampeia
Lamptras
Laodikion
Lappa
Larissa/Argolis
Larissa/Thessalia
Larumna
Las
Lasea
Lassaia
Lato
Laurion
Lebadea
Lebena
Lechaion
Ledon
Lefkadia
Lefkandi
Leibethra
Leipsudrion
Lektos
Leontion
Lepreon
Lerna
Lessa
Letrini
Leukae
Leukas
Leukonion
Leuktra/Boiotia
Leuktra/Lakonia

Levkas
Liatovouni
Lilaia
Limenas
Limera
Limnaia
Limnai
Lindos
Lisos
Lithares
Long Walls/
  Achaia
Long Walls/
  Argolis
Long Walls/
  Attika
Long Walls/
  Megaris
Loukou
Loutraki
Loutsa
Lukuria
Lusi
Lusia
Lukaion
Lukestos
Lukoa
Lukosura
Luktos
Lunkestis
Lurcea
Luttos
Macistus
Madraki
Mainalos
Maira
Makaria
Makistos
Malea
Malia
Malla
Maltepe
Malthi
Mandra
Mani

Manika
Mantineia
Marathon
Marina
Marios
Marmariani
Maroneia
Mases
Matala
Mavromati
Mazarakata
Medeon
Megalopolis/
  Arkadia
Megalopolis/
  Messenia
Megara
Megasa
Mekuberna
Melaineai
Melangea
Meliboia
Melite
Melitia
Menares
Mende
Menelaion
Menidi
Merenda
Meropis
Mesembria
Mesolongion
Messe
Messene
Methana
Methone/
  Macedonia
Methone/
  Messenia
Methudrion
Methumna
Metropolis
Midea
Mieza
Mikalitsi

Mikinae
Mila
Miletos
Minoa
Mitropolis
Mochlos
Modaeoi
Molukrion
Monastiraki
Monemvasia
Moschaton
Mouliana
Mouriatadha
Mukalessos
Mukenae
Munuchia
Muonia
Murkinos
Mursini
Mursinos :
Murrhinos
Murtos
Musaeon
Mutika
Mutilene
Myrleia :
Nafpaktos
Nafplion
Naousa
Naupaktos
Nauplia
Navarino
Naxos
Nea Anchialos
Nea Ionia
Nea Makri
Nea Nicomedia
Neapolis
Negotino
Nemea
Nerikos
Neris
Nestane
Nestor
Nichoria

Nidri
Nigrita
Nikisiani
Nikolaos
Nikopolis
Ninoi
Nirou Khani
Nisa
Nisaia
Nonakris
Nudion
Numphaion
Numphasia
Oaxos
Oianthea
Oichalia/Euboia
Oichalia/
  Messenia
Oichalia/
  Thessalia
Oichaleis
Oineon
Oiniadai
Oinoë/Argolis
Oinoë/NE Attika
Oinoë/NW Attika
Oinoë/Elis
Oinoë/Ikaria
Oinoë/Korinthia
Oinoë/Lokris
Oinoë/
  Macedonia
Oinoë/Phrygia
Oinophuta
Oisume
Oitulos
Okalea
Olen/Achaia
Olen/Aitolia
Olenos/Achaia
Olenos/Aitolia
Olizon
Oloösson
Olophixos
Olous

Olpai
Olumpia
Olunthos
Onchestos
Opoeis
Opos/Elis
Opos/Lokris
Orchomenos/
  Arkadia
Orchomenos/
  Boiotia
Oreathasion
Oreos
Orestheon :
Orestia
Ormenion
Orneiae
Orobiae
Oropos/
  Amphiareion
Oropos/Boiotia
Orthe
Otzaki
Paeania
Pagai
Pagassai
Palaia
Palaiokastro/
  Crete
Palaiokastro/
  Messenia
Palaiopolis
Palaira
Pale
Paleochoria
Pallantion
Pallene
Paluka
Panagurishte
Panakton
Panayia
  Gourtsouli
Pangaion
Panopeios

Panormos/
  Achaia
Panormos/Crete
Panormos/
  Epeiros
Papoura
Parapotamii
Parga
Parrhasia
Pasalimani
Patrai
Patras
Paus
Pautalia
Pedasos
Pedion
Peiraios
Pelagos
Pelinna
Pelion
Pella
Pellana
Pellene
Pelromagula
Pephnos
Perachora
Peraithea
Perati
Pereia
Pergamos
Perinthos
Peristeria
Perivolia
Peteon
Petrosaka
Peuce
Phaedrias
Phagres
Phaia
Phaistos
Phakion
Phalaisia
Phalanna/Crete
Phalanna/
  Thessalia

Phalasarna	Porto Kayio	Rankos
Phaleron	Poseidon	Rezinea
Phanotis	Potamos	Rhaeteai
Pharai/Achaia	Potidaia	Rhaidestos
Pharai/Messenia	Potidania	Rhamnos
Pharis	Potniai	Rheithron
Pharsalos	Praisos	Rheiti
Phelloe	Prasiai/Attika	Rheitos
Pheneos	Prasiai/Lakonia	Rhekaios
Pherai/Messenia	Preveza	Rhipe
Pherai/Phthiotis	Priansos	Rhion/Achaia
Pherusa	Prinias/C Crete	Rhion/Lokris
Phigalia	Prinias/E Crete	Rhitsona
Philippi	Priniatiko	Rhitumna
Philippopolis	Prino	Rhodes
Philister	Prinos	Rhupes
Phlios	Probalinthos	Rhution
Phlua	Prodromos	Rithumna
Phoenikos	Profitis Ilias	Rodopou
Pholoe	Pronnai	Rogozen
Phrearrhioi	Proschion	Rokka
Phrixae	Prospalta	Routsi
Phrukos	Prosumna	Rupei
Phthia	Psamathos	Rutio
Phthiotis	Psiloneron	Sakovouni
Phulake	Psophis	Salamis
Phulakopi	Psuchro	Saliagos
Phule	Pteleos	Salmonia
Phuska	Ptoion	Salonika
Phutia	Ptolis	Same
Pierion	Pudna	Saminthos
Piloros	Pulene	Sandy Pulos
Pindos	Pulos/Messenia	Sane
Piraeus	Pulos/Elis	Sardika
Pisa	Pura	Sarnia
Pitsa	Pura	Sarte
Plataia	Purasos	Schoinias
Platanias	Putho	Selinos
Platanos	Pudna	Sellana
Plati	Purgos/Crete	Sellasia
Pleuron	Purgos/Elis	Selumbria
Polichne	Purrha	Seraglio
Polis	Purrichus	Sermule
Poluchna	Puthion	Servia
Polurrenia	Rachi	Sesklo
Porti		

Sestros	Strepsa	Thermai/
Setaia	Stulari	Chalkidike
Sevaste	Stumphalos	Thermai/Ikaria
Side	Sturia	Therme
Sikuon	Sumetia	Thermi
Sikiona	Sunion	Thermon
Sindos	Subota	Thermopulai
Singos	Sumbola	Thespiai
Siphae	Surie	Thessaloniki
Sirai	Suva	Thisbe
Siris	Suvritos	Thivai
Sisaea	Sveshtari	Thoenis
Sitagroi	Tainaron	Thorikos
Sitia	Talioti	Thouria
Skandia	Tamunae	Thria
Skarphe	Tanagra	Thrimbokambos
Skillos	Tanos	Thronion
Skione	Tarphe	Thruoëssa
Skolos/SE Boiotia	Tarra	Thruon
Skolos/W Boiotia	Tash	Thurea
Skolos/	Tegea/Arkadia	Thuria
Chalkidike	Tegea/Crete	Thussos
Skotussa	Tegura	Tichion
Skope	Teikhos	Tipha
Skoubris	Teleboa	Tiruns
Skupi	Temenion	Titane
Smirtoula	Temple	Tithorea
Sofia	Tenea	Tithronion
Sollion	Teumesos	Tonsos
Sougia	Teuthis	Torone
Souphli	Teuthrone	Toumba/Euboia
Soureza	Thalamae	Toumba/
Sparta	Thamiskia	Phthiotis
Spartalos	Thasos	Tourliditsa
Sphettos	Thaumakia	Trachis
Spilia	Thebes/Boiotia	Tragana
Spiraeon	Thebes/Phthiotis	Traostalos
Stageiros	Theisoa/C	Trapezos
Stavromenos	Arkadia	Trebeniste
Stavros	Theisoa/SW	Triada/Attika
Stenucleros	Arkadia	Triada/Crete
Stiria	Thelpusa	Trianda
Stiris	Theopetra	Trikala
Stobi	Theotokou	Trikolini
Stratos	Therapne	Trikka

Trikorithos
Tripoatis
Tripodiskos
Tripolis
Triteia
Trizina
Troizen
Tsangli
Tsopani-Rachi
Tsoungazi
Tulcea
Tulissos
Tupanaei
Upati
Urtakos

Vai
Vapheio
Vasiliki
Vasiliko
Vathia
Vatupetro
Velestinon
Vergina
Viannos
Vigla
Vitsa
Vlachopoulo
Volos
Vourvoura
Vrakhori

Vranesi
Vrokastro
Vrusinas
Vurgunda
Xeropolis
Xerovrusi
Yambol
Zakinthos
Zakros
Zarax
Zea
Zone
Zou

B. Europe

Abacaenum
Abdera
Abula
Acco
Acradina
Acrae
Acraephnium
Adra
Adrano
Adria
Adrianople
Aegithallos
Aetna
Agatha
Agathurnum
Agrigento
Agurion
Aigussos
Akragas
Alalia
Alea
Aléria
Alesia
Alexandria
Alexandropolis
Aliphera
Almeria

Almunécar
Altinum
Aluntium
Ambrosus
Amudon
Andros
Anemosa
Anthedon
Antigori
Apeire
Aphetae
Aphrodosia
Apodhoulou
Apollonia/
   Sicily
Apollonia/
   Thrace
Apsilaea
Aptera
Aradaena
Araros
Aricia
Arretium
Arrhiana
Asculum
Assorus
Atella

Azov
Bathymasi
Belgrade
Beneventum
Beroia/Thrace
Borysthenes
Brentesion
Bricinniae
Brindisi
Bucharest
Bug
Byzantion
Cacyrum
Cadiz
Caere
Callatis
Callipolis
Camarina
Caralis
Catana
Catania
Centuripa
Cephaloedium
Ceuta
Chersonesos
Clusium
Constanta

Crithote
Croton
Cumae
Daskon
Dicaearchia
Dioskurias
Doriskos
Drapanon
Duvanlij
Dyrrachium
Echetla
Edirne
Egesta
Elea/Calabria
Elea/Lucania
Emporion
Engyum
Enna
Entella
Epidamnos
Epipolae
Eryx
Euboia
Eupatoria
Euryelus
Faesulae
Falerii
Felsina
Frattesina
Galeria
Gallipoli
Gedeira
Gela
Gelibolu
Gelonos
Genoa
Gorgippa
Gravisca
Hadranon
Halaesa
Heloros
Herakleia
Herakleia Minoa
Herbessus

Herbita
Himera
Hippana
Hipponion
Hispalis
Huelva
Huesca
Hybla Geleatis
Hyblaea
Hyccara
Idakos
Ietae
Inycum
Istria/Croatia
Istria/Romania
Istros
Kabyle
Kaffa
Kaleakte
Kallipolis
Kamenskoe
Karanova
Kasmenai
Kaulonia
Kellatis
Kerch
Kerkinitis
Kosovo
Labdalum
Laitas
Laus
Leon
Leontini
Lilybaeum
Limnaia
Lindii
Lissos
Locri
Luni
Lychnidos
Macella
Mactorium
Mainake
Malaca

Mantua
Marsala
Marseille
Massalia
Matauros
Medna
Megara Hyblaea
Melite
Menae
Messana
Metapontion
Metrovika
Minoa
Mirmekion
Morgantina
Motya
Motyum
Mylai
Naples
Narbo
Naxos
Neapolis
Neetum
Nola
Nora
Nympaion
Obia
Odessa
Odessos
Olbia/Sardinia
Olbia/Scythia
Omphace
Omphale
Osca
Ostia
Osuna
Paestum
Palermo
Palestrina
Palice
Panormos
Pantikapaion
Parma
Perusia

Petra/Bulgaria
Petra/Italy
Phalarium
Phasis
Philippopolis
Phintias
Picedo
Pisae
Plemmyrium
Plovdiv
Poseidonia
Praeneste
Poti
Pyrgi
Pyxous
Razlog
Reggio
Rhegion
Rome
Salmudessos
San Filippo
   d'Argiro
Sardika
Satyrion
Scoglio del
   Tonno
Segesta
Selinos
Selymbria
Seuthopolis
Sevilla
Sexi

Siracusa
Siris
Sirmium
Skidros
Smeneous
Smoljan
Sofia
Soloeis
Solontum
Spina
Sremska
   Mitrovica
Sulcis
Sybaris
Syca
Syracuse
Tanais
Tapsus
Taras
Tarentum
Tarquinii
Tarra
Tarraco
Tartaria
Tartessos
Tatarevo
Tauromenium
Terina
Termitito
Thapsus
Tharros
Theodosia

Thermai
Thurii
Tibur
Tirana
Tivoli
Tomis
Trapani
Trieste
Trogilos
Troitilum
Tulcea
Turda
Tyndaris
Tyras
Tyritake
Uskudama
Veii
Venice
Vetulonia
Visentium
Vivara
Voidhokoilia
Volaterrae
Volomandra
Volturnum
Vratsi
Vulci
Xiphonia
Xuthia
Zankle

C. Asia

Abasa
Abudos
Acana
Acre
Adana
Adramuttion
Adrasteia
Aea
Aigai
Aegiae

Aegiroessa
Aegospotami
Agbatana
Agrieliki
Agrigento
Agrileza
Agylla
Agyrium
Aigaeai
Aigaei

Aigiroëssa
Aigospotami
Ai Khanoum
Akko
Akrotiri
Alaca
Alagonia
Alalakh
Aleppo

Alexander's
  Harbor
Alexandretta
Alexandria-in-
  Arachosia
Alexandria-in-
  Areia
Alexandria-in-
  Carmenia
Alexandria-in-
  Caucasus
Alexandria-
  Charax
Alexandria-in-
  Eschate
Alexandria-in-
  India
Alexandria-at-
  Issos
Alexandria-
  Kapisu
Alexandria-
  Nicaea
Alexandria-in-
  Opiene
Alexandria-in-
  Oreitidae
Alexandria-in-
  Prophthasia
Alexandria-at-
  Rambacia
Alexandria-in-
  Rohri
Alexandria-at-
  Susiana
Alexandria
  Margiana
Alexandria Mysia
Alexandria
  Nicaea
Aledandria Troas
Alinda
Al Mina
Alishar

Al-Mygdoniae
Alybe
Amathus
Amastris
Amaxitos
Amisos
Amyclae
Ancyra
Anshan
Antakya
Antalya
Antandros
Antikura/Lokris
Antikura/Malis
Antikura/Phokis
Antioch
Antioch on the
  Maeander
Antiocheia
Antissa
Aornos
Apaisos
Apameia/Lydia
Apameia/Syria
Apostana
Aqaba
Arados ˙
Arae
Arbela
Ardakan
Arethusa
Arginusai
Arigaeum
Arisbe/Lesbos
Arisbe/Troas
Arrapkha
Artacoana
Ascalon
Ashdod
Ashqelon
Askania
Aspadana
Aspendos
Assesus

Assos
Assur
Ataburion
Atarneus
Atok
Attalia
Azotus
Baalbek
Babylon
Bactra
Badis
Bagisara
Bagrām
Balkh
Bam
Bambyce
Barce
Basra
Battus
Bazira
Bagram
Behistun
Beirut
Belen
Bergama
Beroth
Bhagasthena
Bisanthe
Bisitun
Bithynion
Bodrum
Bogaianzköy
Boghazköy
Bolu
Bottia
Branchidai
Bublos
Bukephala
Bukhara
Bursa
Busantion
Cadites
Cadrusi
Cadytis

Callatebos
Calpe
Canate
Carchemish
Carmana
Cartana
Celones
Ceyhan
Chalkedon
Charax
Charman
Charsadda
Chios/Chios
Chios/Propontis
Choarene
Chruse
Cissia
Citium
Cius
Cocala
Comana
Comlekci
Constantinople
Cophas
Critalla
Cromna
Ctesiphon
Curium
Cyreschata
Cyropolis
Cyzicus
Dagaseira
Damascus
Damghan
Dara
Dardanos
Daskylion
Dasteira
Decapolis
Denizli
Diduma
Dina
Dinar
Dirmil
Dokimeion

Dor
Dortyol
Doruk
Drapsaca
Dura Europos
Ecbatana
Edessa
Edremit
Elaeus
Emänshar
Embatum
Ephesos
Erebuni
Erech
Eruthini
Erythrae
Eschate
Esfahan
Eurymedon
Farah
Ferghana
Fethiye
Fevzipasa
Firdawsi
Fraktin
Gadara
Gadara Perea
Gardez
Gargara
Gaugamela
Gaza
Gazaca
Gazara
Gelibolu
Gerasa
Gerrha
Ghazni
Glauke
Gogana
Gordion
Gorgãn
Gordyene
Gorgan
Granikos
Gruneia

Gulashgird
Gwadar
Halab
Halikarnassos
Hama
Hamadan
Hamãh
Hangmatana
Harmozia
Harran
Hasanbeyli
Hasarlik
Hattusa
Hekatompulos
Heliopolis
Heraion
Herakleia
Herat
Hermonassa
Hierapolis
Hieratis
Homs
Houpian
Hupoplakia
Hurria
Hüyük/Alaca
Hüyük/Alishar
Hyde
Hyparna
Hyssus
Iasos
Iduma
Ienysos
Ila
Ilios
Ipsos.
Irbil
Is
Isin
Iskenderun
Islamabad
Isfahan
Issedones
Issos
Istanbul
Jaffa

Jalalkot
Jerabius
Jericho
Jerusalem
Jhelum
Joppa
Kamalia.
Kandahãr
Kapisu
Karachi
Karaoglan
Karasu
Karmenia
Karteria
Kashan
Kassandreia
Kaunos
Kazmaci
Kebrene
Keiros
Kela
Kelainae/Lydia
Kelainae/Phrygia
Kelenderis
Kelif
Keramos
Kerasous
Kerch
Kerman
Khesh
Khirokitia
Khodjend
Khoirokoitia
Killa
Kimmerikon
Kirkuk
Kis Kulesi
Kition
Kizil Kum
Klaros
Klazomenae
Knidos
Kolophon
Kolossai

Konduz
Konya
Koropissos
Korudallos
Korupedion
Kourion
Kozan
Kudrara
Kum
Kumbaca
Kume
Kunaxa
Kunossema
Kurtkulak
Kuthoros
Kyra
Kyrenia
Kyreshkata
Kytoros
Lade
Lagash
Lahore
Lamos
Lamponion
Lampsakos
Laodikeia/Caria
Laodikeia/
    Phoenicia
Lapithos
Larissa
Larnaka
Larsa
Las Bela
Latmos
Lebedos
Leninabad
Levka
Limassol
Loralei
Loruma
Lusimacheia
Lyrnessos
Magarsos
Magnesia/inland

Magnesia/coast
Mainalos
Malakand
Malan
Malli
Mallus
Manisa
Maracanda
Marathus
Margiana
Margush
Mari
Masat
Massaga
Mathura
Mazaka
Mazar-e-Sharif
Mersin
Merv
Meshed
Miletos
Mosarna
Mosul
Mukale
Mulasa
Mundos
Muonessos
Muos
Muros
Murtina
Mut
Murleia
Nagidos
Nautaca
Neandreia
Nicaea/Bactria
Nicaea/Bithynia
Nicephorum
Nikomedia
Nineveh
Nisa
Nisibis
Norsuntepe
Notion

Nuzu
Oenoë
Olba
Opiene
Opis
Oreitidae
Ormara
Orobatis
Osmaniye
Paesos
Paghman
Palaiokastro
Palimbothra
Palmyra
Panopeios
Panormos
Pantikapeion
Paphos
Paraetanece
Parion
Parthaunisa
Pasargadai
Patara
Patna
Pattaia
Pedaion
Pedasos
Pelagus
Pella
Pergamon
Perga
Pergamum
Perkote
Persepolis
Peshāwar
Petra
Peucelaotis
Phaselis
Phoenikos
Phokaia
Phrikonis
Pinaros
Pir Sarai/ancient
Pir Sarai/modern
Pitane

Pitueia
Polichne
Polis
Poseideïon
Praktios
Priapos
Priene
Prusa
Pteleon
Pteleos
Pteria
Pugela
Pura
Pythopolis
Qandahãr
Qomsheh
Qonduz
Quetta
Qom
Qonduz
Rafah
Rambaciam
Raphia
Ras Sharma
Rhagae
Rhoeteum
Rohri/Alexandria
Rohri/Sogda
Sagalassus
Salamis
Salmudessos
Samaria
Samarkand
Samosata
Sangala
Samsun
Sãnghar
Sardis
Saryekshan
Sari
Savnob
Sela
Selge
Sesamos
Sehwan

Shankhar
Shiraz
Shortugai
Sibi
Side
Sidon
Sidoussa
Shahrud
Shahreza
Sillyum
Sindimanao
Sinope
Sigeion
Skepsis
Sminthium
Smyrna
Sochi
Sogda
Soli
Sotera
Spasinou
Susa
Susia
Swat
Syrdarya
Talmena
Tamassos
Taoke
Tarne
Tarsus
Taxila
Tehrãn
Teichioussa
Tel Aviv
Tell Acana
Tell Sankarah
Tell Sukas
Telmessos
Temese
Temnos
Teos
Termessos
Termez
Termita
Teuthrania

Thapsacus   Turrha   Vahlika
Thebe   Tyana   Vounous
Thermiscyra   Tyre   Xanthos
Thospitis   Ugarit   Zadrakarta
Thumbre   Ullais   Zahedan
Tios   Ulu Burun   Zaranj
Toprakkale   Urfa   Zeleia
Trapezos   Urmia   Zeugma
Triopion   Uruk   Ziãrat-e-shah-
Troy   Urfa   Maqsûd
Tsangli   Van   Ziãrat-Gali-Chah

D. Africa

Abu Simbel   Buhen   Esna
Abudos   Busiris   Euesperides
Akhmim   Buto   Faiyum
Alexandria   Cairo   Farafra
Al-Marj   Canobia   Gabès
Amarna   Canopus   Garama
Ammonium   Carthage   Girga
Anthylla   Cercasorus   Gîza
Anysis   Chemmis   Gurob
Aphroditopolis   Cinyps   Habu
Aphtis   Coptos   Halfa
Apis   Critalia   Heliopolis
Apollinopolis   Crocodilônpolis   Herakleopolis
Apollonia   /C   Hermonthis
Archandropolis   Crocodilônpolis   Hermopolis
Aswan   /N   Magna
Asyut   Cusae   Hermopolis
Atarbechis   Dabarosa   Parva
Athribis   Damanhür   Hierakônpolis
Augila   Damietta   Hippo Ihnasya
Avaris   Daphnae   el-Medina
Aziris   Defenneh   Ihnasya
Az-Saqãziq   Dendera   el-Medina
Barce   Edfu   Karnak
Bastah   Egypt/re   Khmunu
Benghazi   Egypt/ri   Kume
Bilbeis   El-Arish   Kyrene
Birket Karûn   Elbo   Labda
Bitter   El-Amarna   Leptis Magna
Bubastis   El-Kab   Leptis Minor

Lëtopolis
Lixus
Luxor
Lykopolis
Marea
Matruh
Medinet Habu
Melissa
Memphis
Mendes
Meroë
Mersa Matruh
Momemphis
Myriandros
Napata
Natho
Naukratis
Oea
Ombos
Omphis
On
Oxyrhynchos
Panopolis

Paprëmis
Paraitonion
Panopolis
Pelusion
Pharbaetus
Philai
Port Said
Prosopitis
Ptolemais
Qasr Ibrim
Qift
Qulzum
Ramsës
Rhinocolura
Rosetta
Sais
San al-Hajar al-
    Qibliyah
Sebennytos
Shahbat
Silë
Sirte
Siwa

Suez/ca
Suez/ci
Suez/gu
Surt
Suto
Syene
Tangier
Tanis
Tapacae
Taucheira
Tell el-Amarna
Thapsus
Thebes
Thinis
Thmuis
Tingis
Tocra
Tombos
Tripoli
Tunis
Utica
Xois
Zeus Ammon

2. ISLANDS, PENINSULAS, ISTHMUSES

A. Grecce, Crete, Aegean Islands

Abantes
Agion Oros
Aigina
Akrotiri
Akte
Akti/Chalkidike
Akti/Piraeus
Alonnisos
Amorgos
Anaphe
Andros
Antikuthera
Aperopia
Aristerae
Asteris
Astupalaia
Atalanta

Attika
Chalkidike
Cranae
Crete
Cyclades
Delos
Dia
Dodekanesoi
Drumoussa
Dulichion
Echinades
Echinae
Elafonissi
Elassa
Euboia
Gaidhouronisi
Gaudos

Gianisadhes
Gla
Grambousa/il
Grambousa/pe
Helene
Hudra
Hudrea
Icos
Ikaria
Ikos
Imbros
Ionian
Ionic
Ios
Isthmos
Ithaka
Kalandriani

B. Europe

Abantis
Aeaea
Aegusa
Aiaia
Aiolia
Albion
Ameselum
Amphiareion
Baleares
Balkans
Berezean
Britain
Calpe
Cassiterides
Chardan
Choerades
Corcyra
Corfu
Corsica
Cotinusa
Crimea
Didume

Elba
England
Epidamnos
Ericussa
Gadira
Gallipoli
Gibraltar
Hephaisti
Hiera
Iberia
Ierne
Ireland
Ischia
Istra
Istria
Leukae
Lipara
Lissa
Majorca
Malta
Melite
Ogugia

Ortugia
Pantellaria
Paropus
Phorbantia
Pillars of
  Herakles
Pithekoussai
Sardinia
Scilly
Sicania
Sicily
Sikilia
Soloeis
Strongule
Tapsus
Taurica
Tin
Trinacria
Ustica
Vis

C. Asia

Akrotiri
Alashiya
Aphousia
Avsa
Bodrum
Bubassos
Chios
Cyprus

Cyzicus
Hormuz
Kapidagi
Kupros
Macetia
Makai
Marmara
Masandam

Mimas
Orracia
Pasalimani
Prokonnesos
Thynias
Tragia

D. Africa

Akhmim
Cercasorus
Demonesi
Elephantine
Kerkennah
Kerkine
Kerkis

Kerkennah
Lampedusa
Mene
Meninx
Myecphoris
Pharos
Phla

Plataia
Plate
Prosopitis
Sinai
Tacompso

3. MOUNTAINS, HILLS, PROMONTORIES, ROCKS, MINES, QUARRIES, CAVES, PLATEAUS, PASSES

A. Greece, Crete, Aegean Islands

Abas
Agios Nikolaos
Agora
Aigai
Aigaleos/Attika
Aigaleos/
  Messina
Akra
Akraia
Akritas
Akrokeraunia
Akrokorinthos
Akropolis/
  Athens
Akropolis/
  Greece
Akte
Aktion
Alepotrupa
Alesion/Arkadia
Alesion/Elis
Anchesia
Anchesmos
Apesas
Arachnaeos
Arakunthos
Araxos
Areiopagos
Arene
Arkolochori
Artemision/
  Argolis
Artemision/
  Euboia
Arvanios
Asia
Aspis
Astupalaia

Atabyrium/
  Phoenicia
Atabyrium/
  Rhodes
Athos
Boreos
Brilessos
Bukephala
Buporthmos
Caphyae
Chaon
Chelidoria
Cynossema
Deiras
Dhikaios
Didumos
Diktaion
Dikte
Drapano
Drepanon
Druoskephalae
Dunax
Dusoron
Eileithuia
Elaios
Erumanthos
Eua
Euboia
Franchti
Geraistos
Geraneia
Gortynios
Grammos
Guphtokastro/
  Aitolia
Guphtokastro/
  Attika
Gurae

Haemos
Helikon
Heraion
Hupatos
Humettos
Hupsos
Ichthos
Ida/Cave
Ida/Mountain
Idi
Ismaros
Istone
Ithome
Kalathios
Kallidromon
Kamares
Kambunion
Kanastraeon
Kaoshan
Katara
Kaza
Kenaion
Kerkine
Kerdulion
Khasia
Kirphis
Kissavos
Kithairon
Klenies
Knakalos
Knemis
Kolias
Kolonos
Koluergia
Korax
Koruphasion
Koruphon
Kotiliusa

Krathis
Krokeae
Kullene
Kunortion
Kunoskephalai
Kunthos
Kuparission
Kuprianon
Laphustios
Larissa
Lasithi
Laurion
Lavka On
Lera
Leukimme
Likodhimon
Lithino
Lukabettos
Lukaion
Lukavittos
Lukone
Luktos
Maenalos
Malea/Argolis
Malea/Lesbos
Matapan
Mathia
Mavrovouni
Megalo Kastelli
Messapios
Mideia
Minoa
Minthe
Munuchia
Muses
Narthakios
Neapolis
Neion
Neriton
Nestor
Nomia
Nusa

Ocha
Oëroë/Euboia
Oëroë/Phokis
Oita/Euboia
Oita/Phokis
Olen
Olumpos
Oneion
Onugnathos
Orbellos
Oruxis
Ossa
Othris
Palaiokastro
Pan
Panachaikon
Panhellenios
Parnassos
Parnes
Parnon
Parium
Parrhasios
Partheneios
Pefkakia
Peirene
Pelion
Pentelikos
Petralona
Petrovouni
Phalanthos
Phanai
Phikios
Pholoe
Pindos
Pieria
Pirin
Plataniston
Pnyx
Pontinos
Pros
Psiloritis
Ptoion

Ptous
Rhodope
Sar
Shipka
Skardos
Skiatos
Skullaion
Siwalik
Skollis
Skombros
Skoteino
Soros
Sphinx
Stavros
Struthos
Sunion
Surie
Tainaron
Taleton
Taygetos
Teügetos
Thermopulai
Thornax
Thuamos
Thurides
Tilphusios
Titan
Titthion
Trachu
Tretos
Triopion
Tsangon
Tupaios
Thuamos
Tuphaoneos
Velatouri
Vermion
Vlichada
Vodomatis
White
Zoster

B. Europe

Aetna	Iapygium	Plagktas
Aigai	Inessa	Plemmyrium
Alps	Ismaros	Pyrenaei
Apennines	Keraunia	Sar
Carpathian	Leukatas	Scardus
Dinaric	Linguetta	Ural
Eryx	Nebrodes	Vesuvius
Heraei	Pelorus	Xiphonia

C. Asia

Akra	Gumal	Olumpos/Cyprus
Aisageia	Harnai	Olumpos/Mysia
Amanos	Hermon	Parachoathras
Anti-Lebanon	Himalayas	Parapomisadai
Aornos	Hindu Kush	Parapamisus
Ararat	Ida	Pergamos
Arginos	Jammu	Persian
Autocane	Jonah	Phthires
Bahce	KalliKolone	Pir Sarai
Batieia	Kaoshan	Plakios
Bolãn	Karakali Dag	Qasiyun
Brahui	Karamenia	Salang
Casius/Palestine	Khyber/ mt	Sandios
Casius/Phoenicia	Khyber/pa	Sanglãkh
Caspian	Korukos	Sardene
Caucasus/Hindu	Kunlun	Senir
Kush	Kush	Sher-Dahan
Caucasus/Russia	Kuthoros	Sialek
Chionistra	Kuwait	Sipulos
Chorienes	Laghman	Sirion
Cudi Dag	Latmos	Sogdiana
Cynossema	Lebanon	Solumi
Dinaric	Lektos	Sulaimãn
Dindymus	Lepte	Symplegades
Elburz	Makrãn	Tahtali
Erumanthos	Malakand	Tamnus
Ferghana/mt	Mimas	Taurus
Ferghana/pa	Mukale	Tereia
Gargaron	Murine	Tmolos
Gelydonia	Nusa	Troödos

Zagros   Zarafshan

D. Africa

Atlas   Kyrenaica   Nusa/Nubia
Kabylia   Nusa/Egypt   Soloeis

4. REGIONS, AREAS, TERRITORIES, VALLEYS, PLAINS, OASES, DESERTS, COUNTRIES

A. Greece, Crete, Aegean Islands

Abantis	Bisaltia	Kaludonia
Achaia/	Boiotia	Kastoria
Peloponnesos	Bottiaia	Kerameikos
Achaia/Phthiotis	Bottike	Kestrine
Achilles	Bouprasion	Kikones
Aetionea	Chaonia	Korinthia
Aitolia	Continental	Koritsa
Agraia	Greece	Korudallos
Agrianes	Dardania	Krestonia
Agrileza	Dassaretis	Krusis
Aigialos	Dii	Kumli
Ainis	Dolopia	Kunosarges
Aithices	Doris	Kunouria
Aitolia	Dotion	Kuparisseis
Akarnania	Driopia	Lakedaimon
Akraiphia	Edonia	Lakonia
Alkimeton	Elimia	Lasithi
Almopia	Elis	Leaia
Ambrakia	Enchelea	Lelantine
Amphaxitis	Enete	Lokris/Opuntian
Amphiareion	Eordaia	Lokris/Ozolian
Amphilochia	Epeiros	Luginos
Amphitus	Eretria	Lunkestis
Anigraia	Eurotas	Lunkos
Arakunthos	Greece	Macedonia
Argolid	Hellas/Greece	Maidi
Argolis	Hellas/Phthiotis	Magnesia
Arkadia	Hellopia	Magna Graecia
Aroanius	Hestiaeotis	Mainland Greece
Atintania	Hua	Malis
Attika	Huampolis	Marathon
Belemina	Kadmeia	Megaris
Bessi		Mesara

Messenia	Paionia/Homeric	Sintia
Minuae/Boiotia	Paionia/Greek	Skiritis
Minuae/Elis	Pannonia	Skordesci
Molossia	Parauaea	Smenus
Molossis	Parnassos	Stenukleros
Molukria	Parrhasia	Taulantii
Muses	Pelagonia	Tembi
Mugdonia	Peloponnese	Tempe
Nestor	Peneios	Tenerion
Nusa	Perrhaibia	Thesprotis.
Odomantia	Phokis	Thessalia/plain
Odrusia	Phthiotis	Thessalia/region
Oëroë	Pieria	Thrace
Opuntian	Pisa	Thria
Oresthis	Plataia	Thureatis
Orestis	Pteleon	Trachis
Oëroë	Rharos	Triphulia
Ozolian	Sapaei	Troizen

B. Europe

Agrianes	Celtic	Hungary
Albania	Chersonesos	Iapygia
Andalusia	Choanes	Iberia/E
Apulia	Croatia	Iberia/W
Ardiaei	Dalmatia	Illyria
Arezzo	Desert	Ireland
Arretium	Dobruja	Italy
Ausonia	Elumi	Kolchis
Austria	England	Korçë
Autariatae	Epipolae	Kosovo
Balkans	Etruria	Labeati
Basilicata	Europe	Latium
Bastarnae	France	Liguria
Belarus	Gades	Lucania
Belgium	Gaul	Lyginus
Bisaltia	Georgia	Macedonia
Bohemia	Germany	Marsi
Bosnia	Getae	Messapia
Britain	Haemos	Moldova
Bulgaria	Hamangia	Montenegro
Calabria	Histriani	Moravia
Camicus	Herzegovina	Paionia
Campania	Holland	Pannonia

Peloponnesos
Picene
Poland
Portugal
Puglia
Romania
Russia
Sacred
Sabina
Sarmatae
Sauromatai

Scythia
Serbia
Sicania
Siculia
Silesia
Skudra
Slovakia
Slovenia
Spain
Switzerland
Thrace

Toscana
Transylvania
Triballi
Trinacria
Turkey
Tyrrhenia
Ukraine
Umbria
Vinca
Walachia

C. Asia

Abii
Abisares
Abu Dhabi
Adana
Afghanistan
Ahhiyawa
Aiolis
Al-Biqā
Aleion
Anatolia
Anshan
Apsilaea
Arabia
Arachosia
Arcia
Areia
Ariaspi
Armenia
Arzawa
Asia
Asia Minor
Aspasii
Assaceni
Assyria
Atok
Atropatene
Attok
Azerbaijan
Babylonia

Bactria
Badakhshan
Bahrain
Balkh
Baluchistan
Bagram
Bebryces
Bekaa
Bhutan
Bithynia
Black
Boudinoi
Brahui
Bukhara
Buner
Cadusia
Canaan
Cappadocia
Caria
Karmania
Cathaei
Chaldaea
Chalibes
China
Choarene
Choaspes
Chorasmia
Cilicia
Cimmeria

Coele Syria
Comisene
Commagene
Cossaea
Cyrrhestis
Dahae
Dardania
Decapolis
Doris
Drangiana
Dubai
Elam
Emirates
Enete
Escharta
Farah
Galatia
Gandhāra
Gaza
Gedrosia
Glausae
Gogarene
Guraei
Halizonia
Harirûd
Harmozia
Hatti
Hellespontine
Herat

Hindu Kush	Lut	Patalene
Hittite	Lycaonia	Perea
Hupoplakia	Lycia/Asia Minor	Persia
Hurria	Lycia/Troas	Persis
Hyrcania	Lydia	Peshāwar
India	Maeonia	Philistia
Ionia	Mago	Phoenicia
Iran	Makrān	Phrygia
Iraq	Malakand	Pisidia
Isauria	Malli	Pontos
Israel	Mardia	Prophthasia
Issos	Margiane	Punjab
Iznik	Mariandyni	Pura
Jammu	Massagetai	Qatar
Jhelum	Matiene	Qonduz
Jordan	Maurya	Rambacia
Kabul	Media	Sacae
Kachi	Media	Salt
Kalāt	Meka	Samaria
Kandahār	Merv	Samarkand
Kapisu	Mesopotamia	Sandy
Kara-Kum	Mongolia	Sangada
Karmania	Mosynoeci	Sānghar
Kunaxa	Mysia	Sarmatia
Karuanda	Nabatea	Sattagydia
Kashmir	Nasamones	Saudi Arabia
Kaska	Negev	Scythia
Kathaei	Nepal	Sibi
Kavir	Nisaia	Sind
Kazakhstan	Oman	Sistan
Khanates	Oreitidae	Sogdia
Khorāsān	Oreitis	Sogdiana
Khulm	Ouxioi	Steppe
Khwārezm	Oxydracae	Sumer
Khyber	Pakistan	Susiana
Kokcha	Palestine	Swat
Konduz	Pamphylia	Syrdarya
Kuh-e Daman	Panjshir	Syria/ancient
Kummuh	Paphlagonia	Syria/modern
Kunar	Parapomisadai	Tadzhikistan
Kuwait	Pareitacae	Tajikistan
Kyrgyzstan	Partheneios	Tapuria
Lagash	Parthia	Tashkurghan
Lebanon	Parthyaea	

Teuthrania
Thal
Thar
Thura
Thyssagetai
Tibareni
Tibet

Tracheia
Troas
Turkey
Turkmenistan
Uzbekistan
Udyana
Urartu

Waziristan.
West Bank
Yemen
Zariaspa
Zranka

D. Africa

Africa
Aiguptos
Aithiopia
Algeria
Arabaya
Bahariya
Chad
Dakhla
Djibouti
Egypt
Eritrea
Ethiopia
Faiyûm

Garamantes
Kabylia
Kharga
Kush
Libya/Africa
Libya/NE Africa
Libyan
Makrobia
Mali
Mauretania
Mauritania
Mersa Matruh
Morocco

Mudraya
Niger
Nigeria
Nubia
Numidia
Sahara
Senegal
Siwa
Somalia
Sudan
Tripolitania
Tunisia

5. RIVERS, STREAMS, SPRINGS, FOUNTAINS, DELTAS, STRAITS, CANALS

A.   Greece, Crete, Aegean Islands

Acheloos
Acheron
Agrianes
Aganippe
Aias
Akidas
Aliakmon
Alope
Alpheios
Amphirho
Amphitos
Anapos
Anigros
Aoos
Apidanos

Apsus
Aradaena
Arda
Ardeskos
Arethusa
Aroanios
Arsen
Artanes
Asopos/Argolis
Asopos/Boiotia
Asopos/Malis
Aspropotamos
Asterion
Atlas
Auras

Avenos
Axios
Balura
Baphuras
Bias
Boagrios
Bolinaeos
Buraikos
Charadra
Charadros/
   Achaia
Charadros/
   Argolis
Charadros/
   Macedonia

Charadros/
  Messenia
Cheimarros
Choerios
Crna
Dardanos
Diagon
Dynamene
Eira
Elaphos
Elektra
Enipeos
Enneakrounos
Erasinos
Ergines
Eridanos
Erigon
Erumanthos
Euenos
Euripos
Eurotas
Garates
Gatheatas
Genusus
Glaukos
Harpinates
Harpus
Hebros
Helisson/Argolis
Helisson/Arkadia
Herkune
Hippokrene
Hissos
Horse's Spring
Hullikos
Hupereia/Argolis
Hupereia/
Iardanos/Crete
Iardanos/Elis
Ikār
Ilisos
Inakhos
Inopos
Ismenos

Kallichoros
Kallirhoe
Karnion
Kastalia
Keladon
Kerunites
Kephisos/Attika
  C
Kephisos/Attika
  NW
Kephisos/Boiotia
Kephisos/Phokis
Kiliaris
Kladeos
Kontadesdos
Krathis
Kreine
Krios
Kuparisseis
Ladon/Arkadia
Ladon/Elis
Ladonas
Lamos
Lankia
Larisos
Leukasia
Leukuanias
Lithaios
Lophis
Loudhias
Louros
Lusios
Maiden Well
Maritsa
Meganitas
Meilichos
Messeis
Mesta
Minueios
Neda
Nemea
Nessos
Nestos
Oëroë

Olmeios
Onchestos
Onochonos
Ophis
+Oskios
Pamisos/
  Messenia
Pamisos/
  Thessalia
Parapotamii
Pasimos/
  Messenia
Pamisos/
  Thessalia
Partheneios
Peiros/Achaia
Peiros/Thessalia
Pellanis
Peneios/Elis
Peneios/
  Thessalia
Permessos
Phalaros
Phoenix
Pieria
Pindos
Pirene
Plataniston
Platanius
Pleistos
Polydora
Puknos
Rhion
Samaria
Samos
Selas
Selemnos
Selinos
Selleis/Achaia
Selleis/Elis
Skirtos
Smenos
Soron

Sperkeios
Stratia
Strumon
Stux
Suthas
Tanaos
Tempe
Termessos

Thespios
Thius
Thuamis
Tiarantus
Tigres
Titarisios
Tripotamos
Tundja

Tunka
Tuthoa
Vardar
Vedea
Vistritsa
Voidomatis

B. Europe

Acesines
Adige
Akragas
Aliakmon
Allia
Anapos
Araros
Arethusa
Arnus
Assinaros
Atlas
Auras
Bonifacio
Borysthenes
Bosporos/Euxine
Bosporos/
   Cimmerian
Bug
Cacyparis
Caicinos
Charente
Charybdis
Cherna
Crimessus
Danube
Dardanelles
Dnestr
Dnieper
Don
Douro
Drago
Drava
Drilon
Drin

Duero
Eordaicus
Eridanos
Erineos
Exampaeus
Garumna
Gelas
Gerrhos
Gibraltar
Gironde
Guadalquivir
Guadiana
Halex
Hellespontos
Himeras
Hylias
Hypacyris
Hypanis/
   Romania
Hypanis/
   Russia
Hypsas
Ingul
Ister
Kerch
Krathis
Kuban
Liger
Loire
Lukos
Maris
Messina
Mesta
Morava

Naparis
Naro
Neretva
Ordessus
Otranto
Pantacyas
Pantikapeion
Phasis
Po
Pyretus
Rhine
Rhone
Rioni
Sava
Scylla
Sikanos
Simeto
Sybaris
Symaethus
Syrgis
Tagus
Tanais
Taulantii
Tearos
Terias
Tiarantus
Tiber
Tibisis
Timis
Tisza
Tunjda
Tyras
Volga

C. Asia

Abanah	Deli	Karesos
Aces	Diyala	Karasu
Acesines	Diz	Karkheh
Acheloos	Enipeus	Kaustros
Adramyttion	Epardus	Kebrene
Aigialos	Erymandrus	Khabur
Aisepos	Euenos	Kizil
Amardus	Eulaeus	Konduz
Amu Darya	Euphrates	Kundar
Anamis	Eurymedon	Kuros
Arabis	Farah	Lamos
Aras	Gandak	Leontes
Araxes/Aras	Ganges	Litani
Araxes/Pulvar	Gediz	Little Maeander
Aridanus	Gerrhos	Lukos/Lydia
Arkturos	Granikos	Lukos/
Askanos	Granis	Mesopotamia
Asopos	Gumal	Maeander
Astraios	Gyndes	Mand
Axios	Halys	Margush
Balkh	Harirûd	Maris
Barada	Helmand	Marmara
Beâs	Heptaporos	Marsyas
Bolãn	Hermos	Meles
Bosporos	Hesidrus	Menderez
Buhtan	Hingol	Midius
Buner	Hormuz	Mulla
Cakitsuya	Hydaspes	Murgab
Calycadnus	Hydraotes	Nari
Ceyhan Nehri	Hyllus	Oroatis
Chenãb	Hyphasis	Orontes
Cheshme-i-Ali	Hyssus	Orsinos
Choaspes/Iran	Indus	Oxus
Choaspes/	Iris	Pactolos
Afghanistan	Is	Pallacopas
Choes	Jaxartes	Panj
Chrusorrhoas	Jhelum	Panjnad
Cophen	Jordan	Pant Kora
Cromna	Jumma	Partheneios
Cydnos	Kabul	Pasitigris
Damietta	Kaikos	Payas
Darya	Kalex	Pediaios

Polytimelus
Pulvar
Purali
Puramos
Puratta
Pyan
Qonduz
Raphina Rãvi
Rhesos
Rhodios
Rhundakos
Samos
Sangarios

Saros
Satmiois
Scylax
Sefid Rud
Selleis
Seyhan Nehri
Simois
Sitaces
Son
Stiboates
Sutlej
Swat
Syrdaria

Tadzen
Tejend
Thermodon
Tigris
Tomerus
Yesil
Waksh
Xanthos
Zab/Great
Zab/Lesser
Zabatos
Zaradros
Zarafshan

D. Africa

Aiguptos
Anthylla
Atbara
Canobia
Cataract 1

Cataract 2
Cataract 3
Cataract 4
Cataract 5
Cinyps

Lixus
Nile
Rosetta
Suez/canal

6. SEAS, GULFS, BAYS, HARBORS, PORTS, INLETS, LAKES, MARSHES, OCEANS

A. Greece, Crete, Aegean Islands

Acherusia
Aegean
Agion Oros
Aigina
Ainos
Almeria
Almirou
Ambrakia
Antikura
Argolis
Argos
Arta
Begoritis
Boibeis
Bolbe
Eleusis
Euboia

Helike
Herakleion
Hulika
Hullaikos
Ianessos
Ikaria
Ioannina
Ionian
Ionic
Kandia
Kantharos
Kassandra
Kastoria
Kavala
Kerkinitis
Kissamos
Kopais

Kophosa
Korinthos/Bay
Korinthos/Gulf
Koroni
Krete
Krisae/Bay
Krisae/Gulf
Lakonia
Larissa
Lechaion
Malis
Mandraki
Marathon
Mediterranean
Megambellou
Melas
Melite

Mesara
Messenia
Mirabellou
Mirtóön
Mikrolimani
Modon
Mounychia
Munuchia
Navarino
Ocean
Ogulia
Okeanos
Orfanou
Oropos
Osmanaga
Pagasitikos

Pagassai
Pasalimani
Patraikos
Peneios
Perachora
Petalion
Phaleron
Pieria
Portomandri
Prasias
Prespa
Samaria
Samarkand
Salamis/Attika
Salamis/Cyprus
Salonika

Salt
Saronic
Singitikos
Souda
Stumphalis
Thermai
Thurea
Trieste
Trikhonis
Vlöre
Voidhokoilia
Volos
Vouliagmeni
Zea

B. Europe

Adriatic
Almeria
Almirou
Antariatae
Atlantic
Azov
Black
Cadiz
English
Euxine

Golovita
Great Prespa
Kvarner
Liguria
Little Prespa
Luchnites
Maeotis
Mediterranean
North
Ochrid

Pachinus
Salerno
Sicilian
Syracusa
Tarentum
Terinaea
Trasimene
Tyrrhenia
Venice

C. Asia

Aden
Adramuttion
Alexandretta
Al-Utaybah
Antalya
Aqaba
Arabian/gulf
Arabian/sea
Aral
Arsissa
Balkhash

Barada
Bengal
Black
Candath
Caspian
Chrisorrhoas
Dead Sea
Edremit
Gwatar
Guge
Hoyran

Hyrcania
Iasos
Ikaria
Indian
Iskenderun
Issos
Iznik
Izmir
Kara-Bogaz
Kerameikos
Larnax

Latmos
Levantine
Lysimeleia
Marmara
Mediterranean
Morphou
Neapolis
Oman

Pacific
Persian
Pontos
Propontis
Rakshastal
Red/gulf
Red/sea
Sidra

Smyrna
Tanais
Thospitis
Urmia
Van
Wular

D. Africa

Alexander's
  Harbor
Algerian
Cyrenic
Egyptian
Gabès
Gennesaret
Hammamet

Libyan
Mareotis
Mediterranean
Moeris
Qabes
Red Sea/
  Egyptian
Red Sea/Persian

Serbonis
Sirte
Suez/gulf
Surt
Syrtis Major
Syrtis Minor
Tritonis
Tunis

7. MYTHOLOGY -- See pp. 268-269

*   *   *

NUMERICAL SUMMARY

1. CITIES, TOWNS, VILLAGES, SITES, SETTLEMENTS

A. Greece, Crete, Aegean Islands 1,199
B. Europe 305
C. Asia 572
D. Africa 152
   TOTAL 2,228

2. ISLANDS, PENINSULAS, ISTHMUSES

A. Greece, Crete, Aegean Islands 167
B. Europe 63
C. Asia 22
D. Africa 19
   TOTAL 271

3. MOUNTAINS, HILLS, PROMONTORIES,ROCKS, MINES, QUARRIES, CAVES, PLATEAUS, PASSES

A. Greece, Crete, Aegean Islands 230
B. Europe 34
C. Asia 91
D. Africa 6
   TOTAL 361

4. REGIONS, AREAS, TERRITORIES, VALLEYS, PLAINS, OASES, DESERTS, COUNTRIES

A. Greece, Crete, Aegean Islands 151
B. Europe 101
C. Asia 237
D. Africa 38
   TOTAL 527

5. RIVERS, STREAMS, SPRINGS, FOUNTAINS, DELTAS, STRAITS, CANALS

A. Greece, Crete, Aegean Islands 190
B. Europe 98
C. Asia 163
D. Africa 14
           TOTAL 465

6. SEAS, GULFS, BAYS, HARBORS, PORTS, INLETS, LAKES, MARSHES, OCEANS

A. Greece, Crete, Aegean Islands 97
B. Europe 29
C. Asia 55
D. Africa 22
           TOTAL 203

7 MYTHOLOGY

A. **Underworld** 16
B. **World** 47
           TOTAL 63

GRAND TOTAL OF NAMES OF PLACES 4,118

Greece 2,034
Europe 630
Asia 1,140
Africa 251
Mythology 63

       *   *   *

SELECT BIBLIOGRAPHY

A. Ancient Literature

Major Sources in chronological order:

1. Hesiod (mid to end of 8th cent. BCE), *Works and Days* et alia; *Homeric Hymns; Epigrams, Epic Cycle, Homerica*:The Loeb Classical Library, Harvard University Press, 57.
2. Homer (end-8th cent. BCE), *Iliad*: Loeb, Ibid., 170-71; *Odyssey* :104-05.
3. Herodotus (ca 485-425 BCE), *Persian Wars* : Loeb, Ibid., 117-120.
4. Thucydides (ca 460-400 BCE), *History of the Peloponnesian War*. Loeb, Ibid., 108-10 & 169.
5. Xenophon (ca 430-355 BCE), *Cyropaedia*: Loeb, Ibid., 51-52; *Hellenica*: 088-089; *Memorabilia*: 168.
6. Strabo (63 BCE-19 CE), *Geography*: Loeb, Ibid., 49-50, 182, 196, 211, 223, 241 & 267.
7. Diodorus Siculus (1st cent, BCE), *Library of History*: Loeb, Ibid., 279
8. Plutarch (46-120 CE), *Parallel Lives*: Loeb, Ibid., 47, 65, 80, 87, 98-103, 128, 137-38, 159-61.
9. Pausanias (2nd cent. CE), *Description of Greece*: Loeb, Ibid., 93, 188, 272, 297-98.
10. Flavianus Arrianus (2nd cent. CE), *Anabasis of Alexander*. Loeb, Ibid., 236 & 269.

Minor Sources, especially noteworthy:

1. Poets, such as Pindar (ca 522-438 BCE)
2. Dramatists, such as Aechylus (ca 524-456 BCE), Euripides (ca 480-406 BCE), Sophokles (496-406 BCE) and Aristophanes (ca 448-380 BCE)
3. Philosophers, such as Plato (ca 427-347 BCE) and Aristotle (384-322 BCE)

B. Select Modern Literature

Baratta, M., P. Fraccard, L. Visintin. *Atlante Storico*. Novara, 1956.
Bengtson, H., V. Milojcic. *Grosser Historisher Weltatlas*, 2 vols. Munich, 1953.
Burn, A. R. and Mary. *The Living Past of Greece*. Little, Brown and Company, 1980.
Carr, Thomas Swinburne. *The History and Geography of Greece*, Simpkin, 1838.
Cleveland, William A., ed et al. *Britannica Atlas*. Encyclopaedia Britannica, Inc.
Crane, Gregory R., editor-in-chief et al. *Perseus Digital Library*. Tufts University, In progress.
Cunliffe, Richard J. *A Lexicon of the Homeric Dialect: Homeric Proper and Place Names*, University of Oklahoma Press, 1977.
Findley, Alexander G. *A Classical Atlas, to Illustrate Ancient Geography*. Harper & Brothers Pub., 1849. Several editions.
Gates, Charles. *Ancient Cities: The Archaeology of Urban Life in the Ancient Near East and Egypt, Greece and Rome*. Routledge, 2003.
Hornblower, Simon and Antony Spawforth, eds. *The Oxford Companion to Classical Civilization*. Oxford University Press, 1998.
Internet Explorer, *Google Maps*, in progress.
Mee, Christopher & Antony Spawforth. *Greece, An Oxford Archaeological Guide*, Select Bibliography, p. 451-453. Oxford University Press, 2001.
Morkot, Robert. *The Penguin Historical Atlas of Ancient Greece*, Penguin Books, 1996.
National Geographic Maps. Online: natgeomaps.com
Smith, William, ed et al. *Dictionary of Greek and Roman Geography*. Introduction by Chris Stray. MacMillan, 2006.
Stier, H. E. et al. *Westermanns Atlas zur Weltgeschichte*. Braunschweig, 1956.
Stillwell, Richard, ed et al. *The Princeton Encyclopedia of Classical Sites*. Princeton University Press, 1976
Strassler, Robert B., ed. *The Landmark Thucydides*, translation of Richard Crawley, introduction by Victor Davis Hanson. The Free Press, 1996.
Talbert, Richard J.A. *Atlas of Classical History*. Routledge, 1985.
Talbert, Richard J.A. et al., eds. *Barrington Atlas of the Greek and Roman World*. Princeton University Press, 2000.
Thompson, J. O. *History of Ancient Geography*. Cambridge University Press, 1948.